the BEST of
Gourmet

the BEST *of*
Gourmet
2004

FROM *the* EDITORS OF GOURMET

CONDÉ NAST BOOKS　●　RANDOM HOUSE, NEW YORK

Random House website address: www.atrandom.com
Gourmet Books website address: www.Gourmetbks.com

Most of the recipes in this work were published previously
in *Gourmet* Magazine.

Printed in the United States of America on acid-free paper.

98765432
First Edition

All informative text in this book was written by Diane
Abrams and Linda M. Immediato.

The text of this book was set in Times Roman. The four-
color separations were done by American Color and
Quad/Graphics, Inc. The book was printed and bound at
R. R. Donnelley and Sons. Stock is Sterling Ultra Web
Gloss, MeadWestvaco.

For Random House
Lisa Faith Phillips, Vice President/General Manager
Tom Downing, Direct Marketing Director
Deborah Williams, Operations Director
Lyn Barris Hastings, Senior Direct Marketing Manager
Fianna Reznik, Direct Marketing Associate
Eric Levy, Inventory Associate
Eric Killer, Direct Marketing Associate
Molly Lyons, Production Manager

For *Gourmet* Books
Diane Abrams, Director
Linda M. Immediato, Senior Associate Editor

For *Gourmet* Magazine
Ruth Reichl, Editor-in-Chief
Diana LaGuardia, Creative Director
Richard Ferretti, Creative Director

Zanne Early Stewart, Executive Food Editor
Kemp Miles Minifie, Senior Food Editor
Alexis M. Touchet, Associate Food Editor
Lori Walther Powell, Food Editor/Stylist
Amy Mastrangelo, Food Editor
Paul Grimes, Food Editor/Stylist
Shelton Wiseman, Food Editor
Ruth Cousineau, Food Editor
Gina Marie Miraglia Eriquez, Food Editor
Melissa Roberts-Matar, Food Editor
Maggie Ruggiero, Food Editor
Lillian Chou, Food Editor
Ian Knauer, Recipe Cross-Tester

Romulo A. Yanes, Photographer

Illustrations by Barry Blitt

Produced in association with Anne B. Wright
and John W. Kern

Front Jacket: Gnocchetti all'Amatriciana (page 16)
Back Jacket: The Big Night (page 58)

ACKNOWLEDGMENTS

*t*he editors of *Gourmet* Books would like to thank everyone who gave us a hand in putting this volume together, especially former *Gourmet* art director Diana LaGuardia, who designed this volume as well as the jacket, and Barry Blitt, whose 80 original drawings are sprinkled throughout our recipe compendium.

Each month *Gourmet*'s photo editor, Helen Cannavale, and associate photo editor, Danielle Vauthy, enlist the many talented photographers who make the pages of the magazine come alive, and, as always, we had a treasure trove of images to chose from (see photo credits). Special thanks to photographer John Kernick for bringing the streets and people of Rome to us in living color in our Cuisines of the World section.

Since the magazine is always evolving, we depend on senior editor Cheryl Brown to keep us abreast of the latest recipe or style changes. Aside from answering our many queries, Cheryl also edited the entire recipe compendium. And deepest thanks to executive food editor Zanne Stewart and senior food editor Kemp Minifie, and all the food editors—Alexis Touchet, Lori Powell, Paul Grimes, Amy Mastrangelo, Shelton Wiseman, Ruth Cousineau, Gina Marie Miraglia Eriquez, Melissa Roberts-Matar, Maggie Ruggiero, and recipe cross-tester Ian Knauer—for all the remarkable recipes in this book.

This year our food editors went to Rome and brought back a vast array of dishes and two memorable menus that are wonderful examples of life imitating art. The Caravaggio-inspired feast came from Gina Marie Miraglia Eriquez, while American-born Roman artist Wendy Artin, whose watercolors adorn the endpapers of this book, shared a lovely little menu of classics from her new hometown.

Thanks to Romulo Yanes, *Gourmet* photographer, and his assistant, Stephanie Foley, for the gnocchi cooking class photos as well as the finished product that graces our jacket, and to Joe Maer, who styled the props with Roman flair. Our sincere gratitude to *Gourmet* production director Stephanie Stehofsky for recipe retrieval and to junior designer Kevin DeMaria, who retrieved images and other electronic information. Thanks also to Molly Lyons, Random House production manager, who handled production and printing.

Last but certainly not least, a very special thanks to Anne Wright, our project director, John Kern, production editor, and Marilyn Flaig, indexer, who have been part of our loyal team for years.

Lazy Days

The Recipe Compendium

Light Fantastic

A Pretty Grill

CONTENTS

tips for using
GOURMET'S RECIPES

MEASURE LIQUIDS
in glass or clear plastic liquid-measuring cups.

MEASURE DRY INGREDIENTS
in nesting dry-measuring cups (usually made of metal or plastic) that can be leveled off with a knife.

MEASURE FLOUR
by spooning (not scooping) it into a dry-measuring cup and leveling off with a knife without tapping or shaking cup.

SIFT FLOUR
only when specified in recipe. If sifted flour is called for, sift flour before measuring. (Many brands say "presifted" on the label; disregard this.)

A SHALLOW BAKING PAN
means an old-fashioned jelly-roll or four-sided cookie pan.

MEASURE SKILLETS AND BAKING PANS
across the top, not across the bottom.

A WATER BATH
for baking is prepared by putting your filled pan in a larger pan and adding enough boiling-hot water to reach halfway up the side of the smaller pan.

METAL PANS
used for baking should be light-colored, unless otherwise specified. If using dark metal pans, including nonstick, your baked goods will likely brown more and the cooking times may be shorter.

ALL PRODUCE
must be washed and dried before using.

FRESH HERBS OR GREENS
are prepped by first removing the leaves or fronds from the stems. The exception is cilantro, which has tender stems.

SALTED WATER
for cooking requires 1 tablespoon of salt for every 4 quarts of water.

BLACK PEPPER
in recipes is always freshly ground.

CHILES
require protective gloves when handling.

ZEST CITRUS FRUITS
by removing the colored part of the rind only (avoid the bitter white pith). For strips, use a vegetable peeler. For grated zest, we prefer using a rasplike Microplane zester, which results in fluffier zest, so pack to measure.

TOAST SPICES
in a dry heavy skillet over moderate heat, stirring, until fragrant and a shade or two darker.

TOAST NUTS
in a shallow baking pan in a 350°F oven until golden, 5 to 10 minutes.

TOAST SEEDS
as you would toast spices or nuts.

CHEESES
such as Parmigiano-Reggiano should be finely grated with the small ($1/8$ inch) teadrop-shaped holes (not the ragged-edged holes) of a box or similar handheld grater. Other shaped holes, a microplane rasp, and pregrated cheese yield different volumes.

INTRODUCTION

*g*ourmet's cooks spend a lot of time, in and out of the kitchen, making sure their recipes are as close to perfection as possible. This volume holds more than 325 recipes that were developed in-house during 2003. Each recipe is delicious; each is meticulously written and guaranteed to work. As you can imagine, "getting it right" takes an amazing amount of effort, and sometimes a great deal of patience.

Since Italian food is so popular and Rome is such a favorite destination, we devoted an entire issue to this great city. Here, in our Cuisines of the World section, you will find two artistic menus, a cache of regional recipes, and a primer on making gnocchi from those pages. Our cooks spent days eating at the finest restaurants in Rome. Between meals they scoured markets for the freshest ingredients and tasted cheeses, oils, and even fava beans at the best purveyors in town. Back in our test kitchens, it was time to spin all this research into great recipes. Who knew that this would prove to be so difficult?

The tale of developing our seemingly simple recipe for *cacio e pepe* (pasta tossed with cheese and crushed black pepper) says it all. As told by senior features editor Jane Daniels Lear, the cooks set out to make this peasant dish with two Roman restaurant versions in mind—a creamy one from Checchino dal 1887, and a dry one from Da Lucia. After a few attempts, it was decided to concentrate on the creamy version. They surmised that olive oil was giving it body and sheen and set out to make a cheesy sauce, finishing the pasta off in a pan on top of the stove. Again and again, the result was a clumpy mess! Could it be the New York water, the cheese, the pasta? When our library of cookbooks failed them, they consulted with their friends, the pros—Lidia Bastianich, Giuliano Bugialli, Fred Plotkin, and Lynne Rossetto Kasper. Four lively conversations later it became clear that the olive oil, sauce, and stovetop cooking were all wrong. They were instructed to just toss the drained (but very wet) pasta with the cheese in a warmed bowl. Further testing proved that the cheese ideally should be a Roman Pecorino and the pasta must be semolina spaghetti. Needless to say, our cooks went the extra mile, but the result on page 35 speaks for itself.

"Getting it right" often includes traveling the world, taking in plenty of cooking lessons and demonstrations along the way. During the year several of our cooks joined cookbook author Diane Kochilas in Crete to learn the secrets of fork-tender octopus, the dry crisp yeast bread known as rusks, spoon fruits, and the fish stew *kakavia*. Diane also led them to Logari taverna, where Katerina Hamilaki and her daughter, Yanna, gave a remarkable pastry demonstration. It so inspired Ruth Cousineau that she recreated their heavenly fried spirals with honey, sesame, and walnuts in her Mediterranean menu (page 72).

Sometimes the cooks pair up and go off to pursue special interests. Last year Shelley Wiseman and Ruth teamed up for a research trip to Veracruz, Mexico. There, chef Ricardo Muñoz Zurita led them down the Filobobos River to visit recently discovered ruins. They set up camp and were treated to a Veracruz feast that included bobo fish and various ancho chiles found in the northern highlands. Later in the year, Alexis Touchet went to Seville, Spain, where she made two discoveries—an incredible dessert wine, Molino Real, accompanied by Torta de Casar, a very soft cheese eaten with a spoon. Then, at the next stop, in Madrid, she tasted an outstanding braised vegetable dish with borage stems and leaves. With the flavors still fresh in her mind, she raced home only to find that cold weather had zapped her borage! Needless to say, as soon as borage is available Alexis will be in the kitchen with her meticulous notes trying to recapture that special bit of Spain.

As with most things in life, getting something to work properly often takes a few tries. Isn't it nice to know that our cooks are doing the necessary footwork and homework for all of us? Come enjoy this year's stash of fully-researched, fully-tested finds.

FROM *the* EDITORS OF GOURMET BOOKS

CUISINES OF THE WORLD

the flavors of ROME

*R*OME IS LIKE AN OPERA—so warm and glorious that you are instantly seduced. The city splashes over you like gorgeous music, tempting you to sit back in its beauty. But when you study the libretto, Rome, like any opera, becomes an especially rewarding experience. The more you know the more it reveals, opening itself layer by layer to bring you messages from the past and promises for the future. Because we want you to love Rome the way that we do, we spent this past year poring over the city, eating, shopping, cooking, looking at art and walking the streets, trying to ferret out the secret places that make being there so much fun. And what we discovered was that no city in the world is kinder to visitors.

First there is its size: Rome is delightfully compact, and you can travel almost everywhere on foot. What seem like distant destinations on the map (and even farther in a taxi) turn out to be quite close; you can walk from Trastevere to the Piazza del Popolo in half an hour, from the Vatican to the Forum in even less. Touring the neighborhoods— Trastevere, Testaccio, and Campo de' Fiori — we uncovered a different side of the Eternal City. In the backstreets, Rome is a village where every person knows his neighbors and every shopkeeper knows your business. Early one morning on the Piazza de Renzi I encountered a young woman standing on the sidewalk, head thrown back, shouting up to her aunt to throw down the key. It came sailing out the window and as I picked it up and handed it to her she smiled, making me feel, if only for one moment, that I was welcome on her street.

Then there's the food: Although other towns in Italy tend to be unkind about *la cucina romana*, they are wrong. The food is not always great, but it is almost always good. And unlike the restaurants of other capitals, it is the humble ones here that truly shine. I've never had more satisfying food than what is served in the simple trattorias spread across the city— or stupider stuff than the "creative cuisine" dished out in some big-deal restaurants.

Roman cooking is a joyous celebration of the Italian way of life. American artist Wendy Artin, who now calls Rome her home, not only takes advantage of the city's beauty on canvas, she also shops daily at her neighborhood market in Campo de' Fiori, where she finds the most exquisite ingredients for dinner (see her menu on page 24). Even if you can't shop at this market, can't heft the heavy artichokes or pile the heavily-scented lemons into your basket, you can make truly remarkable feasts. This collection is filled with wonderful food, inviting food, easy to cook food.

We've enjoyed bringing the city to life in these pages and sharing with you some of the secrets we've uncovered, like how to make gnocchi, or how to create a meal worthy of Caravaggio. You'll find dozens of other Roman favorites, from rich spaghetti alla carbonara to a simple *cacio e pepe* and from tripe to tiramisu. The city courted us with its warmth and generosity and we swooned. We hope you'll fall in love too.

Ruth Reichl
Editor in Chief

10

Piazza Farnese, just a stroll from Campo de' Fiori.

Masterfeast

Serves 8

BACCALÀ FRITTO
Fried Salt Cod

GNOCCHETTI ALL'AMATRICIANA
Tiny Potato Dumplings with
Tomato, Onion, and Guanciale Sauce
Salviano Orvieto Classico Superiore '01

LOMBO DI MAIALE RIPIENO DI MORTADELLA CON PATATE ARROSTO
Mortadella-Stuffed Pork Loin
with Rosemary Roasted Potatoes

CAVOLO ARRICCIATO E SFORMATO DI PORRI
Lacinato Kale and Leek Flan
Collosorbo Rosso di Montalcino '00

INSALATA DI RADICCHIO, FRISÉE, E CARCIOFI
Radicchio, Frisée, and Artichoke Salad

MILLEFOGLIE CON CREMA ALLA GRAPPA E RABARBARO
Millefoglie with Grappa Cream
and Rhubarb

BISCOTTI QUADRATI AL MIELE E ALLE NOCI
Honey Nut Squares

BACCALÀ FRITTO
Fried Salt Cod

Serves 8 (hors d'oeuvre)
Active time: 30 min   Start to finish: 3 days (includes soaking)

1 lb center-cut skinless boneless salt cod,
  rinsed well
1 qt vegetable oil
1 cup all-purpose flour
½ teaspoon salt
2 tablespoons olive oil
½ cup plus 3 tablespoons water
¼ cup finely chopped fresh flat-leaf parsley
1 teaspoon coarse sea salt

Accompaniment: **lemon wedges**
Special equipment: **a deep-fat thermometer**

Soak cod in a large bowl with water to cover by
2 inches, chilled, changing water 3 times a day, 1 to 3
days (see cooks' note, below). Chill cod until ready to use.
Heat vegetable oil in a 5- to 6-quart heavy pot
over moderate heat until it registers 385 to 390°F on
thermometer.
While oil is heating, whisk together flour, salt,
olive oil, water, and parsley in a bowl. Drain cod and
pat dry, then cut into 3- by ½-inch strips. Working in
batches of 4, coat strips in batter, then transfer to oil
with tongs and fry, turning, until golden, 1½ to 2 minutes. Transfer to a paper-towel-lined baking sheet to
drain. (Return oil to 385 to 390°F between batches.)

Sprinkle with sea salt and serve immediately.

Cooks' notes:
• Brands of cod differ in their degree of saltiness: A less
  salty one may need only 1 day of soaking, while
  another could require up to 3. To test it, simply taste a
  small piece after 1 day; you want it to be pleasantly
  salty but not overwhelming.
• If your sea salt is very coarse, lightly crush it with a
  mortar and pestle or the side of a large heavy knife.

GNOCCHETTI ALL'AMATRICIANA
Tiny Potato Dumplings with Tomato, Onion, and Guanciale Sauce

Serves 8 (first course)
Active time: 1½ hr   Start to finish: 2 hr

For sauce
1 tablespoon olive oil
5 oz *guanciale* or pancetta, finely chopped
  (½ cup)
1 large red onion, finely chopped (1¼ cups)
1 small garlic clove, minced
1 (28- to 32-oz) can plum tomatoes, drained
  (reserving juice) and finely chopped
½ cup water
1 teaspoon sugar
½ teaspoon salt
For gnocchetti
1½ lb yellow-fleshed potatoes such as
  Yukon Gold
1½ cups all-purpose flour plus additional
  for dusting
1¼ teaspoons salt

Accompaniment: **finely grated Pecorino Romano**
Special equipment: **a potato ricer**

Make sauce:
Heat olive oil in a 5- to 6-quart heavy pot over
moderately high heat until hot but not smoking, then
sauté *guanciale* and onion, stirring, until onion is golden,
about 6 minutes. Add garlic and sauté, stirring, until
golden, about 1 minute. Add tomatoes with reserved
juice, water, sugar, and salt and simmer, uncovered,
stirring occasionally, until thickened, about 30 minutes.
Make gnocchetti:
Cover potatoes with salted cold water (see Tips,

page 8) by 2 inches in a large pot, then simmer, uncovered, until very tender, about 25 minutes. Drain in a colander and, when cool enough to handle, peel.

Force warm potatoes through ricer into a large bowl. Add flour and salt and stir with a wooden spoon until mixture begins to come together. Gently form dough into a ball and cut in half.

Knead each dough half on a floured surface until smooth, about 1 minute (if dough sticks to surface, dust lightly with additional flour). Cut each half evenly into 10 pieces. Roll 1 piece into a 14-inch-long rope (½ inch thick), keeping remaining pieces covered with a kitchen towel. Cut rope crosswise into ¼-inch pieces and toss pieces lightly with flour on work surface.

Press a piece of dough against tines of a floured fork and push with a floured thumb in a forward rolling motion toward end of tines, letting *gnocchetti* fall from fork into a well-floured shallow baking pan. Make more *gnocchetti* in same manner.

Just before cooking, gently shake *gnocchetti* in 4 batches in a large medium-mesh sieve to knock off excess flour. Cook *gnocchetti* in 4 batches in a 5- to 6-quart pot of boiling salted water until they float, about 1 minute. Transfer with a slotted spoon to a large shallow bowl as cooked and spoon some sauce on top.

Cooks' notes:
• Sauce can be made 2 days ahead and chilled, covered. Reheat before proceeding.
• For visual tips on how to form potato gnocchi, turn to page 43. (Note: *Gnocchetti* will be smaller.)
• *Gnocchetti* can be formed (but not cooked) 1 week ahead and frozen in floured baking pan, covered, until hard, about 3 hours, then put in a sealed plastic bag. Do not thaw before cooking. Boil frozen *gnocchetti* about 2 minutes.

LOMBO DI MAIALE RIPIENO DI MORTADELLA CON PATATE ARROSTO
Mortadella-Stuffed Pork Loin with Rosemary Roasted Potatoes

Serves 8
Active time: 1 hr   Start to finish: 1¼ hr

For pork and potatoes
  2 tablespoons whole black peppercorns
3½ teaspoons kosher salt
  5 garlic cloves
  2 tablespoons unsalted butter, softened
  1 (3½-lb) center-cut boneless pork loin roast
      (4 to 5 inches in diameter), trimmed,
      leaving a ¼-inch layer of fat if possible
  3 tablespoons black truffle butter, softened
  ½ lb thinly sliced mortadella
  4 lb small (2-inch) boiling potatoes
      (preferably yellow-fleshed)
  3 tablespoons extra-virgin olive oil
  1 tablespoon chopped fresh rosemary
  ¼ teaspoon black pepper

For sauce
  ¾ cup chicken broth
  ¼ cup water
1½ teaspoons cornstarch
  1 tablespoon black truffle butter

Special equipment: **a mortar and pestle; kitchen string; a 17- by 11-inch flameproof roasting pan with an adjustable V-rack; an instant-read thermometer**

Prepare pork:
Preheat oven to 450°F.

Coarsely crush peppercorns and 2 teaspoons kosher salt with mortar and pestle, then add garlic and mash until a paste forms. Stir in unsalted butter.

If pork loin has been tied, discard strings. Put loin, fat side down, on a cutting board lined with plastic wrap. Butterfly pork in a spiral cut: Find beginning of a flap on 1 long side of loin (where bone was removed). Starting at inside edge of flap, make a long cut lengthwise down side of loin with a very sharp boning or paring knife, stopping 1 inch from bottom (this is beginning of spiral). Turn knife parallel to bottom of loin and begin to cut your way inward (parallel to bottom), keeping thickness of meat as even as possible,

using your other hand to gently lift and pull top portion of meat away from knife, until loin is 1 long flat piece.

Cover pork with a sheet of plastic wrap and pound to ½ inch thick with a smooth meat pounder or rolling pin. Remove plastic wrap and spread 1 tablespoon truffle butter over pork. Top with half of mortadella, slightly overlapping slices. Spread 1 tablespoon truffle butter over mortadella, then top with remaining mortadella and spread with remaining tablespoon truffle butter. Beginning with end that was interior of loin, roll up loin tightly and arrange, seam side down (fat side up), on cutting board. If fat layer is ¼ inch thick, make very close crosswise cuts in it (about ⅛ inch apart; do not cut through to meat), then tie with kitchen string at 1-inch intervals. Rub roast all over with peppercorn butter, covering fat layer well.

Put pork, fat side up, on oiled rack in roasting pan and roast in middle of oven 20 minutes.

Prepare potatoes:
While pork is roasting, peel and halve potatoes. Parboil potatoes in a 5- to 6-quart pot of boiling salted water (see Tips, page 8) 5 minutes. Drain in a colander 5 minutes, then toss with oil, rosemary, remaining 1½ teaspoons kosher salt, and pepper in a large bowl.

Remove pork from oven and reduce oven temperature to 325°F. Add potatoes to roasting pan, turning them in pan juices to coat, then roast pork with potatoes until thermometer inserted diagonally 2 inches into meat registers 155°F, 45 to 55 minutes. Transfer pork to a platter and let stand 25 minutes.

Increase oven temperature to 450°F and remove rack from roasting pan. Spread potatoes out in pan and roast in middle of oven, stirring every 5 minutes, until golden brown, about 20 minutes more. Transfer to a serving bowl and keep warm.

Make sauce:
Skim as much fat as possible from pan juices. Straddle roasting pan across 2 burners, then add broth and deglaze pan by boiling over high heat, stirring and scraping up brown bits, 1 minute. Stir together water and cornstarch, then add to broth mixture and boil, whisking, 1 minute. Remove from heat and whisk in truffle butter.

Discard string, then slice pork and serve with sauce and potatoes.

Cooks' note:
• **Pork can be butterflied and stuffed 1 day ahead and chilled, covered. Bring to room temperature before proceeding.**

CAVOLO ARRICCIATO E SFORMATO DI PORRI
Lacinato Kale and Leek Flan

Serves 8
Active time: 30 min   Start to finish: 1¼ hr

Although cavolo nero (a.k.a. Tuscan kale, lacinato kale, or dinosaur kale) is what Roman cooks would likely use for this flan, the dish works well with other varieties.

2 large leeks (white parts only), chopped
1 tablespoon unsalted butter
1 tablespoon olive oil
¾ lb *cavolo nero* or other kale,
    stems and center ribs discarded
    and leaves coarsely chopped
1 cup chicken broth
¾ cup water
⅔ cup heavy cream
1½ oz coarsely grated
    Pecorino Romano (½ cup)
1 large whole egg
2 large egg yolks

Special equipment: **8 (3- to 4-oz) ramekins (⅓ to ½ cup)**

Wash leeks in a bowl of cold water, then lift out and drain well. Cook leeks in butter and oil in a 5- to 6-quart heavy pot over moderate heat, stirring occasionally, until softened, about 6 minutes. Stir in kale and cook, covered, until slightly wilted, about 2 minutes. Add broth and water and simmer, uncovered, until kale is tender, about 8 minutes.

Purée kale mixture in 2 batches in a blender until very smooth (use caution when blending hot liquids). Pour through a fine-mesh sieve into a bowl, pressing on and discarding solids.

Preheat oven to 325°F.

Bring cream and cheese just to a boil, then remove from heat. Steep, covered, 10 minutes.

Whisk together whole egg, yolks, and kale purée in a bowl. Pour cream mixture through fine-mesh sieve into kale mixture and whisk to combine. Divide among buttered ramekins and bake, uncovered, in a water bath (see Tips, page 8) until set, 30 to 35 minutes (centers will still be slightly wobbly).

Transfer ramekins with tongs to a rack and cool

5 minutes. If desired, invert custards onto plates by first running a thin sharp knife around edge of each ramekin.

Cooks' note:
• Custards can be made 1 day ahead and chilled, covered. Reheat in a water bath in a 325°F oven until hot, about 15 minutes.

INSALATA DI RADICCHIO, FRISÉE, E CARCIOFI
Radicchio, Frisée, and Artichoke Salad

Serves 8
Active time: 40 min   Start to finish: 1 hr

Including raw artichokes in a salad is an Italian trademark—their flavor is fresher and milder than that of cooked artichokes.

  1 lemon, halved
  4 large artichokes (¾ lb each)
  ½ lb frisée (French curly endive),
      coarse stems discarded and leaves
      torn into bite-size pieces
  ¾ lb radicchio, trimmed, halved
      lengthwise, and thinly sliced
      crosswise
  5 tablespoons extra-virgin olive oil
1¼ teaspoons kosher salt
  ¼ teaspoon black pepper
  2 to 3 tablespoons white-wine vinegar

Special equipment: **a Japanese Benriner or other adjustable-blade slicer**

Squeeze juice from 1 lemon half into a large bowl of cold water. Drop same half into water.

Cut off stem of 1 artichoke and discard. Cut off top inch of artichoke with a serrated knife. Bend back outer leaves until they snap off close to base, then discard several more layers of leaves in same manner until you reach pale yellow leaves with pale green tips.

Cut remaining leaves flush with top of artichoke bottom with a sharp knife, then pull out purple leaves and scoop out fuzzy choke with a melon-ball cutter. Rub cut surfaces with remaining lemon half. Trim remaining dark green fibrous parts from base and sides of artichoke with sharp knife, then rub cut surfaces with same lemon half and drop artichoke into the acidulated water. Repeat with remaining artichokes.

Just before serving, slice artichokes paper-thin crosswise with slicer. Immediately toss with frisée and radicchio in a large bowl. Drizzle with oil and toss. Sprinkle with kosher salt and pepper and toss. Drizzle with vinegar and toss again.

Cooks' notes:
• Dressing ingredients can be whisked together (instead of tossed into salad) 1 day ahead and chilled, covered. Bring to room temperature before using.
• Greens can be washed and trimmed 1 day ahead and chilled in a sealed plastic bag lined with damp paper towels.
• Artichokes can be trimmed (but not sliced) 2 hours ahead and kept in acidulated water.

MILLEFOGLIE
CON CREMA ALLA GRAPPA
E RABARBARO
Millefoglie with Grappa Cream and Rhubarb

Serves 8
Active time: 45 min   Start to finish: 1¾ hr

For custard
2¼ cups whole milk
¼ teaspoon salt
4 large egg yolks
⅔ cup sugar
2 tablespoons all-purpose flour
2 tablespoons cornstarch
2 tablespoons unsalted butter,
   cut into pieces
3 tablespoons grappa (preferably Julia brand)
⅔ cup chilled heavy cream
For rhubarb
1½ lb rhubarb stalks, cut diagonally
   into 1¼-inch pieces
1 cup water
⅓ cup sugar
2 tablespoons grappa (preferably Julia brand)
For pastry
1 (17¼-oz) package frozen puff
   pastry sheets, thawed

Garnish: **confectioners sugar**

Make custard:
Bring 2 cups milk with salt to a boil in a 3-quart heavy saucepan. Meanwhile, whisk together yolks, sugar, flour, cornstarch, and remaining ¼ cup milk in a bowl. Add one third of hot milk to yolk mixture in a

slow stream, whisking, then add to milk remaining in saucepan, whisking.

Bring custard to a boil over moderate heat, whisking, and boil, whisking, 2 minutes. Remove from heat and stir in butter until melted, then stir in grappa. Transfer custard to a bowl and chill, its surface covered with wax paper, until cold, at least 1 hour. (Keep cream chilled.)

Cook rhubarb while custard chills:
Simmer rhubarb, water, sugar, and grappa in cleaned 3-quart heavy saucepan, uncovered, stirring gently once or twice, until rhubarb is tender but not falling apart, about 4 minutes. Set pan in a bowl of ice and cold water and let stand 2 minutes to stop cooking.

Slowly pour rhubarb mixture into a sieve set over a bowl. Return syrup to saucepan, reserving rhubarb, and boil until reduced to about ½ cup, about 10 minutes. Keep rhubarb and syrup, covered, at room temperature until ready to use.

Prepare pastry while rhubarb cooks:
Preheat oven to 400°F.

Unfold 1 puff pastry sheet and gently roll out into a 14-inch square with a rolling pin on a lightly floured surface. Transfer to a buttered large baking sheet and prick all over with a fork. Repeat with remaining sheet.

Bake in upper and lower thirds of oven, switching position of sheets halfway through baking, until pastry is puffed and golden, about 15 minutes total. Cool on baking sheets on racks.

Trim edges of pastry with a large serrated knife. Cut each sheet into 12 (3-inch) squares and break pastry scraps into small shards.

Assemble millefoglie:
Beat cream (for custard) in a bowl with an electric mixer until it just holds soft peaks. Whisk custard to loosen, then fold in whipped cream gently but thoroughly.

Dollop 2 rounded tablespoons of grappa cream on each of 8 dessert plates and top with half of rhubarb. Cover cream and rhubarb on each plate with a pastry square. Make another layer with remaining grappa cream, rhubarb, and pastry squares, then top with pastry shards. Sift confectioners sugar evenly over each serving and drizzle with syrup.

Cooks' notes:
• Custard (without whipped cream) can be
  made 1 day ahead and chilled, covered.
• Rhubarb can be prepared 1 day ahead and
  chilled, covered.
• Pastry can be baked and cut 1 day ahead and kept
  in an airtight container at room temperature. Recrisp
  on 2 baking sheets in a 350°F oven about 5 minutes.

BISCOTTI QUADRATI AL MIELE E ALLE NOCI
Honey Nut Squares

Makes 25 (1-inch) bars
Active time: 30 min   Start to finish: 2 hr

For crust
1¼ cups all-purpose flour
2 tablespoons sugar
½ teaspoon baking powder
¼ teaspoon salt
1 stick (½ cup) cold unsalted butter,
   cut into pieces
1 large egg, lightly beaten

For topping
⅓ cup plus 1 tablespoon mild honey
¼ cup packed light brown sugar
⅛ teaspoon salt
3 tablespoons cold unsalted butter,
   cut into pieces
1 tablespoon heavy cream
½ cup whole almonds with skins (3 oz),
   toasted (see Tips, page 8)
¾ cup hazelnuts (4 oz), toasted and
   any loose skins rubbed off in
   a kitchen towel
¼ cup pine nuts (1½ oz), lightly toasted

Special equipment: **a pastry or bench scraper**

Make crust:

Butter a 9-inch square metal baking pan (2 inches deep) and line with 2 crisscrossed sheets of foil, leaving a 2-inch overhang on all sides. Butter foil.

Blend together flour, sugar, baking powder, salt, and butter with your fingertips or a pastry blender (or pulse in a food processor) until most of mixture resembles coarse meal with small (roughly pea-size) butter lumps. Add egg and stir with a fork (or pulse) until a crumbly dough forms.

Turn out dough onto a work surface and divide into 4 portions. With heel of your hand, smear each portion once or twice in a forward motion to help distribute fat. Gather dough together with scraper.

Preheat oven to 375°F.

Press dough evenly onto bottom (but not up sides) of baking pan and bake in middle of oven until edges are golden and begin to pull away from sides of pan, 15 to 20 minutes. Cool in pan on rack.

Make topping:

Bring mild honey, brown sugar, and salt to a boil in a 2-quart heavy saucepan over moderate heat, stirring until brown sugar is dissolved, then boil, without stirring, 2 minutes. Add butter and cream and boil, stirring, 1 minute. Remove from heat and stir in all nuts until completely coated.

Pour nut mixture over pastry crust, spreading evenly, and bake in middle of oven until topping is caramelized and bubbling, 12 to 15 minutes. Cool completely in pan on a rack. Lift dessert out of pan using foil overhang and cut into 25 squares.

Cooks' note:
• Honey nut squares keep, layered between
  sheets of wax paper, in an airtight container
  at room temperature 1 week.

wendy artin's
STILL LIFE
WITH FLAVOR

Serves 4

**PASTA WITH SQUID,
TOMATOES,
AND CAPERS**

**VEAL BOCCONCINI WITH
PORCINI AND ROSEMARY**

**MÂCHE WITH
OLIVE OIL AND SALT**

Taurino Salice Salentino '99

TIRAMISU

PASTA WITH SQUID,
TOMATOES, AND CAPERS

Serves 4 (first course)
Active time: 45 min   Start to finish: 1 hr

We call for a Thai or serrano *chile because they're easier to find in the United States—try your local supermarket—than the small, thin Italian hot chiles.*

1 lb cleaned squid, bodies and tentacles
    separated but kept intact
6 tablespoons extra-virgin olive oil
4 large garlic cloves, finely chopped
1 (1½-inch) fresh red or green Thai or
    serrano chile, halved crosswise
½ lb grape or cherry tomatoes, halved
⅓ cup dry white wine
½ cup raisins
¼ cup drained bottled capers, rinsed,
    patted dry, and coarsely chopped
½ lb *campanelle* (small bell-shaped pasta)
½ cup loosely packed torn fresh basil leaves
¼ cup pine nuts, lightly toasted
1 (1- by ½-inch) strip fresh lemon zest
    (see Tips, page 8), finely chopped

If squid are large, halve ring of tentacles, then cut longer tentacles, if attached, crosswise into 2-inch pieces. Pull off flaps from squid bodies and cut into ¼-inch-thick slices. Cut bodies crosswise into ¼-inch-thick rings. Pat squid dry.

Heat 3 tablespoons oil in a 12-inch heavy skillet over moderately high heat until hot but not smoking, then sauté garlic and chile, stirring, until fragrant, about 30 seconds. Add squid and sauté, stirring, 1 minute. Add tomatoes and wine and simmer, stirring, 2 minutes. Add raisins and capers and simmer, stirring, 30 seconds. Remove from heat.

Cook pasta in a 6-quart pot of boiling salted water until al dente. Reserve ½ cup pasta cooking water, then drain pasta in a colander.

Add pasta to tomato mixture with ¼ cup reserved cooking water and cook over moderately high heat, stirring constantly, 1 minute. Remove from heat and stir in basil, pine nuts, zest, and salt and pepper to taste. If pasta looks dry, moisten with more cooking water.

Divide pasta among 4 plates, then drizzle each serving with some of remaining 3 tablespoons oil.

VEAL BOCCONCINI
WITH PORCINI AND ROSEMARY

Serves 4
Active time: 35 min   Start to finish: 1¾ hr

Though you may associate bocconcini *with tiny mozzarella balls, the word simply means "little bites" (here the veal is cut into bite-size pieces).*

1¼ oz (30 g) dried porcini (1½ cups), rinsed
1½ cups warm water
1¾ lb boneless veal shoulder, cut into
    1-inch cubes
  3 tablespoons all-purpose flour
  ¼ cup extra-virgin olive oil
  1 cup dry white wine
  ½ cup heavy cream
  ½ cup whole milk
  8 soft dried tomatoes (not packed in oil),
    cut crosswise into ⅛-inch-thick slices
  1 (1½-inch) fresh red or green Thai
    or *serrano* chile, halved crosswise
  2 (4-inch-long) fresh rosemary sprigs
  ¾ teaspoon salt

Soak porcini in warm water in a small bowl until softened, about 20 minutes. Lift porcini out, squeezing liquid back into bowl, then rinse porcini (to remove any grit) and cut into ½-inch pieces. Pour soaking liquid through a sieve lined with a coffee filter or a dampened paper towel into another small bowl.

Pat veal dry. Toss one fourth of veal in flour. Heat oil in a 4- to 5-quart heavy pot over moderately high heat until hot but not smoking, then shake off excess flour and brown veal, turning, until golden brown, about 3 minutes. Transfer with a slotted spoon to a bowl. Coat and brown remaining veal in 3 batches in same manner.

Add wine to pot and deglaze by boiling, stirring and scraping up brown bits, 1 minute. Stir in veal with any juices accumulated in bowl, porcini and soaking liquid, cream, milk, tomatoes, chile, and rosemary sprigs and simmer, partially covered, stirring occasionally, until veal is very tender, about 1¼ hours. Discard rosemary sprigs and chile, then stir in salt.

Cooks' note:
• Stew can be made 1 day ahead and cooled completely, uncovered, then chilled, covered. Bring to room temperature before reheating over moderate heat, stirring occasionally.

TIRAMISU

Serves 4 to 6 generously
Active time: 25 min   Start to finish: 6½ hr (includes chilling)

The popularity of tiramisu has never wavered in Rome, where it continues to be served at dinner parties and restaurants.

    3 large eggs, separated
    ¾ cup sugar
    1 (8-oz) container mascarpone cheese
        (1 scant cup)
    ½ cup chilled heavy cream
    2 cups very strong brewed coffee or brewed
        espresso, cooled to room temperature
    2 tablespoons sweet Marsala wine
    18 *savoiardi* (crisp Italian ladyfingers, 6 oz)
    ¼ cup fine-quality bittersweet chocolate
        shavings (not unsweetened; made with
        a vegetable peeler) or 2 tablespoons
        unsweetened cocoa powder

Beat together yolks and ½ cup sugar in a large bowl with an electric mixer at medium speed until thick and pale, about 2 minutes. Beat in mascarpone until just combined.

Beat whites with a pinch of salt in another bowl with cleaned beaters until they just hold soft peaks. Add remaining ¼ cup sugar a little at a time, beating. Continue to beat whites until they just hold stiff peaks. Beat cream in another bowl with cleaned beaters until it just holds soft peaks. Fold cream into mascarpone mixture gently but thoroughly, then fold in whites.

Stir together coffee and Marsala in a shallow bowl. Dip 1 ladyfinger in coffee mixture, soaking it about 4 seconds on each side, and transfer to an 8-inch glass baking dish (2-quart capacity). Repeat with 8 more ladyfingers and arrange in bottom of dish, trimming to fit snugly. Spread half of mascarpone mixture evenly over ladyfingers. Make another layer in same manner with remaining ladyfingers and mascarpone mixture. Chill tiramisu, covered, at least 6 hours.

Just before serving, sprinkle with chocolate.

Cooks' notes:
• The eggs in this recipe are not cooked, which may be of concern if there is a problem with salmonella in your area.
• Tiramisu can be chilled up to 1 day.

MÂCHE WITH OLIVE OIL AND SALT

Serves 4
Active time: 5 min   Start to finish: 5 min

Mâche is so delicate that tossing it with vinegar would not only wilt it instantly but would completely mask its subtle flavor.

    3 oz *mâche* (lamb's lettuce),
        trimmed (12 cups)
    ⅛ teaspoon fine sea salt, or to taste
    ¼ teaspoon black pepper, or to taste
    2 to 3 tablespoons extra-virgin olive oil

Gently toss together *mâche*, sea salt, pepper, and 1 tablespoon oil. Mound salad on plates and drizzle with remaining oil (to taste).

MORE RECIPES FROM ROME

FAVA BEAN, ASPARAGUS, AND ARUGULA SALAD WITH SHAVED PECORINO

Serves 4 (first course or lunch main course)
Active time: 1½ hr   Start to finish: 1½ hr

This salad was inspired by a couple of dishes our food editors encountered at restaurants in Rome.

½ lb medium asparagus, trimmed
2 cups shelled fresh fava beans (2½ lb in pods) or shelled *edamame* (fresh soybeans)
2 tablespoons extra-virgin olive oil
¼ lb arugula, coarse stems discarded
1 (½-lb) piece Pecorino Romano or Parmigiano-Reggiano
2 teaspoons balsamic vinegar

Cut asparagus stalks on a long diagonal into ⅛-inch-thick slices, leaving 1-inch-long tips (reserve tips separately).

Blanch asparagus tips (but not sliced stalks) in a 4-quart pot of boiling salted water (see Tips, page 8) 2 minutes, then immediately transfer with a slotted spoon to a bowl of ice and cold water to stop cooking.

Return water to a boil and blanch fava beans 1 minute, then immediately transfer with slotted spoon to ice water to stop cooking. Drain asparagus tips and beans and gently peel skins from beans (it's not necessary to peel *edamame*, if using).

Toss beans and asparagus (blanched tips and raw sliced stalks) in a bowl with 1 tablespoon oil and salt and pepper to taste, then divide among 4 plates. Toss arugula with remaining tablespoon oil and salt and pepper to taste and mound on top of vegetables. Shave thin slices of cheese over salad with a vegetable peeler (use about half of piece), then drizzle with vinegar.

Cooks' notes:
• Fava beans can be blanched and peeled 1 day ahead and chilled in a sealed plastic bag.
• Be aware that fava beans can cause a potentially fatal food intolerance in some people of Mediterranean, African, and Pacific Rim descent.

FRIED ARTICHOKES

Serves 4 (hors d'oeuvre)
Active time: 1 hr   Start to finish: 1 hr

Fried artichokes are usually served whole in Rome as a primo piatto, *but we found that cutting them into wedges before frying made them a finger-friendly and addictive hors d'oeuvre.*

2 lemons, halved
4 large artichokes (¾ lb each)
6 cups olive oil or vegetable oil

Special equipment: **a deep-fat thermometer**

Fill a large bowl with cold water and squeeze juice from 2 lemon halves into bowl.

Keep stem attached and, at opposite end, cut off top inch of 1 artichoke with a serrated knife. Bend back outer leaves until they snap off close to base, then discard several more layers of leaves in same manner until you reach pale yellow leaves with pale green tips. Trim dark green fibrous parts from base and side of artichoke with a paring knife, then rub cut surfaces with a remaining lemon half.

Trim ¼ inch from end of stem to expose inner core. Trim sides of stem (still attached) down to pale inner core (don't worry if remaining stem is very thin). Cut off pale green top of artichoke, then cut artichoke lengthwise into 6 wedges. Cut out purple leaves and fuzzy choke. Rub cut surfaces with remaining lemon half and put in bowl of acidulated water. Trim remaining artichokes in same manner.

Drain artichokes well on paper towels and pat dry. Heat oil in a 4-quart deep heavy saucepan over moderate heat until thermometer registers 220°F, then simmer artichokes in oil, gently stirring occasionally, until tender, about 15 minutes. Transfer with a slotted spoon to paper towels to drain.

Continue to heat oil over moderate heat until thermometer registers 375°F, then fry artichokes in 4 batches until leaves are curled, browned, and crisp, 30 to 40 seconds. (Return oil to 375°F between batches.) Drain well on paper towels and season with salt.

INDIVIDUAL ZUCCHINI FRITTATAS WITH PECORINO AND CHIVES

Serves 6 (main course)
Active time: 25 min   Start to finish: 25 min

1½ tablespoons olive oil
 3 medium zucchini (1 lb total), halved
    lengthwise and cut crosswise
    into ⅛-inch-thick slices
 ¼ teaspoon salt
 ¼ teaspoon black pepper
 ¼ cup chopped fresh chives
1½ oz finely grated Pecorino Romano or
    Parmigiano-Reggiano
    (¾ cup; see Tips, page 8)
10 large eggs, lightly beaten

Special equipment: **a nonstick muffin pan with
   6 (1-cup) muffin cups**

Preheat oven to 375°F.
    Heat oil in a 12-inch nonstick skillet over moderately high heat until hot but not smoking, then sauté zucchini with salt and pepper, stirring occasionally, until just tender, about 4 minutes.
    Whisk chives, zucchini, and ½ cup cheese into eggs. Divide mixture among oiled muffin cups and bake in middle of oven until tops are puffed and set, about 14 minutes. Remove pan from oven and turn on broiler. Sprinkle frittatas with remaining ¼ cup cheese and broil 3 to 4 inches from heat until cheese is melted and tops are golden, 1 to 2 minutes.

SPINACH AND CHEESE CANNELLONI

Serves 8 (first course) or 4 (main course)
Active time: 2 hr   Start to finish: 4 hr (includes making fresh pasta)

For sauce
1½ tablespoons unsalted butter
1½ tablespoons all-purpose flour
 2 cups whole milk
 ¼ teaspoon salt
 ¼ teaspoon black pepper
    Pinch of freshly grated nutmeg
 ¾ oz finely grated Pecorino Romano
    or Parmigiano-Reggiano
    (about ⅓ cup; see Tips, page 8)
For cannelloni
 3 tablespoons extra-virgin olive oil
 1 small onion, chopped
 2 garlic cloves, finely chopped
10 oz baby spinach
1¾ cups ricotta (12 oz fresh or
    15 oz supermarket-style)
 1 large egg, lightly beaten
 ½ cup chopped fresh flat-leaf parsley
 3 oz thinly sliced prosciutto (optional),
    chopped
 ¼ teaspoon salt
 ¼ teaspoon black pepper
 1 oz finely grated Pecorino Romano or
    Parmigiano-Reggiano (½ cup)
 8 (6- by 4-inch) fresh pasta rectangles
    (recipe follows) or 8 oven-ready (sometimes
    labeled "no-boil") lasagne noodles

Special equipment: **a 13- by 9- by 2-inch ceramic
   baking dish or other shallow 3-qt
   flameproof baking dish (not glass)**

Make sauce:
    Melt butter in a 1½- to 2-quart heavy saucepan over moderately low heat. Whisk in flour and cook roux, whisking, 2 minutes. Add milk in a stream, whisking, and bring to a boil over high heat, whisking constantly (sauce will thicken). Reduce heat and simmer, whisking occasionally, 2 minutes, then whisk in salt, pepper, and nutmeg. Remove from heat and whisk in cheese, then cover pan.

Make cannelloni:

Heat oil in a 5- to 6-quart heavy pot over moderately high heat until hot but not smoking, then sauté onion and garlic, stirring occasionally, until lightly browned, about 5 minutes. Add spinach and sauté, stirring, until just wilted, about 3 minutes. Remove from heat and cool completely.

Stir together ricotta, egg, parsley, prosciutto (if using), salt, pepper, and ⅓ cup cheese in a bowl, then stir in spinach mixture.

Boil pasta 2 pieces at a time in a 6- to 8-quart pot of boiling salted water (see Tips, page 8), stirring to separate, until just tender, about 2 minutes for fresh pasta or about 6 minutes for oven-ready noodles. Gently transfer with a slotted spoon to a large bowl of cold water to stop cooking, then remove from bowl, shaking off water, and lay flat on kitchen towels (not terry cloth). Pat dry with paper towels. Trim oven-ready noodles (if using) as closely as possible to 6¼- by 5½-inch rectangles.

Preheat oven to 425°F.

Spread ⅔ cup sauce in buttered baking dish. Spread about ⅓ cup ricotta filling in a line along 1 short side of 1 pasta rectangle, then roll up to enclose filling. Transfer, seam side down, to baking dish. Make 7 more cannelloni in same manner, arranging snugly in 1 layer. Spread ½ cup more sauce over cannelloni and sprinkle with remaining cheese. Bake, covered with foil, in middle of oven until sauce is bubbling, about 20 minutes.

Turn on broiler.

Remove foil and broil cannelloni about 5 inches from heat until lightly browned, 2 to 4 minutes. Let stand 5 minutes before serving. Reheat remaining sauce and serve on the side.

Cooks' note:
• Cannelloni can be assembled (but not baked) 1 day ahead and chilled, covered with plastic wrap. Let stand at room temperature 15 minutes before baking. Remaining sauce will need to be thinned slightly.

FRESH PASTA

Makes 8 fresh pasta rectangles
Active time: 1 hr   Start to finish: 2 hr

Some of the tenderest pasta is made with Italian "00" soft wheat flour. Since this flour can be hard to find, we used a combination of cake flour and all-purpose flour with good results.

    1 cup cake flour (not self-rising)
    ¼ cup all-purpose flour plus
        additional for kneading
    ½ teaspoon salt
    2 large egg yolks
    1½ tablespoons extra-virgin olive oil
    ¼ cup water

Special equipment: **a pasta machine**

Make dough:

Blend all ingredients in a food processor until mixture begins to form a ball. Knead dough on a lightly floured surface, incorporating only as much additional flour as necessary to keep dough from sticking, until smooth and elastic, 6 to 8 minutes. Wrap dough in plastic wrap and let stand 1 hour.

Roll out dough:

Set smooth rollers of pasta machine on widest setting. Cut dough into 4 pieces. Cover 3 pieces with plastic wrap, then form remaining piece into a rectangle and feed through rollers. Fold rectangle in half and feed, folded end first, through rollers 8 more times, folding in half each time and dusting with flour if necessary to prevent sticking.

Turn dial to next (narrower) setting and feed dough through without folding. Catch pasta sheet with your hand as it feeds through rollers instead of letting it crumple at base of machine. Continue to feed through without folding, making space between rollers narrower each time and dusting with flour if it begins to stick, until second narrowest setting is reached.

Lay 1 pasta sheet on a floured surface and cut into 2 (6- by 4-inch) rectangles. Roll out and cut remaining 3 pieces of dough in same manner to form a total of 8 pasta squares.

Cooks' note:
• Pasta trimmings can be cut into odd-shaped pieces and used in soup. In Italian they're called *maltagliati*, which means "badly cut."

PIZZA BIANCA

Serves 4 (makes 1 very thin 12- by 8-inch pizza)
Active time: 25 min   Start to finish: 25 min

This pizza is made with no toppings other than oil and salt and should be served as a snack. It's not really a cracker, but it's crisper than focaccia.

1 teaspoon hot water
1 teaspoon kosher salt
2 tablespoons extra-virgin olive oil
1 lb fresh or thawed frozen pizza dough
  (not from a tube)
All-purpose flour for dusting

Preheat oven to 500°F.

Whisk together hot water and ½ teaspoon kosher salt until most of salt is dissolved, then whisk in 1 tablespoon oil.

Coat dough lightly with flour, then stretch with floured hands on a floured surface into a 12- by 8-inch rectangle. Transfer dough to an oiled 15- by 10- by 1-inch baking pan, stretching dough to cover bottom of pan. Dimple dough by pressing your fingertips all over, then brush with oil mixture.

Bake pizza in pan on bottom rack of oven until golden brown on top and bottom, 10 to 12 minutes. Transfer pizza to a rack, then brush with remaining tablespoon oil and sprinkle with remaining ½ teaspoon kosher salt. Serve warm, torn into pieces.

TRIPPA ALLA ROMANA

Serves 4 (main course)
Active time: 45 min Start to finish: 7 hr

3 lb raw beef honeycomb tripe
  (not partially cooked)
⅓ cup extra-virgin olive oil
1 large onion, chopped
2 carrots, chopped
2 celery ribs, chopped
2 garlic cloves, chopped
½ teaspoon salt
¼ teaspoon black pepper
⅔ cup dry white wine
1 (32-oz) can whole tomatoes in juice
2 cups cold water
¼ cup chopped fresh mint

Garnish: **finely grated Pecorino Romano; chopped fresh mint**

Trim any fat from tripe, then rinse under cold water. Soak tripe in a large bowl of fresh cold water 1 hour, then rinse again. Put tripe in an 8-quart pot of cold water and bring to a boil, then drain and rinse. Bring tripe to a boil again in pot filled with fresh cold water, then reduce heat and simmer, uncovered, turning tripe occasionally and adding more hot water to pot if necessary to keep tripe covered, until very tender, about 4 hours (tripe will have a pungent aroma while simmering). Drain in a colander and cool completely.

While tripe is cooking, heat oil in a 6- to 8-quart heavy pot over moderate heat until hot but not smoking, then cook onion, carrots, celery, and garlic, stirring frequently, until softened, about 8 minutes. Add salt, pepper, and wine and boil, stirring, 1 minute. Pour juice from tomatoes into sauce, then chop tomatoes and add to sauce with water and mint. Simmer sauce, uncovered, 30 minutes.

Trim any remaining fat from tripe and cut tripe into 2- by ½-inch strips. Add to sauce and simmer, uncovered, stirring occasionally, until tripe is a little bit more tender but still slightly chewy, 45 minutes to 1 hour. Season with salt and pepper.

Serve tripe sprinkled with cheese and mint.

Cooks' notes:
• Tripe in sauce can be cooked 2 days ahead and chilled, covered. Reheat before serving.
• Tripe is delicious served over pasta.

CACIO E PEPE
Spaghetti with Pecorino Romano and Black Pepper

Serves 4 (first course)
Active time: 20 min   Start to finish: 20 min

*For this recipe, you need to grate the cheese
with the ragged-edged holes of a box grater for
ease of melting. Don't use the teardrop-shaped
holes recommended in Tips (page 8), or a rasp,
as your cheese will clump up in the bowl.*

2 teaspoons black peppercorns
½ lb spaghetti
**2½ oz very finely grated Pecorino Romano
    (¾ cup plus 2 tablespoons) or Parmigiano-
    Reggiano plus additional for serving**

Toast black peppercorns in a dry small skillet over
moderately high heat, swirling skillet, until fragrant and
peppercorns begin to jump, 2 to 3 minutes. Coarsely
crush peppercorns with a mortar and pestle or wrap in a
kitchen towel and press on peppercorns with bottom of
a heavy skillet.

Cook spaghetti in a 6- to 8-quart pot of boiling
salted water (see Tips, page 8) until al dente.

Fill a large glass or ceramic bowl with some hot
water to warm bowl. Just before spaghetti is finished
cooking, drain bowl but do not dry.

Reserve ½ cup pasta cooking water, then drain
pasta quickly in a colander (do not shake off excess
water) and add to warm pasta bowl. Sprinkle ¾ cup
cheese and 3 tablespoons cooking water evenly over
spaghetti and toss quickly. If pasta seems dry, toss
with some additional cooking water.

Divide pasta among 4 plates, then sprinkle with
pepper and 2 tablespoons cheese (total). Serve immediately with additional cheese on the side.

RICOTTA ORANGE FRITTERS

Serves 2 to 4
Active time: 30 min   Start to finish: 30 min

   1 large egg
   3 tablespoons granulated sugar
   ½ teaspoon finely grated fresh orange zest
   ½ teaspoon fresh orange juice
   ½ cup whole-milk ricotta
   ⅓ cup all-purpose flour
   ⅛ teaspoon salt
   1 cup olive oil
     Confectioners sugar for dusting

   Whisk together egg and granulated sugar, then whisk in zest, juice, ricotta, flour, and salt until just combined. Heat oil in a 10-inch heavy skillet over moderately high heat until hot but not smoking. Working in batches of 4, spoon 1 tablespoon of batter per fritter into oil and fry, turning over once, until golden on both sides, about 2 minutes. Transfer with a slotted spoon to paper towels to drain and cool slightly.

   Dust fritters with confectioners sugar and serve immediately.

GREEN BEANS WITH LEMON AND OIL

Serves 6 (side dish)
Active time: 20 min   Start to finish: 20 min

   1 lb thin green beans such as
     haricots verts, trimmed
   1 tablespoon extra-virgin olive oil
   ¼ teaspoon salt
   1 teaspoon fresh lemon juice
   ½ teaspoon finely grated fresh lemon zest

   Cook beans in a 5-quart pot of boiling salted water (see Tips, page 8) until crisp-tender, about 5 minutes. Drain in a colander and immediately transfer to a bowl of ice and cold water to stop cooking. Drain and pat dry.

   Toss beans with oil, salt, and pepper to taste, then toss with lemon juice and half of zest. Serve beans sprinkled with remaining zest.

SPICY SAUTÉED DANDELION GREENS

Serves 4 (side dish)
Active time: 30 min   Start to finish: 30 min

   2 lb dandelion greens, tough stems removed
     and leaves cut crosswise into 4-inch pieces
   ¼ cup extra-virgin olive oil
   2 large garlic cloves, smashed
   ½ teaspoon dried hot red pepper flakes
   ½ teaspoon salt

   Cook greens in a 6- to 8-quart pot of boiling salted water (see Tips, page 8) until ribs are tender, 4 to 5 minutes, then drain in a colander. Rinse under cold water to stop cooking and drain well, gently pressing out excess water.

   Heat oil in a 12-inch heavy skillet over moderate heat until hot but not smoking, then cook garlic, stirring, until pale golden, about 30 seconds. Increase heat to moderately high, then add greens, red pepper flakes, and salt and sauté, stirring, until liquid greens give off is evaporated, about 4 minutes.

ROASTED POTATOES
WITH ANCHOVIES AND LEMON

Serves 4 to 6
Active time: 20 min   Start to finish: 35 min

2 lb small (2-inch) white boiling
    potatoes, quartered
½ teaspoon salt
¼ teaspoon black pepper
3 tablespoons extra-virgin olive oil
1½ tablespoons minced anchovy fillets
1½ tablespoons fresh lemon juice
1½ tablespoons finely chopped garlic
    (3 large cloves)
⅓ cup chopped fresh flat-leaf parsley

Preheat oven to 450°F.

Toss potatoes with salt, pepper, and 2 tablespoons oil in a large shallow baking pan (1 inch deep). Roast in lower third of oven, without turning or stirring, until undersides are golden brown, about 20 minutes.

While potatoes are roasting, whisk together anchovies, lemon juice, and remaining tablespoon oil.

Turn potatoes over and roast in lower third of oven 10 minutes more. Toss potatoes with garlic and roast 5 minutes. Transfer to a bowl and stir in anchovy mixture, parsley, and salt and pepper to taste. Serve warm.

FISH SOUP WITH PASTA
AND BROCCOLI

Serves 4 to 6 (first course)
Active time: 20 min   Start to finish: 20 min

This classic soup appears on many menus in Rome, but we were disappointed with the versions we were served there. Our recipe is more of a crowd pleaser.

4 cups chicken broth (32 fl oz)
2 cups water
1 lb skinless skate or flounder fillet,
    halved crosswise if large
1 garlic clove, finely chopped
1 cup small shell pasta (5 oz)
2 cups ½-inch broccoli florets
1 tablespoon fresh lemon juice, or to taste
3 tablespoons extra-virgin olive oil,
    or to taste

Bring broth and water to a simmer with fish and garlic in a 4-quart heavy pot. Add pasta and simmer until al dente, about 5 minutes (fish will break apart). Add broccoli and simmer (still uncovered) until pasta and broccoli are tender, 2 to 3 minutes.

Add lemon juice and season soup with salt and pepper. Serve soup drizzled with oil.

ARTICHOKE
AND OLIVE CROSTINI

Serves 4 (makes 12 hors d'oeuvres)
Active time: 15 min   Start to finish: 15 min

12 (½-inch-thick) slices from a long
    Italian loaf (3 inches wide)
3½ tablespoons extra-virgin olive oil
2 (6½-oz) jars marinated artichoke hearts,
    drained, rinsed well, and patted dry
2 tablespoons heavy cream
6 tablespoons chopped pitted green olives
    (½ cup)
3 tablespoons finely chopped red onion

Preheat broiler.

Arrange bread slices in 1 layer on a baking sheet and brush tops with 1½ tablespoons oil (total). Broil 4 to 6 inches from heat until golden on top, about 30 seconds. Turn toasts over and broil until golden, about 30 seconds more. Transfer toasts to a rack to cool.

Pulse artichokes with cream in a food processor until finely chopped. Transfer mixture to a bowl and stir in salt and pepper to taste.

Stir together olives, onion, and ½ tablespoon oil in a small bowl. Spread toasts evenly with artichoke cream and top with olive mixture. Drizzle with remaining 1½ tablespoons oil just before serving.

SPAGHETTI ALLA CARBONARA

Serves 4 (main course)
Active time: 40 min Start to finish: 40 min

5 oz *guanciale* (unsmoked cured hog jowl)
   or pancetta, cut into ⅓-inch dice
1 medium onion, finely chopped
¼ cup dry white wine
1 lb spaghetti
3 large eggs
1½ oz finely grated Parmigiano-Reggiano
   (¾ cup; see Tips, page 8)
¾ oz finely grated Pecorino Romano
   (⅓ cup)
¼ teaspoon salt
1 teaspoon coarsely ground black pepper

Cook *guanciale* in a deep 12-inch heavy skillet over moderate heat, stirring, until fat begins to render, 1 to 2 minutes. Add onion and cook, stirring occasionally, until onion is golden, about 10 minutes. Add wine and boil until reduced by half, 1 to 2 minutes.

Cook spaghetti in a 6- to 8-quart pot of boiling salted water (see Tips, page 8) until al dente.

While pasta is cooking, whisk together eggs, cheeses, salt, and pepper in a small bowl.

Drain spaghetti in a colander and add to onion mixture, then toss with tongs over moderate heat until coated. Remove from heat and add egg mixture, tossing to combine. Serve immediately.

Cooks' note:
• The eggs in this recipe will not be fully cooked, which may be of concern if there is a problem with salmonella in your area.

HAZELNUT GELATO

Makes 1 scant quart
Active time: 30 min Start to finish: 4 hr
(includes chilling and freezing)

5 oz hazelnuts, toasted
   (1 cup; see Tips, page 8)
¼ cup sugar
Pinch of salt
2½ cups whole milk
⅓ cup heavy cream
4 large egg yolks
¼ cup plus 2 tablespoons sugar

Special equipment: an instant-read thermometer; an ice-cream maker

Pulse cooled hazelnuts with sugar and salt in a food processor until finely chopped. Transfer to a 3-quart heavy saucepan and add milk and cream. Bring just to a simmer over moderate heat, stirring occasionally, then remove from heat and let steep, covered, 1 hour.

Pour mixture through a fine-mesh sieve into a bowl, pressing hard on and discarding solids.

Beat together egg yolks and sugar with an electric mixer at medium speed until thick and pale, 2 to 3 minutes. Beat in milk mixture and transfer to cleaned saucepan. Cook custard over moderately low heat, stirring constantly, until thermometer registers 175°F (do not let boil). Immediately pour custard through cleaned sieve into a metal bowl, then set bowl in a larger bowl of ice and cold water and cool, stirring occasionally. Chill custard, covered, until cold. Freeze in an ice-cream maker, then transfer to an airtight container and put in freezer to harden.

Cooks' note:
• Gelato can be made 1 week ahead.

VIGNAROLA
Fava Bean, Pea, and Artichoke Stew

Serves 4 (main course)
Active time: 1 hr   Start to finish: 1¾ hr

You'll find this dish in trattorias all over Rome during the spring. The long, slow cooking causes the vegetables to lose their bright color, but the sweet flavor of the stew makes up for its rather bland appearance.

2 cups shelled fresh fava beans
    (2½ lb in pods) or shelled
    edamame (fresh soybeans)
2 lemons, halved
4 large artichokes (¾ lb each)
2 oz *guanciale* or pancetta, cut into
    ⅛-inch-thick matchsticks (½ cup)
2 cups thinly sliced onion
5 tablespoons extra-virgin olive oil
2 cups fresh or frozen peas (not thawed)
2 teaspoons finely chopped fresh oregano
2 cups water
1 teaspoon salt
½ teaspoon black pepper
½ teaspoon fresh lemon juice, or to taste

Prepare fava beans:
Blanch beans in a 2-quart pot of boiling water 1 minute, then drain in a sieve and immediately transfer to a bowl of ice and cold water to stop cooking. Gently peel off skins (it's not necessary to peel *edamame*, if using).

Prepare artichokes:
Fill a large bowl with 4 cups cold water and squeeze juice from 2 lemon halves into bowl.

Cut off stem of 1 artichoke and reserve. Cut off top inch of artichoke with a serrated knife. Bend back outer leaves until they snap off close to base, then discard several more layers of leaves in same manner until you reach pale yellow leaves with pale green tips.

Cut remaining leaves flush with top of artichoke bottom using a paring knife, then quarter bottom. Cut out fuzzy choke and purple leaves with paring knife. Trim dark green fibrous parts from base and side of artichoke. Rub cut surfaces with a remaining lemon half and put artichoke bottom in bowl of acidulated water.

Trim ¼ inch from end of reserved stem to expose inner core, then trim sides of stem down to pale inner core (don't worry if remaining stem is very thin). Rub cut surfaces with lemon half and put in bowl of acidulated water. Trim remaining artichokes, including stems, in same manner.

Prepare stew:
Drain artichokes and cut crosswise into ¼-inch-thick slices, including stems. Cook *guanciale* and onion in oil in a 5-quart heavy pot over moderate heat, stirring occasionally, until onion is softened, about 6 minutes. Add sliced artichokes, fava beans, and remaining ingredients and simmer, covered, stirring occasionally, until vegetables are tender, about 45 minutes.

Cooks' notes:
• Stew can be made 1 day ahead and chilled, covered. Stew will thicken slightly; add water to thin to desired consistency.
• Be aware that fava beans can cause a potentially fatal food intolerance in some people of Mediterranean, African, and Pacific Rim descent.

APRICOT CROSTATA

Serves 6 to 8
Active time: 45 min Start to finish: 3¼ hr

1½ sticks (¾ cup) softened unsalted butter
⅓ cup sugar
1 large egg
1 teaspoon vanilla
2¼ cups all-purpose flour
½ teaspoon salt
2 teaspoons finely grated fresh lemon zest
1 cup fine-quality apricot preserves (11 oz)
4 teaspoons fresh lemon juice
⅛ teaspoon almond extract

Beat together butter and sugar with an electric mixer at medium speed until pale and fluffy, about 3 minutes. Beat in egg and vanilla. Reduce speed to low and mix in flour, salt, and zest until mixture just forms a dough. Shape dough into 2 balls, 1 slightly larger than the other. Flatten each ball into a 5-inch disk, then wrap each in wax paper and chill 30 minutes.

Stir together preserves, lemon juice, and extract in a small bowl. Roll out thicker piece of dough (keep remaining piece chilled) between 2 sheets of wax paper into an 11-inch round. Remove top sheet of paper and invert dough into a 9-by 1-inch fluted round tart pan with removable bottom. Peel off paper and fit dough into pan, trimming side to ¼ inch below top of rim. Chill shell.

Roll out remaining dough in same manner and remove top sheet of paper, then cut dough into 10 (1-inch-wide) strips. Slide strips on wax paper onto a baking sheet and chill until firm, about 10 minutes.

Preheat oven to 375°F.

Spread apricot filling in tart shell and arrange 5 strips across filling (about 1 inch apart), trimming excess dough at ends of strips. Arrange remaining 5 strips on top (about 1 inch apart) to form a lattice (do not weave), trimming ends. Press ends onto edge of tart shell and bake *crostata* in middle of oven until golden, 40 to 50 minutes. Cool completely in pan on a rack.

CHICKEN WITH SWEET AND HOT RED PEPPERS

Serves 4
Active time: 45 min Start to finish: 45 min

8 small chicken thighs with skin and bones (2½ lb)
¾ teaspoon salt
2 tablespoons extra-virgin olive oil
3 red bell peppers, cut lengthwise into ⅓-inch-wide strips
1 onion, sliced
2 garlic cloves, smashed and peeled
¼ to ½ teaspoon dried hot red pepper flakes
¼ cup dry white wine

Pat chicken dry and sprinkle with ½ teaspoon salt. Heat oil in an ovenproof 12-inch heavy skillet over moderately high heat until just beginning to smoke, then cook chicken, skin sides down, until browned, about 5 minutes. Turn chicken over and cook 2 minutes more, then transfer to a plate.

Pour off all but 2 tablespoons fat from skillet and cook bell peppers, onion, garlic, red pepper flakes (to taste), and remaining ¼ teaspoon salt over moderate heat, stirring, until softened, about 10 minutes. Add wine and boil 1 minute. Nestle chicken, skin sides up, into pepper mixture and cook, covered, over moderate heat until cooked through, about 15 minutes.

Turn on broiler. Remove lid from skillet and broil chicken 4 to 6 inches from heat until skin is crisp, about 1½ minutes.

cooking class
GNOCCHI

*e*VERY COUNTRY HAS a dumpling it can call its own. Italians call theirs gnocchi and they're eaten, as you might imagine, like pasta (topped with sauce). Gnocchi come in all different sizes and shapes and are made with various ingredients, from potatoes, ricotta, and semolina to pumpkin and even prunes. All varieties make excellent vehicles for flavor. We've capitalized on this to great effect; our tender potato gnocchi carry juicy tomato and salty *guanciale* (cured hog jowl) in every bite—that's

meat and potatoes the Italian way. And we couldn't think of a better way to bring a healthy dose of Parmigiano-Reggiano to our taste buds than on our buttery, crispy disks of semolina gnocchi *alla romana*.

The word gnocchi comes from the Venetian "*gnocco*" meaning "knot" or "knuckle" (historians have traced the word back to Lombardy from an old German word for knuckle "*knoche*"). Looking at the curved shapes of gnocchi it's easy to see where the inspiration came from. Another, possibly unrelated, connection is the Northern Italian slang "*gnocca*" meaning "an attractive woman"—which gives those curvy shapes a very different interpretation. Many towns along the boot-shaped peninsula claim to have invented gnocchi, and each has its own version.

The first dumplings in Italy, said to have originally appeared in the 14th century, were made with a flour/water mixture (other ingredients were capriciously added depending on who was doing the cooking). This variety often appears under the curious moniker (curious for a country that houses the Pope) of "priest strangler" in many towns. In Naples it's called *strangulaprievete*, in Lucano it's *strangulapreti*, and in Tuscany *strozzapreti* is made with spinach in the dough. Legend has it a prominent, gluttonous priest choked to death on these dumplings.

Nowadays, it's common to find gnocchi made with potatoes all over Italy, but this variety made its gastronomic debut relatively recently—in the 1860's, with the arrival of the potato from the New World. And slowly but surely the lowly tuber (first feared by Italians because it was thought to carry leprosy) assimilated into the cuisine. It has gone on to become a staple.

Most recipes call for boiling the potatoes, like ours on page 16, but in Florence where the dish is called *topini*, or "field mice," it is common to find the potatoes baked first. Older potatoes are preferred because they are drier and starchier which makes the gnocchi less gummy. In our own kitchens we found that using a yellow-fleshed potato, like a Yukon Gold, offers beautiful golden color and buttery flavor. We avoided adding eggs which can cause potato dumplings to be heavy. We also avoid overkneading the dough. The more flour that gets incorporated, the tougher the "knuckles." The same theory applies to rolling the dough into a log—roll gently. And as you'll see, flicking gnocchi off the tines of a fork takes some practice, it's all in the wrist.

Not to be out done, the Eternal City of Rome has a gnocchi all its own—no potatoes or flour here. It's made with semolina (polenta) dough (enhanced with butter, Parmigiano-Reggiano, and an egg) that is simply chilled, cut into rounds, then baked. The crisp cheesy topping gives way to a smooth, rich center—addictive enough to eat every week. In fact, in Rome, every Thursday is gnocchi day.

—Linda Immediato

GNOCCHI ALLA ROMANA
Serves 6 (first course)
Active time: 30 min Start to finish: 2 hr

- **3 cups whole milk**
- **¾ cups semolina (sometimes labeled "semolina flour"; resembles fine yellow cornmeal)**
- **1 teaspoon salt**
- **¼ cup unsalted butter plus 2 tablespoons, melted**
- **3 oz finely grated Parmigiano-Reggiano (1½ cups; see Tips, page 8)**
- **1 large egg**

Special equipment: **a 2-inch round cookie cutter**

Whisk together milk, semolina, and salt in a 2-quart heavy saucepan and bring to a boil over moderate heat, whisking. Simmer, stirring constantly with a wooden spoon, until very stiff, 5 to 8 minutes. Remove from heat and stir in 2 tablespoons butter and half of cheese. Beat in egg.

Spread gnocchi mixture ½ inch thick on an oiled baking sheet and chill, uncovered, until very firm, about 1 hour.

Preheat oven to 425°F.

Cut out rounds from gnocchi mixture with cookie cutter (push scraps into remaining mixture as you go) and arrange, slightly overlapping, in a well-buttered 13-by 9-inch baking dish. Make a small second layer in center of dish with any remaining rounds. Brush gnocchi with remaining ¼ cup butter and sprinkle with remaining half of cheese.

Bake in middle of oven until gnocchi begins to brown, 15 to 20 minutes. Let stand 5 minutes before serving.

SEMOLINA GNOCCHI (Roman-Style)

Roman-style gnocchi (recipe on preceding page) are easier to make than the kind that must be shaped with a fork.

1. The semolina thickens up almost right away, but continue to cook for 5 to 8 minutes, or until it's very stiff. Otherwise, it won't hold its shape while being cut.

2. Immediately spread the mixture ½ inch thick on a lightly oiled baking sheet, then chill. (The colder it is, the easier it is to cut.)

3. Cut out rounds with a 2-inch cookie cutter. You can't reroll scraps, so push the trimmings into the remaining mixture as you proceed.

4. Overlap rounds in a single layer in a well-buttered baking dish, then sprinkle with cheese.

POTATO GNOCCHI

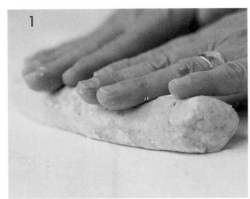

Follow this procedure for the potato *gnocchetti all'amatriciana*, page 16.

1. Roll gnocchi dough into a log very gently. If it's overhandled, the end result will be tough and heavy.

2. If your knife begins to stick while you're cutting each log into pieces, dip the blade into flour.

3. To form gnocchi, push with a floured thumb as you simultaneously roll a piece of dough against the curve of the fork tines. (You want to flick, not drag, the gnocchi off the fork.)

4. Gnocchi ready for the pot.

the menu COLLECTION

*n*o one ever said that entertaining was easy. Having friends over for wine and cheese before a movie is one thing—*real* entertaining is something altogether different. If you are planning to serve a formal meal, it can take hours just to decide what you want to cook, and then there are the details, like choosing wines, figuring out when to prepare the various dishes, and creating the perfect atmosphere. This section, filled with hundreds of full-color photographs, offers *all* the entertaining menus created by *Gourmet*'s food editors during 2003. Now, in minutes, you'll be able to review more than thirty menus, complete with wine selections, game plans for involved parties, and lovely table settings.

So, what will it be? If casual elegance is what you are looking for, simply turn this page to discover *French Connection*—a warming cool-weather menu that you'll undoubtedly turn to again and again whenever you yearn for comfort food. Gather everyone around the fire for tiny Camembert and walnut-filled puff pastries, a teaser of Gallic flavors to come. Then, settle into a leisurely evening at the table with pampering broiled scallops in a velvety white-wine sauce, followed by tender roasted pork chops in a buttery shallot and hard cider sauce served simply with a carrot and potato purée. Dessert is a free-form apple tart unlike any other. (The secret is a layer of Calvados applesauce hidden under golden sliced Gala apples).

Or, perhaps you'd like to host an hors d'oeuvres party? Every year *Gourmet* throws at least one showstopper, and in 2003 it was *Light Fantastic*. Our candle-lit party, set around a fabulous pool that reflects towering white linen-canopied tables laden with pyramids of fanciful drinks and hors d'oeuvres, is dramatic, to say the least. At a glance, one might think that form surpasses substance, but that's not the case; the food is as dazzling as the setting. How about sugar snap peas fried in beer batter and served with soy dipping sauce? Or asparagus rolls in parmesan-sprinkled puff pastry sheets sitting up on a plate? Or rich crab combined with the heat of wasabi and radish in cool little cucumber holders? If you want to impress, this is the party for you.

Maybe you've been thinking about inviting friends out for *A Weekend in the Country*, but thought it was too daunting a task? Five menus and a detailed game plan take the guesswork out of what to serve and how to organize your cooking. *A Friday Welcome* sets a relaxed tone with a kale and potato Spanish tortilla, and this ease continues with a *Saturday Night Supper* of green *pozole* with chicken, and, for dessert, Mexican chocolate ice cream. On Sunday, everyone will *Rise and Shine* to an unforgettably-good cranberry coffeecake; that evening, *The Big Night*, you'll set the dining room table for osso buco with tomatoes, olives, and *gremolata*; creamy polenta, and an luscious candied kumquat and ricotta tart. *A Morning Send Off* of tangerine mimosas and pecan waffles indulges everyone, including the cook.

As always, there are plenty of alfresco dining ideas, perfect for warm weather entertaining. Be sure to look at our *Lazy Days* menu for refreshing (and beautiful) shellfish watermelon ceviche; our *Smiles of a Summer Day* for juicy bacon-wrapped Cornish hens with raspberry balsamic glaze; and *A Pretty Grill* for a spice-rubbed skirt steak that's so good you'll end up bringing out your grill pan to prepare it long after the outdoor grill is put away.

When it comes to everyday meals, two low-fat meals and six one-dish dinners are ready for inspection. (There are even a few dinners for one, for those rare times when you manage to have an evening to yourself). After all, everybody can use a little help with those meals, too.

Come, let this collection save your precious time with great menu-planning ideas. We want you to enjoy the process of entertaining as much as the party itself.

french CONNECTION

Roasted pork chop with hard cider jus.
Opposite: Apple and Calvados tart.

it's a
KICK

51

A WEEKEND IN THE COUNTRY

friday
WELCOME

Serves 6

saturday night SUPPER

Serves 6

WARM TORTILLA CHIPS WITH SPICY CHEESE DIP
page 138

GREEN POZOLE WITH CHICKEN
page 177

Hoegaarden White beer

MEXICAN CHOCOLATE ICE CREAM
page 245

ORANGE SHORTBREAD
page 233

GAME PLAN

These menus are all about cooking with friends—you'll have the most fun if you enlist them to help out. If you're among people who love to cook, let everyone choose a recipe they'd like to make; if not, you can divvy up some of the shopping and prep work.

1 week ahead
· Make maple apricot granola
· Make shell (if freezing) for candied kumquat and ricotta tart

4 days ahead
· Make smoky tomato confit
· Make almond crunch for roasted pears
· Make Mexican chocolate ice cream

3 days ahead
· Make vanilla brown sugar syrup for pecan waffles
· Make orange shortbread

2 days ahead
· Make broth and filling for mushroom tortellini

1 day ahead
· Make spicy cheese dip
· Cook and shred chicken and make broth for *pozole*
· Make pasta dough and form tortellini
· Make osso buco
· Make shell (if chilling) for candied kumquat and ricotta tart
· Candy kumquats and make ricotta filling for tart
· Make cranberry coffeecake
· Make orange, grapefruit, and grape compote
· Make waffle batter and toast and chop pecans
· Form sausage patties

sunday
RISE
AND SHINE

Serves 6

MAPLE APRICOT
GRANOLA
page 182

CRANBERRY
COFFEECAKE
page 230

ORANGE, GRAPEFRUIT,
AND GRAPE COMPOTE
page 250

A WEEKEND IN THE COUNTRY
the
BIG NIGHT

Serves 8 to 10

Candied kumquat and ricotta tart.

A WEEKEND IN THE COUNTRY

morning send-off

Serves 6

TANGERINE MIMOSAS
page 262

CAFÉ AU LAIT
page 263

**PECAN WAFFLES WITH
SAUTÉED PINEAPPLE AND
VANILLA BROWN SUGAR SYRUP**
page 183

**HOMEMADE
SAUSAGE PATTIES**
page 167

spring fling

Serves 8

GOAT CHEESE SOUFFLÉS
IN PHYLLO CUPS
WITH FRISÉE SALAD
page 134

Firepeak Vineyard Carpe Diem Chardonnay '01

ROAST CAPON
WITH LEMON AND THYME
page 178

SPRING
VEGETABLE SAUTÉ
page 206

GARLIC
ROASTED POTATOES
page 202

SPIRAL ROLLS
page 140

Beaulieu Vineyard Tapestry Reserve '99

COCONUT
CREAM TART
page 241

CHOCOLATE ORANGE
PETITS FOURS
page 233

Château Guiraud Sauternes '99

Coconut cream tart. Opposite: Goat cheese soufflé
in phyllo cup with frisée salad; chocolate orange petits fours;
roast capon with lemon and thyme; spiral rolls.

a Passover SEDER

island
ELEGANCE

69

Mint juleps and pimento cheese sticks.
Opposite: Frozen mocha rum parfait with
walnut thins; deviled ham on celery;
shrimp in Sherry butter sauce; and hot crab and
artichoke dip with benne seed pita toasts.

under a MEDITERRANEAN SKY

73

light FANTASTIC

Schramsberg Brut Rosé Schloss
Saarstein Kabinett Riesling '01

Château de Montmirail
Cuvée des Deux Frères '00

GAME PLAN

Here is a game plan to help you take full advantage of the make-ahead possibilities. If you have helpers in the kitchen, you need only start the day before, marinating the pork and perhaps starting the tomato water for the shooters. But why not keep your sanity and prepare things at a more leisurely pace so you can relax and enjoy your party? This menu has been developed with the idea that you will have help for last-minute cooking, assembling, and serving.

2 weeks ahead:
· Make *arepas* (if freezing)

1 week ahead:
· Make rhubarb syrup with lime juice for cocktails (if freezing)
· Assemble and steam dumplings (if freezing)

3 days ahead:
· Make soy dipping sauce

2 days ahead:
· Bake cloverleaf potato chips
· Make tomato water for clam shooters
· Marinate pork for *arepas*
· Make pickled onion for *arepas*
· Roast and slice beets for goat cheese stacks

1 day ahead:
· Make rhubarb syrup
· Trim sugar snap peas for tempura
· Assemble asparagus parmesan pastry rolls
· Make cauliflower purée for caviar hors d'oeuvres

· Form cucumber cups
· Make wasabi mayonnaise for crab salad
· Cut radishes and trim sprouts for crab salad
· Pick over crabmeat for crab salad
· Assemble clam shooters
· Cook and shred pork for *arepas*
· Make *arepas*
· Assemble beet and goat cheese stacks
· Trim sorrel leaves for beet and goat cheese stacks
· Assemble and steam dumplings

4 to 6 hours ahead:
· Bake asparagus parmesan pastry rolls
· Wrap beet and goat cheese stacks in sorrel leaves
· Add lime juice, gin, and Cointreau to rhubarb syrup and chill
· Chill white wine and Champagne

2 hours ahead:
· Make tempura batter for sugar snap peas
· Add scallion to soy dipping sauce
· Bring cauliflower purée to room temperature
· Recrisp potato chips in oven (if made ahead)

Before serving:
· Assemble caviar hors d'oeuvres
· Combine crab filling ingredients
· Deep-fry sugar snap pea tempura
· Bake or reheat and cut asparagus parmesan pastry rolls
· Reheat *arepas* and pork and assemble hors d'oeuvres
· Steam dumplings

Sugar snap pea tempura. Opposite
(above): Asparagus parmesan pastry
rolls; rhubarb Collins; and steamed pork
and jicama dumplings. Below:
tomato ginger gelée clam shooters.

a PRETTY GRILL

lazy days

Serves 6

**SHELLFISH
WATERMELON
CEVICHE**
page 131

WillaKenzie Estate Willamette Valley Pinot Gris '01

**HEIRLOOM TOMATOES
WITH BACON,
BLUE CHEESE, AND BASIL**
page 220

**GRILLED STEAKS
WITH RED CHILE SAUCE**
page 158

**PICKLED RED ONIONS
WITH CILANTRO**
page 159

**CORN AND
HARICOTS VERTS
IN LIME SHALLOT BUTTER**
page 198

Concha y Toro Don Melchor Reserva Privada '98

**FRESH FIG TART
WITH ROSEMARY CORNMEAL
CRUST AND LEMON
MASCARPONE CREAM**
page 240

Essensia California Orange Muscat '01

Shellfish watermelon ceviche.
Oppossite: Grilled steaks (topped with pickled red onions) served with corn and haricot verts; heirloom tomatoes; and fresh fig tart.

forecast:
CHILE AND CRISP

smiles of a SUMMER DAY

Serves 8

HERBAL WHITE SANGRIA
page 261

CHEDDAR DILL PUFFS
page 118

CORN FRITTERS WITH ARUGULA AND WARM TOMATO SALAD
page 132

Château Routas Rouvière Rosé Coteaux Varois '02

BACON-WRAPPED CORNISH HENS WITH RASPBERRY BALSAMIC GLAZE
page 178

ORZO WITH SUMMER SQUASH AND TOASTED HAZELNUTS
page 191

Kent Rasmussen Carneros Pinot Noir '00

THREE-BERRY PIE WITH VANILLA CREAM
page 236

Three-berry pie with vanilla cream. Opposite: Bacon-wrapped Cornish hens with raspberry balsamic glaze and orzo with summer squash and toasted hazelnuts.

brunch and ALL THAT JAZZ

the VIRGINIAN

thanks for THE MEMORY

Serves 8

ESCAROLE, FENNEL, AND ORANGE SALAD
page 214

EGGPLANT LASAGNE WITH PARSLEY PESTO
page 188

Castello di Luzzano Bonarda dell'Oltrepò '00

APRICOT FROZEN YOGURT
page 244

SPICED TUILES
page 235

flavors of the AMERICAN HEARTLAND

Serves 8 to 10

ROASTED CHESTNUTS
page 115

BOURBON CHICKEN LIVER PÂTÉ
page 136

Alvear Carlos VII Amontillado

**ROAST TURKEY
WITH CIDER SAGE GRAVY**
page 180

**WILD RICE, APPLE,
AND DRIED-CRANBERRY
STUFFING**
page 194

JELLIED CRANBERRY SAUCE
page 224

**SHREDDED BRUSSELS SPROUTS
WITH MAPLE HICKORY NUTS**
page 196

CREAMED PEARL ONIONS
page 200

**MOLASSES HORSERADISH
SWEET-POTATO SPEARS**
page 204

POTATO PARSNIP PURÉE
page 202

Chappellet Napa Valley Cabernet Sauvignon '00

**BRANDIED SOUR CHERRY
AND PEAR TARTLETS**
page 238

PUMPKIN GINGER RICE PUDDING
page 256

Dow's 10-year-old Tawny Port

Turkey dinner. Opposite: Roasted chestnuts and bourbon chicken liver pâté; jelllied cranberry sauce; brandied sour cherry and pear tartlets; wild-rice, apple, and dried-cranberry stuffing.

winter LIGHT

Herb-braised ham; glazed chestnuts and haricot verts; buckwheat crêpe noodles with chive butter. Opposite: plated dinner; oyster soup with frizzled leeks; miniature tourtières with spicy tomato cranberry preserves; and maple walnut bûche de Noël.

103

sophisticated RHYTHM

low-fat: MOOD MEXICO

Each serving about 701 calories and 15 grams fat

low-fat:
COMFORTING
RESOLUTION

Serves 6

TURKEY MEATLOAF
page 179

**ROASTED RED PEPPER
TOMATO SAUCE**
page 179

**LEMON POPPY SEED
NOODLES**
page 190

**RED LEAF LETTUCE,
WATERCRESS,
AND CUCUMBER SALAD
WITH BUTTERMILK DRESSING**
page 215

**APRICOT GINGER
PEAR PARFAITS**
page 249

Each serving about 680 calories
and 19 grams fat

Grilled Pizza Margherita

Finnan Haddie Gratin

Grilled Tuna Salade Niçoise

Spinach and Cheese Strata

Pasta Primavera

six
ONE-DISH
DINNERS

Island Pork Tenderloin Salad

dinner for one:
MAJOR FLAVORS

Serves 1

dinner for one:
TRAY CHIC

Serves 1

OVEN-FRIED CHICKEN

GARLIC
MASHED POTATOES

SNAP PEAS
AND CARROTS

BAKED APPLE

the recipe
COMPENDIUM

*h*ere we've gathered all the recipes featured in The Menu Collection and hundreds of others from favorite columns like Gourmet Every Day, The Last Touch, and Seasonal Kitchen. You'll also find a host of recipes from *Gourmet*'s five special issues that appeared in 2003. Each of these editions was designed to showcase a remarkable place or memorable thing that inspires great cooking, and as you'll see, our food editors were indeed inspired. Our hope is that the recipes in this compendium will have the same effect on you.

After months of planning an extensive research trip, The Rome Issue became a reality. The menus and recipes from its pages appear in our Cuisines of the World section, but here you'll discover even more of our favorite dishes from the Eternal City, such as mozzarella in carrozza (little finger sandwiches filled with gooey cheese dotted with salty capers) and rich classic fettuccine Alfredo.

When summer was on the horizon, but not close enough, we found ourselves thinking of vacations, of sultry locales with sunny beaches and warm breezy nights. From these daydreams came The Island Issue—a joyous celebration of water-bound paradises from the Caribbean to the Greek Isles. To us, these idyllic places were fertile ground for vibrant flavors. Seared mahimahi fillets topped with a tangy hot-and-sour relish; a Grecian dessert of pastry spirals drizzled with honey and sprinkled with crunchy sesame seeds and walnuts; a not-as-sweet-as-you-might-think coconut bread; and a robust and spicy island pork tenderloin salad are just a sampling. You might want to mix up a welcoming Mai Tai or Blue Hawaiian cocktail as you consider your options.

In July, summer was in full-bloom and once again we couldn't keep our hands off everything the garden was turning up—corn, tomatoes, cherries, melons, apricots, greens, and so much more. Our annual Produce Issue was filling up quickly with tons of recipes featuring farm fresh flavors. Cherries found a home in a cherry balsamic sauce drizzled over seasoned lamb chops; melons were shaved into thin slices and topped with sea salt and fresh tarragon; collard greens and bacon were tossed with pasta; and a fresh apricot upside-down cake gave us a new twist on an old favorite. We've included these and scores of exceptional dishes of the season.

In the fall, while discussing bread during an editorial meeting, someone suddenly remembered an old "I Love Lucy" episode that ended in a yeast disaster. One by one, each editor added another television food mishap and another special issue was born—The Television Issue. So look for Elaine's blueberry muffin tops (the best part of the muffin) from *Seinfeld*; Bill Cosby's ding-dong eight-alarm chili; and Ricky Ricardo's *arroz con pollo*. They're all here.

And that's not all. We've included loads of recipes from our One-Dish Dinner column, such as a light yet filling tuna salade niçoise and an unctuous finnan haddie. Also sprinkled throughout are surprisingly tempting recipes from our Low-Fat Menus—like a succulent sea bass and spicy tomato sauce over braised fennel or moist delicious mini chocolate cupcakes—with calorie and fat information listed. All of *Gourmet*'s recipes from the Quick Kitchen column can be made in under 45 minutes (start to finish). But most can be made in even less time, which means you can serve up blade steaks with mushrooms in just 25 minutes or panfried chicken breasts with oregano garlic butter in only 30. And for those times when you have the house all to yourself, check out one of our Dinner For One recipes, like chicken legs with achiote garlic sauce served with black beans. Top it off with a tequila and lime baked pineapple for dessert—believe us, you won't miss the company.

So go ahead, take your time leafing through this section. You just might be surprised by what you find.

APPETIZERS

hors d'oeuvres

ASPARAGUS PARMESAN PASTRY ROLLS

Makes about 96 hors d'oeuvres
Active time: 2 hr   Start to finish: 2½ hr

The rolls should be served warm, so reheat them in batches as platters need replenishing.

1 (17¼-oz) package frozen puff pastry sheets, thawed
2 large egg yolks, lightly beaten with 2 tablespoons cold water
5 oz finely grated Parmigiano-Reggiano (1¾ cups packed)
28 (¾-inch-thick) asparagus (2 lb), stalks trimmed to 6-inch lengths and tips reserved if desired
3 tablespoons white or black truffle oil (1½ oz; optional)

Unfold pastry sheets and halve each parallel to fold lines. Roll out 1 half (keep remaining 3 halves chilled, covered with plastic wrap) into a 20- by 7-inch rectangle with a floured rolling pin on a well-floured surface. (Pastry will shrink slightly after rolling.) Brush off excess flour from work surface and both sides of pastry, then trim all edges with a sharp knife to make even. Cut crosswise into 6 (6½- by 3-inch) rectangles.

Brush rectangles with some egg wash and sprinkle each evenly with 1 packed tablespoon cheese, leaving a ½-inch border on long sides. Lay an asparagus stalk along 1 long side, then roll up asparagus in pastry, pressing seam to seal. Make more rolls with remaining pastry, cheese, and asparagus.

Arrange rolls, seam sides down, about 1 inch apart on lightly oiled baking sheets and brush top and sides lightly with egg wash. Chill rolls until pastry is firm, at least 15 minutes.

Put oven rack in middle position and preheat oven to 400°F.

Bake rolls in batches until puffed and golden, about 16 minutes.

Transfer with a metal spatula to a cutting board and trim about ½ inch from ends. Halve each roll crosswise, then, starting about ½ inch from either end, cut each section diagonally in half. Stand asparagus rolls on end, 2 by 2 on platters, and drizzle each with 1 drop of truffle oil (if using). Serve warm.

Cooks' notes:
· Unbaked asparagus rolls can be chilled, loosely covered with plastic wrap, up to 1 day.
· Asparagus rolls can be baked (but not cut) 4 hours ahead and kept, uncovered, at room temperature. Reheat in a preheated 350°F oven 8 to 10 minutes.
PHOTO ON PAGE 76

CAMEMBERT AUX NOIX AMUSE-BOUCHES
Miniature Camembert Walnut Pastries

Makes 40 hors d'oeuvres (serves 8)
Active time: 30 min   Start to finish: 50 min

For pastry
¼ cup walnuts (1 oz), minced
2 teaspoons unsalted butter, melted
⅛ teaspoon fine sea salt
1 sheet frozen puff pastry (from a 17¼-oz package), thawed
1 large egg, lightly beaten with 1 tablespoon water
For cheese filling
6 oz Camembert (not runny), rind discarded
⅓ cup walnuts (1¼ oz), finely chopped, toasted (see Tips, page 8), and cooled

Special equipment: **parchment paper; a 1½-inch round cookie cutter**

Make pastry:
Put oven rack in middle position and preheat oven to 400°F. Line a large baking sheet with parchment.
Stir together minced walnuts, butter, and sea salt.
Roll out pastry on a lightly floured surface with a lightly floured rolling pin into a 14- by 12-inch rectangle. Cut out 40 rounds with lightly floured cookie cutter and discard trimmings.

Brush tops of rounds with egg wash, then sprinkle each with about ¼ teaspoon walnut mixture and transfer to baking sheet. Bake rounds in oven until golden and puffed, 10 to 15 minutes, then slide pastries on parchment onto a rack to cool. (Leave oven on.)

While pastries are still warm, gently pull each one apart to make a top and a bottom. Lightly press down any puffed inner layers on tops and bottoms if necessary.

Make filling while pastry bakes:
Mash together cheese and walnuts with a fork.
Fill pastries:
Sandwich a ½-teaspoon mound of cheese filling inside each pastry (between top and bottom), then bake on parchment-lined baking sheet (it's not necessary to use a clean sheet of parchment) until cheese begins to melt, 2 to 3 minutes. Season tops of pastries with pepper and serve immediately.

Cooks' notes:
• Puff pastry can be baked and rounds separated into tops and bottoms 1 day ahead, then cooled completely and kept at room temperature in an airtight container.
• Pastries can be filled (but not baked) 1 hour ahead and kept, loosely covered, at room temperature.

CHEDDAR CAYENNE CHIPS

Makes about 28 chips (serves 6)
Active time: 35 min   Start to finish: 35 min

Cheddar is much easier to grate when it's very cold, so keep your cheese in the refrigerator until you are ready to proceed. Also, don't be tempted to use anything other than a nonstick skillet, or the chips will stick.

1 (6-oz) piece cold sharp Cheddar
Rounded ¼ teaspoon cayenne

Using largest holes on a box grater, coarsely shred enough cheese to measure 2½ cups.

Toss together cheese and cayenne in a bowl, then make 4 mounds of cheese (1 tablespoon each) about 2 inches apart in a 12-inch nonstick skillet. Cook over low heat (cheese will melt and spread), undisturbed, until bubbling and firm enough to lift, 4 to 5 minutes (do not turn over). Quickly transfer with a metal spatula to a rolling pin, allowing chips to drape over pin, and cool completely. Pour off fat from skillet and wipe clean with paper towels. Make more Cheddar chips in same manner.

Cooks' notes:
• You can make flat chips instead of curved ones by transferring them to a rack to cool instead of to a rolling pin.
• Chips can be made 3 days ahead and kept, layered between sheets of wax paper, in an airtight container at room temperature.
PHOTO ON PAGE 79

ROASTED CHESTNUTS

Serves 8 to 10
Active time: 30 min   Start to finish: 30 min

1½ to 2 lb whole chestnuts in shell
1 teaspoon vegetable oil
¼ cup water

Special equipment: **a chestnut knife (optional); a large heavy skillet (preferably cast-iron) with a lid**

Make a large X in each chestnut with chestnut knife or a sharp paring knife, cutting through shell. Toss chestnuts with oil in a bowl.

Heat dry skillet over moderately low heat until hot, then roast chestnuts in skillet on stovetop, covered, stirring every few minutes, 15 minutes.

Add water and continue to roast, covered, stirring occasionally, until water is evaporated and chestnuts are tender, about 5 minutes more. Serve hot.
PHOTO ON PAGE 98

TOMATO GINGER GELÉE CLAM SHOOTERS

Makes 60 hors d'oeuvres

Active time: 2 hr   Start to finish: 9½ hr (includes chilling)

We decided to serve these shooters in small glasses, so in order for the gelée to slide out easily we made sure the tomato ginger water is thickened but not set. We call for 60 glasses in this recipe, but for simplicity the clams can be served in their shells: Double the amount of gelatin, keeping all other measurements the same, and chill the mixture with cilantro and clams in well-scrubbed shells instead. Whichever presentation you choose, it is very important to cook the ginger thoroughly and to clean the food processor because otherwise the enzymes from the raw ginger will inhibit the action of the gelatin.

　4 lb ripe tomatoes, quartered
½ cup finely grated peeled fresh ginger (5 oz)
　2 fresh *serrano* chiles, finely chopped
　　　(including seeds)
　1 tablespoon salt
　1 tablespoon sugar
　1 cup water
60 small hard-shelled clams such as littlenecks
　　　(less than 2 inches in diameter; 7 lb),
　　　scrubbed well
　2 teaspoons unflavored gelatin (from a
　　　¼-oz envelope)
¾ cup loosely packed fresh cilantro leaves

Special equipment:　4 (20-inch) squares of
　　　cheesecloth; kitchen string; 60 (1- to
　　　1½-oz) tiny stemmed glasses or
　　　shot glasses

Make tomato ginger water:
　Purée one fourth of tomatoes with ginger in a food processor until smooth, about 2 minutes. Transfer to a small heavy saucepan and simmer, covered, stirring occasionally, 5 minutes.
　Clean processor thoroughly, then purée remaining tomatoes in batches with chiles, salt, and sugar until smooth, 2 to 3 minutes. Transfer to a bowl and stir in cooked tomato ginger purée.
　Line a large sieve with stacked cheesecloth squares and set over a deep nonreactive pot or a large clean bucket. Carefully pour purée into center of cheesecloth. Gather sides of cheesecloth up over purée to form a large sack and tie sides together securely with string as close to purée as possible but without squeezing purée. Tie sack to a wooden spoon longer than diameter of pot and remove sieve. Set spoon across top of pot, suspending sack inside pot and leaving a couple of inches underneath sack so that it will not sit in any tomato water that accumulates. (Alternatively, transfer tomato water to another container as it accumulates.) Let sack hang 4 hours at room temperature.

Prepare clams:
　Bring 1 cup water to a boil in a 7- to 8-quart heavy pot. Add clams and cook, covered, over moderately high heat, until clams are opened wide, stirring and checking frequently after 6 minutes and transferring clams as opened to a bowl. (Discard any clams that have not opened after 10 minutes.) When cool enough to handle, shuck clams.

Assemble shooters:
　Discard cheesecloth sack and its contents without squeezing. Pour tomato water through large sieve lined with a dampened paper towel into a bowl. Measure out 4 cups tomato water and reserve remainder for another use.
　Transfer ½ cup tomato water to a small saucepan, then sprinkle with gelatin and let soften 1 minute. Heat over low heat, stirring, just until gelatin is dissolved, then stir into remaining 3½ cups tomato water.
　Arrange glasses on trays and put 1 or 2 cilantro leaves in each, then a clam, and then 1 or 2 more cilantro leaves. Add about 1 tablespoon tomato water to each glass (stir water each time so gelatin remains well distributed) and chill, loosely covered with plastic wrap, at least 3 hours. (Gelatin will be thickened but not set; it needs to slide easily out of glass.)

Cooks' notes:
- Tomato water (without gelatin) can be made 2 days ahead. Pour through paper-towel-lined sieve, then chill, covered.
- Shooters can be chilled up to 1 day.

PHOTO ON PAGE 76

MOROCCAN-STYLE CHICKEN PHYLLO ROLLS

Makes 32 hors d'oeuvres
Active time: 1¼ hr   Start to finish: 2¼ hr

These rolls are based loosely on b'stilla—*a phyllo-crusted "pie" of shredded chicken that's been simmered with spices and then mixed with egg and nuts. The egg lends a custardlike richness.*

    1 small onion, finely chopped
    1 tablespoon olive oil
      Scant teaspoon salt
    ¾ teaspoon ground cumin
    ½ teaspoon ground ginger
    ½ teaspoon turmeric
    ½ teaspoon black pepper
    ¼ teaspoon ground coriander
 1¼ lb chicken thighs (with skin and bones)
    ¾ cup low-sodium chicken broth
    ½ cup water
    1 (3-inch) cinnamon stick
    ¼ cup sliced almonds, toasted (see Tips,
       page 8), cooled, and coarsely chopped
    2 large eggs, lightly beaten
    1 stick (½ cup) unsalted butter, melted
    8 (17- by 12-inch) phyllo sheets, thawed
       if frozen
    1 teaspoon ground cinnamon
    2 teaspoons brown mustard seeds

Accompaniment: **spiced tomato sauce (page 118)**

Make filling:

Cook onion in oil along with salt, cumin, ginger, turmeric, pepper, and coriander in a 3-quart heavy saucepan over moderate heat, stirring, until softened, about 5 minutes. Add chicken, broth, water, and cinnamon stick and simmer, covered, turning chicken over once, until meat is very tender, about 45 minutes total. Transfer chicken with tongs to a bowl, reserving cooking liquid.

When cool enough to handle, shred chicken, discarding skin and bones, and transfer to a large bowl. Transfer cooking liquid to a 2-cup glass measure (do not clean saucepan) and let stand 1 minute, then skim off fat and discard cinnamon stick. Return liquid to saucepan and simmer over moderately high heat, uncovered, until reduced to about ¼ cup (liquid will look like a glaze in bottom of pan), about 8 minutes, then stir into shredded chicken along with almonds.

Reserve 2 tablespoons beaten egg in a cup for egg wash. Lightly season remaining egg with salt and pepper, then cook in ½ tablespoon butter in an 8- to 10-inch nonstick skillet over moderately high heat, stirring, until just set but still slightly soft. Stir scrambled egg into filling.

Make rolls:

Put oven racks in upper and lower thirds of oven and preheat oven to 450°F.

Put 1 phyllo sheet on a work surface, keeping remaining phyllo covered with overlapping sheets of plastic wrap and a damp kitchen towel, and brush generously with some melted butter. Evenly sift ¼ teaspoon cinnamon over buttered phyllo using a fine-mesh sieve, then top with another phyllo sheet and generously brush with butter.

Halve buttered phyllo stack crosswise, then arrange 1 half with a long side nearest you. Spread ¼ cup chicken filling in a narrow strip along edge nearest you, then roll up filling tightly in phyllo, leaving ends open. Transfer roll, seam side down, to a cutting board set inside a baking pan (to help contain mustard seeds when sprinkling). Make another roll with remaining half stack. Make 6 more rolls in same manner, transferring to cutting board.

Lightly brush top of rolls with egg wash and immediately sprinkle with mustard seeds, pressing lightly on seeds to help adhere. Cut each roll crosswise into 4 pieces and arrange pieces 1 inch apart on 2 baking sheets. Bake, switching position of sheets halfway through baking, until phyllo is golden brown, about 12 minutes total.

Transfer rolls to a rack to cool slightly.

Cooks' notes:
• Rolls can be assembled (but not coated or cut) 1 day ahead and chilled, covered.
• Rolls can be assembled and cut (but not coated or baked) 2 weeks ahead and frozen, wrapped well in plastic wrap. Coat frozen rolls, then bake (do not thaw) in a preheated 350°F oven about 20 minutes.

PHOTO ON PAGE 105

SPICED TOMATO SAUCE

Makes about 1½ cups
Active time: 20 min   Start to finish: 1 hr

This Moroccan-style dipping sauce would also be delicious on grilled chicken or fish.

⅓ cup finely chopped onion
1 garlic clove, finely chopped
1½ teaspoons finely chopped peeled fresh ginger
¾ teaspoon ground cumin
½ teaspoon hot paprika
¼ teaspoon ground cinnamon
   Pinch of cayenne
   Pinch of ground cloves
1 tablespoon olive oil
1½ tablespoons cider vinegar
1 (14½- to 15-oz) can whole tomatoes in juice, coarsely chopped (reserving juice)
2 tablespoons light brown sugar

Cook onion, garlic, ginger, and spices in oil in a 1- to 2- quart heavy saucepan over moderately low heat, stirring, until onion is softened, about 4 minutes. Stir in vinegar and simmer over moderately low heat 1 minute. Add tomatoes (with juice) and brown sugar, then increase heat to moderate and simmer, stirring occasionally, until slightly thickened, about 30 minutes. Cool slightly, about 5 minutes.

Purée sauce in a blender until smooth (use caution when blending hot liquids). Serve at room temperature.

Cooks' note:
• Sauce can be made 3 days ahead and cooled completely, then chilled, covered.

CHEDDAR DILL PUFFS

Makes about 60 hors d'oeuvres
Active time: 20 min   Start to finish: 1¼ hr

We like to think of these as an American version of gougères.

1 cup water
1 stick (½ cup) unsalted butter, cut into tablespoon pieces
½ teaspoon salt
1 cup all-purpose flour
4 to 5 large eggs
6 oz extra-sharp Cheddar (preferably yellow), finely grated (1½ cups)
2 tablespoons finely chopped fresh dill

Special equipment: **parchment paper (optional); a pastry bag fitted with ½-inch plain tip (optional)**

Put oven racks in upper and lower thirds of oven and preheat oven to 375°F. Line 2 large baking sheets with parchment or lightly butter sheets.

Bring water to a boil with butter and salt in a 3-quart heavy saucepan over high heat, then reduce heat to moderate. Add flour all at once and cook, stirring vigorously with a wooden spoon, until mixture pulls away from side of pan, about 2 minutes. Remove from heat and cool slightly, about 3 minutes, then add 4 eggs 1 at a time, beating well after each addition (batter will appear to separate but will then become smooth). Mixture should be glossy and just stiff enough to hold soft peaks and fall softly from a spoon. If batter is too stiff, beat remaining egg in a small bowl and add to batter 1 teaspoon at a time, beating and then testing batter until it reaches proper consistency. Stir in cheese and dill.

Fill pastry bag with batter and pipe 15 (1-inch-diameter) mounds (or spoon level tablespoons) about 1 inch apart onto each sheet. Bake in upper and lower thirds of oven, switching position of sheets halfway through baking, until puffed, golden, and crisp, about 30 minutes total. Make more puffs in same manner. Serve warm.

Cooks' note:
• Puffs can be made 2 days ahead and cooled completely, then chilled in sealed plastic bags or frozen 1 week. Reheat, uncovered, on baking sheets in a 350°F oven 10 minutes if chilled or 15 minutes if frozen.

PARMESAN CUSTARD TART WITH BUTTERNUT SQUASH

Makes 32 hors d'oeuvres
Active time: 45 min   Start to finish: 4 hr
(includes making tart shell)

For tart shell
1¼ cups all-purpose flour
2½ teaspoons finely chopped fresh sage
    Rounded ¼ teaspoon salt
¾ stick (6 tablespoons) cold unsalted butter,
    cut into cubes
2 tablespoons cold vegetable shortening,
    cut into pieces
2 to 4 tablespoons ice water
1 large egg white, lightly beaten
For filling
2 oz finely grated Parmigiano-Reggiano
    (1 cup; see Tips, page 8)
1 cup heavy cream
1½ tablespoons olive oil
¾ lb piece butternut squash, peeled, seeded,
    and cut into ½-inch pieces (2 cups)
⅜ teaspoon salt
¼ teaspoon coarsely ground black pepper
1 whole large egg
1 large egg yolk

Special equipment: **a pastry or bench scraper; a
    13½- by 4-inch rectangular or 8½-inch
    round fluted tart pan with a removable
    bottom; pie weights or raw rice**
Garnish: **fried sage leaves (page 120)**

Make shell:
Combine flour, sage, and salt in a food processor, then add butter and shortening and pulse until mixture resembles coarse meal with some small (roughly pea-size) butter lumps. Drizzle with 2 tablespoons ice water and pulse until just incorporated.

Squeeze a small handful of dough: If it doesn't hold together, add more ice water, 1 tablespoon at a time, pulsing until just incorporated, then test again. (Do not overwork, or pastry will be tough.)

Turn out dough onto a lightly floured surface and divide into 4 portions. With heel of your hand, smear each portion once or twice in a forward motion to help distribute fat. Gather dough into a ball with scraper, then flatten into a 5-inch square. Chill dough, wrapped in plastic wrap, until firm, at least 1 hour.

Put oven rack in middle position and preheat oven to 375°F.

Roll out dough on a lightly floured surface with a floured rolling pin into a 17- by 8-inch rectangle and fit into tart pan. Trim excess dough, leaving a ½-inch overhang, then fold overhang inward and press against side of pan to reinforce edge. Lightly prick bottom and sides of shell all over with a fork. Chill until firm, about 30 minutes.

Line pastry shell with foil and fill with pie weights. Bake until sides are set and edges are pale golden, 18 to 20 minutes. Carefully remove foil and weights and bake shell until bottom is pale golden, 10 to 15 minutes more. Lightly brush bottom and sides of shell with egg white and continue to bake until dry and shiny, about 5 minutes. Cool completely in pan on a rack, about 15 minutes.

Reduce oven temperature to 325°F.
Make filling while shell bakes:
Bring cheese and cream just to a boil in a small heavy saucepan over moderate heat, stirring occasionally. Remove from heat and steep, covered, 30 minutes. Pour steeped cream through a fine-mesh sieve into a bowl, pressing hard on cheese solids and then discarding them.

While cream steeps, heat oil in a 10-inch heavy nonstick skillet over moderately high heat until hot but not smoking, then sauté squash with ⅛ teaspoon salt and ⅛ teaspoon pepper, turning, until lightly browned on all sides, 8 to 10 minutes. Transfer with a slotted spoon to paper towels to drain and cool slightly.

Whisk together whole egg, yolk, remaining ¼ teaspoon salt, and remaining ⅛ teaspoon pepper in a bowl until combined. Add steeped cream, whisking until smooth.

Fill and bake tart:
Scatter squash evenly in tart shell and pour custard over. Bake until custard is just set and golden in patches, 30 to 35 minutes. Cool tart in pan on rack at least 20 minutes. Halve tart crosswise, then cut in half lengthwise and cut each quarter into 8 pieces. Serve warm or at room temperature.

Cooks' notes:
• **Pastry dough can be chilled up to 1 day. Let stand
   at room temperature until slightly softened, about
   20 minutes, before rolling out.**
• **Tart can be baked 6 hours ahead and cooled
   completely, then kept, loosely covered with plastic
   wrap, at room temperature.**

FRIED SAGE LEAVES

Makes 32 leaves (garnish)
Active time: 5 min   Start to finish: 15 min

**1½ cups vegetable oil
32 small fresh sage leaves**

Special equipment: **a deep-fat thermometer**

Heat oil in a 1- to 1½-quart heavy saucepan until it registers 365°F on thermometer. Fry sage in 5 or 6 batches, stirring, 5 seconds (leaves will crisp as they cool). Transfer with a slotted spoon to paper towels to drain and season with salt.

Cooks' note:
• Sage leaves can be fried 2 days ahead and cooled completely, then kept in an airtight container at room temperature.

SORREL-WRAPPED GOAT CHEESE AND BEET STACKS

Makes about 60 hors d'oeuvres
Active time: 1 hr   Start to finish: 2½ hr

If you can't get sorrel at your local market, arugula leaves or large basil leaves are a good alternative.

**6 medium yellow or red beets (2½ lb with greens), trimmed, leaving 1 inch of stems attached
¼ cup extra-virgin olive oil
2 (1½-inch-diameter) logs fresh mild goat cheese (herbed or plain; 8 oz total), chilled
30 fresh sorrel leaves (about 4 by 2 inches), leaves halved lengthwise and center ribs and stems discarded**

Special equipment: **a 1½-inch round cookie cutter (at least 1 inch deep); wooden picks**

Put oven rack in middle position and preheat oven to 425°F.
Wrap beets in foil in 2 packages (3 per package) and roast until tender, 1¼ to 1½ hours. When cool enough to handle, peel beets and cut off stems and root ends. Halve beets crosswise and arrange, cut sides down, on a work surface. Cut out a cylinder from each half with cookie cutter. Halve each cylinder lengthwise,

then cut crosswise into generous ¼-inch-thick slices.
Line a tray with plastic wrap and brush plastic wrap with some oil. Cut cheese logs crosswise into ¼-inch-thick slices with an oiled knife, then halve slices. Arrange cheese slices in 1 layer on tray and brush with some oil, then top each with a slice of beet.
Arrange sorrel leaf halves, veined sides up, on work surface. Put a cheese and beet stack in middle of each leaf half, then wrap sorrel over stack and secure with a pick.

Cooks' notes:
• Beets can be roasted and sliced 2 days ahead and chilled in a sealed plastic bag.
• Cheese and beet stacks (without sorrel) can be assembled 1 day ahead and chilled on tray, covered with plastic wrap.
• Sorrel leaves can be trimmed 1 day ahead and chilled in a sealed plastic bag lined with dampened paper towels.
• Hors d'oeuvres can be assembled 4 hours ahead and chilled, loosely covered with plastic wrap.

FRIED PORTABELLA MUSHROOMS

Makes about 30 hors d'oeuvres
Active time: 30 min   Start to finish: 30 min

**4 cups fresh rye bread crumbs (from 6 large oval slices of rye with seeds, finely ground in a food processor)
½ teaspoon salt
¼ teaspoon black pepper
3 large eggs
2 (6-oz) packages sliced portabella mushrooms or 5 large portabella mushroom caps, cut crosswise into ½-inch-thick slices
About 4 cups vegetable oil**

Special equipment: **a deep-fat thermometer**
Accompaniment: **lemon wedges**

Toss crumbs with salt and pepper in a bowl and spread on a large plate.
Lightly beat eggs in a bowl. Dip mushroom slices 3 or 4 at a time into egg, letting excess drip off, then dredge in bread crumbs, pressing mushroom slices into crumbs to help adhere and turning to coat. (Coating will be uneven.) Transfer to a tray.
Heat 1 inch oil in a 3- to 4-quart heavy saucepan

over moderate heat until it registers 350°F on a deep-fat thermometer. Fry mushrooms in batches of 7 or 8, turning over occasionally, until golden, 1 to 2 minutes per batch, returning oil to 350°F between batches. Transfer mushrooms with a slotted spoon to paper towels to drain. Season with salt and serve warm.

Cooks' note:
• Mushrooms can be fried 2 hours ahead and kept, loosely covered with foil, on fresh paper towels at room temperature. Transfer to a large baking sheet, arranging in 1 layer, and reheat in a preheated 350°F oven until warm, 10 to 15 minutes.

DEVILED HAM ON CELERY

Makes about 32 hors d'oeuvres
Active time: 35 min   Start to finish: 35 min

We wanted to give this savory starter a modern look, so we cut away the curved edges of the celery to make flat pieces. If you're short on time, it looks just as nice with the edges left on. You will have about ¼ cup deviled ham left over—you can make a few more celery hors d'oeuvres or simply put it in the fridge to serve on crackers the next day.

 10 celery ribs, strings discarded if desired
 ½ lb thinly sliced (⅛-inch-thick) cooked
      smoked ham
 ¼ cup minced fresh flat-leaf parsley
 ¼ cup mayonnaise
  2 tablespoons Dijon mustard
 ½ teaspoon Worcestershire sauce
 ½ teaspoon Sherry vinegar or cider vinegar

Trim a thin strip down length of rounded side of each celery rib to form a flat bottom, then rest celery on flat bottom. Cut away curved edges with a large knife to form flat-sided pieces of celery, discarding trimmings. Diagonally cut celery into 32 (1¼-inch) lengths.

Pulse half of ham in a food processor until finely chopped, then mince remaining ham with a sharp large knife. Stir together finely chopped and minced ham with remaining ingredients and pepper to taste in a bowl, then mound 1 teaspoon of filling onto each piece of celery.

Cooks' notes:
• Celery can be cut 6 hours ahead and chilled, wrapped tightly in plastic wrap.
• Deviled ham can be made 1 day ahead and chilled, covered.

PHOTO ON PAGE 71

MOZZARELLA IN CARROZZA

Makes 24 hors d'oeuvres
Active time: 20 min   Start to finish: 20 min

 ¼ cup drained bottled capers, chopped
 12 slices firm white sandwich bread
  6 oz fresh mozzarella, cut into ¼-inch-thick
      slices, at room temperature
 ¼ cup all-purpose flour
  2 large eggs
  2 tablespoons milk
  1 tablespoon unsalted butter
  2 tablespoons olive oil

Divide capers among 12 bread slices and spread evenly. Divide mozzarella among 6 slices and sprinkle with pepper to taste. Make into 6 sandwiches, then cut off and discard crusts to form 3-inch squares.

Coat sandwiches with flour, knocking off excess. Beat together eggs, milk, and a pinch each of salt and pepper in another small shallow bowl.

Heat ½ tablespoon butter with 1 tablespoon oil in a 10-inch heavy skillet over moderate heat until foam subsides. Meanwhile, coat 3 sandwiches, 1 at a time, with egg mixture. Fry, turning over once, until golden brown, about 5 minutes total, then drain on paper towels. Coat and fry remaining 3 sandwiches in same manner.

Cut fried sandwiches into quarters and serve immediately.

MUSTARD AND CHEESE CRACKERS

Makes about 5 dozen crackers
Active time: 25 min   Start to finish: 3 hr (including chilling)

1 stick (½ cup) unsalted butter, cut into
    tablespoon pieces
½ lb Swiss cheese, coarsely grated (2¼ cups)
1 cup all-purpose flour
3 tablespoons Dijon mustard
2 teaspoons dry mustard
1½ teaspoons mustard seeds
1 teaspoon salt

Blend butter and cheese in a food processor until almost smooth. Add remaining ingredients and pulse until just combined. Divide dough between 2 sheets of wax paper and roll each half into an 8-inch log. Freeze, wrapped in wax paper and then foil, until firm, 1½ to 2 hours.

Put oven racks in upper and lower thirds of oven and preheat oven to 350°F. Butter 2 large baking sheets.

Cut 1 log crosswise into ¼-inch-thick slices and arrange about 1 inch apart on baking sheets. Bake in upper and lower thirds of oven, switching position of sheets halfway through baking, until edges are golden brown, about 15 minutes total. Transfer crackers to a rack to cool. Repeat with remaining dough.

SUGAR SNAP PEA TEMPURA

Makes about 120 hors d'oeuvres
Active time: 45 min   Start to finish: 45 min

These tempura hors d'oeuvres should be served warm, so fry a couple of batches at a time as needed.

1 cup all-purpose flour
1 cup beer (8 oz; not dark)
1 to 1½ qt vegetable oil
1 lb sugar snap peas, trimmed

Special equipment: **a deep-fat thermometer**
Accompaniment: **soy dipping sauce (recipe follows)**

Whisk together flour and beer in a bowl until smooth.

Heat 2 inches oil in a 4-quart heavy pot over moderate heat until it registers 365°F on thermometer.

Working in batches of about 15, toss sugar snaps in batter until coated. Lift sugar snaps out of batter 1 at a time, letting excess batter drip off, and transfer to oil. Fry sugar snaps, turning with a slotted spoon, until golden, about 1½ minutes. Transfer with slotted spoon to paper towels to drain. (Return oil to 365°F between batches.)

Serve sugar snaps warm.

Cooks' notes:
• Peas can be trimmed 1 day ahead and chilled in a sealed plastic bag lined with dampened paper towels.
• Batter can be made 2 hours ahead and chilled, covered. Whisk before using.

PHOTO ON PAGE 77

SOY DIPPING SAUCE

Makes about 2 cups
Active time: 5 min   Start to finish: 5 min

We serve this sauce with both the sugar snap pea tempura (recipe precedes) and the pork and jicama dumplings (page 124). If you make only one of these hors d'oeuvres, however, this recipe should be halved.

1 cup soy sauce
½ cup water
¼ cup plus 2 tablespoons seasoned
    rice vinegar
4 teaspoons sugar
¼ cup thinly sliced scallion

Stir together soy sauce, water, vinegar, and sugar until sugar is dissolved. Just before serving, stir in sliced scallion.

Cooks' note:
• Dipping sauce (without scallion) can be made 3 days ahead and chilled, covered. Stir in scallion and bring to room temperature before serving.

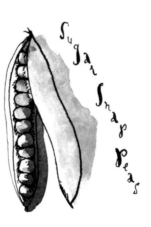

PIMENTO CHEESE STICKS

Makes about 64 hors d'oeuvres
Active time: 1 hr   Start to finish: 1¼ hr

These cheese sticks are a spin on the beloved southern spread "pimento cheese." Made from shredded Cheddar, mayonnaise, and chopped pimento peppers from a jar, it's used on everything from sandwiches to crackers and celery to burgers.

½ cup plus 1 tablespoon all-purpose flour
¼ teaspoon baking powder
⅛ teaspoon salt
⅛ teaspoon cayenne
½ stick (¼ cup) unsalted butter, softened
½ lb sharp Cheddar cheese, grated (2 cups)
1 (4-oz) jar sliced pimentos, rinsed, minced, and patted dry (½ cup)

Put oven racks in upper and lower thirds of oven and preheat oven to 350°F.

Whisk together flour, baking powder, salt, and cayenne in a bowl. Beat together butter and cheese in a large bowl with an electric mixer at high speed until combined well, then beat in pimentos. Reduce speed to low, then add flour mixture and mix just until a dough forms.

Roll 1 level teaspoon dough into a ball with lightly floured hands, then roll ball on a lightly floured surface into a 5-inch-long rope and transfer to a large baking sheet (ungreased). Make more ropes with remaining dough, arranging them about 1 inch apart on 2 large baking sheets.

Bake cheese sticks in upper and lower thirds of oven, switching position of sheets halfway through baking, until pale golden, 15 to 18 minutes total (sticks will flatten slightly). Carefully transfer with a metal spatula to racks to cool.

Cooks' note:
• **Cheese sticks can be made 1 day ahead and kept in an airtight container at room temperature. Recrisp in a preheated 375°F oven 2 to 3 minutes before serving.**
PHOTO ON PAGE 70

SCALLION CILANTRO PANCAKES

Makes 32 hors d'oeuvres
Active time: 35 min   Start to finish: 35 min

For dipping sauce
⅓ cup soy sauce
2 tablespoons rice vinegar (not seasoned)
⅜ teaspoon Asian sesame oil
1 teaspoon sesame seeds, toasted (see Tips, page 8)
For pancakes
¾ cup all-purpose flour
¼ cup rice flour (not from sweet rice)
    Slightly rounded ½ teaspoon salt
1 whole large egg
1 large egg yolk
1 cup water
1 small fresh green Thai or serrano chile, minced
⅛ teaspoon black pepper
⅛ teaspoon Asian sesame oil
1 tablespoon vegetable oil
4 scallions (pale green and dark green parts only), diagonally sliced into 1½-inch pieces
¼ cup loosely packed small fresh cilantro leaves

Make sauce:
Stir together soy sauce, vinegar, and oil in a bowl, then stir in sesame seeds.

Make pancakes:
Whisk together flours, salt, whole egg, yolk, water, chile, black pepper, and sesame oil in a bowl (batter will be thin). Heat ¾ teaspoon vegetable oil in an 8-inch nonstick skillet over moderately high heat until hot but not smoking. Pour in ⅓ cup batter, then scatter one fourth of scallions and one fourth of cilantro leaves over top, gently pressing into pancake. Fry pancake until underside is pale golden, about 2 minutes. Turn pancake over and cook until scallions are lightly browned, about 1 minute, then transfer to paper towels. Make 3 more pancakes in same manner, adding vegetable oil to skillet each time (there may be some leftover batter).

Transfer pancakes to a cutting board and cut each into 8 wedges. Serve warm or at room temperature, with dipping sauce.

Cooks' note:
• **Sauce can be made 1 day ahead and chilled, covered.**

STEAMED PORK AND JICAMA DUMPLINGS

Makes about 60 hors d'oeuvres
Active time: 1½ hr   Start to finish: 1¾ hr

These dumplings are traditionally cooked in stacked Asian bamboo or metal steamers; you can also use a pasta pot with a deep perforated colander-steamer insert. If your pot has a second shallow colander-steamer insert, you can steam 2 batches at once. The dumplings should be served warm, so reheat them in batches as platters need replenishing.

  1 large egg white
  2 tablespoons minced peeled fresh ginger
  1 tablespoon minced garlic
  1 tablespoon peanut or vegetable oil
  1 tablespoon Asian sesame oil
  1 tablespoon soy sauce
  1 tablespoon cornstarch
  2 teaspoons sugar
  ½ teaspoon salt
  1 cup diced (¼ inch) peeled jicama
  ½ cup minced scallion
  1½ lb ground pork (not lean)
  60 wonton wrappers (from two 12- to 14-oz
    packages), thawed if frozen
  2 tablespoons black sesame seeds, toasted
    (see Tips, page 8)
  2 tablespoons white sesame seeds, toasted

Special equipment: **a 2½-inch round cookie cutter; a pasta pot with a deep perforated colander-steamer insert or a metal steamer**
Accompaniment: **soy dipping sauce (page 122)**

  Make filling:
  Lightly whisk egg white in a large bowl, then add ginger, garlic, peanut oil, sesame oil, soy sauce, cornstarch, sugar, and salt and whisk until sugar and salt are dissolved. Add jicama, scallion, and pork and mix together with your hands until combined well.
  Assemble dumplings:
  Separate wonton wrappers and restack in piles of 10. Cut through each stack with cookie cutter and discard trimmings. Arrange 6 rounds on a work surface (keep remaining rounds covered with plastic wrap) and mound a scant tablespoon filling in center of each. Lightly moisten edge of wrappers with a finger dipped in water. Working with 1 at a time and leaving dumpling on flat surface, gather edge of wrapper around side of filling, pleating wrapper to form a cup and pressing pleats against filling (leave dumpling open at top). Flatten filling flush with edge of wrapper with wet finger and transfer dumpling to a tray. Make more dumplings with remaining rounds and filling.
  Steam dumplings:
  Generously oil bottom of colander-steamer insert and bring a few inches of water to a boil in pot so that bottom of insert sits above water. Arrange 10 dumplings, about ½ inch apart, in insert and steam over moderate heat, covered, until dough is translucent and filling is just cooked through, about 6 minutes.
  Stir together black and white sesame seeds and sprinkle over dumplings. Serve immediately.

  Cooks' note:
  • Dumplings (without sesame seeds) can be formed and steamed 1 day ahead and cooled completely, then chilled, covered. Steamed dumplings can also be frozen 1 week; freeze in 1 layer on a plastic-wrapped tray until hardened, then transfer to a sealable plastic bag. Reheat (do not thaw if frozen) in colander-steamer insert over simmering water (over low heat) until heated through, about 6 minutes.
  PHOTO ON PAGE 76

BAKED SHRIMP TOASTS

Makes 32 hors d'oeuvres
Active time: 20 min   Start to finish: 1¾ hr
(includes marinating shrimp)

  4 teaspoons minced garlic
  1 tablespoon minced peeled fresh ginger
  1 tablespoon vegetable oil
  1 tablespoon mirin
  2 teaspoons soy sauce
  ½ teaspoon salt
  ¾ lb medium shrimp in shell (31 to 35 per lb),
    peeled, deveined, and cut into
    ½-inch pieces
  3 tablespoons chopped fresh cilantro
  1 (9- by 4-inch) white Pullman loaf,
    unsliced

  Cook garlic and ginger in oil in an 8- to 9-inch heavy skillet over moderate heat, stirring, until softened and fragrant, about 1 minute. Add mirin, soy sauce, and salt (omit salt if making ahead; see cooks' note, below) and simmer, stirring, 15 seconds. Transfer marinade to a bowl and cool to room temperature.

Add shrimp and cilantro, tossing to coat well, and marinate, covered and chilled, 1 hour.

Put oven rack in upper third of oven and preheat oven to 350°F.

Turn bread loaf on its side and evenly cut crust from bottom of loaf using a long serrated knife, discarding crust, then cut a ⅜-inch-thick slice from bottom and trim crust from sides of slice. Put slice on a baking sheet (reserve rest of loaf for another use) and bake, turning over once, until dry but not colored, 8 minutes total. Remove bread from oven but leave on baking sheet. Immediately increase oven temperature to 475°F.

Spread top of hot toast with all of shrimp mixture, packing it down into a thick even layer and covering surface entirely. Make sure oven temperature has reached 475°F, then bake shrimp toast until topping is cooked through, 12 to 15 minutes. Transfer with a large flat spatula to a rack to cool 5 minutes, then transfer to a cutting board.

Halve shrimp toast crosswise with a very sharp knife, then cut each half lengthwise into fourths, making 8 strips total. Cut each strip into 4 pieces. Serve toasts warm or at room temperature.

Cooks' note:
- Shrimp can be marinated (without salt in marinade) up to 4 hours. Stir in salt before proceeding.

PHOTO ON PAGE 104

MINIATURE TOURTIÈRES
Pork Pies

Makes 24 hors d'oeuvres
Active time: 40 min   Start to finish: 1¼ hr

Every French-Canadian home serves a version of tourtière *during the holidays. Various thickeners (such as flour, crushed crackers, or even oats) can be used to bind the filling. Our version is made with flour, and the filling is enclosed in a tender biscuit crust. We decorated our pies with a maple-leaf-shaped cutout.*

For filling
 1 lb lean ground pork
 1 medium onion, finely chopped (¾ cup)
 1 garlic clove, minced
 ½ teaspoon dried savory, crumbled
 ½ teaspoon salt
 ¼ teaspoon ground allspice
 ¼ teaspoon black pepper
 3 tablespoons all-purpose flour

For pastry
 1½ cups all-purpose flour
 1½ teaspoons baking powder
 1 teaspoon salt
 3 tablespoons cold vegetable shortening
 2 tablespoons cold unsalted butter, cut into ½-inch cubes
 ½ cup whole milk

Special equipment: **a 3-inch round cookie cutter; a 1¼- to 1½-inch leaf-shaped cookie cutter (preferably maple); 2 mini-muffin pans, each with 12 (⅛-cup) muffin cups**
Accompaniment: **spicy tomato cranberry preserves (page 126)**

Make filling:
Cook pork with onion, garlic, savory, salt, allspice, and pepper in a 12-inch nonstick skillet over moderate heat, stirring frequently and breaking up lumps with a fork, until pork is no longer pink, 5 to 7 minutes. Sprinkle with flour and cook, stirring, until thickened, 3 to 4 minutes. Cool filling completely.

Make pastry while filling cools:
Put oven rack in middle position and preheat oven to 425°F.

Whisk together flour, baking powder, and salt in a bowl. Blend in shortening and butter with a pastry blender or your fingertips until mixture resembles coarse meal. Add milk and stir with a fork just until a dough forms. Turn out dough onto a lightly floured surface and gently knead 10 to 12 times. Roll out dough on lightly floured surface with a floured rolling pin into a rough 18-inch round (⅛ inch thick), dusting with just enough additional flour to keep dough from sticking. Cut out 24 rounds with 3-inch cutter and 24 leaves with leaf-shaped cutter. Make decorative lines on leaves with tip of a sharp paring knife.

Fit each round into a muffin cup and fill with a rounded tablespoon of filling. Arrange leaves on filling.

Bake pies until crusts are golden, 15 to 17 minutes. Lift pies out of muffin cups and transfer to a rack. Cool to warm, about 15 minutes.

Cooks' notes:
- Filling can be made 1 day ahead and chilled, covered. Bring to room temperature before using.
- Pies can be assembled and baked 6 hours ahead and cooled, uncovered, then chilled, uncovered. Serve at room temperature or reheat in 350°F oven until warm.

PHOTO ON PAGE 103

SPICY TOMATO CRANBERRY PRESERVES

Makes about 2 cups
Active time: 20 min   Start to finish: 9½ hr
(includes cooling and chilling)

1 small red onion, chopped (½ cup)
1 (14- to 16-oz) can whole tomatoes in juice,
   including juice
1 cup fresh or frozen cranberries, coarsely
   chopped in a food processor
⅔ cup sugar
⅓ cup cider vinegar
2 (4- by 1-inch) strips fresh orange zest
1 (4- by 1-inch) strip fresh lemon zest
¼ teaspoon dried hot red pepper flakes, or
   to taste
⅛ teaspoon salt

Bring all ingredients to a boil in a 2-quart heavy nonreactive saucepan over moderate heat, stirring and breaking up tomatoes. Reduce heat and simmer, uncovered, stirring frequently, until thick, 20 to 25 minutes. Cool preserves, then chill, covered, at least 8 hours (for flavors to develop).

Cooks' note:
• Preserves can be chilled up to 1 week.

AREPAS WITH PULLED PORK AND PICKLED ONION

Makes about 60 hors d'oeuvres
Active time: 2 hr   Start to finish: 12½ hr
(includes pickling and marinating)

These hors d'oeuvres should be served warm, so reheat the arepas *in batches as platters need replenishing.*

For pickled onion
1 medium red onion, cut into ¾-inch-wide
   wedges, then very thinly sliced crosswise
1 to 2 fresh *habanero* or Scotch bonnet chiles,
   seeded, deveined, and very finely chopped
½ cup distilled white vinegar
½ teaspoon dried oregano (preferably
   Mexican), crumbled
½ teaspoon salt, or to taste
For pork
½ teaspoon cumin seeds

¼ teaspoon whole allspice
½ teaspoon whole black peppercorns
2 tablespoons achiote (annatto) seeds
6 large garlic cloves, coarsely chopped
1½ teaspoons salt
1 teaspoon dried oregano (preferably
   Mexican), crumbled
⅓ cup fresh orange juice
⅓ cup distilled white vinegar
3 lb pork shoulder chops (¾ inch thick)
½ cup water
   For arepas
3 cups whole milk
½ stick (¼ cup) unsalted butter, cut into
   tablespoon pieces
1½ cups white *arepa* flour
1 tablespoon sugar
1 teaspoon salt
5 oz coarsely grated mozzarella (1 cup)
2½ tablespoons vegetable oil

Make pickled onion:
Stir together all pickled onion ingredients in a bowl and chill, covered, at least 12 hours.
Marinate pork while onion chills:
Toast cumin, allspice, and peppercorns together in a dry heavy skillet over moderate heat, stirring, until fragrant, 1 to 2 minutes. Finely grind toasted spices with achiote in an electric coffee/spice grinder or with a mortar and pestle. Mince garlic and mash to a paste with salt using a heavy knife, then transfer to a 2½- to 3-quart shallow glass or ceramic baking dish. Stir in spice mixture, oregano, orange juice, and vinegar. Add pork and rub meat all over with marinade. Marinate, covered and chilled, at least 2 hours.
Cook pork while onion chills:
Put oven rack in middle position and preheat oven to 325°F.
Bring pork to room temperature, then add water to baking dish and cover tightly with foil. Bake until very tender, 1¾ to 2 hours. (Leave oven on.)
Uncover pork and, when cool enough to handle, shred meat on a cutting board, discarding bones and excess fat. Transfer meat and any juices accumulated on cutting board to baking dish.
Make arepas *while pork cooks:*
Bring milk to a simmer in a small saucepan, then remove from heat and reserve ½ cup in a small bowl. Add butter to remaining 2½ cups hot milk and stir until melted.

Toss together white *arepa* flour, sugar, salt, and mozzarella in a large bowl. Add hot milk with butter and stir until combined. Let mixture stand until milk is absorbed, 1 to 2 minutes (dough will be soft; it will continue to stiffen as it stands).

Line a large tray with wax paper. Form 1 level tablespoon dough into a ball. Flatten ball to a 1½- to 1¾-inch-diameter disk and transfer to tray. Form more disks with remaining dough in same manner, stirring in some of reserved milk if dough becomes too stiff and edges of disks crack when flattened.

Heat ½ tablespoon oil in a 12-inch nonstick skillet over moderately low heat until hot, then cook *arepas* in batches of 10 to 12, turning over once, until golden in patches, 8 to 12 minutes total. (Add more oil to skillet between batches as needed.) Transfer to baking sheets as cooked.

Reheat *arepas* in batches as needed, covered with foil, until heated through, 10 to 15 minutes, then top with pork and pickled onion. Serve warm.

Cooks' notes:
• Pickled onion can be chilled up to 2 days.
• Pulled pork can be made 2 days ahead, first marinated (up to 1 day), then cooked and shredded 1 day ahead and chilled, covered. Reheat, covered, in a preheated 350°F oven 10 to 15 minutes.
• *Arepas* can be made 1 day ahead and cooled completely, then chilled, covered. Reheat in oven before serving. *Arepas* can also be made 2 weeks ahead and frozen, layered between sheets of plastic wrap, in an airtight container. Thaw 30 minutes at room temperature before reheating.

ONION, TOMATO, AND OLIVE PIZZAS

Makes 32 hors d'oeuvres
Active time: 45 min   Start to finish: 5 hr (includes thawing dough)

These quick and easy pizzas make great use of store-bought pizza dough, which is available in your grocer's freezer.

 2 medium onions, halved lengthwise and
   thinly sliced lengthwise
 2 garlic cloves, finely chopped
 1 teaspoon anchovy paste
 ¼ teaspoon salt
 ¼ teaspoon black pepper
 ¼ teaspoon sugar
 2 tablespoons extra-virgin olive oil

 ½ lb frozen pizza dough, thawed
 ¾ cup grape tomatoes (4½ oz), cut crosswise
   into ¼-inch-thick slices
 ¼ cup Kalamata olives (1½ oz), pitted and
   cut into slivers
 1 teaspoon fresh thyme leaves
   Scant ½ teaspoon flaky sea salt such
   as Maldon

Special equipment: **parchment paper**

Put oven rack in middle position and preheat oven to 475°F. Line a baking sheet with parchment paper.

Cook onions, garlic, anchovy paste, salt, pepper, and sugar in oil in a 12-inch heavy skillet over moderate heat, stirring frequently, until onions are caramelized and very soft, 25 to 30 minutes.

Divide dough into 4 pieces and gently stretch each into a 5-inch square, then transfer to baking sheet. Spread onion mixture over each square, leaving a ¼-inch border around edges, then top with tomato slices. Bake pizzas until edges of dough are golden, 12 to 18 minutes.

Toss together olives and thyme and sprinkle over pizzas. Quarter each square diagonally, making 4 triangles, then cut each triangle in half. Sprinkle with sea salt.

Cooks' notes:
• Onion mixture can be made 1 day ahead and cooled completely, then chilled, covered.
• Pizzas can be assembled (but not baked) 2 hours ahead and chilled, loosely covered with plastic wrap.
PHOTO ON PAGE 104

ZUCCHINI CHIPS

Serves 8 to 10
Active time: 30 min   Start to finish: 30 min

3 to 4 cups vegetable oil
1 cup all-purpose flour
1 large or 2 medium zucchini

Special equipment: **a deep-fat thermometer;**
   a Japanese Benriner or other adjustable-
   blade slicer; 2 sieves

Fill a deep 10- to 12-inch heavy skillet (preferably cast-iron) halfway with oil and heat over moderate heat until it registers 360°F on thermometer.

Put flour in a shallow bowl, then fill another bowl halfway with cold water. Cut zucchini into paper-thin rounds with slicer, then separate slices. Put 12 slices in 1 sieve and dip into water, shaking off excess. Transfer slices to flour and dredge, then gently shake in second sieve to remove excess flour.

Fry coated slices in oil, turning and separating, until golden brown, 1 to 2 minutes. Transfer zucchini chips with a wire-mesh or slotted spoon to paper towels to drain, then season lightly with salt. Coat and fry remaining slices in same manner. Serve warm.

Cooks' note:
• Chips can be made 2 hours ahead and kept at room temperature. Reheat in a preheated 350°F oven 8 to 10 minutes.

SPICED PARTY MIX

Makes about 14 cups
Active time: 20 min   Start to finish: 1 hr

2 large egg whites
1½ teaspoons Worcestershire sauce
¼ cup sugar
2 tablespoons sweet paprika
1½ teaspoons cayenne
9 cups freshly popped unsalted popcorn
2 cups miniature pretzels
1½ cups salted roasted peanuts
1½ cups whole almonds, toasted (see Tips,
   page 8)
1½ cups pecans, toasted
1½ cups salted roasted cashews

Put oven racks in upper and lower thirds of oven and preheat oven to 325°F. Butter 2 large shallow baking pans (1 inch deep).

Whisk together egg whites, Worcestershire sauce, sugar, paprika, and cayenne in a large bowl. Add popcorn, pretzels, nuts, and salt to taste and toss until thoroughly coated. Spread evenly in baking pans and bake in upper and lower thirds of oven, switching position of pans halfway through baking, until coating is crisp, about 20 minutes total.

Spread mixture on 2 large sheets of parchment paper or oiled foil and cool completely.

Cooks' note:
• Spiced party mix can be made 3 days ahead and kept in an airtight container at room temperature.
PHOTO ON PAGE 51

CAULIFLOWER PURÉE AND CAVIAR ON CLOVERLEAF POTATO CHIPS

Makes about 60 hors d'oeuvres
Active time: 1 hr   Start to finish: 1¼ hr

Though the chips and purée can be served at room temperature, the caviar should be chilled, so assemble these hors d'oeuvres in batches as platters need replenishing.

4 large russet (baking) potatoes (2 lb total)
½ stick (¼ cup) unsalted butter, melted
2 cups chopped cauliflower
⅓ cup sour cream
¼ teaspoon salt
2 tablespoons finely chopped fresh chives
   (optional)
150 g caviar (5 oz; preferably osetra), chilled

Special equipment: **a Japanese Benriner or other**
   adjustable-blade slicer; a 1½- to 2-inch
   cloverleaf or other small decoratively
   shaped cookie cutter
Garnish: **fresh chives**

Make potato chips:
Put oven rack in middle position and preheat oven to 375°F.

Peel potatoes and transfer to a bowl of cold water. Cut 2 potatoes lengthwise into ⅛- to 1⁄16-inch-thick slices with slicer, then stack slices in piles of 6. Cut out as many cloverleafs as possible from each stack, pressing cutter through stacks, and toss with half of melted butter in a bowl. Arrange chips in 1 layer in a large shallow baking pan (1 inch deep) and season very lightly with salt.

Bake until edges are pale golden, 10 to 15 minutes, then turn chips over with a metal spatula and bake until golden all over, 5 to 10 minutes more, checking frequently after 5 minutes and transferring chips as baked to a rack to cool.

While first batch bakes, slice and cut shapes from remaining 2 potatoes. Toss with remaining butter and bake in another shallow baking pan.

Make cauliflower purée:

Cook cauliflower in a 3-quart saucepan of boiling salted water (see Tips, page 8) until very tender, 5 to 7 minutes, and drain in a colander. Purée cauliflower in a food processor until smooth, then transfer to a bowl and whisk in sour cream and salt. Just before serving, stir in chives (if using).

Assemble hors d'oeuvres:

Top potato chips with 1 teaspoon cauliflower purée and ½ teaspoon caviar, then garnish with chives.

Cooks' notes:
- **Chips can be made 2 days ahead and kept in an airtight container at room temperature. Recrisp in a preheated 350°F oven 5 minutes.**
- **Cauliflower purée (without chives) can be made 1 day ahead and chilled, covered. Bring to room temperature and stir in chives before serving.**

FIG AND GOAT CHEESE CROSTINI

Makes 24 hors d'oeuvres
Active time: 40 min   Start to finish: 1 hr

 3 tablespoons minced shallot
 2 (3-inch) fresh thyme sprigs plus ½ teaspoon minced fresh thyme
 ½ Turkish or ¼ California bay leaf
 1½ tablespoons unsalted butter
 ¼ lb dried Black Mission figs, finely chopped
 ¾ cup Port
 ¼ teaspoon salt
 ⅛ teaspoon black pepper
 12 (½-inch-thick) diagonally cut baguette slices
 1 tablespoon olive oil
 6 oz soft mild goat cheese at room temperature
 2 fresh ripe figs, cut into ½-inch pieces

Garnish: **fresh thyme leaves**

Make savory fig jam:

Cook shallot, thyme sprigs, and bay leaf in butter in a 1- to 1½-quart heavy saucepan over moderately low heat, stirring, until shallot is softened, about 2 minutes. Add dried figs, Port, salt, and pepper and bring to a boil. Reduce heat and simmer, covered, until figs are soft, about 10 minutes. If there is still liquid in saucepan, remove lid and simmer, stirring, until most of liquid is evaporated, 3 to 4 minutes more. Discard bay leaf and thyme sprigs and transfer jam to a bowl. Cool, then stir in minced thyme and salt and pepper to taste.

Make toasts while jam cools:

Put oven rack in middle position and preheat oven to 350°F.

Halve each baguette slice diagonally, then arrange on a baking sheet and brush tops lightly with oil. Bake until lightly toasted, about 7 minutes. Cool on baking sheet on a rack.

Assemble crostini:

Spread each toast with 1 teaspoon fig jam and top with about 1½ teaspoons goat cheese and 2 pieces fresh fig.

Cooks' notes:
- **Fig jam can be made 1 day ahead and chilled, covered. Bring to room temperature before using.**
- **Toasts can be made 1 day ahead and cooled, then kept in an airtight container at room temperature.**

PHOTO ON PAGE 93

VIRGINIA HAM AND MELON APPLE CHUTNEY ON CORN BREAD ROUNDS

Makes 24 hors d'oeuvres
Active time: 1¼ hr   Start to finish: 2½ hr

For corn bread rounds
⅔ cup yellow cornmeal
⅓ cup all-purpose flour
2 tablespoons sugar
½ teaspoon baking powder
½ teaspoon salt
5 tablespoons unsalted butter, melted
  and cooled
2 tablespoons milk
1 large egg
For topping
  About 2 tablespoons Dijon mustard
¼ lb sliced cooked Virginia country ham,
  cut into 1½- by ⅓-inch strips
½ cup melon apple chutney (recipe follows)

Special equipment: **a 1½-inch round cookie
  cutter**

Make corn bread rounds:
Put oven rack in middle position and preheat oven
to 350°F. Generously grease a 13- by 9- by 2-inch
metal baking pan.

Whisk together cornmeal, flour, sugar, baking powder, and salt in a bowl. Whisk together butter, milk, and
egg in a small bowl, then add to cornmeal mixture and
stir just until combined. Spread (or pat out) batter in a
very thin even layer in baking pan (preferably using an
offset spatula).

Bake until firm and pale golden, 20 to 25 minutes.
Cut out 24 rounds from hot corn bread with cookie cutter and transfer rounds to a rack to cool. (Reserve
remaining corn bread for another use.)

Top rounds:
Spread each round with a thin layer of mustard and
top with a few strips of ham and about 1 teaspoon
melon apple chutney.

Cooks' note:
• Corn bread rounds can be made 1 day ahead and
  cooled, then kept in an airtight container at room
  temperature.

MELON APPLE CHUTNEY

Makes about 1 cup
Active time: 20 min   Start to finish: 1¼ hr

1 (1½-inch) piece cinnamon stick
2 whole cloves
5 whole allspice
¾ cup diced (¼ inch) cantaloupe or
  honeydew, or a combination
1 Granny Smith apple, peeled and cut into
  ¼-inch dice
½ cup sugar
¼ cup plus 2 tablespoons distilled white
  vinegar
3 tablespoons dried currants
2 tablespoons minced peeled fresh ginger

Special equipment: **a 6-inch piece of cheesecloth;
  kitchen string**

Wrap cinnamon stick, cloves, and allspice in
cheesecloth and tie with string to form a bag. Crush
spices gently in bag with a rolling pin or bottom of a
heavy skillet.

Bring melon, apple, sugar, vinegar, currants, ginger, cheesecloth bag, and a pinch of salt to a boil in a
1- to 1½-quart heavy saucepan, then reduce heat and
simmer, uncovered, stirring occasionally, until syrup is
thick and most of liquid is evaporated, 30 to 35 minutes. Discard cheesecloth bag and cool chutney. (Syrup
will continue to thicken as it cools.)

Cooks' note:
• Chutney can be made 2 days ahead and chilled,
  covered. Bring to room temperature before using.

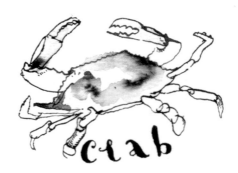

130

WASABI LIME CRAB SALAD IN CUCUMBER CUPS

Makes about 60 hors d'oeuvres
Active time: 1 hr   Start to finish: 1 hr

4 seedless cucumbers (usually plastic-
    wrapped; 3½ lb total), peeled
¼ cup mayonnaise
4 teaspoons wasabi paste (Japanese
    horseradish paste)
2 tablespoons fresh lime juice
¾ teaspoon salt, or to taste
6 medium radishes
1 (3-oz) container radish sprouts or baby
    pea shoots
½ lb jumbo lump crabmeat, picked over

Special equipment: a 1½-inch fluted round
    cookie cutter; a melon-ball cutter
    (optional); a Japanese Benriner or other
    adjustable-blade slicer

Prepare cucumber cups:
Cut cucumbers crosswise into generous ½-inch-thick slices. Cut a fluted round from each slice with cookie cutter, then scoop out some flesh from center of each round with melon-ball cutter or a small spoon, creating an indentation but leaving bottom intact.
Prepare filling:
Whisk together mayonnaise and wasabi, then whisk in lime juice and salt.
Cut radishes into very thin slices with slicer. Halve slices, then cut crosswise into very thin strips. Trim radish sprouts to 1-inch lengths, measuring from top of sprout, and discard remaining stems. (If using pea shoots, cut sections with leaves into 1-inch pieces.)
Stir together crab, wasabi mayonnaise, radish strips, and radish sprouts, then put a small spoonful of filling into each cucumber cup.

Cooks' notes:
• Cucumber cups can be formed (but not filled) 1 day ahead and chilled, covered with plastic wrap.
• Wasabi mayonnaise can be made 1 day ahead and chilled, covered.
• Radishes can be cut and sprouts trimmed 1 day ahead and chilled separately in sealed plastic bags lined with dampened paper towels.
• Crabmeat can be picked over 1 day ahead and chilled, covered.

first courses

SHELLFISH WATERMELON CEVICHE

Serves 6
Active time: 45 min   Start to finish: 1¾ hr

1 navel orange
½ cup plus 2 tablespoons fresh orange juice
¼ cup fresh lime juice
½ cup diced (¼ inch) seeded watermelon
½ teaspoon finely grated peeled fresh ginger
1½ tablespoons finely diced red onion
2 to 3 teaspoons finely chopped fresh
    jalapeño chile
½ teaspoon salt
¼ lb sea scallops, tough muscles removed and
    scallops cut into ½-inch pieces
¼ lb large shrimp in shell (21 to 25 per lb),
    peeled, deveined, and cut into
    ½-inch pieces
¼ lb cooked lobster meat, cut into
    ½-inch pieces
1½ tablespoons chopped fresh mint
4 heads Bibb or 2 heads Boston lettuce (1¼ lb)

Cut peel and white pith from orange with a sharp paring knife, then cut segments free from membranes. Chop enough segments to measure ¼ cup. Stir together chopped orange, orange juice, lime juice, watermelon, ginger, onion, jalapeño (to taste), and salt in a large bowl.
Bring a 1-quart saucepan three-fourths full of salted water (see Tips, page 8) to a boil, then add scallops. Reduce heat to a bare simmer and poach scallops until just cooked through, about 1 minute. Transfer with a slotted spoon to a bowl of ice and cold water to stop cooking. Return water in saucepan to a boil and poach shrimp in same manner. Drain shrimp in a colander and transfer to bowl of ice and cold water to stop cooking. Drain scallops and shrimp well and pat dry.
Add scallops, shrimp, lobster, and mint to watermelon mixture and toss to combine, then season with salt. Chill ceviche, covered, at least 1 hour.
Trim and separate lettuce leaves. Serve ceviche with lettuce leaves on the side (use a slotted spoon to transfer ceviche to lettuce).

Cooks' note:
• Ceviche can be chilled up to 3 hours.
PHOTO ON PAGE 82

CORN FRITTERS WITH ARUGULA AND WARM TOMATO SALAD

Serves 8
Active time: 1 hr   Start to finish: 1 hr

We found that using finely stone-ground cornmeal yielded a denser, slightly heavier fritter than regular stone-ground cornmeal. Though both tasted the same, we preferred the texture of the fritter made with regular cornmeal.

For tomatoes
6 scallions, white and pale green parts separated from dark green parts and both finely chopped
2 tablespoons olive oil
1 lb cherry or grape tomatoes, halved (3 to 4 cups)
¼ teaspoon salt
¼ teaspoon black pepper
For fritters
⅔ cup corn (cut from 2 ears)
⅔ cup yellow cornmeal
3 tablespoons all-purpose flour
¼ teaspoon salt, or to taste
⅛ teaspoon baking soda
    Pinch of sugar
½ cup whole milk
1 large egg
⅓ cup vegetable oil
For arugula
2½ teaspoons white-wine vinegar
½ teaspoon whole-grain mustard
¼ teaspoon salt, or to taste
¼ teaspoon black pepper
3 tablespoons olive oil
1 lb arugula, coarse stems discarded (8 cups)

Prepare tomatoes:
Cook white and pale green scallions in oil in a 10- to 12-inch nonstick skillet over moderate heat, stirring, until softened, 1 to 2 minutes. Add tomatoes, salt, and pepper and cook, stirring, until tomatoes begin to soften, 3 to 5 minutes. Remove from heat and stir in scallion greens. Transfer to a bowl and cool to warm.
Make fritters while tomatoes cool:
Cook corn in a small saucepan of boiling water until tender, about 3 minutes. Drain in a sieve, then rinse under cold water and pat dry.
Whisk together cornmeal, flour, salt, baking soda,

and sugar in a bowl. Whisk together milk and egg in another bowl, then add to dry ingredients and stir until just combined (do not overmix). Stir in corn.
Heat oil in cleaned skillet over moderate heat until hot but not smoking. Working in batches of 4, spoon 1 heaping tablespoon batter per fritter into skillet and fry, turning over once, until lightly browned, about 4 minutes total. Transfer with a spatula to paper towels to drain.
Prepare arugula:
Whisk together vinegar, mustard, salt, and pepper in a large bowl, then add oil in a slow stream, whisking until emulsified. Add arugula and toss to coat.
Divide arugula, fritters, and tomatoes among 8 small plates.

CRISPY SHREDDED DUCK AND NOODLE SALAD

Serves 6
Active time: 45 min   Start to finish: 45 min

It's important to use large lettuce leaves (about 6 inches) for this salad, so you may need to buy 2 heads of lettuce in order to get 6 good leaves.

2 oz dried rice-stick noodles (rice vermicelli)
1½ tablespoons rice vinegar (not seasoned)
1½ teaspoons sugar
¼ teaspoon salt
¼ cup plus 1 tablespoon vegetable oil
2 (6- to 7-oz) confit duck legs, meat (with skin attached) removed from bone in large pieces

1 large shallot, thinly sliced crosswise and
    separated into rings (⅓ cup)
1 (6-inch) piece seedless cucumber (usually
    plastic-wrapped), peeled
1 firm-ripe medium peach or nectarine,
    halved lengthwise and pitted
6 large Boston lettuce leaves
24 fresh mint leaves
24 fresh cilantro leaves
18 Thai basil leaves or small Italian basil
    leaves

Special equipment: **a Japanese Benriner or other**
    adjustable-blade slicer
Accompaniment: **nuoc cham and/or sweet chile**
    dipping sauce (recipes follow)

Cook noodles in a 4-quart pot of boiling salted water (see Tips, page 8) until just tender, 2 to 3 minutes. Drain in a colander, then rinse under cold water and drain well. Stir together vinegar, sugar, and salt in a bowl until sugar is dissolved, then add noodles and toss well.

Heat 1 tablespoon oil in a 10- to 12-inch heavy skillet over moderately high heat until hot but not smoking, then sauté duck pieces, starting with skin sides down and turning occasionally, until skin and meat are crisp, 3 to 5 minutes. Transfer with tongs to a cutting board. (Do not clean skillet.)

When duck is cool enough to handle, remove crisp skin from meat and thinly slice skin. Remove and discard any excess fat from meat, then shred meat into ¼-inch-wide pieces.

Heat remaining ¼ cup oil in skillet over moderately high heat until hot but not smoking, then fry shallot, stirring occasionally, until golden brown, about 2 minutes (watch closely, as shallot can burn easily). Quickly transfer with a slotted spoon to paper towels to drain.

Working around core of cucumber, cut thin lengthwise slices (about ⅛ inch thick) with slicer, then stack slices. Halve stack crosswise, then cut slices lengthwise into ¼-inch-wide matchsticks.

Cut each peach half lengthwise into ⅛-inch-thick wedges with slicer or a sharp knife.

Put 1 lettuce leaf on each of 6 plates, then divide noodles among leaves and top with duck (meat and skin), cucumber, peach, shallot, and herbs. To eat, roll lettuce leaf into a cylinder to enclose filling.

PHOTO ON PAGE 84

Our food editors were evenly divided concerning which dipping sauce they preferred with the shredded duck and noodle salad. Some liked the nuoc cham *because of the depth of flavor imparted by the fish sauce; others leaned toward the sweetness and heat of the sweet chile sauce. Make one or both, depending on your taste.*

NUOC CHAM

Makes about ½ cup
Active time: 5 min   Start to finish: 5 min

¼ cup fresh lime juice
 3 tablespoons Asian fish sauce
 2 tablespoons water
 1 tablespoon packed brown sugar

Stir together all ingredients in a bowl until sugar is dissolved.

Cooks' note:
• Sauce can be made 2 hours ahead and kept, covered, at room temperature.

SWEET CHILE DIPPING SAUCE

Makes about ¾ cup
Active time: 5 min   Start to finish: 1½ hr
(includes chilling)

¼ cup water
¼ cup sugar
½ cup rice vinegar (not seasoned)
¾ teaspoon salt
½ teaspoon *sambal oelek* (chile garlic sauce)
    or ½ teaspoon dried hot red pepper flakes

Bring water and sugar to a boil in a small saucepan over moderate heat, stirring until sugar is dissolved. Remove from heat and stir in rice vinegar, salt, and *sambal oelek*. Cool sauce, then chill, covered, at least 1 hour.

Cooks' note:
• Sauce can be chilled up to 3 days.

GOAT CHEESE SOUFFLÉS IN PHYLLO CUPS WITH FRISÉE SALAD

Serves 8
Active time: 45 min   Start to finish: 1 hr

For phyllo cups
**6 (17- by 12-inch) phyllo sheets, thawed
    if frozen**
½ stick (¼ cup) unsalted butter, melted
    For soufflé filling
2 tablespoons unsalted butter
2 tablespoons all-purpose flour
¾ cup whole milk
2 teaspoons Dijon mustard
2 large eggs, separated
**1 oz finely grated Parmigiano-Reggiano
    (½ cup; see Tips, page 8)**
5 oz soft mild goat cheese, crumbled (⅔ cup)
    For salad
1½ tablespoons cider vinegar
1½ teaspoons Dijon mustard
¼ teaspoon salt
5 tablespoons extra-virgin olive oil
8 oz frisée, torn into bite-size pieces (8 cups)
6 radishes, cut into very thin wedges
3 tablespoons chopped fresh chives

Special equipment: **a muffin pan with 12 (½- or
    ⅓-cup) muffin cups**

Make cups:
Put oven rack in middle position and preheat oven to 375°F.

Cover stack of phyllo with 2 overlapping sheets of plastic wrap and a dampened kitchen towel. Put 1 phyllo sheet on a work surface and brush with some butter, then top with 2 more sheets of phyllo, brushing each with butter.

Cut buttered stack into 6 (4½-inch) squares with a sharp knife, trimming sides as needed. Line each of 6 muffin cups with a square. Make 6 more phyllo cups (4 are extra, in case of breakage) in same manner with remaining pastry sheets and butter.

Bake cups until golden, about 8 minutes, then cool completely in pan on a rack.
Make filling:
Increase oven temperature to 400°F.

While cups cool, melt butter in a 3-quart heavy saucepan over moderately low heat, then add flour and cook roux, whisking, 3 minutes. Add milk in a stream, whisking, and bring to a boil, whisking. Reduce heat and simmer, whisking occasionally, 5 minutes. Remove from heat and whisk in mustard, yolks, and ¼ cup Parmigiano-Reggiano until combined, then fold in goat cheese. (Cover surface of mixture with wax paper if not using immediately.)

Beat egg whites in a large bowl with an electric mixer until they just hold stiff peaks. Fold one third of whites into sauce to lighten, then fold in remaining whites gently but thoroughly.

Spoon batter into 8 phyllo cups and sprinkle with remaining Parmigiano-Reggiano. Bake until soufflés are puffed and golden, about 15 minutes.
Make salad while soufflés bake:
Whisk together vinegar, mustard, and salt in a bowl, then add oil in a slow stream, whisking until emulsified.

Just before soufflés are ready, toss frisée and radishes in a large bowl with just enough dressing to coat. Mound salad onto 8 plates and sprinkle with chives, then make a small nest in center of each.

Place a soufflé cup in each salad and serve immediately.

Cooks' notes:
• Phyllo cups can be made 1 day ahead and kept in pan, carefully wrapped in plastic wrap, at room temperature. (Extra phyllo cups can be filled with ice cream or fruit for dessert the next day.)
• Soufflé filling (without egg whites) can be made 1 day ahead and chilled, covered. Bring to room temperature and stir (to loosen) before proceeding.
PHOTO ON PAGE 64

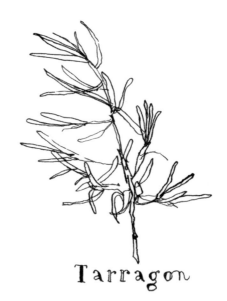

Tarragon

MELON CARPACCIO

Serves 6
Active time: 20 min   Start to finish: 20 min

1 (3-lb) cantaloupe, halved lengthwise
   and seeded
1½ teaspoons fresh lime juice
1 tablespoon extra-virgin olive oil
60 small fresh tarragon leaves
   Coarse sea salt (lightly crushed if
   grains are large) to taste
6 thin lime wedges

Special equipment: **a Y-shaped vegetable peeler**

Cut each cantaloupe half lengthwise into 3 wedges (6 total). Shave thin slices from seeded side of a melon wedge with vegetable peeler, stopping when you get close to rind. Arrange slices, overlapping slightly, on a plate. Repeat with remaining cantaloupe, putting slices from each wedge on a separate plate.

Drizzle each serving with ¼ teaspoon lime juice and ½ teaspoon oil, then scatter 10 tarragon leaves on top. Season with sea salt and pepper and serve with lime wedges.

COQUILLES ST.-JACQUES
Scallops with Mushrooms in White-Wine Sauce

Serves 8
Active time: 30 min   Start to finish: 1 hr

¼ cup coarse fresh bread crumbs from a
   baguette
½ oz finely grated Parmigiano-Reggiano
   (¼ cup)
1¼ cups dry white wine
1 cup water
½ small onion, sliced
½ Turkish or ¼ California bay leaf
½ teaspoon salt
¼ teaspoon black pepper
1 lb sea scallops, tough muscle removed from
   side of each if necessary and scallops cut
   into ¾-inch pieces
½ lb small mushrooms, halved lengthwise,
   then thinly sliced lengthwise
¾ stick (6 tablespoons) unsalted butter
½ cup heavy cream

1 large egg yolk
1 tablespoon all-purpose flour
8 cups kosher salt to stabilize scallop shells
   (if using)
1½ tablespoons minced fresh flat-leaf parsley

Special equipment: **16 (2½-inch) scallop shells or
   8 (2-oz) ramekins**

Put oven rack in middle position and preheat oven to 350°F.

Toast bread crumbs on a baking sheet until pale golden, 6 to 8 minutes, then toss with cheese.

Simmer wine, water, onion, bay leaf, salt, and pepper in a 2½-quart heavy saucepan, uncovered, 5 minutes. Add scallops and simmer, uncovered, stirring occasionally, until just cooked through, 2 to 3 minutes. Transfer scallops to a platter with a slotted spoon to cool, returning any onions to pan, then boil cooking liquid until reduced to about 1 cup, 8 to 10 minutes. Pour cooking liquid through a sieve into a bowl.

Cook mushrooms in 2 tablespoons butter in a 10- to 12-inch heavy skillet over moderate heat, stirring occasionally, until most of liquid mushrooms give off is evaporated, about 5 minutes. Season with salt and pepper to taste.

Whisk together cream and yolk in a heatproof bowl. Melt 2 tablespoons butter in cleaned 2½- to 3-quart saucepan over moderately low heat, then add flour and cook roux, whisking, 2 minutes. Remove pan from heat and add reduced cooking liquid in a stream, whisking constantly. Return pan to heat and simmer, whisking, 1 minute. Pour sauce in a slow stream into cream mixture, whisking constantly, then pour sauce back into pan and simmer, whisking, 1 minute. Remove from heat and season with salt and pepper.

Preheat broiler.

Stir scallops and mushrooms into sauce, then divide among scallop shells or ramekins and sprinkle with bread crumb mixture. If using shells, spread kosher salt evenly in a large shallow baking pan, then nestle shells in salt. Dot scallops with remaining 2 tablespoons butter, then broil about 4 inches from heat until golden, about 2 minutes.

Sprinkle with parsley and serve immediately.

Cooks' note:
• Scallop mixture can be made (but not spooned into
  shells or ramekins) 1 day ahead and chilled, covered.
  Reheat over moderate heat before proceeding.

dips and spreads

HOT CRAB AND ARTICHOKE DIP

Serves 8
Active time: 1 hr   Start to finish: 1½ hr

1 (9-oz) package frozen artichoke hearts
1 red bell pepper, finely chopped
3 tablespoons unsalted butter
2 tablespoons all-purpose flour
1¼ cups half-and-half
3 scallions, thinly sliced
2 oz finely grated parmesan (½ cup)
1½ teaspoons fresh lemon juice, or to taste
1½ tablespoons minced drained pickled
    jalapeño chiles
½ teaspoon salt
¼ teaspoon celery salt
¾ lb jumbo lump crabmeat, picked over

Accompaniment: **benne seed pita toasts (recipe follows)**

Put oven rack in middle position and preheat oven to 375°F. Butter a 1½-quart baking dish.

Cook artichoke hearts according to package instructions, then drain well and finely chop. Cook bell pepper in 1 tablespoon butter in a 2- to 3-quart heavy saucepan over moderately low heat, stirring occasionally, until softened, about 5 minutes. Stir in artichokes and transfer mixture to a bowl.

Melt remaining 2 tablespoons butter in saucepan over moderately low heat, then add flour and cook roux, stirring, 3 minutes. Add half-and-half in a stream, whisking, and bring to a boil, whisking. Reduce heat and simmer, whisking, 3 minutes. Remove from heat and stir in artichoke mixture, scallions, ⅓ cup parmesan, lemon juice, jalapeños, salt, and celery salt. Gently stir in crab. Transfer to baking dish and sprinkle with remaining parmesan.

Bake crab dip until bubbling, 20 to 25 minutes. Serve warm.

Cooks' note:
• Dip can be prepared (but not baked) 1 day ahead and chilled, covered.
PHOTO ON PAGE 71

BENNE SEED PITA TOASTS

Makes 48 hors d'oeuvre toasts
Active time: 20 min   Start to finish: 35 min

1 tablespoon cornstarch
¾ stick (6 tablespoons) unsalted butter,
    melted and cooled
¾ teaspoon salt
⅓ cup sesame (benne) seeds, toasted
    (see Tips, page 8)
4 (6- to 7-inch) pita loaves with pockets,
    halved horizontally

Put oven racks in upper and lower thirds of oven and preheat oven to 375°F.

Whisk together cornstarch and 2 tablespoons butter in a small bowl until smooth, then whisk in salt, remaining 4 tablespoons butter, and sesame seeds.

Brush rough sides of pita halves with butter mixture, stirring mixture well before brushing each half. Cut each pita half into 8 wedges and arrange, seeded sides up, in 1 layer on 2 baking sheets. Bake in upper and lower thirds of oven, switching position of sheets halfway through baking, until golden, 10 to 12 minutes total. Cool toasts on a rack.

Cooks' note:
• Pita toasts can be made 1 day ahead and kept in an airtight container at room temperature. Recrisp in a preheated 375°F oven 4 to 5 minutes before serving.

BOURBON CHICKEN LIVER PÂTÉ

Serves 8 to 10
Active time: 25 min   Start to finish: 3 hr (includes chilling)

Though this pâté can be eaten the day it's made, we find it even more flavorful when made 1 or 2 days ahead. If you use several small ramekins instead of a pâté crock or terrine, you may need more clarified butter to seal the tops.

1½ sticks (¾ cup) unsalted butter
1 cup finely chopped onion
1 large garlic clove, minced
1 teaspoon minced fresh thyme or
    ¼ teaspoon dried
1 teaspoon minced fresh marjoram or
    ¼ teaspoon dried

1 teaspoon minced fresh sage or
    ¼ teaspoon dried
¾ teaspoon salt
¼ teaspoon black pepper
⅛ teaspoon ground allspice
1 lb chicken livers, trimmed
2 tablespoons bourbon

Special equipment: **a 2½-cup crock or terrine or
    several small ramekins**
Accompaniment: **crackers or toasted baguette
    slices**
Garnish: **a fresh thyme, marjoram, or sage sprig**

Melt 1 stick butter in a large nonstick skillet over
moderately low heat, then cook onion and garlic, stirring, until softened, about 5 minutes. Add herbs, salt,
pepper, allspice, and livers and cook, stirring, until livers are cooked outside but still pink when cut open,
about 8 minutes. Stir in bourbon and remove from heat.
Purée mixture in a food processor until smooth, then
transfer pâté to crock and smooth top.

Melt remaining ½ stick butter in a very small heavy
saucepan over low heat, then remove pan from heat and
let butter stand 3 minutes. If using herb garnish, put
sprig on top of pâté. Skim froth from butter, then spoon
enough clarified butter over pâté to cover its surface,
leaving milky solids in bottom of pan.

Chill pâté until butter is firm, about 30 minutes.
Cover with plastic wrap and chill at least 2 hours more.

   Cooks' notes:
• Pâté can be chilled up to 2 weeks.
• Once butter seal has been broken, pâté keeps, its
  surface covered with plastic wrap and chilled, 1 week.
PHOTO ON PAGE 98

CUCUMBERS IN YOGURT

Serves 4
Active time: 15 min   Start to finish: 1¼ hr (includes draining)

*Greek yogurt, if you can find it, is incredibly thick and
creamy and a delight to eat. It shows up in several
guises on the Greek table — as a savory dip, in sauces,
or for dessert.*

2 cups plain whole-milk yogurt (14 to 16 oz;
    preferably Greek)
1 (14- to 16-oz) seedless cucumber (usually
    plastic-wrapped), peeled, halved
    lengthwise, and cored
1½ teaspoons kosher salt
2 medium garlic cloves

If using a regular supermarket brand of yogurt
(not Greek), drain in a paper-towel-lined sieve set over
a bowl 1 hour. Discard liquid.

While yogurt drains, cut cucumber into ½-inch
cubes. Transfer to another sieve set over a bowl and
toss with 1 teaspoon kosher salt, then drain 1 hour.
Rinse cucumber and pat dry.

Mince garlic and mash to a paste with remaining
½ teaspoon kosher salt using a large heavy knife. Stir
together yogurt, cucumbers, garlic paste, and salt to
taste in a bowl.

   Cooks' note:
• Cucumbers in yogurt can be made 2 hours ahead
  and chilled, covered. Bring to room temperature
  before serving.
PHOTO ON PAGE 73

WARM TORTILLA CHIPS WITH SPICY CHEESE DIP

Serves 6
Active time: 15 min   Start to finish: 2¾ hr (includes chilling dip)

½ cup finely chopped drained bottled
    roasted red peppers
2 fresh *serrano* chiles, minced (including
    seeds)
3 scallions, finely chopped
1 cup sour cream
2½ oz crumbled *cotija* cheese or feta (½ cup)
1 teaspoon cumin seeds, toasted (see Tips,
    page 8) and finely ground in an electric
    coffee/spice grinder
¼ teaspoon salt
1 large bag tortilla chips

Stir together all ingredients (except chips) in a bowl and chill, covered, at least 2 hours (for flavors to develop). Bring to room temperature before serving.

Put oven rack in middle position and preheat oven to 350°F.

Spread tortilla chips in a large shallow baking pan and bake until warm, about 5 minutes.

Serve chips with dip.

Cooks' note:
• Dip can be chilled up to 1 day.

PHOTO ON PAGE 54

PESTO, OLIVE, AND ROASTED-PEPPER GOAT CHEESE TORTA

Serves 8 to 10
Active time: 20 min   Start to finish: 9 hr (includes chilling)

¼ cup prepared basil pesto
    Vegetable oil for brushing pan
¼ cup finely chopped rinsed drained bottled
    roasted red peppers
20 oz soft mild goat cheese (2 cups), at room
    temperature
3 tablespoons bottled black olive paste or
    tapenade

Special equipment: a 2¼-cup loaf pan (5¾ by
    3½ by 2¼ inches)
Accompaniment: crackers or toasts

Drain pesto in a small fine-mesh sieve set over a bowl 15 minutes, then discard excess oil.

While pesto drains, lightly oil loaf pan and line with a sheet of plastic wrap large enough to allow a generous overhang on all 4 sides. Blot peppers well between paper towels to remove excess liquid.

Spread about one fourth (½ cup) of cheese evenly onto bottom of loaf pan and top with all of pesto, spreading evenly. Drop ½ cup cheese by tablespoons over pesto and spread gently to cover pesto, then top with peppers, spreading evenly. Drop another ½ cup cheese by tablespoons over peppers and spread gently to cover peppers.

Spread olive paste evenly on top, then drop remaining cheese by tablespoons over olive paste, spreading gently to cover olive paste. Cover pan with another sheet of plastic wrap and chill at least 8 hours.

Remove plastic wrap from top of pan and invert torta onto a serving plate, then peel off remaining plastic wrap. Let torta stand at room temperature 20 minutes before serving.

Cooks' notes:
• For a smoother-looking torta, oiled loaf pan can be lined with parchment paper instead of plastic wrap. Cut 1 long piece of parchment to line bottom and ends, leaving a 2-inch overhang, then trace and cut out 2 more pieces for sides of pan plus a 2-inch overhang.
• Torta can be chilled in pan up to 24 hours.

SOURDOUGH TOASTS WITH SMOKY TOMATO CONFIT

Serves 6 (makes about 1 cup confit)
Active time: 40 min   Start to finish: 1 hr

1 small onion, finely chopped
6 tablespoons extra-virgin olive oil
1 (28- to 32-oz) can whole tomatoes in juice,
    drained, seeded, and finely chopped
½ teaspoon sweet Spanish smoked paprika
½ teaspoon sugar
⅛ teaspoon salt
1 (20-inch) baguette (preferably sourdough),
    cut diagonally into ½-inch-thick slices

Cook onion in 3 tablespoons oil in a 10-inch heavy skillet over moderate heat, stirring occasionally, 4 minutes. Reduce heat to low and cook, covered, stirring occasionally, until onion is golden and soft, 8 to 10 minutes more. Add tomatoes, paprika, sugar, and salt and cook, uncovered, over moderately low heat, stirring frequently, until mixture is very thick (jamlike), 25 to 30 minutes. Purée in a blender or food processor, then transfer to a bowl to cool.

Put oven rack in middle position and preheat oven to 350°F.

Brush both sides of bread slices with remaining 3 tablespoons oil, then arrange in 1 layer on a baking sheet and bake, turning once, until lightly toasted, about 15 minutes total.

Serve toasts with confit.

Cooks' note:
• Confit can be made 4 days ahead and chilled, covered. Bring to room temperature before using.
PHOTO ON PAGE 52

GARLIC ROASTED POTATO SKINS

Serves 8
Active time: 30 min   Start to finish: 1¾ hr

3 lb russet (baking) potatoes (6 to 8 medium; preferably organic)
1 small head garlic (2 inches in diameter)
¾ stick (6 tablespoons) unsalted butter, softened
1 teaspoon salt
¼ teaspoon black pepper

Accompaniment: **onion and spinach dip (recipe follows)**

Put oven rack in lower third of oven and preheat oven to 350°F.

Prick each potato once or twice with a fork. Cut off and discard top fourth of garlic head, then wrap garlic tightly in foil. Bake garlic and potatoes on same rack until potatoes are tender, 50 minutes to 1 hour. Remove potatoes from oven and cool on a metal rack 15 minutes. Continue to bake garlic until tender, about 15 minutes more, then cool in foil on rack.

While garlic cools, halve potatoes lengthwise, then quarter each half (to form short wedges). Scoop out potato flesh (reserving it for another use), leaving ¼-inch-thick potato skins.

Increase oven temperature to 425°F.

Squeeze garlic into a small bowl, discarding garlic

skins, and mash to a paste with butter, salt, and pepper using a fork.

Divide garlic paste among potato skins (about ½ teaspoon each), spreading evenly, then roast skins in a large shallow baking pan (1 inch deep) until golden and crisp, 20 to 25 minutes.

Cooks' note:
• Potato skins can be scooped out and spread with garlic paste (but not baked) 1 day ahead and chilled, loosely covered with foil. Bring to room temperature before baking.
PHOTO ON PAGE 51

ONION AND SPINACH DIP

Makes about 3½ cups
Active time: 30 min   Start to finish: 1¾ hr (includes chilling)

3 tablespoons extra-virgin olive oil
1 large onion, chopped (1¾ cups)
½ lb shallots, chopped
½ lb baby spinach, coarsely chopped
3 oz cream cheese, softened
1 (16-oz) container sour cream
½ teaspoon salt
¼ teaspoon black pepper

Heat oil in a 12-inch heavy skillet over moderately high heat until hot but not smoking, then sauté onion and shallots, stirring, until lightly browned, about 2 minutes. Reduce heat to moderate and continue to cook, stirring occasionally, until softened, about 8 minutes more. Add spinach and cook, stirring, just until wilted, about 2 minutes. Remove from heat and cool slightly.

Transfer spinach mixture to a bowl, then stir in cream cheese, sour cream, salt, and pepper until combined well. Chill, covered, at least 1 hour.

Cooks' note:
• Dip can be chilled up to 1 day (though the spinach will lose some of its color). Let stand at room temperature 15 minutes before serving.

BREADS

WHOLE-WHEAT PITA BREAD

Makes 8 (6-inch) pita loaves
Active time: 30 min   Start to finish: 3 hr

Why make your own pita when it's readily available at supermarkets? One bite of these, fresh and warm from the oven, will tell you exactly why. The dough is simple to make, and because the dough rounds are thin, they bake in less than 5 minutes.

1 (¼-oz) package active dry yeast
   (2½ teaspoons)
1 teaspoon honey
1¼ cups warm water (105–115°F)
2 cups bread flour or high-gluten flour,
   plus additional for kneading
1 cup whole-wheat flour
¼ cup extra-virgin olive oil
1 teaspoon salt
   Cornmeal for sprinkling baking sheets

Stir together yeast, honey, and ½ cup warm water in a large bowl, then let stand until foamy, about 5 minutes. (If mixture doesn't foam, discard and start over with new yeast.)

While yeast mixture stands, stir together flours in another bowl. Whisk ½ cup flour mixture into yeast mixture until smooth, then cover with plastic wrap and let stand in a draft-free place at warm room temperature until doubled in bulk and bubbly, about 45 minutes. Stir in oil, salt, remaining ¾ cup warm water, and remaining 2½ cups flour mixture until a dough forms.

Turn out dough onto a floured surface and knead, working in just enough additional flour to keep dough from sticking, until dough is smooth and elastic, 8 to 10 minutes. Form dough into a ball and put in an oiled large bowl, turning to coat. Cover bowl with plastic wrap and let dough rise in draft-free place at warm room temperature until doubled in bulk, about 1 hour.

Lightly sprinkle 2 baking sheets with cornmeal. Punch down dough and cut into 8 pieces. Form each piece into a ball. Flatten 1 ball, then roll out into a 6½- to 7-inch round on floured surface with a floured rolling pin. Transfer round to 1 of 2 baking sheets. Make 7 more rounds in same manner, arranging them on baking sheets. Loosely cover pitas with 2 clean kitchen towels (not terry cloth) and let stand at room temperature 30 minutes.

Put oven rack in lower third of oven and remove other racks. Preheat oven to 500°F.

Transfer 4 pitas, 1 at a time, directly onto oven rack. Bake until just puffed and pale golden, about 2 minutes. Turn over with tongs and bake 1 minute more. Cool pitas on a cooling rack 2 minutes, then stack and wrap loosely in a kitchen towel to keep pitas warm. Bake remaining 4 pitas in same manner. Serve warm.

Cooks' note:
• Pitas can be baked 1 week ahead and cooled completely, then frozen, wrapped well in foil in a sealed plastic bag. Thaw before reheating, wrapped in foil, 10 to 12 minutes in a preheated 350°F oven.

PHOTO ON PAGE 73

SPIRAL ROLLS

Makes 12 rolls
Active time: 40 min   Start to finish: 3¼ hr

¾ cup plus 1 tablespoon warm whole milk
   (105–110°F)
2¼ teaspoons active dry yeast (from a ¼-oz
   package)
2½ tablespoons sugar
3 cups all-purpose flour
1½ sticks (¾ cup) unsalted butter, cut into
   ½-inch cubes
1½ teaspoons salt
1 large egg, lightly beaten with 1 teaspoon
   water

Special equipment: **a muffin pan with 12 (½- to
   ⅓-cup) muffin cups**

Stir together milk, yeast, and ½ tablespoon sugar and let stand until foamy, about 5 minutes. (If mixture doesn't foam, discard and start over with new yeast.)

Pulse flour and butter in a food processor until mixture resembles fine bread crumbs, then stir together with salt and remaining 2 tablespoons sugar in a

140

large bowl. Add yeast mixture and stir just until a dough forms.

Turn out dough onto a work surface (not floured) and knead until smooth and elastic, 8 to 10 minutes. Transfer to an oiled large bowl and turn dough to coat. Cover bowl with plastic wrap and let dough rise in a draft-free place at warm room temperature until doubled in bulk, about 1 hour.

Punch down dough and turn out onto work surface (not floured). Divide into 12 equal portions.

Roll out 1 piece of dough into a 9- by 1-inch strip with a rolling pin, rolling and folding lengthwise and crosswise to make sides as straight as possible. Starting with 1 end, roll up strip and put, a spiral side up, in a muffin cup. Make 11 more rolls in same manner.

Cover rolls loosely with oiled plastic wrap and let rise in draft-free place at warm room temperature until doubled in bulk, 1 to 1½ hours.

Put oven rack in middle position and preheat oven to 375°F.

Gently brush tops of rolls with some egg wash. Bake rolls until tops are golden and bottoms are golden brown and sound hollow when tapped, 18 to 20 minutes. Transfer to racks to cool completely.

Cooks' note:
• Rolls can be made 1 day ahead and frozen in a sealed plastic bag. Thaw before reheating.
PHOTO ON PAGE 64

COCONUT BREAD

Makes 1 loaf (serves 8)
Active time: 50 min   Start to finish: 4 hr (includes cooling)

This bread is slightly sweet, like some corn breads. It also makes a nice island-style tea bread when served in the afternoon with lime marmalade and hibiscus tea.

4 cups sweetened flaked coconut (10 oz)
2 cups self-rising flour (not cake flour)
1 stick (½ cup) unsalted butter, softened
½ cup sugar
2 large eggs
1 cup water

Put oven rack in middle position and preheat oven to 350°F. Butter and flour a 9- by 5- by 3-inch loaf pan, knocking out excess flour.

Toast and grind coconut:

Spread 3 cups coconut in a large shallow baking pan (1 inch deep) and toast, stirring occasionally, until evenly golden brown, 20 to 25 minutes. (Watch flakes carefully; edges burn quickly.) Cool completely in pan on a rack, about 15 minutes, then grind in a food processor to a coarse meal, about 40 seconds (you will have about 1¼ cups). Leave oven on.

Make batter:

Stir together flour, ground coconut, and remaining cup (untoasted) coconut in a large bowl. Beat together butter and sugar in another bowl with an electric mixer at medium speed until pale and creamy, 1 to 2 minutes. Add eggs 1 at a time, beating well after each addition. Whisk water into flour mixture, then add egg mixture, whisking just until well blended.

Bake bread:

Pour batter into loaf pan, smoothing top with a spatula, and bake until a wooden pick or skewer inserted in center comes out clean and top is evenly brown, 1 hour to 1 hour and 10 minutes. Cool bread to warm in pan on a rack, 10 to 15 minutes, then turn out of pan and set right side up on rack to cool completely, about 2 hours more. Cut into 1-inch-thick slices.

Cooks' note:
• Bread can be served the day it is made, but it slices more easily if kept, wrapped in plastic wrap, at room temperature 1 day.

Doughnuts

WARM MINIATURE DOUGHNUTS

Makes about 40 doughnuts
Active time: 30 min   Start to finish: 45 min

1¼ cups all-purpose flour
1½ teaspoons baking powder
¼ teaspoon baking soda
¼ teaspoon freshly grated nutmeg
¼ teaspoon ground cinnamon or allspice
   Rounded ¼ teaspoon salt
½ cup packed light brown sugar
½ cup well-shaken buttermilk
2 tablespoons unsalted butter, melted
1 large egg
   About 6 cups vegetable oil for frying
   Confectioners sugar for coating (optional)

Special equipment: **a deep-fat thermometer**

Sift together flour, baking powder, baking soda, spices, and salt into a bowl. Whisk in brown sugar, breaking up any lumps. Whisk together buttermilk, butter, and egg in a small bowl, then add to flour mixture, whisking until just combined.

Heat 2 inches oil in a deep 3-quart heavy saucepan until it registers 375°F on thermometer. Working in batches of 6, scoop out a rounded teaspoon (not a measuring spoon) of batter per doughnut and scrape batter from spoon into oil with another spoon, keeping ball as round as possible. Once 6 balls are in oil, turn them over with a slotted spoon and continue to cook, turning occasionally, until deep brown and cooked through, 1½ to 2 minutes. Transfer doughnuts as fried with slotted spoon to paper towels to drain and return oil to 375°F between batches. Cool doughnuts to warm, at least 10 minutes.

If desired, coat with confectioners sugar just before serving: Put sugar in a small sealed plastic bag and shake doughnuts, a few at a time, to coat.

BLUEBERRY MUFFIN TOPS

Makes 12
Active time: 35 min   Start to finish: 1¼ hr

This recipe, which originally ran in our Television Issue, was inspired by the sitcom Seinfeld *and the character Elaine's penchant for muffin tops.*

For batter
¾ stick (6 tablespoons) unsalted butter
⅓ cup whole milk
1 whole large egg
1 large yolk
¾ teaspoon vanilla
1½ cups all-purpose flour
¾ cup sugar
1½ teaspoons baking powder
¾ teaspoon salt
2 cups fresh blueberries (12 oz)
   For topping
3 tablespoons cold unsalted butter, cut into
   ½-inch cubes
½ cup all-purpose flour
3½ tablespoons sugar

Special equipment: **2 muffin-top pans, each with 6 (4- by ½-inch) muffin-top cups (½-cup capacity); or regular muffin pans**

Make batter:
Put oven rack in upper third of oven and preheat to 375°F. Generously butter muffin pans.

Melt butter in a small saucepan over moderately low heat, then remove from heat. Whisk in milk, then whole egg, yolk, and vanilla until combined well.

Whisk together flour, sugar, baking powder, and salt in a bowl, then add milk mixture and stir until just combined. Fold in blueberries gently but thoroughly.

Divide muffin batter among 12 muffin cups, spreading evenly.
Make topping and bake muffins:
Rub together all topping ingredients in a bowl with your fingertips until crumbly, then sprinkle evenly over batter in cups.

Bake until golden and crisp and a wooden pick or skewer inserted diagonally into center of a muffin comes out clean, 18 to 20 minutes.

Cool in pans on a rack 15 minutes, then run a knife around edge of each muffin top and carefully remove from cups. Serve warm or at room temperature.

GRILLED PIZZA MARGHERITA

Makes 2 (9-inch) pizzas

Active time: 1¼ hr   Start to finish: 2¾ hr (includes making dough)

If you aren't able to grill outdoors, you can cook these pizzas indoors in a grill pan (see cooks' note, below).

- 1 lb plum tomatoes or 1 (28- to 32-oz) can whole tomatoes in juice, drained
- ¼ teaspoon salt
- 3 tablespoons extra-virgin olive oil plus additional for brushing
- 6 oz mozzarella, coarsely grated (1½ cups)
  Flour for dusting
  Pizza dough (page 144) or 1 lb thawed frozen pizza dough, divided and formed into 2 balls
  Flour for dusting
- 6 to 8 medium fresh basil leaves, torn

Special equipment: **a 22½-inch charcoal kettle grill, a large charcoal chimney starter, and a 10-lb bag of charcoal (preferably hardwood); or a gas grill**

Make sauce and prepare cheese:

If using fresh tomatoes, cut an X (just through skin) in each, at end opposite stem, and immerse in a saucepan of boiling water 10 seconds. Transfer to a bowl of cold water with a slotted spoon, then peel.

Seed and chop tomatoes (fresh or canned).

Simmer tomatoes, salt, and 2 tablespoons oil in a 10-inch heavy skillet over moderate heat, stirring occasionally, until very thick and reduced to about 1 cup, 10 to 15 minutes. Transfer to a bowl to cool.

Toss together mozzarella and remaining tablespoon oil in a bowl.

Form pizza rounds:

Flour a large tray. Do not punch down dough. Gently dredge 1 ball of dough in a bowl of flour to coat, then transfer to a lightly floured work surface. Holding 1 edge of floured dough in the air with both hands and letting bottom touch work surface, carefully move hands around edge of dough (like turning a steering wheel), allowing weight of dough to stretch round to roughly 7 inches in diameter. Lay dough round flat on floured surface and continue to stretch by pressing dough with your fingertips, working from center outward to edge, stretching it into a 9-inch round. Transfer to tray and make another round in same manner, then

place it next to other round. Lightly rub a long sheet of plastic wrap with flour, then invert loosely over pizza rounds and let them stand to puff slightly while preparing grill, 10 to 20 minutes.

Prepare charcoal grill:

Open vents on bottom of grill and on lid. Light a heaping chimneyful of charcoal and pour it evenly over 2 opposite sides of bottom rack (you will have a double or triple layer of charcoal), leaving clear a 9-inch-wide strip in middle (for grilling over indirect heat).

Charcoal fire is medium-hot when you can hold your hand 5 inches above rack for 3 to 4 seconds.

Prepare gas grill:

Preheat burners on high, covered, 10 minutes, then reduce heat to moderate.

To grill pizzas by either method:

Remove plastic wrap from both rounds of dough and lightly brush dough with some oil. Carefully flip dough rounds, oiled sides down, with your hands onto middle of lightly oiled grill rack and brush tops of each with oil. Grill crusts, uncovered, until undersides are golden brown (rotate them if 1 side of grill is hotter than the other), 4 to 6 minutes on charcoal grill or 2 to 3 minutes on gas grill.

Flip crusts over with tongs and a spatula and top each crust with half of tomato sauce, spreading evenly over dough and leaving a ½-inch border around edge. Sprinkle mozzarella evenly over sauce and grill pizzas, covered with lid, until undersides are golden brown and cheese is melted, about 5 minutes on charcoal grill or 3 minutes on gas grill.

Scatter basil over pizzas.

Cooks' note:
- Pizzas can also be cooked in a well-seasoned 10- to 12-inch ridged grill pan. Heat pan over high heat until hot, about 5 minutes, then cook pizzas 1 at a time over moderately high heat, following grilling instructions in recipe above, covering pan after sprinkling with cheese, and using cooking times for charcoal grill.

PHOTO ON PAGE 108

PIZZA DOUGH

Makes 1 lb dough, enough for 2 (9-inch) pizzas
Active time: 20 min   Start to finish: 1¾ hr

Chris Bianco, the owner of Pizzeria Bianco, in Phoenix, makes our favorite pizza dough. Here, we've adapted his recipe slightly to make it work on the grill.

1 (¼-oz) package active dry yeast
    (2¼ teaspoons)
1¾ to 2 cups unbleached all-purpose flour plus
    additional for kneading and dredging
¾ cup warm water (105–115°F)
1½ teaspoons salt
½ tablespoon olive oil

Stir together yeast, 1 tablespoon flour, and ¼ cup warm water in a measuring cup and let stand until mixture appears creamy on surface, about 5 minutes. (If it doesn't, discard and start over with new yeast.)

Stir together 1¼ cups flour and salt in a large bowl, then add yeast mixture, oil, and remaining ½ cup warm water and stir until smooth. Stir in enough remaining flour (¼ to ½ cup) for dough to come away from side of bowl. (This dough will be slightly wetter than other pizza doughs you may have made.)

Knead dough on a floured surface with floured hands, reflouring surface and hands when dough becomes too sticky, until dough is smooth, soft, and elastic, about 8 minutes. Divide dough in half and form into 2 balls, then generously dust balls all over with

flour and put each in a bowl. Cover bowls with plastic wrap and let dough rise until doubled in bulk, about 1¼ hours.

Cooks' note:
• Dough can be allowed to rise, covered and chilled, 1 day. Bring to room temperature before kneading.

WHOLE-WHEAT CRISPS

Serves 8
Active time: 15 min   Start to finish: 1¼ hr

1 (22- to 24-inch) baguette (1¼ lb; preferably
    whole-wheat)
About ¼ cup extra-virgin olive oil
Kosher salt for sprinkling

Put oven rack in middle position and preheat oven to 350°F.

Cut bread on a long diagonal into ⅛- to ¼-inch-thick slices with a serrated knife and arrange in 1 layer on 3 large baking sheets. Brush top of each slice with some oil.

Bake slices 1 sheet at a time until golden and crisp, 15 to 17 minutes. Sprinkle toasts lightly with kosher salt and cool on sheets on racks.

Cooks' note:
• **Toasts can be made 1 week ahead and kept in an airtight container at room temperature.**
PHOTO ON PAGE 90

pizza margherita

SOUPS

ROASTED-TOMATO SOUP WITH PARMESAN WAFERS

Makes about 8 cups
Active time: 20 min   Start to finish: 1¾ hr

Using plum tomatoes for this recipe will yield an intensely flavored soup—good for the chilly months—while other tomatoes make for a refreshingly lighter, more delicately flavored soup that is perfect for warm weather. The soups are equally delicious.

  4 lb tomatoes, halved lengthwise
  6 garlic cloves, left unpeeled
  3 tablespoons olive oil
  ½ teaspoon salt
  ¼ teaspoon black pepper
  1 medium onion, finely chopped
  ½ teaspoon dried oregano, crumbled
  2 teaspoons sugar
  2 tablespoons unsalted butter
  3 cups chicken stock or low-sodium broth
  ½ cup heavy cream

Accompaniment: **parmesan wafers (recipe follows)**
Garnish: **fresh oregano sprigs**

Put oven rack in middle position and preheat oven to 350°F.

Arrange tomatoes, cut sides up, in 1 layer in a large shallow baking pan and add garlic to pan. Drizzle tomatoes with oil and sprinkle with salt and pepper. Roast tomatoes and garlic 1 hour, then cool in pan on a rack. Peel garlic.

Cook onion, oregano, and sugar in butter in a 6- to 8-quart heavy pot over moderately low heat, stirring frequently, until onion is softened, about 5 minutes. Add tomatoes, garlic, and stock and simmer, covered, 20 minutes.

Purée soup in batches in a blender (use caution when blending hot liquids), then force through a sieve into cleaned pot, discarding solids. Stir in cream and salt and pepper to taste and simmer 2 minutes.

Divide soup among 8 bowls and float 1 wafer in center of each.

PARMESAN WAFERS

Makes 8 wafers
Active time: 10 min   Start to finish: 35 min

1½ cups coarsely grated Parmigiano-Reggiano (4 to 5 oz; do not use a food processor)
1 tablespoon all-purpose flour

Special equipment: **a nonstick baking pad such as Silpat**

Put oven rack in middle position and preheat oven to 350°F. Line a large baking sheet with nonstick pad.

Stir together cheese and flour in a bowl. Make 4 mounds (3 tablespoons each) about 5 inches apart on baking sheet and spread each mound to form a 4- to 5-inch round.

Bake until golden, about 10 minutes. Cool 2 minutes on baking sheet on a rack, then carefully transfer each wafer (they are very delicate) with a wide metal spatula to rack to cool completely.

Stir cheese in bowl (to redistribute flour) and make 4 more wafers in same manner.

  Cooks' note:
· Wafers can be made 2 days ahead and kept, layered between sheets of wax paper, in an airtight container at room temperature.

MUSHROOM TORTELLINI IN MUSHROOM BROTH

Serves 8 to 10 (makes about 80 tortellini)
Active time: 3 hr   Start to finish: 3½ hr

2 cups boiling-hot water
1½ oz dried porcini mushrooms (1½ cups)
1 large leek
1 piece Parmigiano-Reggiano with rind
(at least 6 oz)
½ lb fresh cremini mushrooms, caps and
stems chopped separately
¼ lb fresh shiitake mushrooms, caps and
stems chopped separately
2 teaspoons minced garlic
¾ teaspoon salt
2 tablespoons unsalted butter
1 tablespoon finely chopped fresh
flat-leaf parsley plus 2 fresh flat-leaf
parsley sprigs
2 fresh thyme sprigs
1 (3- to 4-inch) piece celery rib
4 cups cold water
4 cups beef broth
8 black peppercorns, cracked
Fresh pasta dough (recipe follows) at
room temperature
All-purpose flour for dusting

Special equipment: **kitchen string; cheesecloth
(optional); a pasta machine; a 2-inch
round cookie cutter**
Garnish: **small fresh flat-leaf parsley leaves**

Prepare vegetables for stuffing and broth:
Pour boiling-hot water over porcini in a bowl and
let stand until softened, about 20 minutes. Lift out
porcini, squeezing excess liquid back into bowl, and
rinse to remove any grit. Finely chop porcini. Pour
soaking liquid through a sieve lined with a dampened
paper towel into another bowl.

Trim leek, reserving about 5 inches of green leaves,
and rinse greens well. Halve rest of leek lengthwise,
then rinse well under cold water and pat dry. Coarsely
chop greens and finely chop white and pale green parts,
reserving greens separately.

Finely grate enough Parmigiano-Reggiano cheese
to measure ¼ cup, then cut off and reserve rind.
Reserve remaining piece of cheese.

Make filling for tortellini:
Pulse cremini caps, shiitake caps, ⅓ cup chopped
porcini, white and pale green parts of leek, garlic, and
½ teaspoon salt in a food processor until finely minced.

Heat butter in a 12-inch nonstick skillet over moderate heat until foam subsides, then cook mushroom
mixture, stirring constantly, until liquid mushrooms
give off is evaporated and mushrooms are golden,
about 10 minutes. Transfer to a bowl and cool completely. Stir in ¼ cup grated cheese, 1 tablespoon
parsley, and salt and pepper to taste.

Make broth:
Tuck parsley and thyme sprigs into celery and tie
together tightly with string to make a *bouquet garni.*
Bring cold water, beef broth, *bouquet garni,* cracked
peppercorns, cremini stems, shiitake stems, leek greens,
remaining chopped porcini, porcini soaking liquid,
cheese rind, and remaining ¼ teaspoon salt to a simmer
in a 3-quart heavy saucepan, stirring occasionally.
Reduce heat and cook at a bare simmer, partially covered, 45 minutes.

Pour broth through a large sieve lined with a double thickness of rinsed and squeezed cheesecloth (or
dampened paper towels) into a large bowl, pressing on
and discarding solids. Return broth to saucepan.

Roll out pasta and form tortellini:
Line a large baking sheet with waxed paper and
lightly flour paper. Set smooth rollers of pasta machine
at widest setting. Cut pasta dough into 4 pieces and
keep 3 pieces covered with plastic wrap. Flatten
unwrapped piece of dough into a rectangle and feed
through rollers. Fold rectangle in half and feed through
rollers 8 more times, folding in half each time and dusting with flour as necessary to prevent sticking.

Turn dial to next (narrower) setting and feed dough
through without folding. Continue to feed dough
through without folding, making space between rollers
narrower each time, until narrowest setting is used.
(Cut sheet of dough in half if it gets too long.)

Cut out as many rounds as possible from sheet with
cookie cutter (reserve trimmings for another use, such
as chicken noodle soup). Transfer rounds in 1 layer to
baking sheet and cover with plastic wrap.

Working with 5 pasta rounds at a time, put ¼ teaspoon filling in center of each round, keeping remaining rounds covered tightly with plastic wrap. Moisten
edges of filling-topped rounds with a fingertip dipped
in water and fold in half, letting bottom edge protrude
slightly beyond top edge, then press top edge to bottom

half to seal. Holding straight edge of half-moon against nail of your little finger, wrap half-moon around finger-tip (curved edge will flip up), overlapping corners and pinching to seal. Transfer tortellini to a dry kitchen towel (not terry cloth).

Roll out and cut remaining pasta dough and make more tortellini in same manner, working with 1 piece at a time.

Cook tortellini:

Bring broth to a boil and season with salt and pepper. Add tortellini and cook at a strong simmer, stirring gently once or twice, until tender, 3 to 5 minutes.

Ladle broth with 8 to 10 tortellini per person into bowls and serve remaining piece of Parmigiano-Reggiano on the side for grating.

Cooks' notes:
- Tortellini can be formed (but not cooked) 1 day ahead and chilled, arranged in 1 layer in a kitchen-towel-lined shallow baking pan and covered with plastic wrap.
- Broth and filling can be made 2 days ahead. Cool completely, then chill separately, covered.
- If you don't have time to make fresh pasta, you can cut rounds from wonton wrappers (thawed if frozen).

PHOTO ON PAGE 58

FRESH PASTA DOUGH

Makes 1 lb dough
Active time: 15 min   Start to finish: 1¼ hr

2 cups cake flour (not self-rising)
½ cup all-purpose flour plus additional for kneading
1 teaspoon salt
4 large egg yolks
3 tablespoons extra-virgin olive oil
½ cup water

Blend all ingredients in a food processor until mixture just begins to form a ball. Knead dough on a lightly floured surface, incorporating only as much additional flour as necessary to keep dough from sticking, until smooth and elastic, 6 to 8 minutes. Wrap dough in plastic wrap and let stand at room temperature 1 hour.

Cooks' note:
- Pasta dough, though best used immediately, can be made (but not rolled out) 1 day ahead and chilled, wrapped in plastic wrap.

CHAYOTE SOUP

Serves 4
Active time: 30 min   Start to finish: 45 min

The delicately flavored fruit chayote is ubiquitous in the central highlands of Mexico. It varies greatly in size, ranges in color from white to dark green, and can have prickly or smooth skin. The variety most commonly available in the United States (also known as a vegetable pear or mirliton) has smooth, pale green skin that can be eaten but is sometimes removed.

2 scallions, minced
1 small garlic clove, minced
¼ teaspoon minced small fresh hot green chile such as *serrano* or Thai, or to taste
½ tablespoon unsalted butter
1½ lb chayotes (2 to 3), peeled, quartered lengthwise, and pitted if necessary, then cut into ½-inch pieces (4 cups)
½ teaspoon salt
2 tablespoons finely chopped fresh cilantro
1¾ cups water

Garnish: fresh cilantro sprigs

Cook scallions, garlic, and chile in butter in a 3-quart heavy saucepan over moderately low heat, stirring, until softened, about 3 minutes. Add chayotes, salt, and 1 tablespoon cilantro and cook, stirring, 2 minutes. Add water and simmer, covered, until chayotes are very tender, 15 to 20 minutes.

Stir in remaining tablespoon cilantro and purée soup in 2 batches in a blender until smooth (use caution when blending hot liquids). Season with salt.

Cooks' note:
- Soup can be made 1 day ahead and cooled, uncovered, then chilled, covered.

Each serving about 41 calories and 2 grams fat

PHOTO ON PAGE 106

OYSTER SOUP WITH FRIZZLED LEEKS

Serves 8 (makes about 11 cups)
Active time: 1 hr   Start to finish: 1¼ hr

It's very important to use small oysters—such as Kumamoto or Prince Edward Island—in this soup. The oysters themselves (not the shell) should be no more than 1 to 1½ inches in diameter. When we tested the recipe with larger ones, the flavor was much too briny.

For fried leeks
2 large leeks (white and pale green parts only), trimmed
4 cups vegetable oil
For soup
1½ cups shucked small oysters (6 dozen) with 1½ cups of their liquor (if necessary, add enough bottled clam juice to bring total to 1½ cups)
2 medium leeks (white and pale green parts only), chopped
2 large russet (baking) potatoes (1 lb total)
1 teaspoon salt
3 tablespoons unsalted butter
3½ cups water
1 cup half-and-half
Pinch of cayenne

Special equipment: **a deep-fat thermometer**

Fry leeks:
Cut leeks crosswise into 2-inch lengths, then cut lengthwise into enough very thin strips to measure 2 cups. Wash leek strips in a bowl of cold water, agitating them, then lift out and pat dry.

Heat oil in a deep 4-quart heavy saucepan until it registers 360°F on thermometer. Fry leeks in 8 batches, stirring, until golden, about 10 seconds per batch. Transfer as fried with a slotted spoon to paper towels to drain. Cool completely (leeks will crisp as they cool).

Make soup:
Pick over oysters, discarding any bits of shell, and rinse well. Wash chopped leeks in a bowl of cold water, agitating them, then lift out and drain well. Peel potatoes and cut into ½-inch cubes. Cook leeks, potatoes, and salt in butter in a 4-quart heavy saucepan, covered, over low heat, stirring occasionally, until leeks are golden and potatoes are beginning to soften, about 15 minutes. Add water and simmer, covered, over moderate heat until potatoes are very tender, about

10 minutes. Purée soup in batches in a blender until very smooth (use caution when blending hot liquids), transferring to a bowl.

Return soup to saucepan. Add oyster liquor and half-and-half and bring to a simmer over moderate heat, stirring occasionally (do not boil). Add oysters and cayenne and cook, stirring occasionally, just until oysters become plump and edges curl, about 3 minutes. Season with salt.

Serve soup topped with fried leeks.

Cooks' notes:
• Fried leeks can be made 3 days ahead and kept in a sealed plastic bag at room temperature.
• Soup base (without oyster liquor, half-and-half, oysters, and cayenne) can be made 2 days ahead and cooled, uncovered, then chilled, covered.
PHOTO ON PAGE 103

SPANISH ALMOND SOUP

Serves 4
Active time: 15 min   Start to finish: 25 min

3 tablespoons extra-virgin olive oil
½ cup blanched almonds (3 oz)
2 cups ½-inch bread cubes (from a baguette)
2 tablespoons chopped fresh flat-leaf parsley
2 large garlic cloves, finely chopped
¼ teaspoon coarsely crumbled saffron threads
2 cups chicken broth
2 cups water
½ teaspoon salt, or to taste
1 teaspoon Sherry vinegar (optional)

Heat olive oil in a 10-inch heavy skillet over moderately high heat until hot but not smoking, then sauté almonds, stirring constantly, until golden, about 4 minutes. Transfer sautéed almonds with a slotted spoon to a blender.

Add bread cubes, parsley, garlic, and saffron to oil in skillet and cook over moderate heat, stirring constantly, until golden, about 2 minutes. Transfer about one fourth of crouton mixture to a small bowl for garnish, then transfer remainder to blender. Add broth to blender and purée mixture until smooth.

Transfer purée to a 2- to 3-quart heavy saucepan and stir in water. Simmer, uncovered, stirring occasionally, until slightly thickened, about 5 minutes. Stir in salt and vinegar and serve soup topped with croutons.

CREAMY CHINESE CELERY SOUP

Serves 6
Active time: 30 min   Start to finish: 1½ hr

This celery looks very much like the variety found in most supermarkets, but its stems are thinner and it has an abundance of leaves that resemble Italian parsley. Cooking mellows Chinese celery's pronounced flavor— for a stir-fry, it's often blanched first.

For soup
1 medium leek (white and pale green parts
    only), chopped
1 medium russet (baking) potato
½ cup chopped shallot
2 tablespoons unsalted butter
1 tablespoon olive oil
2 bunches Chinese celery (1½ lb total),
    top leaves discarded and stalks cut into
    2-inch pieces
½ cup dry white wine
4 cups chicken stock or low-sodium chicken
    broth (32 fl oz)
½ cup heavy cream
½ teaspoon salt
¼ teaspoon black pepper
For croutons
6 (¼-inch-thick) diagonal baguette slices
¼ cup extra-virgin olive oil
    Kosher salt to taste

Garnish: fresh Chinese parsley leaves or flat-leaf
    parsley leaves

Make soup:
Wash leek well in a bowl of cold water, then lift out and drain well. Peel and chop potato. Cook shallot in butter and oil in a 3-quart heavy saucepan over moderate heat, stirring, until softened, about 2 minutes. Add leek and cook, stirring, until softened, about 5 minutes. Add celery and potato and cook, stirring, 2 minutes. Add wine and boil 1 minute. Add broth and simmer, covered, until celery is very tender, about 1 hour.

Purée soup in batches in a blender until very smooth (use caution when blending hot liquids), then pour through a large medium-mesh sieve into a bowl, pressing hard on solids. Discard solids. Transfer soup to cleaned saucepan, then stir in cream, salt, and pepper and heat over low heat until hot. Thin with water if desired.

Make croutons while soup simmers:
Put oven rack in middle position and preheat oven to 350°F.

Brush baguette slices with oil and season generously with kosher salt and pepper. Arrange in 1 layer on a baking sheet, then bake until golden brown and crisp, 12 to 15 minutes.

Serve soup topped with croutons.

Cooks' notes:
• Soup can be made 1 day ahead and cooled, uncovered,
  then chilled, covered.
• Croutons keep in an airtight container at room
  temperature 2 days.

CHICKEN SOUP WITH ASPARAGUS,
PEAS, AND DILL

Makes about 13 cups
Active time: 25 min   Start to finish: 4 hr (includes making stock)

Sephardim (Jewish people of Middle Eastern and Mediterranean extraction) eat peas during Passover; those from eastern European Jewish backgrounds do not. Feel free to omit the peas—the soup is just as delicious without them. It's important to use a flavorful chicken stock for this recipe, so if you have a stash of homemade in your freezer, this is the time to use it.

14 cups chicken stock (page 150)
8 fresh dill stems (stripped of leaves) plus
    3 tablespoons chopped dill leaves
1½ lb asparagus, trimmed and thinly sliced
    diagonally, leaving tips intact
3 cups frozen baby green peas (1 lb; not
    thawed)

Simmer stock with dill stems in a 4- to 5-quart saucepan, uncovered, until reduced to about 8 cups, 25 to 30 minutes. Discard dill stems. Add asparagus and peas, then bring to a boil, partially covered. Reduce heat and simmer, uncovered, until asparagus is crisp-tender, about 3 minutes. Stir in dill leaves and season with salt and pepper.

PHOTO ON PAGE 66

CHICKEN STOCK

Makes about 14 cups
Active time: 30 min   Start to finish: 3½ hr

16½ cups cold water
 1 (3½- to 4-lb) chicken, cut into 8 pieces,
   plus neck and giblets (except liver)
 2 onions, left unpeeled, halved
 2 whole cloves
 4 garlic cloves, left unpeeled
 1 celery rib, halved
 2 carrots, halved
 1 teaspoon salt
 6 long fresh flat-leaf parsley sprigs
 8 whole black peppercorns
 ½ teaspoon dried thyme, crumbled
 1 Turkish or ½ California bay leaf

Bring 16 cups cold water to a boil with chicken pieces (including neck and giblets) in an 8-quart pot, skimming froth. Add remaining ½ cup cold water and bring to a simmer, skimming froth. Add remaining ingredients and simmer stock, uncovered, skimming froth, 3 hours.

Pour stock through a fine-mesh sieve into a large bowl, discarding solids. If using stock right away, skim off and discard any fat. If not, cool stock completely, uncovered, before skimming fat, then chill, covered.

Cooks' note:
• Stock keeps, covered and chilled, 1 week, or frozen, 3 months.

BUTTERNUT SQUASH AND WHITE BEAN SOUP

Serves 4 (main course)
Active time: 15 min   Start to finish: 35 min

 1 large garlic clove, minced
 2 tablespoons extra-virgin olive oil
 ½ small butternut squash (1 lb), peeled,
   seeded, and cut into ½-inch pieces (2 cups)
1¾ cups low-sodium chicken broth (14 fl oz)
 2 cups water
 1 (16- to 19-oz) can white beans (preferably
   cannellini), rinsed and drained
 2 canned whole tomatoes, coarsely chopped
 1 teaspoon finely chopped fresh sage

 1 oz finely grated Parmigiano-Reggiano
   (½ cup) plus additional for serving
 ¼ cup hulled green pumpkin seeds (not
   roasted; optional)

Cook garlic in 1 tablespoon oil in a 3-quart heavy saucepan over moderate heat, stirring frequently, until golden, about 1 minute. Add squash, broth, water, beans, tomatoes, and sage and simmer, covered, stirring occasionally, until squash is tender, about 20 minutes. Mash some of squash against side of saucepan to thicken soup. Remove from heat and stir in ½ cup cheese and salt and pepper to taste.

While soup simmers, cook pumpkin seeds in remaining tablespoon oil in a small skillet over moderately low heat, stirring, until seeds are plump and lightly toasted, 2 to 4 minutes. Season with salt.

Serve soup sprinkled with pumpkin seeds and additional cheese.

SCALLOP CHOWDER

Serves 4 (main course)
Active time: 1¼ hr   Start to finish: 1¼ hr

 2 large leeks (white and pale green parts
   only), finely chopped (1½ cups)
 1 tablespoon unsalted butter
 1 large russet (baking) potato
 2 tablespoons dry white wine
 1 (6-inch) fresh thyme sprig
 ¼ teaspoon white pepper
 ¾ lb sea scallops, tough muscle removed from
   side of each if necessary and scallops cut
   into ⅓-inch dice
3½ cups bottled clam juice (28 oz)
 1 medium carrot, cut into ⅓-inch dice
 1 large celery rib, cut into ⅓-inch dice
 1 oz sliced bacon (2 slices), chopped
 ½ cup whole milk
 ¼ teaspoon salt, or to taste

Accompaniment: herbed oyster crackers (recipe
   follows)

Wash leeks well in a bowl of cold water, then lift out and drain well. Cook half of leeks in butter in a 3-quart heavy saucepan over low heat, covered, stirring occasionally, until very soft, about 10 minutes.

While leeks cook, peel potato and cut into ⅓-inch dice. Add wine, thyme sprig, and white pepper to leeks and boil until most of liquid is evaporated, about 1 minute. Add ⅓ cup potato (reserve remaining diced potato in a bowl of cold water), ½ cup scallops, and clam juice, then simmer, uncovered, until potato is tender, about 15 minutes.

Drain remaining potatoes in a colander and cook with carrot, celery, and remaining leeks in a 1-quart saucepan of boiling salted water (see Tips, page 8) until just tender, about 5 minutes, then drain.

Cook bacon in a skillet over moderate heat, stirring occasionally, until crisp, about 3 minutes, and transfer to paper towels to drain.

Remove and discard thyme sprig and purée soup in 2 batches in a blender until very smooth (use caution when blending hot liquids), then transfer to a bowl. Return soup to cleaned saucepan, then add vegetable mixture, remaining scallops, milk, and salt and cook over moderate heat (do not let boil), stirring, until scallops are just cooked through, about 2 minutes.

Serve sprinkled with bacon.

Each serving (not including crackers) about 229 calories and 6 grams fat

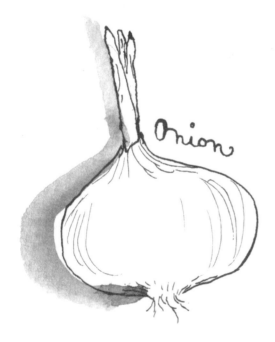

HERBED OYSTER CRACKERS

Makes about 4 cups
Active time: 45 min   Start to finish: 3 hr

Even if your crackers fail to puff, they'll still taste delicious.

- ½ **teaspoon active dry yeast (from a ¼-oz package)**
  Pinch of sugar
- ½ **cup lukewarm (105–115°F) water**
- 1⅓ **to 1½ cups all-purpose flour**
- 2 **teaspoons chopped fresh thyme or 1 teaspoon dried, crumbled**
- ½ **teaspoon salt**
- ⅛ **teaspoon cayenne**
- 2 **teaspoons extra-virgin olive oil**
- ½ **teaspoon kosher salt**

Stir yeast and sugar into warm water in a measuring cup and let stand until foamy, about 5 minutes. (If mixture doesn't foam, discard and start over with new yeast.) Stir together 1¼ cups flour, thyme, salt, and cayenne, then make a well in center and add yeast mixture and oil, stirring to form a dough.

Turn out dough onto a lightly floured surface and knead in 2 to 3 tablespoons flour (dough should be moist but not sticky). Knead until smooth and elastic, about 6 minutes, then transfer to a lightly oiled large bowl and let rise, covered with plastic wrap, in a draft-free place at warm room temperature until doubled in bulk, 1½ to 2 hours.

Put oven rack in middle position and preheat oven to 450°F. Lightly oil 3 baking sheets.

Roll out dough as thin as possible (into an 18-inch square) with a lightly floured rolling pin on a lightly floured surface. Sprinkle with kosher salt and gently press salt to help adhere. Cut dough into 1-inch squares with a pizza wheel or large sharp knife. Transfer with a lightly floured metal spatula to baking sheets, placing squares close together.

Bake crackers in batches, rotating sheets halfway through baking, until bottoms are golden (tops will remain pale), 6 to 7 minutes. Transfer to a rack to cool completely. (Crackers will crisp as they cool.)

Each ¾-cup serving about 177 calories and 3 grams fat

FISH AND SHELLFISH

fish

SEA BASS AND SPICY TOMATO SAUCE OVER BRAISED FENNEL

Serves 4
Active time: 30 min   Start to finish: 1¼ hr

2 large fennel bulbs, preferably with fronds
 (sometimes called anise; 2 lb total), fronds
 reserved and stalks discarded
1 large onion, halved lengthwise, one half cut
 lengthwise into ¼-inch-thick slices and the
 other half chopped
½ teaspoon anchovy paste
2½ teaspoons extra-virgin olive oil
1 cup fat-free chicken broth
¼ to ½ teaspoon dried hot red pepper flakes
1 (14-oz) can whole tomatoes in juice
4 (5-oz) skinless sea bass fillets (¾ inch thick),
 bones removed

Chop enough fennel fronds, if using, to measure 2 tablespoons. Quarter fennel bulbs lengthwise, then cut lengthwise into ¼-inch-thick slices.

Cook fennel bulbs, sliced onion, and anchovy paste in 1½ teaspoons oil in a 12-inch heavy nonstick skillet over moderate heat, stirring, until coated, about 1 minute. Season with salt and pepper, then add broth and braise, covered, stirring occasionally, until vegetables are tender, about 20 minutes.

Remove lid and boil, stirring occasionally, until liquid is evaporated, about 10 minutes. Transfer fennel mixture to a 1½-quart shallow gratin or other shallow 9-inch ceramic or glass baking dish.

Put oven rack in middle position and preheat oven to 450°F.

While fennel mixture braises, cook chopped onion, red pepper flakes, and salt to taste in remaining teaspoon oil in an 8-inch nonstick skillet over moderate heat, stirring occasionally, until onion is softened, 3 to 4 minutes. Add tomatoes with juice and simmer, breaking up tomatoes with a spoon and stirring occasionally, until very thick, 15 to 20 minutes.

Arrange fish fillets on top of fennel mixture and season with salt. Spoon tomato sauce over fish. Cover with a sheet of wax paper or parchment, then cover baking dish tightly with foil and bake until fish is just cooked through, 20 to 25 minutes. Sprinkle with fennel fronds, if using.

Each serving about 218 calories and 6 grams fat

FINNAN HADDIE GRATIN
Potato and Celery-Root Gratin with Smoked Haddock

Serves 6 to 8
Active time: 40 min   Start to finish: 2¼ hr

2 medium onions, halved lengthwise, then
 thinly sliced lengthwise
2 tablespoons unsalted butter
½ lb smoked haddock fillet (finnan haddie;
 thawed if frozen), shredded with your
 fingers into ½-inch pieces, discarding any
 tough parts
2 tablespoons chopped fresh flat-leaf parsley
1½ lb celery root (sometimes called celeriac),
 peeled with a knife
2 lb large potatoes (preferably russet or
 Yukon Gold), peeled
2 cups heavy cream
½ cup whole milk
1 teaspoon salt
¼ teaspoon black pepper

Special equipment: **a Japanese Benriner or other
 adjustable-blade slicer**

Put oven rack in middle position and preheat oven to 375°F. Butter a 13- by 9- by 2-inch or other shallow 2½- to 3-quart glass or ceramic baking dish.

Cook onions in butter in a 12-inch heavy skillet over moderate heat, stirring occasionally, until softened and just beginning to brown, 7 to 8 minutes. Remove from heat and stir in haddock, 1 tablespoon parsley, and salt and pepper to taste.

Halve or quarter celery root to fit slicer. Thinly slice celery root and potatoes (about ⅛ inch thick) with slicer. Layer one third of potatoes and celery root in baking dish. Spread half of haddock mixture on top, then repeat layering with half of remaining vegetables, all of remaining haddock mixture, and then remaining vegetables. Stir together cream, milk, salt, and pepper and pour over top of gratin, then cover dish tightly with buttered foil.

Bake gratin until vegetables are just tender, about 1 hour. Uncover and bake, basting 2 or 3 times with pan juices, until top is golden, about 30 minutes more. Let stand 10 minutes, then sprinkle with remaining tablespoon parsley.

PHOTO ON PAGE 108

SEARED MAHIMAHI WITH HOT-AND-SOUR MANGO RELISH

Serves 4 (main course)
Active time: 40 min   Start to finish: 40 min

This tangy relish also goes well with chicken or pork.

⅓ cup finely chopped shallot
3 tablespoons peanut or vegetable oil
1 (1½- to 2-inch) fresh chile, minced
   (including seeds)
2 (1-lb) firm-ripe mangoes, peeled, pitted,
   and cut into ¾-inch pieces (3½ cups)

1½ tablespoons Asian fish sauce such as Thai
   nam pla or Vietnamese *nuoc mam*
1 tablespoon sugar
¼ teaspoon salt
2 tablespoons fresh lime juice, or to taste
4 (6-oz) pieces mahimahi fillet (1 to
   1½ inches thick) with skin

Accompaniment: **lime wedges**

Cook shallot in 2 tablespoons oil in a 12-inch non-stick skillet over moderate heat, stirring occasionally, until golden, 3 to 5 minutes. Add chile and cook, stirring, until softened, about 1 minute. Add mangoes, fish sauce, sugar, and salt and cook, stirring occasionally, until mango is softened and mixture is slightly thickened, 3 to 7 minutes. Remove from heat and stir in lime juice. Transfer relish to a bowl.

Pat fish dry and season with salt and pepper. Heat remaining tablespoon oil in cleaned skillet over moderately high heat until it just begins to smoke, then cook fish, starting with skin sides down and turning over once, until golden and just cooked through, 12 to 16 minutes total. Serve fish topped with relish.

SALMON WITH MUSTARD MAPLE SAUCE

Serves 4
Active time: 20 min   Start to finish: 20 min

4 (6- to 7-oz) pieces center-cut salmon fillet
   (1¼ inches thick), skinned
1 tablespoon vegetable oil
3 tablespoons water
2 tablespoons Dijon mustard
2 tablespoons pure maple syrup
2 garlic cloves, finely chopped
2 teaspoons mustard seeds
¼ cup chopped scallion greens

Pat salmon dry and season with salt and pepper. Heat oil in a 12-inch nonstick skillet over moderately high heat until hot but not smoking, then sauté salmon in 2 batches, starting with skinned sides up and turning over once, until just cooked through, 6 to 9 minutes per batch. Transfer to a platter and keep warm, covered.

Remove skillet from heat and cool 1 minute. Whisk in remaining ingredients and salt and pepper to taste. Pour sauce over salmon.

PAN-SEARED TILAPIA WITH CHILE LIME BUTTER

Serves 6
Active time: 25 min   Start to finish: 25 min

For chile lime butter
½ stick (¼ cup) unsalted butter, softened
1 tablespoon finely chopped shallot
1 teaspoon finely grated fresh lime zest
2 teaspoons fresh lime juice
1 teaspoon minced fresh Thai or *serrano* chile (preferably red), including seeds
½ teaspoon salt
For fish
6 (5- to 6-oz) pieces skinless tilapia fillet or farm-raised striped bass fillets with skin
½ teaspoon salt
2 tablespoons vegetable oil

Make chile lime butter:
Stir together butter, shallot, zest, lime juice, chile, and salt in a bowl.

Prepare fish:
If using striped bass, score skin in 3 or 4 places with a thin sharp knife to prevent fish from curling (do not cut through flesh). Pat fish dry and sprinkle with salt. Heat 1 tablespoon oil in a 12-inch nonstick skillet over moderately high heat until just smoking, then sauté 3 pieces of fish, turning over once with a spatula, until golden and just cooked through, 4 to 5 minutes total, and transfer to a plate. Sauté remaining fish in remaining tablespoon oil in same manner.

Serve each piece of fish with a dollop of chile lime butter.

Cooks' note:
• Chile lime butter can be made 1 day ahead and chilled, covered. Bring to room temperature before using.
PHOTO ON PAGE 84

SALMON FILLET WITH SOY GLAZE

Serves 6
Active time: 10 min   Start to finish: 30 min

¼ cup soy sauce
¼ cup pure maple syrup
1 (2-lb) piece center-cut salmon fillet with skin (1½ inches thick)

Put oven rack in middle position and preheat oven to 450°F. Line bottom of a broiler pan with foil, then oil rack of pan.

Boil soy sauce and maple syrup in a small saucepan over moderate heat until glaze is reduced to about ⅓ cup, about 5 minutes.

Arrange salmon, skin side down, on rack of broiler pan and pat dry. Reserve 1½ tablespoons glaze in a small bowl for brushing after broiling. Brush salmon generously with some of remaining glaze. Let stand 5 minutes, then brush with more glaze.

Roast salmon 10 minutes. Turn on broiler and brush salmon with glaze again, then broil 4 to 5 inches from heat until just cooked through, 3 to 5 minutes.

Transfer salmon with 2 wide metal spatulas to a platter, then brush fillet with reserved glaze using a clean brush.

GRILLED SWORDFISH WITH CUCUMBER LIME SALSA

Serves 1
Active time: 30 min   Start to finish: 40 min

For swordfish
1 tablespoon fresh lime juice
1 teaspoon honey
1 teaspoon vegetable oil plus additional
1 teaspoon ground coriander
1 (1-inch-thick) swordfish steak (6 oz)
For salsa
1 lime
1 (¼-lb) Kirby cucumber, peeled, seeded, and cut into ¼-inch dice (¾ cup)
1 tablespoon finely chopped fresh cilantro
1 tablespoon finely chopped scallion greens
1 teaspoon finely chopped fresh jalapeño or *serrano* chile (including seeds)
1 teaspoon sugar, or to taste
¼ teaspoon salt

Special equipment: **a well-seasoned ridged grill pan (preferably cast-iron)**

Marinate swordfish:
Stir together lime juice, honey, oil, and coriander in a shallow dish. Add swordfish, turning to coat, and marinate at room temperature, turning over once, 15 minutes. (Do not marinate longer.)
Make salsa while swordfish marinates:
Remove peel, including all white pith, from lime with a sharp paring knife. Cut segments free from membranes and finely chop segments, then combine with remaining salsa ingredients in a bowl.
Grill swordfish:
Lightly brush grill pan with oil and heat over moderately high heat until just beginning to smoke. Remove swordfish from marinade and season both sides with salt and pepper. Grill fish, turning over once, until just cooked through, 6 to 8 minutes total.
Serve fish topped with salsa.

Cooks' note:
• Salsa can be made 2 hours ahead and chilled, covered.

RED SNAPPER WITH LEMON MARJORAM BUTTER

Serves 4
Active time: 15 min   Start to finish: 20 min

½ stick (¼ cup) unsalted butter, softened
1 teaspoon finely grated fresh lemon zest
2 teaspoons fresh lemon juice
1 teaspoon chopped fresh marjoram or oregano
¼ teaspoon salt
⅛ teaspoon black pepper
4 (7-oz) red snapper fillets with skin
  Olive oil for brushing

Preheat broiler. Line a shallow baking pan (1 to 1½ inches deep) with foil.
Stir together butter, zest, juice, marjoram, salt, and pepper in a small bowl.
Brush both sides of each snapper fillet with oil. Arrange fillets, skin sides down, in baking pan and season with salt and pepper. Broil 4 to 6 inches from heat until cooked through, about 5 minutes. Serve immediately, topped with marjoram butter.

PANFRIED TROUT WITH PECAN BUTTER SAUCE

Serves 2 to 4
Active time: 40 min   Start to finish: 40 min

At the opening of every episode of The Andy Griffith Show, *we see Andy and Opie walking to the creek, fishing rods slung over their shoulders. This simple and delicious recipe from our Television Issue is one way that Aunt Bee might have prepared Andy's freshly caught trout.*

1 stick (½ cup) unsalted butter
2 (½- to ¾-lb) whole brook, rainbow, or brown trout, cleaned, keeping head and tail intact
1 teaspoon salt
¾ cup all-purpose flour
3 tablespoons vegetable oil
¼ cup pecans, coarsely chopped
2 tablespoons chopped fresh flat-leaf parsley
¼ teaspoon black pepper
1 tablespoon fresh lemon juice

Garnish: **lemon wedges**

Put oven rack in middle position and preheat oven to 200°F.
Melt 2 tablespoons butter in a 12-inch heavy skillet (preferably oval) over low heat and remove from heat.
Rinse trout and pat dry. Brush with melted butter inside and out and season with ¾ teaspoon salt (total for both fish). Mound flour on a sheet of wax paper, then dredge each fish in flour to coat completely, shaking off excess.
Add oil and 2 tablespoons butter to skillet and heat over moderately high heat until foam subsides, then sauté both trout, gently turning over once using 2 spatulas, until golden brown and almost cooked through, about 8 minutes total (fish will continue to cook as it stands). Transfer each trout to a plate and keep warm in oven.
Pour off fat from skillet and wipe skillet clean. Melt remaining ½ stick butter over moderately low heat, then cook pecans, stirring, until fragrant and a shade darker, 1 to 2 minutes. Add parsley, pepper, and remaining ¼ teaspoon salt, swirling skillet to combine, and remove from heat. Add lemon juice, swirling skillet to incorporate, and spoon over trout.
Serve immediately.

shellfish

GRILLED NEW ORLEANS–STYLE SHRIMP

Serves 4 (main course)
Active time: 40 min   Start to finish: 40 min

Serve these spicy grilled shrimp with bread for sopping up all the sauce.

  1½ lb large shrimp in shell (21 to 25 per lb)
  2 tablespoons olive oil
  3 medium garlic cloves, minced
  ¾ teaspoon salt
  ¾ stick (6 tablespoons) unsalted butter
  2 teaspoons chili powder
  2 teaspoons black pepper
  4 teaspoons Worcestershire sauce
  1 tablespoon fresh lemon juice

Special equipment: **7 (12-inch) wooden skewers**
Accompaniments: **a baguette and lemon wedges**

Snip shells of shrimp with scissors down middle of back, leaving tail and first segment of shell intact. Make an incision along length of back where shells are cut and devein, leaving shells in place. (Shells will prevent shrimp from becoming tough on outside when grilled.) Toss shrimp with oil, garlic, and ½ teaspoon salt and marinate at cool room temperature 15 minutes.

While shrimp marinate, prepare grill for cooking. If using a charcoal grill, open vents on bottom of grill, then light charcoal. Charcoal fire is medium-hot when you can hold your hand 5 inches above rack for 3 to 4 seconds. If using a gas grill, preheat burners on high, covered, 10 minutes, then reduce heat to moderately high.

Heat butter, chili powder, pepper, Worcestershire sauce, and remaining ¼ teaspoon salt in a small heavy saucepan over moderately low heat, stirring, until butter is melted. Remove from heat and stir in lemon juice.

Thread 4 or 5 shrimp onto each skewer and grill, uncovered (covered if using a gas grill), turning over once, until just cooked through, 3 to 4 minutes total. Push shrimp off skewers into a bowl, then pour butter mixture over them and toss to combine well.

Cooks' note:
• If you're unable to grill outdoors, shrimp can be broiled on a broiler pan 6 inches from heat, turning over once, about 6 minutes total.

BRAISED SHRIMP AND CREAMY ENDIVE

Serves 2
Active time: 45 min   Start to finish: 45 min

  1 lb Belgian endives (4 or 5), trimmed and
    quartered lengthwise
  1 teaspoon sugar
  ¾ teaspoon salt
  1½ tablespoons fresh lemon juice
  2 tablespoons unsalted butter
  10 oz large shrimp in shell, peeled
    and deveined
  ¼ cup heavy cream

Garnish: **chopped fresh herbs**

Cut out and discard endive cores, then cut endives diagonally into ½-inch-wide strips. Toss with sugar, ½ teaspoon salt, and 1 tablespoon lemon juice in a bowl.

Melt butter in a 10-inch nonstick skillet over moderately low heat and add endive mixture, tossing to coat. Cook, covered, stirring occasionally, until endive is tender, 10 to 12 minutes.

While endive cooks, toss shrimp with remaining ¼ teaspoon salt and remaining ½ tablespoon lemon juice in a bowl.

When endive is tender, increase heat to moderate and cook, uncovered, stirring, until juices evaporate, about 2 minutes. Stir in cream and simmer 1 minute.

Scatter shrimp over endive and cook, covered, over low heat, without stirring, until shrimp are just cooked through, 3 to 5 minutes.

SEARED SCALLOPS WITH
BRUSSELS SPROUTS AND BACON

Serves 4
Active time: 30 min   Start to finish: 30 min

If they are available, purchase dry-packed scallops, which exude less liquid.

  10 oz Brussels sprouts, trimmed and halved
    lengthwise
  3 bacon slices (3 oz), cut crosswise into
    ½-inch pieces
  1 cup low-sodium chicken broth
  ¼ cup plus 2 teaspoons water
  1½ tablespoons unsalted butter

¼ teaspoon salt
   Pinch of sugar
12 large sea scallops (1¼ lb), tough muscle
      removed from side of each if necessary
 2 teaspoons olive oil
¾ teaspoon cornstarch
 2 teaspoons fresh lemon juice

Blanch Brussels sprouts in a 3- to 4-quart saucepan of boiling salted water (see Tips, page 8), uncovered, 3 minutes, then drain.

Cook bacon in a 10-inch heavy skillet over moderate heat, turning over occasionally, until crisp. Transfer bacon with a slotted spoon to a small bowl and reserve bacon fat in another small bowl.

Add ¼ cup broth and ¼ cup water to skillet and bring to a simmer, scraping up any brown bits. Add butter, salt, sugar, a pinch of pepper, and Brussels sprouts and simmer, covered, 4 minutes. Remove lid and cook over moderately high heat, stirring occasionally, until all liquid is evaporated and Brussels sprouts are tender and golden brown, about 8 minutes more. Stir in bacon and remove from heat.

While Brussels sprouts brown, pat scallops dry and season with salt and pepper. Heat oil with 2 teaspoons bacon fat in a 12-inch heavy skillet over moderately high heat until hot but not smoking, then sear scallops, turning over once, until golden brown and just cooked through, 4 to 6 minutes total. Transfer to a platter and keep warm, loosely covered with foil.

Pour off and discard any fat from skillet used to cook scallops. Add remaining ¾ cup broth and simmer, stirring and scraping up any brown bits, 1 minute. Stir cornstarch into remaining 2 teaspoons water in a cup, then stir into sauce along with any scallop juices accumulated on platter. Simmer, stirring, 1 minute, then remove from heat and stir in lemon juice and salt and pepper to taste.

Serve Brussels sprouts topped with seared scallops and sauce.

Shrimp

SHRIMP IN SHERRY BUTTER SAUCE

Serves 8 (main course)
Active time: 45 min   Start to finish: 2 hr

 1 tablespoon vegetable oil
 3 lb medium shrimp in shell (31 to 35 per lb),
      rinsed, peeled, and shells reserved
 8 cups water
 1 onion, halved, plus ½ cup minced onion
 1 carrot, halved
 1 Turkish or ½ California bay leaf
 2 fresh flat-leaf parsley sprigs
 1 fresh thyme sprig
½ teaspoon whole black peppercorns
1½ teaspoons salt
1½ tablespoons all-purpose flour
 1 stick (½ cup) unsalted butter, cut into
      tablespoon pieces and softened
½ cup medium-dry Sherry
 2 teaspoons fresh lemon juice, or to taste

Heat oil in a 4- to 5-quart heavy pot over moderately high heat until hot but not smoking, then cook shrimp shells, stirring, 1 minute. Add water, onion halves, carrot, bay leaf, parsley, thyme, peppercorns, and salt and simmer, uncovered, 30 minutes.

Pour stock through a large sieve lined with a dampened paper towel into a large bowl, discarding solids. Return stock to cleaned pot. Add shrimp and cook over high heat (stock will be hot but not boiling), stirring frequently, until just cooked through, about 2 minutes. Transfer shrimp with a slotted spoon to a large shallow baking pan, spreading in 1 layer to cool quickly. Boil stock until reduced to about 1½ cups, 30 to 40 minutes, then transfer to a bowl.

Stir together flour and 1½ tablespoons butter until a paste forms, then set aside. Cook minced onion in 1 tablespoon butter in cleaned pot over moderately low heat, stirring, until softened, about 3 minutes. Add Sherry and boil until liquid is reduced to about ⅓ cup, about 2 minutes. Add shrimp stock and bring to a simmer, then reduce heat to low and whisk in remaining 5½ tablespoons butter until just incorporated. Whisk in flour paste, bit by bit, and simmer sauce, whisking, until slightly thickened, about 2 minutes. Add lemon juice, shrimp, and salt and pepper to taste and cook over moderate heat, stirring, until shrimp are just heated through, about 1 minute.

PHOTO ON PAGE 71

MEATS

beef

BLADE STEAKS WITH MUSHROOMS

Serves 4
Active time: 25 min   Start to finish: 25 min

Top blade steaks—great for a weeknight supper—are inexpensive and cook in just minutes.

4 (½-inch-thick) top blade chuck steaks
   (1¼ lb total)
¼ teaspoon salt
⅛ teaspoon black pepper
1 tablespoon olive oil
1 tablespoon unsalted butter
10 oz cremini or white mushrooms, cut into
   ¾-inch-thick wedges
1 tablespoon finely chopped shallot
¼ cup balsamic vinegar
2 tablespoons soy sauce
½ cup plus 2 teaspoons beef broth
¾ teaspoon cornstarch

Pat steaks dry and cut 3 (1-inch-long) slits, 1 inch apart, across center cartilage (to keep meat from curling), then sprinkle steaks with salt and pepper.

Heat oil in a 12-inch heavy skillet over moderately high heat until hot but not smoking, then cook steaks, turning over once, until meat is just medium-rare, 4 to 6 minutes total. Transfer steaks to a platter and cover loosely with foil.

Add butter to skillet and sauté mushrooms and shallot, stirring frequently, until mushrooms are browned and tender, about 4 minutes, then transfer to platter with steaks.

Add vinegar and soy sauce to skillet and simmer, stirring and scraping up any brown bits, 2 minutes. Add ½ cup beef broth and simmer 2 minutes.

While sauce simmers, stir cornstarch into remaining 2 teaspoons broth in a cup. Stir cornstarch mixture into sauce and simmer, stirring, 1 minute. Return steaks and mushrooms, along with any juices accumulated on platter, to skillet and simmer, turning steaks over in sauce, until just heated through, about 1 minute.

GRILLED STEAKS WITH RED CHILE SAUCE

Serves 6
Active time: 1 hr   Start to finish: 1½ hr

3 oz dried *guajillo* chiles
4 cups boiling-hot water
1 (12-oz) jar roasted red peppers, drained,
   seeded, and coarsely chopped
3 garlic cloves, minced
1 teaspoon cumin seeds, toasted (see Tips,
   page 8) and ground in an electric
   coffee/spice grinder
1 tablespoon chopped fresh oregano or
   ¾ teaspoon dried, crumbled
1 teaspoon salt, or to taste
2 tablespoons unsalted butter
1 tablespoon all-purpose flour
1 teaspoon cider vinegar, or to taste
6 (¾-inch-thick) boneless rib-eye steaks
   (7 to 8 oz each)

Accompaniment: **pickled red onions with cilantro
   (recipe follows)**

Make sauce:
Rinse chiles and remove stems, then split open and discard seeds and ribs. Heat a dry well-seasoned cast-iron skillet or heavy skillet over moderate heat, then toast chiles in batches, turning them, about 30 seconds per batch. Transfer chiles to a heatproof bowl and pour boiling water over them. Cover bowl and soak chiles, stirring occasionally, until softened, about 20 minutes.

Reserve 2 cups soaking liquid, then drain chiles in a colander. Purée chiles, reserved soaking liquid, and roasted peppers in 2 batches in a blender until smooth (use caution when blending hot liquids). Force purée through a fine-mesh sieve into a bowl, pressing on and discarding solids.

Cook garlic, cumin, oregano, and salt in butter in a 4-quart heavy saucepan over moderately low heat, stirring, 1 minute. Add flour and cook roux, stirring, 2 minutes. Whisk in chile mixture and simmer, whisking occasionally, until reduced to about 2½ cups, 15 to 20 minutes. Add vinegar and salt to taste. Keep warm, covered.

Grill steaks:

Prepare grill for cooking. If using a charcoal grill, open vents on bottom of grill, then light charcoal. Charcoal fire is medium-hot when you can hold your hand 5 inches above rack for 3 to 4 seconds. If using a gas grill, preheat burners on high, covered, 10 minutes, then reduce heat to moderately high.

Pat steaks dry and season with salt. Grill steaks, uncovered, on lightly oiled grill rack, turning over once, 6 to 8 minutes total for medium-rare. Transfer to a platter and let steaks stand, loosely covered with foil, 5 minutes.

Serve steaks with sauce.

PHOTO ON PAGE 83

PICKLED RED ONIONS WITH CILANTRO

Serves 6
Active time: 15 min   Start to finish: 1¼ hr (includes cooling)

  1 cup cider vinegar
½ cup sugar
  1 teaspoon cumin seeds, toasted (see Tips, page 8)
  1 teaspoon salt
  3 medium red onions, cut into 1-inch pieces
  3 tablespoons chopped fresh cilantro

Bring vinegar, sugar, cumin, and salt to a boil in a 2-quart nonreactive heavy saucepan, then reduce heat and simmer, stirring occasionally, 5 minutes. Add onions and simmer, stirring occasionally, 2 minutes, then transfer to a bowl and cool completely. Stir in chopped cilantro.

Cooks' note:
• Pickled onions can be made 1 week ahead and chilled, covered.

GRILLED SPICE-RUBBED SKIRT STEAK

Serves 6
Active time: 25 min   Start to finish: 7 hr (includes marinating)

Because skirt steaks can be very long, it's much easier to handle them when they are cut in half.

  3 garlic cloves
1½ teaspoons kosher salt
1½ teaspoons paprika
1½ teaspoons ground cumin
1½ teaspoons ground coriander
  1 teaspoon black pepper
½ teaspoon ground cinnamon
    Pinch of ground cloves
  1 tablespoon olive oil
2¼ lb skirt steak (2 steaks), each halved crosswise

Accompaniments: sweet-potato salad with mustard vinaigrette (page 220); arugula with lemon and olive oil (page 213)

Mince garlic and mash to a paste with kosher salt. Stir together spices in a bowl, then stir in garlic and oil until a paste forms. Pat steak dry, then rub all over with paste. Marinate steak in a sealed large plastic bag, chilled, at least 6 hours.

Bring steak to room temperature, about 30 minutes.

While steak comes to room temperature, prepare grill for cooking. If using a charcoal grill, open vents on bottom of grill, then light charcoal. Charcoal fire is hot when you can hold your hand 5 inches above rack for 1 to 2 seconds. If using a gas grill, preheat burners on high, covered, 10 minutes, then reduce heat to moderately high.

Grill steak on lightly oiled grill rack, uncovered, turning over once, 4 to 6 minutes total for medium-rare.

Cut steak diagonally across grain into ¼-inch-thick slices. Divide sweet-potato salad among 6 plates, then top with steak and arugula.

Cooks' notes:
• Steak can marinate up to 1 day.
• If you're unable to grill outdoors, steak can be grilled in batches in a hot lightly oiled well-seasoned ridged grill pan over moderately high heat. (Steaks may have to be quartered instead of halved to fit in pan.)
PHOTO ON PAGE 78

DING DONG EIGHT-ALARM CHILI

Serves 8

Active time: 1¾ hr   Start to finish: 6½ hr
(plus 1 to 2 days for flavors to develop)

This is another recipe from our Television Issue; this time the inspiration was the hit TV show The Cosby Show *and Cliff Huxtable's famous chili.*

- 2 oz dried *ancho* chiles (4 large), stemmed and seeded
- 6 large garlic cloves, 3 of them finely chopped
- 1 tablespoon salt, or to taste
- 1½ tablespoons ground cumin
- 1½ tablespoons chili powder (not pure chile)
- 4 lb well-marbled beef brisket or boneless chuck, trimmed and cut into 1½- to 2-inch pieces
- 3 to 4 tablespoons vegetable oil
- 1 (28- to 32-oz) can whole tomatoes in juice
- ¼ cup canned *chipotle* chiles in *adobo*
- ½ cup coarsely chopped fresh cilantro
- 1½ lb white onions, chopped (4 cups)
- 1 tablespoon dried oregano (preferably Mexican), crumbled
- 1 to 4 fresh *serrano* or other small green chiles, finely chopped, including seeds (1 is fine for most tastes; 4 is the eight-alarm version)
- 1 (12-oz) bottle beer (not dark)
- 2 cups water
- 2½ cups cooked pinto beans, rinsed if canned

Accompaniments: cubed avocado; chopped white onion; shredded Cheddar; chopped fresh cilantro; sour cream

Soak *ancho* chiles in hot water to cover until softened, about 30 minutes. Drain well.

While chiles soak, mince 1 whole garlic clove and mash to a paste with ½ tablespoon salt, ½ tablespoon cumin, and ½ tablespoon chili powder. Pat beef dry and toss with spice mixture in a large bowl until coated.

Heat 2 tablespoons oil in a wide 6- to 7-quart heavy pot over moderately high heat until hot but not smoking. Brown beef in 3 or 4 batches, without crowding, turning occasionally, about 5 minutes per batch (lower heat as needed; spice mixture burns easily). Transfer beef as browned to another bowl. (Do not clean pot.)

Purée *anchos* in a blender along with tomatoes (including juice), *chipotles* in *adobo*, cilantro, remaining 2 whole garlic cloves, and remaining ½ tablespoon salt until smooth.

Add enough oil to fat in pot to total 3 tablespoons, then cook onions and chopped garlic over moderate heat, stirring and scraping up brown bits from beef, until softened, 8 to 10 minutes. Add oregano, remaining tablespoon cumin, and remaining tablespoon chili powder and cook, stirring, 2 minutes. Add chile purée and 1 chopped *serrano* and simmer, stirring, 5 minutes. Stir in beer, water, and beef along with any juices accumulated in bowl and gently simmer, partially covered, stirring occasionally and checking often to make sure chili is not scorching, 2 hours.

Taste sauce, then add more *serrano* if desired and continue to simmer, partially covered, until beef is very tender and sauce is slightly thickened, 1 to 2 hours more. (If chili becomes very thick before meat is tender, thin with water as needed.)

Coarsely shred meat (still in pot) with 2 forks and cool chili completely, uncovered, then chill, covered, 1 to 2 days to allow flavors to develop.

Reheat over low heat, partially covered, stirring occasionally, until hot, about 30 minutes. Add beans (if using) and simmer, stirring, 5 minutes.

veal

MATZO-STUFFED BREAST OF VEAL

Serves 6
Active time: 45 min   Start to finish: 4½ hr

For stuffing
2 medium onions, chopped
3 carrots, cut into ¼-inch dice
2 celery ribs, cut into ¼-inch dice
¼ cup vegetable oil
3 (6- by 6-inch) matzos, broken into ½-inch pieces
2 tablespoons chopped fresh flat-leaf parsley
1 large egg, lightly beaten
¾ teaspoon salt
¼ teaspoon black pepper
For veal
1 (3½- to 4-lb) boneless veal breast (1½ inches thick)
1 small onion, quartered
2 garlic cloves, smashed
1 tablespoon vegetable oil
2 teaspoons paprika (preferably sweet Hungarian)
1½ teaspoons salt
1 teaspoon black pepper
2 fresh thyme sprigs
1½ cups water

Special equipment: **a carpet, darning, or upholstery needle; kitchen string**

Make stuffing:
Cook onions, carrots, and celery in oil in a wide 3½- to 5-quart heavy pot over moderate heat, stirring occasionally, until vegetables begin to brown, 8 to 10 minutes.

While vegetables cook, put matzos in a colander and run under hot water until softened. Cool stuffing.

Remove pot from heat and transfer half of vegetables to a bowl. Cool vegetables in bowl 5 minutes, then stir in matzos, parsley, egg, salt, and pepper.

Prepare veal while stuffing cools:
Put oven rack in middle position and preheat oven to 350°F.

Trim as much excess fat as possible from veal. Cut a large pocket in veal breast: Beginning at center of thickest side, insert a large knife horizontally and cut into center of veal as evenly as possible, leaving a 1-inch border on 3 sides.

Stuff and braise veal:
Purée onion, garlic, oil, paprika, salt, and pepper in a food processor or blender. Put veal breast on a cutting board and rub inside of pocket with 2 tablespoons purée. Fill pocket loosely with matzo stuffing, leaving a 1-inch border on cut side. Sew pocket closed with carpet needle and string.

Pat veal dry and rub both sides with remaining purée. Put thyme sprigs over vegetables remaining in pot, then top with veal. Add water and bring to a boil.

Cover pot with lid and braise in oven until meat is very tender, 3 to 3½ hours. Transfer veal with a wide metal spatula to a clean cutting board and let stand, loosely covered with foil, 30 minutes.

Discard thyme sprigs and skim any fat from sauce. Discard string, then cut stuffed veal across the grain into 1-inch-thick slices and serve with sauce.

Cooks' note:
• Veal improves in flavor if braised 2 days ahead. Cool in sauce, uncovered, then chill, surface covered with wax paper or parchment and pot covered with lid. Remove any solidified fat before reheating. Slice cold meat across the grain and reheat in oven with sauce in a shallow baking pan, covered, 45 minutes.

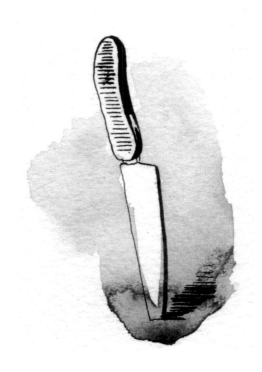

OSSO BUCO WITH TOMATOES, OLIVES, AND GREMOLATA

Serves 8 to 10
Active time: 45 min   Start to finish: 3¾ hr

For stew
8 to 10 (10-oz) meaty cross-cut veal shanks (osso buco; 5 to 6½ lb total), each tied with kitchen string
½ cup all-purpose flour
2 tablespoons olive oil
3 tablespoons unsalted butter
2 medium onions, halved lengthwise and thinly sliced
1 small carrot, finely chopped
1 celery rib, finely chopped
2 garlic cloves, finely chopped
1 cup dry white wine
1 cup low-sodium chicken broth
1 (28- to 32-oz) can whole plum tomatoes with juice (not in purée), coarsely chopped
1 cup Kalamata or other brine-cured black olives, pitted and halved
1½ teaspoons fresh thyme leaves
2 fresh flat-leaf parsley sprigs
1 Turkish or ½ California bay leaf
2 (2- by ½-inch) strips fresh lemon zest (see Tips, page 8), cut crosswise into fine julienne
1 teaspoon salt, or to taste
½ teaspoon black pepper, or to taste
For gremolata
3 tablespoons chopped fresh flat-leaf parsley
1 large garlic clove, minced
1 teaspoon finely grated fresh lemon zest (see Tips, page 8)

Special equipment: **a 7- to 9-quart heavy ovenproof pot (wide enough to hold shanks in 1 layer)**

Make stew:
Put oven rack in middle position and preheat oven to 325°F.

Pat shanks dry and season with salt and pepper. Divide shanks and flour between 2 large sealable plastic bags and shake to coat, then remove shanks from bags, shaking off excess flour. Heat oil and 2 tablespoons butter in ovenproof pot over moderately high heat until foam subsides, then brown shanks well in 2 batches, 10 to 12 minutes per batch, transferring to a plate as browned.

Reduce heat to moderate and add remaining tablespoon butter to pot along with onions, carrot, celery, and garlic and cook, stirring, until onions are pale golden, about 5 minutes. Add remaining stew ingredients and bring to a boil, stirring. Arrange shanks in pot in 1 layer and return to a simmer.

Cover pot and braise shanks in oven until very tender, about 2½ hours. Remove strings from osso buco and discard along with parsley sprigs and bay leaf.

Make gremolata *and serve osso buco:*
Stir together *gremolata* ingredients in a small bowl and sprinkle over osso buco. Serve immediately.

Cooks' notes:
• Osso buco (without *gremolata*) can be made 1 day ahead. Cool completely, uncovered, then chill, covered. Reheat, covered, in a preheated 325°F oven 30 to 40 minutes.
• Osso buco can also be cooked in a large roasting pan. Straddle pan across 2 burners for browning and boiling, then cover pan tightly with foil for braising.
PHOTO ON PAGE 59

pork

PORK CHOPS WITH MUSTARD CRUMBS

Serves 4
Active time: 25 min   Start to finish: 25 min

3 tablespoons olive oil
1⅓ cups coarse rye bread crumbs (2 to 3 slices)
2 garlic cloves, minced
1 tablespoon finely chopped fresh sage or ½ teaspoon dried
½ teaspoon salt
¼ teaspoon black pepper
4 (¾- to 1-inch-thick) rib pork chops (2 lb total)
2 tablespoons Dijon mustard

Put oven rack in middle position and preheat oven to 425°F.

Heat 2 tablespoons oil in a 10-inch heavy skillet over moderately high heat until hot but not smoking, then sauté bread crumbs, garlic, sage, salt, and pepper, stirring, until crumbs are golden brown, 3 to 5 minutes. Transfer crumbs to a bowl and wipe skillet clean.

Pat pork dry. Heat remaining tablespoon oil in skillet over moderately high heat, then brown chops in batches, turning over once, about 4 minutes per batch. Transfer chops to a baking pan and spread tops with mustard and then bread crumbs. Roast in oven until meat is just cooked through, 5 to 7 minutes.

PORK CHOPS AND APPLESAUCE

Serves 4 to 8
Active time: 50 min   Start to finish: 1½ hr

The predicaments of six kids growing up under one suburban roof were the cornerstone of each Brady Bunch *episode. In "The Personality Kid," which first aired in 1971, Peter thinks he's dull and goes looking for a new image. Trying on Humphrey Bogart for size, he asks Alice what's for dinner. "Pork chops and applesauce," Peter repeats à la Bogart. "Ain't that swell."*

For pork chops
2 cups milk
3 teaspoons salt
8 (½-inch-thick) pork chops (with or without bone; 2 lb total)
3½ cups fresh bread crumbs (from 10 slices firm white sandwich bread, ground in a food processor)
1 tablespoon minced garlic

2 teaspoons chopped fresh rosemary or ½ teaspoon dried, crumbled
2 teaspoons chopped fresh thyme or ½ teaspoon dried, crumbled
2 to 3 tablespoons vegetable oil
2 to 3 tablespoons unsalted butter
For applesauce
3 lb mixed McIntosh and Gala apples
¼ cup water
3 tablespoons sugar
1 tablespoon cider vinegar
1 Turkish or ½ California bay leaf
¼ teaspoon ground allspice

Marinate pork chops:
Stir together milk and 2 teaspoons salt in a shallow 3-quart dish, then add pork chops. Marinate, covered and chilled, turning over once, at least 1 hour.

Make applesauce while chops marinate:
Peel, core, and coarsely chop apples, then stir together with remaining applesauce ingredients in a 3-quart heavy saucepan. Bring to a simmer, stirring occasionally, then reduce heat to moderately low and cook, covered, stirring occasionally, until apples are falling apart, 15 to 20 minutes. Discard bay leaf and mash apples. Keep applesauce warm, covered.

Fry pork chops:
Put oven rack in middle position and preheat oven to 200°F.

Stir together bread crumbs, garlic, rosemary, thyme, and remaining teaspoon salt in a shallow bowl.

Lift pork chops from milk 1 at a time, letting excess drip off, and dredge in bread crumbs, lightly patting crumbs to help adhere, then transfer to a tray, arranging in 1 layer.

Heat 2 tablespoons oil and 2 tablespoons butter in a 12-inch heavy skillet over moderately high heat until foam subsides, then sauté pork chops in 2 or 3 batches, without crowding, turning over once, until golden brown and just cooked through, 5 to 6 minutes per batch. Transfer as cooked to a platter and keep warm in oven. (Add more oil and butter to skillet as needed.)

Serve pork chops with applesauce.

Cooks' notes:
• Pork chops can be marinated in milk up to 4 hours.
• Applesauce can be made 1 day ahead and chilled, covered. Reheat before serving.

RED-COOKED PORK WITH FRIZZLED GINGER

Serves 6
Active time: 40 min   Start to finish: 14½ hr (includes chilling)

The flavorful broth that results from cooking the pork is known in Chinese cuisine as a master sauce—save any that's left over in the freezer and use it for braising other meats, such as duck or chicken. Allowing the pork to cool overnight in the broth ensures its succulence—and because it's made ahead, this dish is ideal for entertaining.

6 cups water
1 cup soy sauce
1 cup Chinese rice wine or medium-dry Sherry
½ cup Chinese rock sugar or packed light brown sugar
1 bunch scallions, white parts smashed and greens reserved
2 (1-inch-thick) pieces fresh ginger, smashed
2 garlic cloves, smashed
10 fresh cilantro stems (reserve leaves for garnish)
2 (4- by 1-inch) strips fresh orange zest
2 whole star anise
1 (5- to 6-lb) boneless pork butt, shoulder, or blade roast, tied
1 teaspoon finely grated fresh orange zest

Accompaniment: **frizzled ginger (recipe follows)**

Stir together water, soy sauce, wine, rock sugar, white parts of scallions, ginger, garlic, cilantro stems, zest strips, and star anise in a deep 6- to 8-quart heavy pot and bring to a boil. Reduce heat and simmer, uncovered, 10 minutes. Add pork, then cover and reduce heat to low. Simmer gently, turning pork over every 30 minutes, until very tender, 4 to 4½ hours.

Cool pork in cooking liquid, uncovered, about 1 hour, then chill, covered, at least 8 hours.

Put oven rack in middle position and preheat oven to 350°F.

Transfer chilled pork to a clean cutting board, then remove string and cut meat across the grain into ½-inch-thick slices. Arrange pork in overlapping slices in a 13- by 9-inch glass or ceramic baking dish.

Discard fat from cooking liquid and reheat liquid over low heat until warm, then pour through a sieve into a bowl (discard solids). Transfer 2 cups cooking liquid to a 1-quart saucepan, reserving remainder for another use. Bring to a simmer, then pour over pork. Cover dish tightly with foil and heat in oven until heated through, about 30 minutes.

Cut scallion greens diagonally into thin slices. Carefully pour hot broth from baking dish into a bowl and stir in scallion greens and grated zest. Serve pork with broth, topped with reserved cilantro leaves and frizzled ginger.

Cooks' note:
• Pork can be chilled, covered with lid, in cooking liquid up to 2 days.

FRIZZLED GINGER

Makes about 1¼ cups
Active time: 20 min   Start to finish: 30 min

½ lb fresh ginger, peeled
1 cup vegetable oil

Special equipment: **a Japanese Benriner or other adjustable-blade slicer; a deep-fat thermometer**

Cut ginger lengthwise into very thin slices with slicer, then cut slices lengthwise into very fine shreds with a sharp knife.

Heat oil in a 1-quart heavy saucepan over moderate heat until it registers 360°F on thermometer. Fry ginger in 4 batches, stirring frequently, until crisp and golden, 1 to 2 minutes per batch. Transfer with a slotted spoon or skimmer to paper towels to drain. Return oil to 360°F between batches.

Cooks' note:
• Frizzled ginger can be made 1 day ahead and kept, covered, at room temperature.

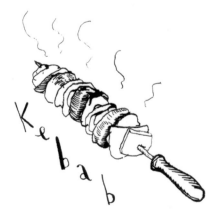

GRILLED PORK KEBABS WITH GINGER MOLASSES BARBECUE SAUCE

Serves 4
Active time: 45 min   Start to finish: 1¼ hr
(includes soaking skewers)

For barbecue sauce
6 tablespoons cider vinegar
2 tablespoons sugar
2 tablespoons ketchup
1½ tablespoons molasses (regular or robust; not blackstrap)
1 tablespoon minced garlic
1 tablespoon minced fresh *serrano* or other small hot green chile (1 or 2), including seeds
½ tablespoon minced peeled fresh ginger
½ teaspoon salt
For pork
1 (1-lb) pork tenderloin, trimmed
¼ teaspoon salt

Special equipment: **about 30 (8-inch) wooden skewers, soaked in water for 30 minutes**

Make barbecue sauce:
Stir together all sauce ingredients in a 1- to 1½-quart heavy saucepan and briskly simmer, uncovered, stirring occasionally, until thickened and reduced to about ½ cup, about 3 minutes. Transfer sauce to a bowl and cool to room temperature.
Prepare and grill pork kebabs:
Put tenderloin on a cutting board. Starting about 5 inches from narrow end of tenderloin and holding a large sharp knife at a 30-degree angle to cutting board, cut a thin slice (⅛ to ¼ inch thick) from tenderloin, slicing diagonally toward narrow end and cutting through to cutting board. Continue to cut thin slices from tenderloin following same diagonal, starting each consecutive slice closer to wide end. (You will have about 12 slices. Cut any slices more than 2 inches wide in half lengthwise.)
Thread 2 skewers, 1 at a time and ½ to 1 inch apart, lengthwise through each slice of pork and transfer to a tray lined with plastic wrap.
Prepare grill for cooking. If using a charcoal grill, open vents on bottom of grill, then light charcoal. Charcoal fire is hot when you can hold your hand 5 inches above rack for 1 to 2 seconds. If using a gas grill, preheat burners on high, covered, 10 minutes.
Sprinkle pork slices with salt and brush both sides with barbecue sauce, then grill on oiled grill rack, uncovered, turning over once, until just cooked through, 2 to 3 minutes total. Discard any leftover barbecue sauce.

Each serving about 241 calories and 8 grams fat

CÔTELETTES DE PORC AVEC SON JUS AU CIDRE
Roasted Pork Chops with Hard Cider Jus

Serves 8
Active time: 30 min   Start to finish: 45 min

8 (1-inch-thick) rib pork chops (4 lb total)
1 teaspoon fine sea salt
1¼ teaspoons black pepper
2½ tablespoons unsalted butter
1 lb large shallots (8), bulbs separated if necessary and each bulb halved lengthwise
1 cup hard cider

Special equipment: **an instant-read thermometer**

Put oven rack in lower third of oven and preheat oven to 450°F.
Pat pork chops dry and sprinkle both sides with sea salt and pepper. Heat 1½ tablespoons butter in a 12-inch heavy skillet over moderately high heat until foam subsides, then brown chops in 3 batches, turning over once, 6 minutes per batch, and transfer with tongs to a large shallow baking pan (1 inch deep).
Add shallots and remaining tablespoon butter to skillet and cook over moderate heat, turning occasionally, until shallots are golden brown and tender, 6 to 8 minutes. Add cider and boil, stirring and scraping up brown bits, until reduced to about ¾ cup, about 3 minutes.
Spoon shallots and sauce around chops and roast until thermometer inserted horizontally into center of 1 chop (do not touch bone) registers 150°F, 7 to 9 minutes.
Let chops stand, loosely covered with foil, 5 minutes (temperature will rise to 155°F while standing).
Serve chops with shallots and sauce.

PHOTO ON PAGE 48

PORK WITH PRUNES

Serves 4
Active time: 20 min   Start to finish: 1½ hr

2 lb (½-inch-thick) pork shoulder chops
½ teaspoon salt
¼ cup all-purpose flour
3 tablespoons vegetable or olive oil
¾ cup chopped shallot (4½ oz)
½ cup cider vinegar
3 cups water
1¾ cups low-sodium chicken broth
1 teaspoon whole allspice
1½ cups dried pitted prunes (11 oz)

Put oven rack in middle position and preheat oven to 350°F.

Pat chops dry and sprinkle with salt. Dredge in flour, shaking off excess. Heat oil in a wide 3½- to 4-quart heavy saucepan over moderately high heat until hot but not smoking, then brown chops in batches, turning over once, about 5 minutes per batch. Transfer to a plate. Add shallot to saucepan and sauté until golden, 2 to 3 minutes. Add vinegar and boil, scraping up brown bits, until reduced by half. Stir in water, broth, and allspice and bring to a simmer. Return chops to saucepan along with prunes. Cover saucepan, then transfer to oven and braise until very tender, about 45 minutes. Transfer chops to a platter using a slotted spoon.

Boil sauce until reduced to 1 cup, about 20 minutes. Season with salt and pepper and pour over chops.

BRAISED PORK WITH FUYU PERSIMMON

Serves 6
Active time: 35 min   Start to finish: 2½ hr

2½ lb boneless pork shoulder, cut into
    1½-inch pieces
¾ teaspoon salt
1 to 3 tablespoons vegetable oil
1 onion, chopped
1 green bell pepper, chopped
1 celery rib, chopped
1 large garlic clove, minced
1 tablespoon ground cumin
2 teaspoons ground coriander
1 teaspoon ground turmeric
⅛ teaspoon cayenne
2 cups water
4 plum tomatoes (¾ lb total), peeled
    (see cooks' note, below) and chopped,
    or 1 (14- to 16-oz) can whole tomatoes,
    drained and chopped
1½ lb firm-ripe Fuyu persimmons, peeled,
    seeded if necessary, and cut into
    ¼-inch-thick wedges
½ cup chopped scallion greens

Accompaniment: **cooked white rice**

Put oven rack in lower third of oven and preheat oven to 350°F.

Pat pork dry and sprinkle with salt. Heat 1 tablespoon oil in a wide 6-quart heavy pot over moderately high heat until hot but not smoking, then brown pork in 3 batches, turning, about 5 minutes per batch, transferring to a bowl as browned. (Add more oil to pot as needed between batches.)

Pour off all but 1 tablespoon fat from pot. Add onion, bell pepper, and celery and cook over moderate heat, stirring, until softened, 3 to 5 minutes. Stir in garlic, cumin, coriander, turmeric, and cayenne and cook, stirring, 1 minute. Add pork with any juices accumulated in bowl, water, and tomatoes and bring to a simmer.

Cover pot, then transfer to oven and braise pork until very tender, about 1¾ hours.

Scatter persimmons over pork and braise in oven, partially covered, 10 minutes more. Stir in scallion greens and salt and pepper to taste.

Cooks' notes:
• Stew can be made (without persimmons or scallions) 1 day ahead and cooled, uncovered, then chilled, covered. Reheat in a preheated 350°F oven, about 30 minutes, before proceeding.
• To peel a tomato, first cut an X in the end opposite the stem and immerse in boiling water 10 seconds. Transfer to ice water, then peel.

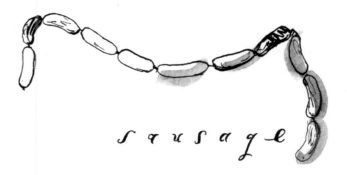

sausage

CHINESE BROCCOLI WITH SAUSAGE AND POLENTA

Serves 6
Active time: 25 min   Start to finish: 45 min

2 lb Chinese broccoli, thick ends trimmed
For polenta
6 cups water
1½ teaspoons salt
1½ cups polenta (not instant) or yellow
   cornmeal
3 tablespoons unsalted butter, softened
½ cup heavy cream
2 tablespoons finely grated parmesan
For sausage and garlic
2 tablespoons olive oil
¾ lb hot Italian sausage, casings removed
2 garlic cloves, thinly sliced
1 teaspoon salt
½ teaspoon black pepper

Cook broccoli:
Cut broccoli stems diagonally into 1-inch pieces and coarsely chop leaves. Cook stems in a large pot of boiling salted water (see Tips, page 8) until just tender, about 4 minutes, then stir in leaves and cook 1 minute. Drain in a colander, then rinse under cold water to stop cooking. (Do not squeeze out excess water.)

Cook polenta:
Bring water with salt to a boil in a 3-quart heavy saucepan, then add polenta in a thin stream, whisking constantly. Cook over moderate heat, whisking, 2 minutes. Reduce heat to low and simmer polenta, covered, stirring for 1 minute after every 10 minutes of cooking, 45 minutes total. Stir in butter, cream, and cheese and remove from heat.

Sauté sausage and garlic while polenta cooks:
Heat oil in a 12-inch heavy skillet over moderately high heat until hot but not smoking, then sauté sausage, stirring and breaking up meat into large pieces with a spoon, until browned and cooked through, about 5 minutes. Transfer with a slotted spoon to a plate. Reduce heat to moderate, then cook garlic in fat remaining in skillet, stirring, until golden, about 2 minutes.

Add broccoli and cook, stirring and scraping up brown bits from bottom of skillet, 2 minutes. Return sausage to skillet and toss with greens, salt, and pepper. Serve over polenta.

HOMEMADE SAUSAGE PATTIES

Makes about 18 (3-inch) patties
Active time: 50 min   Start to finish: 1 hr

1 medium onion, finely chopped
2 tablespoons plus 1 teaspoon vegetable oil
½ cup coarse fresh bread crumbs
2 tablespoons milk
2 lb ground pork (not lean)
2 teaspoons salt
1 teaspoon white pepper
¼ teaspoon freshly grated nutmeg
¼ teaspoon cinnamon
¼ teaspoon cayenne
⅛ teaspoon ground cloves
1 teaspoon finely chopped fresh thyme
1 teaspoon finely chopped fresh sage
2 large egg yolks

Cook onion in 2 tablespoons oil in a small heavy skillet over moderately low heat, stirring occasionally, until softened and beginning to brown, 8 to 10 minutes. Cool 10 minutes.

While onions cool, stir together bread crumbs and milk in a large bowl and let stand until bread crumbs have absorbed milk.

Add onions and remaining ingredients (except remaining oil) to crumb mixture and stir with a fork until blended well.

Put oven rack in middle position and preheat oven to 250°F.

Line a tray with wax paper. Form sausage mixture into 3-inch patties (about ½ inch thick) with dampened hands and arrange on tray. Heat ½ teaspoon remaining oil in a 12-inch heavy skillet over moderately high heat until hot but not smoking, then cook patties in 3 batches, turning once, until browned and just cooked through, 4 to 6 minutes per batch. Drain patties briefly on paper towels as cooked, then transfer to a shallow baking pan and keep warm, covered with foil, in oven while cooking remaining batches. (Add remaining ½ teaspoon vegetable oil to skillet between batches if needed.)

Cooks' note:
• Sausage patties can be formed (but not cooked) 1 day ahead and chilled, covered with plastic wrap.
PHOTO ON PAGE 61

HERB-BRAISED HAM

Serves 8
Active time: 1½ hr   Start to finish: 4½ hr

Smoked pork shoulder is available partially or fully cooked. This will affect the braising time.

1 (11- to 13-lb) bone-in smoked pork
    shoulder (sometimes called picnic ham)
2 medium leeks (white and pale green parts
    only), chopped
1 large onion, chopped
3 medium carrots, cut into ½-inch cubes
2 celery ribs, cut into ½-inch cubes
2 garlic cloves, finely chopped
6 (5-inch) fresh thyme sprigs plus
    2 tablespoons finely chopped leaves
6 fresh flat-leaf parsley stems plus ¼ cup
    finely chopped leaves
¼ whole nutmeg, smashed with side of knife
1 teaspoon whole black peppercorns
4 whole cloves
5 tablespoons unsalted butter, softened
2 cups dry white wine
4 cups water
⅓ cup all-purpose flour

Special equipment: **a deep 10- to 20-qt pot (such as a stockpot, lobster pot, or canning pot); a wide 7-qt heavy ovenproof pot (if you have an 11-lb ham) or a wide 9- to 10-qt heavy ovenproof pot (if you have a 13-lb ham); an instant-read thermometer (preferably remote digital with probe)**

Put ham in deep 10- to 20-quart pot and cover with cold water (don't worry if bone sticks out). Bring to a boil, then drain ham.

Put oven rack in lower third of oven (remove any other racks) and preheat oven to 350°F.

Wash leeks in a bowl of cold water, then lift out and drain well. Cook leeks, onion, carrots, celery, garlic, thyme sprigs, parsley stems, nutmeg, peppercorns, and whole cloves in 2 tablespoons butter in wide 7- to 10-quart heavy pot (see "special equipment," above) over moderately high heat, stirring occasionally, until vegetables are softened and beginning to brown, about 10 minutes. Add wine and bring to a boil, then add ham, skin side down, and water (liquid will not cover ham) and return to a boil.

Cover pot tightly with lid or, if ham sticks up over top of pot, with heavy-duty foil. Braise ham in oven 1 hour.

Turn ham skin side up and continue to braise in oven, covered, until thermometer inserted into center of ham (do not touch bone) registers 120°F, about 1 hour more (if ham was labeled "fully cooked"), or 160°F, about 2 hours more (if ham was labeled "partially cooked").

While ham braises, mash together flour and remaining 3 tablespoons butter with a fork to make a *beurre manié*.

Transfer ham to a platter and let stand, loosely covered with foil, 45 minutes.

While ham stands, pour braising liquid through a fine-mesh sieve into a 3-quart saucepan, pressing on and discarding solids, and skim off any fat. Bring braising liquid to a simmer and whisk in *beurre manié* ½ tablespoon at a time (sauce will become lumpy). Continue to simmer, whisking, until sauce is smooth and slightly thickened, about 5 minutes. Remove from heat and stir in chopped thyme and parsley.

Remove skin from ham, then slice meat and serve with sauce.

Cooks' note:
• Ham can be braised 2 days ahead and cooled in braising liquid, uncovered, then chilled, covered. Skim any fat before reheating ham, in braising liquid, on top of stove.
PHOTO ON PAGE 102

lamb

LAMB AU POIVRE

Serves 1
Active time: 15 min   Start to finish: 15 min

1 teaspoon whole black peppercorns
3 (¾- to 1-inch-thick) rib lamb chops (1 lb
    total), bones frenched if desired and fat
    trimmed
1 tablespoon vegetable oil
1 medium shallot, finely chopped
½ cup low-sodium chicken broth
1 tablespoon Cognac or balsamic vinegar
1 teaspoon unsalted butter

Coarsely crush peppercorns with a mortar and pestle or wrap in a kitchen towel and press on peppercorns with bottom of a heavy skillet.

Pat chops dry and season with salt. Rub one side of each chop with peppercorns, pressing peppercorns into meat to adhere.

Heat oil in a 12-inch heavy skillet over moderately high heat until hot but not smoking, then cook chops, peppered sides up, 2 minutes. Turn chops over with tongs and cook, pressing down on each chop with side of tongs to help pepper adhere to meat, about 2 minutes more (for medium-rare). Transfer chops with tongs to a plate and let stand while making sauce.

Pour off all but 2 teaspoons of fat from skillet if necessary, then sauté shallot over moderately high heat, stirring, until golden brown, about 30 seconds. Add broth and Cognac and boil until reduced to about ¼ cup, 2 to 3 minutes. Remove skillet from heat and swirl in butter. Add any meat juices that have accumulated on plate and season with salt. Serve sauce over lamb.

PHOTO ON PAGE 110

carrot

SPICED BRAISED LAMB WITH CARROTS AND SPINACH

Serves 8

Active time: 50 min   Start to finish: 3 hr

Sephardim eat coriander seeds during Passover; if you do not because you are from an eastern European Jewish background, you can simply leave the coriander out of this recipe.

3½ lb boneless lamb shoulder, trimmed and
    cut into 2-inch pieces
1 teaspoon black pepper
1½ teaspoons salt
1 to 3 tablespoons olive oil
1 large onion, chopped
1 celery rib, chopped
3 garlic cloves, finely chopped
4 teaspoons ground cumin
2 teaspoons ground coriander
2 cups water
1 (14- to 16-oz) can whole tomatoes in juice
6 medium carrots, cut crosswise into
    2½-inch pieces
1½ lb spinach, coarse stems discarded

Accompaniments: **matzo scallion pancakes
(page 170) and haroseth (page 170)**

Put oven rack in middle position and preheat oven to 350°F.

Pat lamb dry and sprinkle with pepper and 1 teaspoon salt. Heat 1 tablespoon oil in a 10-inch heavy skillet (preferably cast-iron) over moderately high heat until hot but not smoking, then brown lamb in 5 batches, turning occasionally, about 4 minutes per batch, adding more oil as needed. Transfer as browned to a wide 6- to 7-quart heavy ovenproof pot.

Pour off all but 1 tablespoon fat from skillet, then cook onion and celery in remaining fat over moderate heat, stirring occasionally, until golden, about 3 minutes. Add garlic, cumin, and coriander and cook, stirring, 1 minute. Add 1 cup water and deglaze skillet by boiling, stirring and scraping up any brown bits, 1 minute, then pour mixture over lamb in pot.

Pour juice from can of tomatoes into stew, then coarsely chop tomatoes and add to stew along with remaining cup water and remaining ½ teaspoon salt and bring to a boil (liquid should almost cover meat).

Cover pot and braise lamb in oven 1½ hours. Stir in carrots and continue to braise until carrots and lamb are tender, 20 to 30 minutes. Transfer pot to top of stove and, working over moderately high heat, stir in spinach by handfuls to soften it. Cook, uncovered, stirring occasionally, until spinach is tender, 5 to 8 minutes. Season with salt and pepper.

Cooks' note:
• Braised lamb improves in flavor when made 1 day ahead. Prepare without spinach and cool, uncovered, then chill, covered. Remove any solidified fat before reheating and add spinach once stew is hot.

PHOTO ON PAGE 67

MATZO SCALLION PANCAKES

Makes 30 (3-inch) pancakes
Active time: 30 min   Start to finish: 30 min

½ cup thinly sliced scallion (white and pale
   green parts only) plus ½ cup finely
   chopped scallion greens (from 1 bunch)
¾ cup plus 2 teaspoons olive oil
5 large eggs
1½ cups plus 1 tablespoon water
1½ cups matzo meal
1 teaspoon salt
¼ teaspoon black pepper

Cook sliced scallion in 2 teaspoons oil in a small
heavy saucepan over moderate heat, stirring occasionally, until pale golden, 2 to 3 minutes. Remove from heat
and stir in scallion greens.

Whisk eggs in a bowl until combined well, then
whisk in water. Stir in matzo meal, salt, pepper, and
scallion mixture until combined well.

Line a baking sheet with paper towels and set a
large rack on top. Heat ½ cup oil in a 12-inch nonstick
skillet over moderate heat until hot but not smoking.
Working in batches of 4, fill a ¼-cup measure three-
fourths full (3 tablespoons) for each pancake, then drop
batter carefully into hot oil and spread with back of a
spoon to form a 3-inch round. Cook pancakes until
undersides are golden, 1½ to 2 minutes. Turn over with
a slotted spatula and cook until undersides are golden,
about 1½ minutes more, then transfer to rack. Add
some of the remaining ¼ cup olive oil as needed
between batches.

Cooks' note:
• Pancakes can be made 4 hours ahead and chilled,
  covered. Reheat on a baking sheet in a preheated
  350°F oven 10 minutes.

PHOTO ON PAGE 67

HAROSETH
Dried-Fruit and Nut Paste

Makes about 3 cups
Active time: 20 min   Start to finish: 20 min

*The Passover meal typically includes haroseth, which
symbolizes the mortar used by Israelite slaves in
Egypt. Recipes can vary greatly, depending on the
country of origin. Haroseth is used as a condiment—
almost like a chutney—and would be good with many
kinds of roasted meat or poultry. This spicy version is
based on a recipe from Yemen.*

⅔ cup dried Mission figs (6 oz)
⅔ cup dried apricots (6 oz)
⅓ cup pitted dates (4 oz)
1⅓ cups walnuts (4 oz), finely chopped, toasted
   (see Tips, page 8), and cooled
¼ cup sweet red wine such as Manischewitz
   Extra Heavy Malaga
¼ teaspoon cinnamon
¼ teaspoon cayenne
⅛ teaspoon ground ginger

Pulse together figs, apricots, and dates in a food
processor until finely chopped, then transfer to a bowl
and stir in walnuts and wine. Sprinkle spices evenly
over mixture and stir until combined well.

Cooks' note:
• Haroseth can be made 3 days ahead and kept, covered,
  at room temperature.

LAMB CHOPS WITH CHERRY BALSAMIC
SAUCE AND MINT

Serves 4
Active time: 20 min   Start to finish: 30 min
(or 2 hr if using frozen cherries)

1½ cups fresh or frozen (not thawed) pitted
   sour cherries (½ lb)
1 tablespoon sugar
8 (¾-inch-thick) rib lamb chops (2 lb total),
   trimmed of excess fat
¼ teaspoon salt
¼ teaspoon black pepper
2 tablespoons vegetable oil
1 cup thinly sliced shallot (4 oz)
½ cup beef broth
2 tablespoons balsamic vinegar
2 tablespoons unsalted butter
4 tablespoons finely chopped fresh mint

Stir fresh cherries together with sugar and macerate
while browning chops. If using frozen cherries, stir
with any juices and sugar and thaw, about 1½ hours.

Pat lamb dry and sprinkle with salt and pepper. Heat 1 tablespoon oil in a 12-inch nonstick skillet over moderately high heat until hot but not smoking, then sauté 4 chops, turning over once, about 6 minutes total for medium-rare. Transfer to a plate and loosely cover with foil. Cook remaining 4 chops in same manner.

Pour off fat from skillet. Heat remaining tablespoon oil in skillet until hot but not smoking, then sauté shallot, stirring, until golden brown, about 3 minutes. Add cherries with juices, broth, and vinegar and bring to a boil, stirring occasionally and scraping up brown bits, then reduce heat and simmer 3 minutes. Add salt and pepper to taste, then add butter and 2 tablespoons mint, stirring just until butter is melted.

Spoon sauce over chops and sprinkle with remaining 2 tablespoons mint.

BRAISED LAMB SHANKS WRAPPED IN EGGPLANT

Serves 8
Active time: 1½ hr   Start to finish: 5½ hr

For eggplant
2 (1½-lb) eggplants (at least 10 inches long and 4 inches in diameter), trimmed
⅓ **cup extra-virgin olive oil**
1 teaspoon salt
½ **teaspoon black pepper**
For shanks
6 lb lamb shanks, trimmed of excess fat
1½ **teaspoons salt**
1 teaspoon black pepper
2 tablespoons extra-virgin olive oil
½ **large green bell pepper, cut into ½-inch pieces**
2 garlic cloves, chopped
1 (1½-inch) piece cinnamon stick
16 whole allspice
15 whole black peppercorns
2 Turkish bay leaves or 1 California
1 cup dry white wine
1 (28- to 32-oz) can whole tomatoes in purée, coarsely chopped (including purée) in a food processor

Bake eggplant:
Put oven racks in upper and lower thirds of oven and preheat oven to 350°F.

Remove 2-inch-wide strips of skin from opposite sides of each eggplant with a vegetable peeler and discard. Holding knife parallel to a peeled side, cut each eggplant lengthwise into 8 (⅓-inch-thick) slices.

Brush eggplant slices on both sides with oil and arrange in 1 layer in 2 shallow baking pans. Sprinkle with salt and pepper and bake in upper and lower thirds of oven, switching position of pans halfway through baking, until eggplant is tender and lightly browned, 30 to 40 minutes total. Cool eggplant in pans. (Leave oven on.)

Brown shanks while eggplant bakes:
Pat shanks dry and sprinkle with salt and pepper. Heat oil in a 12-inch heavy skillet over moderately high heat until hot but not smoking, then brown shanks in 2 batches, turning occasionally, about 5 minutes per batch. Transfer as browned to a roasting pan just large enough to hold shanks in 1 layer. Reserve skillet.

Cook bell pepper, garlic, spices, and bay leaves in fat remaining in skillet over moderate heat, stirring occasionally, until garlic is golden, about 3 minutes. Add wine and bring to a boil, stirring and scraping up any brown bits. Add chopped tomatoes and bring to a boil. Season sauce with salt and pepper and pour over shanks (liquid should come about halfway up sides of meat).

Cover roasting pan tightly with foil and braise in oven until very tender, 2½ to 3 hours. Cool shanks, uncovered. (Leave oven on.)

Assemble eggplant and lamb bundles:
Remove shanks from sauce. Discard bones and gristle, then cut meat into 1½-inch pieces. Skim fat from sauce and season sauce with salt and pepper. Spoon one third of sauce into a 13- by 9- by 2-inch glass or ceramic baking dish.

Move oven rack to middle position.

Arrange 2 eggplant slices end to end lengthwise on a work surface so that ends overlap by about 2 inches. Put one eighth of lamb on eggplant where it overlaps, then wrap ends of eggplant over lamb to form a bundle. Transfer bundle to baking dish with a wide metal spatula. Make 7 more bundles in same manner, arranging them in 1 layer in dish. Spoon remaining sauce over and around bundles and cover dish tightly with foil.

Braise bundles in oven 30 minutes.

Cooks' note:
• Lamb and eggplant bundles can be assembled 2 days ahead and chilled in sauce, surface covered with wax paper or parchment and dish covered with foil. Bring to room temperature before braising.

171

MUSTARD AND HERB CRUSTED RACK OF LAMB

Serves 8
Active time: 25 min   Start to finish: 1½ hr

1½ cups fine fresh bread crumbs
 3 tablespoons finely chopped fresh
    flat-leaf parsley
 1 tablespoon finely chopped fresh mint
1½ teaspoons minced fresh rosemary
 ½ teaspoon salt
 ¼ teaspoon black pepper
3½ tablespoons olive oil
 3 frenched racks of lamb (8 ribs and 1½ lb
    each rack), trimmed of all but a thin layer
    of fat, then brought to room temperature
 2 tablespoons Dijon mustard

Special equipment: **an instant-read thermometer**

Stir together bread crumbs, parsley, mint, rosemary, salt, and pepper in a bowl, then drizzle with 2½ tablespoons oil and toss until combined well.

Put oven rack in middle position and preheat to 400°F.

Season lamb with salt and pepper. Heat remaining tablespoon oil in a large heavy skillet over moderately high heat until hot but not smoking, then brown lamb 1 rack at a time, turning once, about 4 minutes per rack. Transfer to a 13- by 9- by 2-inch roasting pan, arranging fatty sides up.

Spread fatty sides of each rack with 2 teaspoons mustard. Divide bread crumb mixture into 3 portions and pat each portion over mustard coating on each rack, gently pressing to adhere.

Roast lamb until thermometer inserted diagonally 2 inches into center (do not touch bone) registers 130°F (for medium-rare), 20 to 25 minutes, and transfer to a cutting board. Let lamb racks stand 10 minutes, then cut into chops.

PHOTO ON PAGE 92

other meats

CALF'S LIVER WITH BACON AND ONIONS

Serves 4
Active time: 35 min   Start to finish: 35 min

We recommend asking the butcher for the freshest calf's liver available, since it can vary in quality. Soaking the liver in milk, a method typically used for pork liver, helps soften and mellow its flavor.

 1 lb calf's liver (½ inch thick), cut into
    4 pieces
 1 cup whole milk
 8 bacon slices, halved crosswise
 3 medium onions, halved lengthwise,
    then cut lengthwise into ¼-inch slices
 ½ cup all-purpose flour
 1 teaspoon salt
 ½ teaspoon black pepper

Soak liver in milk in a bowl 20 minutes.

While liver soaks, cook bacon in a 12-inch nonstick skillet over moderate heat, turning over occasionally, until crisp. Transfer bacon to paper towels to drain and reserve 2½ tablespoons fat in skillet, transferring remaining fat to small bowl.

Cook onions with salt and pepper to taste in fat in skillet over moderate heat, stirring frequently, until golden brown, 12 to 15 minutes. Transfer onions to a bowl and add bacon. Keep warm, covered.

Pat liver dry and discard milk. Stir together flour, salt, and pepper on a sheet of wax paper and dredge liver in flour mixture, shaking off excess.

Add 1½ tablespoons reserved bacon fat to skillet and heat over moderately high heat until hot but not smoking, then sauté liver, turning over once, until browned but still pink inside, about 4 minutes total.

Serve liver topped with onions and bacon.

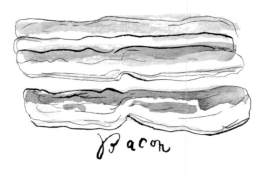

Bacon

BRAISED RABBIT WITH EGG NOODLES

Serves 4
Active time: 40 min   Start to finish: 1¾ hr

More supermarkets are carrying fresh rabbit, as people rediscover its delicate flavor. Braising helps to keep it moist and tender. If you have trouble finding rabbit, however, you can substitute bone-in chicken, skin removed.

1 (2½- to 3½-lb) rabbit, cut into
    8 serving pieces
1 teaspoon salt
½ teaspoon black pepper
¼ cup extra-virgin olive oil
2 medium onions, halved lengthwise and
    then cut lengthwise into ¼-inch slices
2 garlic cloves, finely chopped
2 (4- by 1-inch) strips fresh orange zest
1 (3- to 4-inch) cinnamon stick
2 Turkish bay leaves or 1 California
½ cup dry red wine
2 cups canned crushed tomatoes (from
    a 28-oz can)
½ cup water
8 oz dried egg tagliatelle or egg fettuccine
1 tablespoon chopped fresh flat-leaf parsley

Special equipment: **a deep 12-inch ovenproof skillet (preferably with a lid) or a 5-qt wide heavy pot**

Put oven rack in middle position and preheat oven to 350°F.

Pat rabbit pieces dry and sprinkle with ½ teaspoon salt and ¼ teaspoon pepper. Heat 2 tablespoons oil in skillet over moderately high heat until hot but not smoking, then brown rabbit in 2 batches, turning over once, about 6 minutes per batch. Transfer as browned to a plate.

Reduce heat to moderate and cook onions, garlic, zest, cinnamon stick, and bay leaves in remaining 2 tablespoons oil, stirring frequently, until onions are beginning to brown, 4 to 5 minutes. Add wine and deglaze skillet by boiling, stirring and scraping up any brown bits, until wine is reduced by about half, about 2 minutes. Stir in tomatoes, water, remaining ½ teaspoon salt, and remaining ¼ teaspoon pepper. Nestle rabbit pieces in sauce and bring to a simmer.

Cover skillet tightly with lid or heavy-duty foil, then braise in oven 30 minutes. Turn rabbit over and continue to braise, covered, until rabbit is tender, 25 to 30 minutes more.

While rabbit braises, cook pasta in a large pot of boiling salted water (see Tips, page 8) until al dente. Drain pasta well in a colander and transfer to a large platter. Discard zest, cinnamon stick, and bay leaf from sauce. Arrange rabbit over pasta, then spoon sauce over top and sprinkle with parsley.

Cooks' note:
• Rabbit can be braised 1 day ahead and cooled, uncovered, then chilled, covered. Reheat on top of stove until hot.

PHOTO ON PAGE 73

POULTRY

chicken

HONEY-ROASTED CHICKEN WITH LEMON AND TARRAGON

Serves 4 to 6
Active time: 30 min   Start to finish: 1½ hr

2 lemons
2 tablespoons unsalted butter, softened
2 tablespoons finely chopped fresh tarragon
¾ teaspoon salt
½ teaspoon black pepper
1 (3½-lb) chicken, rinsed and patted dry
1 head garlic, left unpeeled and halved
　　horizontally
¼ cup mild honey
1 tablespoon olive oil

Special equipment: **kitchen string; an instant-read thermometer**

Put oven rack in middle position and preheat oven to 425°F.

Finely grate enough zest from 1 lemon (see Tips, page 8) to measure 1 tablespoon, then squeeze enough juice from same lemon to measure 2 tablespoons.

Stir together butter, tarragon, zest, ½ teaspoon salt, and pepper.

Put chicken, breast side up, in a small roasting pan. Starting from neck cavity, work your fingers gently between skin and flesh of breast to loosen skin all the way to thighs without tearing. Put one fourth of tarragon butter under skin of each breast, then rub skin from outside to spread evenly.

Starting from large cavity, loosen skin on both sides of cavity with a paring knife (to provide access to thighs), then work your fingers gently between skin and flesh of thighs and drumsticks. Divide remaining tarragon butter among thighs and drumsticks, rubbing skin from outside to spread evenly. Season cavity and skin with salt and pepper, then halve remaining lemon and put inside cavity along with garlic. Tie drumsticks together with kitchen string.

Whisk together honey, lemon juice, oil, and remaining ¼ teaspoon salt. Roast chicken 30 minutes, then brush pan juices and half of honey mixture over chicken and roast 10 minutes more. Brush chicken again with pan juices and remaining honey mixture and continue to roast until thermometer inserted in fleshy part of a thigh (do not touch bone) registers 170°F, about 20 minutes more.

Transfer chicken to a cutting board and let stand 10 to 15 minutes before carving. Skim fat from pan juices and serve juices with chicken.

PANFRIED CHICKEN BREASTS WITH OREGANO GARLIC BUTTER

Serves 4
Active time: 20 min   Start to finish: 30 min

Cooking chicken breasts on the bone keeps them exceptionally juicy.

1 garlic clove
¼ teaspoon salt
5 tablespoons unsalted butter, softened
1 tablespoon chopped fresh oregano
¼ teaspoon dried hot red pepper flakes
4 chicken breast halves with skin and bones
　　(2 to 2¼ lb)
1 tablespoon olive oil

Mince garlic and mash to a paste with salt using a large heavy knife.

Mash together butter, oregano, red pepper flakes, and garlic paste with a fork until well blended.

Pat chicken dry. Cut a 2-inch-long pocket horizontally in side of each chicken breast half and fill each pocket with 2 teaspoons oregano garlic butter. Season chicken with salt and pepper.

Heat oil in a 12-inch heavy skillet over moderately high heat until hot but not smoking, then cook chicken, skin sides down, uncovered, until well browned, 8 to 10 minutes. Turn chicken over and cover skillet, then cook until chicken is just cooked through, about 10 minutes more. Spread remaining oregano garlic butter over skin of chicken.

ARROZ CON POLLO

Serves 4

Active time: 1¼ hr   Start to finish: 2½ hr (includes marinating)

When Ricky and Fred switch roles with Lucy and Ethel on the I Love Lucy *show, Ricky decides he wants to make his native Cuban* arroz con pollo *for dinner. Here's one approach from our Television Issue.*

For chicken
- 3 large garlic cloves, coarsely chopped
- 2 tablespoons fresh orange juice
- 2 tablespoons fresh lime juice
- 1½ teaspoons salt
- ¾ teaspoon black pepper
- 1 (3½- to 4-lb) chicken, cut into 8 serving pieces
- 1 tablespoon vegetable oil
- 1 tablespoon unsalted butter

For rice
- 1 lb onions, chopped (2½ cups)
- 2 green bell peppers, chopped
- 3 large garlic cloves, minced
- ¼ teaspoon crumbled saffron threads
- ¼ cup dry white wine
- 2 teaspoons ground cumin
- 2 teaspoons salt
- 1 Turkish or ½ California bay leaf
- 1 (14- to 15-oz) can diced tomatoes, including juice
- 1½ cups low-sodium chicken broth (12 fl oz)
- 1½ cups water
- 2 cups long-grain white rice (¾ lb)
- 1 cup frozen baby peas (not thawed; 5 oz)
- ½ cup small or medium pimiento-stuffed green olives (2 oz), rinsed
- ¼ cup drained chopped bottled pimientos (2 oz), rinsed

Special equipment: **a wide 6- to 7-qt heavy pot (about 12 inches in diameter and 4 inches deep)**

Prepare chicken:
Purée garlic, orange juice, lime juice, salt, and pepper in a blender until smooth. Put chicken pieces in a large bowl and pour purée over them, turning to coat. Marinate chicken, covered and chilled, turning occasionally, 1 hour.

Transfer chicken, letting excess marinade drip back into bowl, to paper towels. Pat dry. Reserve marinade.

Heat oil and butter in 6- to 7-quart pot over moderately high heat until foam subsides, then brown chicken in 2 or 3 batches, without crowding, turning occasionally, about 6 minutes per batch. Transfer chicken as browned to a plate, reserving fat in pot.

Prepare rice and bake arroz con pollo:
Put oven rack in middle position and preheat to 350°F.

Sauté onions, bell peppers, and garlic in fat in pot over moderately high heat, stirring occasionally and scraping up brown bits from chicken, until vegetables are softened, 6 to 8 minutes.

While vegetables cook, heat saffron in a dry small skillet over low heat, shaking skillet, until fragrant, about 30 seconds. Add wine and bring to a simmer, then remove from heat.

Add cumin and salt to vegetables and cook over moderately high heat, stirring, 2 minutes. Stir in saffron mixture, bay leaf, tomatoes (including juice), broth, water, and reserved marinade and bring to a boil.

Add all chicken except breast pieces, skin sides up, and gently simmer, covered, over low heat 10 minutes. Stir in rice, then add breast pieces, skin sides up, and arrange chicken in 1 layer. Return to a simmer.

Cover pot tightly, then transfer to oven and bake until rice is tender and most of liquid is absorbed, about 20 minutes.

Scatter peas, olives, and pimientos over rice and chicken (do not stir) and let stand, pot covered with a kitchen towel, until peas are heated through and any remaining liquid is absorbed by rice, about 5 minutes. Discard bay leaf.

CHICKEN LEGS WITH ACHIOTE GARLIC SAUCE

Serves 4
Active time: 30 min   Start to finish: 1¾ hr

This dish, flavored with achiote seeds, garlic, and spices, is based on chicken pibil, *from Mexico's Yucatán Peninsula. Traditionally, the chicken is baked in banana leaves, but here we've used collard leaves because they are more readily available. They add moisture and a bit of flavor but do not get tender enough to eat.*

  1 tablespoon achiote (annatto) seeds
  ½ teaspoon cumin seeds
  ¼ teaspoon whole allspice
  ¼ teaspoon whole black peppercorns
  ½ teaspoon dried oregano (preferably
      Mexican)
  4 garlic cloves
  1 teaspoon salt
  ¼ cup fresh orange juice
  ¼ cup fresh lime juice
  ½ tablespoon olive oil
  4 small whole chicken legs (1¾ lb total),
      separated into thighs and drumsticks
  6 to 8 large collard leaves, stems trimmed
      flush with leaves

Special equipment: **an electric coffee/spice
    grinder; a 24- by 18-inch sheet of
    heavy-duty foil**
Accompaniments: **2 cups cooked white rice;
    pickled onions (page 225)**

Put oven rack in middle position and preheat oven to 350°F.

Toast seeds, spices, and oregano together in a dry heavy skillet over moderate heat, stirring, until fragrant, 1 to 2 minutes. Cool slightly, then finely grind mixture in grinder.

Mince garlic and mash to a paste with salt using a large heavy knife, then transfer to a large bowl and whisk in ground spices, juices, and oil.

Remove skin and all visible fat from chicken, then add chicken to juice mixture and turn to coat.

Lay foil loosely on top of a 13- by 9-inch baking dish and arrange collard leaves, overlapping, to create a 14-inch round in center of foil. Press foil and leaves loosely into dish to form a well, then mound chicken with sauce in well and fold collards over chicken to enclose. Wrap collard package snugly in foil, crimping edges to seal completely.

Transfer foil package from baking dish directly to rack in oven and bake until chicken is cooked through, 1 to 1¼ hours.

Transfer foil package to a serving dish, then open foil. (If desired, carefully pull out foil from under collard package.) Open collards and serve chicken with rice and pickled onions.

Each serving (including ½ cup rice) about 359 calories and 9 grams fat
PHOTO ON PAGE 106

OVEN-FRIED CHICKEN

Serves 1
Active time: 20 min   Start to finish: 1 hr

  1 cup bread crumbs (from 3 slices firm
      white sandwich bread, coarsely ground
      in a food processor)
  ¾ teaspoon salt
  ⅜ teaspoon black pepper
  2 tablespoons unsalted butter, softened
  1 tablespoon Dijon mustard
  1 tablespoon mayonnaise
  ½ teaspoon fresh lemon juice
      Rounded ⅛ teaspoon curry powder
  1 (8- to 10-oz) chicken breast and
      1 (8-oz) whole leg, both with skin
      and bones

Put oven rack in middle position and preheat oven to 450°F.

Bake bread crumbs in a small shallow baking pan until dry but not browned, 2 to 4 minutes. Transfer to a shallow bowl and mix in ½ teaspoon salt and ¼ teaspoon pepper. (Leave oven on.)

Stir together butter, mustard, mayonnaise, lemon juice, curry powder, remaining ¼ teaspoon salt, and remaining ⅛ teaspoon pepper in a small bowl.

Brush butter mixture all over chicken, then transfer chicken to bowl of crumbs to coat evenly on both sides, pressing crumbs to help adhere.

Bake chicken, skin sides up, in baking pan until well browned and cooked through, 30 to 40 minutes. Let chicken stand 5 to 10 minutes (do not cover).
PHOTO ON PAGE 111

GREEN POZOLE WITH CHICKEN

Serves 6 generously
Active time: 1½ hr   Start to finish: 2 hr

9 cups water
1 Turkish or ½ California bay leaf
1 large white onion, halved lengthwise and
  thinly sliced
6 garlic cloves, chopped
2½ teaspoons salt
3 lb skinless boneless chicken thighs
½ cup hulled (green) pumpkin seeds
  (not roasted; 2¼ oz)
1 lb tomatillos, husked
2 fresh jalapeño chiles, quartered
  (including seeds)
¾ cup chopped fresh cilantro
1 teaspoon dried epazote or oregano
  (preferably Mexican), crumbled
2 tablespoons vegetable oil
2 (15-oz) cans white hominy, rinsed and
  drained

Special equipment: **an electric coffee/spice
  grinder**
Accompaniments: **diced radish; cubed avocado
  tossed with lime juice; shredded romaine;
  chopped white onion; lime wedges; dried
  oregano**

Cook chicken:

Bring 8 cups water, bay leaf, half of onion, half of garlic, and 1 teaspoon salt to a boil, covered, in a 6-quart heavy pot, then reduce heat and simmer 10 minutes. Add chicken and poach at a bare simmer, uncovered, skimming off any foam, until just cooked through, about 20 minutes. Transfer chicken to a cutting board to cool. Pour broth through a fine-mesh sieve into a large bowl, discarding solids, and reserve. When chicken is cool enough to handle, coarsely shred with your fingers.

Make sauce while chicken cools:

Cook pumpkin seeds in a dry small skillet over low heat, stirring occasionally, until puffed but not browned (seeds will pop as they puff), 6 to 7 minutes. Transfer to a bowl to cool completely, then finely grind in coffee/spice grinder.

Simmer tomatillos and remaining onion in remaining cup water in a 3-quart saucepan, covered, until

tender, about 10 minutes. Drain vegetables and purée in a blender with jalapeños, ¼ cup cilantro, epazote, remaining garlic, and remaining 1½ teaspoons salt.

Heat oil in a 4- to 5-quart heavy pot over moderately high heat until hot but not smoking, then add purée (use caution as it will splatter and steam). Cook, uncovered, stirring frequently, until thickened, about 10 minutes. Stir in pumpkin seeds and 1 cup reserved broth and simmer 5 minutes. Stir in shredded chicken, hominy, and 3 more cups reserved broth and simmer, partially covered, 20 minutes.

Stir in remaining ½ cup cilantro and serve *pozole* in deep bowls with accompaniments.

Cooks' note:
• Chicken can be cooked and shredded 1 day ahead and chilled in 4 cups reserved broth. Measure out 1 cup broth before proceeding.
PHOTO ON PAGE 54

SESAME CRUSTED CHICKEN

Serves 6
Active time: 10 min   Start to finish: 35 min

6 skinless boneless chicken breast halves
  (1½ lb total)
2 large egg whites
1¼ teaspoons salt
1 cup sesame seeds (4½ oz)
⅓ cup vegetable oil

If chicken breasts are more than ½ inch thick, gently pound them between 2 sheets of plastic wrap with flat side of a meat pounder or with a rolling pin until ½ inch thick.

Line a tray with wax paper. Whisk together egg whites and ½ teaspoon salt in a shallow dish until whites are loosened but not foamy. Put sesame seeds in another shallow dish. Pat chicken dry and sprinkle with remaining ¾ teaspoon salt. Dip chicken, 1 piece at a time, in egg whites, letting excess drip off, then dredge in sesame seeds. Transfer to tray.

Heat oil in a 12-inch heavy skillet over moderately high heat until hot but not smoking. Reduce heat to moderate and cook 3 pieces of chicken, turning over once with tongs, until coating is golden and chicken is cooked through, 10 to 12 minutes, then transfer to a plate. Remove any browned sesame seeds from skillet, then cook remaining chicken in same manner.

assorted fowl

ROAST CAPON WITH LEMON AND THYME

Serves 8
Active time: 45 min   Start to finish: 3 hr

1 (8-lb) capon or roasting chicken
¾ stick unsalted butter, softened
1 tablespoon finely grated fresh lemon zest
1 teaspoon chopped fresh thyme
1½ teaspoons salt
½ teaspoon black pepper
4 whole lemons, quartered lengthwise
1 cup water
2 teaspoons red-currant jelly

Special equipment: **kitchen string; an instant-read thermometer**
Garnish: **fresh flat-leaf parsley and thyme sprigs**

Put oven rack in middle position and preheat oven to 375°F.

Rinse capon inside and out and discard any excess fat from cavity. Pat capon dry and season cavity with salt and pepper. Put in a large roasting pan and let stand at room temperature 20 minutes.

While capon stands, stir together butter, zest, thyme, salt, and pepper in a small bowl.

Turn capon so neck cavity is nearest you. To loosen breast skin, lift neck flap and work your fingers gently between skin and flesh, being careful not to tear skin. Slide your fingers down breast and along both sides all the way to thighs. Put half of butter mixture evenly under skin of each breast, then rub outside of capon to distribute evenly.

Place 6 lemon wedges in cavity of bird and tie legs together with string.

Roast capon, basting with pan juices every 30 minutes, 1½ hours. Skim most of fat from pan, then add remaining 10 lemon wedges to pan, tossing with pan juices. Continue roasting capon, basting every 15 minutes, until thermometer inserted 2 inches into fleshy part of a thigh (do not touch bone) registers 170°F, about 45 minutes more.

Tilt capon in pan to pour out juices in cavity, then transfer capon and lemon wedges to a carving platter and let stand 20 to 30 minutes before carving. (Do not clean pan.)

Skim fat from pan juices and straddle roasting pan across 2 burners. Add water and jelly and deglaze pan by boiling over moderately high heat, stirring and scraping up brown bits, 1 minute. Continue to boil, stirring occasionally, until reduced to about 1 cup, about 5 minutes. Season sauce with salt and pepper, then pour through a fine-mesh sieve into a bowl.

Carve capon and serve with sauce.

PHOTO ON PAGE 64

BACON-WRAPPED CORNISH HENS WITH RASPBERRY BALSAMIC GLAZE

Serves 8
Active time: 25 min   Start to finish: 1 hr

Sweet, sour, and meaty, this is summer food to eat with your hands.

⅔ cup seedless raspberry jam
½ cup balsamic vinegar
16 bacon slices (¾ lb)
4 (1½- to 1¾-lb) Cornish hens

Briskly simmer raspberry jam and vinegar in a small saucepan, uncovered, stirring occasionally, until glaze is reduced to about ½ cup, about 8 minutes. Cool to room temperature (glaze will thicken slightly as it cools).

Put oven rack in middle position and preheat oven to 450°F.

Cook bacon in batches in a large heavy skillet over moderate heat, turning occasionally, until some of fat is rendered but bacon is still translucent and pliable, 5 to 7 minutes. Transfer to paper towels to drain.

Cut out and discard backbone from each hen with kitchen shears, then halve each hen lengthwise. Pat hens dry and season with salt and pepper, then arrange, cut sides down, in a large roasting pan. Brush hens liberally with glaze, reserving remainder, and wrap 2 slices of bacon around each half hen, tucking ends under. Roast, brushing with pan juices and reserved glaze twice (every 10 minutes), until juices run clear when a thigh is pierced, 30 to 35 minutes.

PHOTO ON PAGE 88

TURKEY MEATLOAF

Serves 6
Active time: 30 min   Start to finish: 1½ hr

1½ cups finely chopped onion
1 tablespoon minced garlic
1 teaspoon olive oil
1 medium carrot, cut into ⅛-inch dice
¾ lb cremini mushrooms, trimmed and very
   finely chopped in a food processor
1 teaspoon salt
½ teaspoon black pepper
1½ teaspoons Worcestershire sauce
⅓ cup finely chopped fresh flat-leaf parsley
¼ cup plus 1 tablespoon ketchup
1 cup fine fresh bread crumbs (from
   2 slices firm white sandwich bread)
⅓ cup 1% milk
1 whole large egg, lightly beaten
1 large egg white, lightly beaten
1¼ lb ground turkey (mix of dark and light
   meat)

Special equipment: **an instant-read thermometer**
Accompaniment: **roasted red pepper tomato**
   sauce (recipe follows) or ketchup

Put oven rack in middle position and preheat oven to 400°F. Lightly oil a 13- by 9- by 2-inch metal baking pan.

Cook onion and garlic in oil in a 12-inch nonstick skillet over moderate heat, stirring, until onion is softened, about 2 minutes. Add carrot and cook, stirring, until softened, about 3 minutes. Add mushrooms, ½ teaspoon salt, and ¼ teaspoon pepper and cook, stirring occasionally, until liquid mushrooms give off is evaporated and mushrooms are very tender, 10 to 15 minutes. Stir in Worcestershire sauce, parsley, and 3 tablespoons ketchup, then transfer all vegetables to a large bowl and cool.

Stir together bread crumbs and milk in a small bowl and let stand 5 minutes. Stir in whole egg and egg white, then add to vegetables. Add turkey, remaining ½ teaspoon salt, and remaining ¼ teaspoon pepper to vegetable mixture and mix well with your hands. (Mixture will be very moist.)

Form into a 9- by 5-inch oval loaf in baking pan and brush meatloaf evenly with remaining 2 tablespoons ketchup. Bake until thermometer inserted into meatloaf registers 170°F, 50 to 55 minutes.

Let meatloaf stand 5 minutes before serving.

Each serving (not including sauce) about 230 calories and 9 grams fat
PHOTO ON PAGE 107

ROASTED RED PEPPER TOMATO SAUCE

Makes about ¾ cup
Active time: 10 min   Start to finish: 1½ hr

1 small head garlic (2 inches in diameter)
½ lb plum tomatoes, halved lengthwise
1 large red bell pepper (½ lb)
1 teaspoon olive oil
1½ teaspoons fresh lemon juice
½ teaspoon balsamic vinegar, or to taste

Put oven rack in middle position and preheat oven to 375°F. Line a 13- by 9- by 2-inch metal baking pan with foil.

Cut off and discard top quarter of garlic head and wrap remainder in foil. Arrange tomatoes, cut sides up, in baking pan and season lightly with salt. Add whole bell pepper and garlic (in foil) to pan and roast vegetables 1 hour.

Transfer bell pepper to a bowl and cover bowl with plastic wrap, then let stand about 20 minutes. When cool enough to handle, peel pepper, discarding stem and seeds, and transfer to a food processor or blender along with tomatoes.

Unwrap garlic and squeeze roasted cloves from skins into food processor. Add remaining ingredients and salt and black pepper to taste, then purée sauce until smooth.

Cooks' note:
• **Sauce can be made 1 day ahead and chilled, covered.**

Each 2-tablespoon serving about 30 calories and 1 gram fat
PHOTO ON PAGE 107

ROAST TURKEY WITH CIDER SAGE GRAVY

Serves 8 to 10
Active time: 1¼ hr   Start to finish: 4½ hr (includes making stock)

Everyone wants the juiciest turkey possible for Thanksgiving, and we find that brined or kosher turkeys are best for this. If you'd like to try brining, stir together 8 quarts water with 2 cups kosher salt in a 5-gallon bucket lined with a large heavy-duty plastic garbage bag, then soak raw turkey, covered and chilled, 10 hours. (Kosher turkeys, which are salted during the koshering process, are just as succulent.)

For turkey
- 1 (3-inch) piece celery
- 2 fresh flat-leaf parsley sprigs
- 2 fresh thyme sprigs
- 2 fresh marjoram sprigs
- 2 large fresh sage leaves
- 1 Turkish or ½ California bay leaf
- 1 (12- to 14-lb) turkey (preferably kosher), any feathers and quills removed with tweezers or needlenose pliers, and neck and giblets (excluding liver) reserved for making turkey stock (recipe follows)
- 1 tablespoon salt
- 1 teaspoon black pepper
- 1 onion, peeled and stuck with 2 whole cloves
- ½ stick (¼ cup) unsalted butter, softened, plus additional if necessary for basting

For gravy
- 1 cup hard cider or sparkling hard cider
  About 4 cups turkey stock (recipe follows)
- 1 lb onions, finely chopped (2 cups)
- 3 tablespoons unsalted butter
- 1 tablespoon finely chopped fresh sage or ¾ teaspoon dried
- ⅓ cup all-purpose flour

Special equipment: kitchen string; a metal flat rack (use a cooling rack if necessary) small enough to just fit inside roasting pan; an instant-read thermometer or remote digital thermometer

Cook turkey:
Put oven rack in lowest position and preheat oven to 425°F.

Tie celery, parsley, thyme, marjoram, sage, and bay leaf into a bundle with kitchen string to make a *bouquet garni*.

Rinse turkey inside and out and pat dry. Rub turkey inside and out with salt and pepper, then put onion and *bouquet garni* in large cavity. Working from large cavity end, run your fingers between skin and flesh of breast to loosen skin without tearing. Put 1 tablespoon butter under skin of each side of breast and massage skin from outside to spread butter evenly. Tie drumsticks together with kitchen string and fold wings under body. Put turkey on rack in a large flameproof roasting pan and, if using remote thermometer, insert it into thickest part of a thigh (do not touch bone).

Brush remaining 2 tablespoons butter over turkey, then roast 30 minutes.

Reduce oven temperature to 350°F. Baste turkey with pan drippings or butter, then continue to roast, basting every 30 minutes, until a thigh registers 165°F on thermometer, 2 to 2½ hours more.

Carefully tilt turkey so juices from inside cavity run into roasting pan. Transfer turkey to a serving platter and discard onion and *bouquet garni* from cavity. Let turkey stand 30 to 40 minutes (thigh temperature will rise to 175°F).

Make gravy while turkey stands:
Remove rack from roasting pan and pour pan juices through a sieve into a 1-quart glass measure. Straddle roasting pan across two burners, then add cider and deglaze pan by boiling over high heat, stirring and scraping up brown bits, until reduced to about ½ cup, 3 to 5 minutes. Pour cider through sieve into glass measure with pan juices, then skim fat, reserving ¼ cup of it. (Reserve 6 tablespoons total if using turkey fat for wild rice stuffing; page 194.) Add enough turkey stock to drippings to total 4 cups.

Cook chopped onions in butter in a 12-inch heavy skillet over moderate heat, stirring occasionally, until golden brown, about 10 minutes. Add sage and cook, stirring, 1 minute. Add turkey stock mixture and any turkey juices accumulated on platter and bring to a boil. Stir together flour and reserved ¼ cup fat in a small bowl, then whisk into gravy. Reduce heat and simmer gravy, uncovered, whisking occasionally, 10 minutes. Season with salt and pepper.

Serve turkey with gravy on the side.
PHOTO ON PAGE 96

TURKEY STOCK

Makes about 5 cups
Active time: 10 min Start to finish: 2¼ hr

5 cups water
2 cups chicken broth (16 fl oz)
  Neck and giblets (excluding liver) from
    turkey (recipe precedes)
1 onion, peeled and stuck with 2 whole cloves
1 (3-inch) piece celery
2 fresh thyme sprigs or ¼ teaspoon dried,
    crumbled
2 fresh flat-leaf parsley sprigs
2 fresh marjoram sprigs or ¼ teaspoon dried,
    crumbled
1 Turkish or ½ California bay leaf
5 whole black peppercorns

Bring all ingredients to a boil in a 3-quart saucepan, skimming froth, then reduce heat and gently simmer, partially covered, until reduced to about 5 cups, 1½ to 2 hours.

Pour stock through a large sieve into a bowl and discard solids.

Cooks' note:
• Stock can be made 1 day ahead and cooled completely, uncovered, then chilled, covered.

TURKEY SAUSAGE PATTIES

Serves 4
Active time: 30 min   Start to finish: 45 min

¾ lb ground turkey (not labeled "all breast
    meat")
1 medium Bosc pear (6 oz), peeled, cored,
    and coarsely grated
¼ cup chopped fresh flat-leaf parsley
2 tablespoons finely chopped fresh sage
¾ teaspoon salt
¼ teaspoon black pepper
¼ teaspoon ground allspice
1 large egg, lightly beaten
  Vegetable oil for brushing skillet

Stir together all ingredients except oil in a large bowl until combined well.

Line a tray with wax paper. Form ¼ cups of sausage mixture into patties (3 inches in diameter; about 8 total) using moistened hands and arrange on tray.

Lightly brush a 12-inch nonstick skillet with oil and heat over moderate heat until hot but not smoking. Cook patties in 2 batches, turning over once, until browned and cooked through, about 6 minutes per batch. Transfer to a plate as cooked and keep warm, covered with foil.

Each serving (2 patties) about 160 calories and 6 grams fat

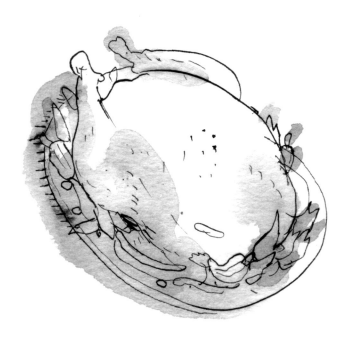

BREAKFAST, BRUNCH, AND SANDWICHES

breakfast and brunch dishes

MAPLE APRICOT GRANOLA

Makes about 10 cups
Active time: 20 min   Start to finish: 1 hr

¼ cup flaxseeds (1¼ oz)
6 cups old-fashioned oats (18 oz)
2 cups sliced almonds (8 oz)
1 cup hulled (green) pumpkin seeds
    (not roasted; 5 oz)
½ cup hulled sunflower seeds (not roasted;
    2½ oz)
1 teaspoon salt
¾ cup vegetable oil
¾ cup pure maple syrup
⅓ cup crystallized ginger (2½ oz; optional),
    finely chopped
2 cups dried apricots (11 oz), finely chopped

Special equipment: **an electric coffee/spice
    grinder**
Accompaniments: **plain yogurt or milk; honey
    or maple syrup**

Put oven racks in upper and lower thirds of oven
and preheat oven to 350°F.

Finely grind flaxseeds in coffee/spice grinder, then
stir together with oats, almonds, pumpkin seeds, sunflower seeds, salt, oil, and syrup in a large bowl.

Spread mixture evenly in 2 large shallow baking
pans (1 inch deep) and bake in upper and lower thirds
of oven, stirring and switching position of pans halfway
through baking, until mixture is golden brown, about
30 minutes total.

Cool granola completely in pans on racks, then stir
in ginger (if using) and apricots.

Cooks' note:
• Granola can be made 1 week ahead and kept in an
  airtight container at cool room temperature, or frozen
  1 month.

PHOTO ON PAGE 57

HONEYDEW IN LEMON THYME SYRUP

Serves 8
Active time: 15 min   Start to finish: 55 min

1 cup water
½ cup sugar
¼ cup chopped fresh lemon thyme
1½ firm-ripe honeydew melons, seeded and cut
    lengthwise into 1½-inch-wide wedges

Garnish: **tender lemon thyme sprigs; lemon
    wedges**

Bring water, sugar, and lemon thyme to a boil in
a 1-quart heavy saucepan over moderate heat, stirring
until sugar is dissolved. Boil syrup until reduced to
about ¾ cup, 5 to 10 minutes. Remove pan from heat
and steep syrup, covered, 30 minutes. Pour through a
sieve into a bowl, pressing on and discarding thyme.

While syrup steeps, remove rind from honeydew
wedges, then halve each wedge crosswise on a slight
diagonal.

Put melon in a shallow bowl and drizzle with
lemon thyme syrup.

Cooks' notes:
• Strained syrup can be made 1 week ahead and chilled,
  covered. Bring to room temperature before using.
• Melon in syrup can be made 1 hour ahead and kept at
  room temperature, covered.

PECAN WAFFLES WITH SAUTÉED PINEAPPLE

Serves 6
Active time: 35 min   Start to finish: 9 hr

Allowing the batter to chill overnight gives the yeast time for a long, slow rise, which makes the waffles light and crisp and develops their malty flavor.

For waffles
1 (¼-oz) package active dry yeast
   (2¼ teaspoons)
¼ cup warm water (105–115°F)
2 tablespoons plus 1 teaspoon sugar
6 large eggs
1 qt well-shaken buttermilk
⅓ cup vegetable oil plus additional for
   brushing waffle iron
3¼ cups all-purpose flour
1 teaspoon baking powder
1 teaspoon baking soda
½ teaspoon salt
1½ cups pecans (6 oz), toasted (see Tips, page
   8), then 1 cup finely chopped and ½ cup
   coarsely chopped
For pineapple topping
3 tablespoons unsalted butter
½ vanilla bean
1 pineapple (preferably labeled "extra
   sweet"), peeled (reserving rind for syrup,
   recipe follows), cut into 8 wedges, cored,
   and cut crosswise into ½-inch slices

Special equipment: **a waffle iron (preferably**
   Belgian-style)
Accompaniment: **vanilla brown sugar syrup**
   (recipe follows)

Make waffle batter:
Stir together yeast, warm water, and 1 teaspoon sugar in a small bowl and let stand until foamy, about 5 minutes. (If mixture doesn't foam, discard and start over with new yeast.)

Whisk together eggs, buttermilk, and oil. Sift together flour, baking powder, baking soda, salt, and remaining 2 tablespoons sugar into a large bowl. Add egg mixture and whisk until combined but still lumpy. Add yeast mixture and whisk until combined but still lumpy. Chill batter, covered, at least 8 hours. Bring batter to room temperature, then stir in 1 cup finely chopped pecans.

Prepare pineapple topping while batter comes to room temperature:
Melt butter in a 12-inch heavy skillet over low heat and scrape seeds from vanilla bean into butter (save pod for another use). Increase heat to moderately high, then cook pineapple, stirring occasionally, until heated through, 8 to 10 minutes. Keep warm, covered.
Cook waffles:
Put oven rack in middle position and preheat oven to 250°F. Preheat waffle iron.

Brush waffle iron lightly with vegetable oil and spoon batter into iron, using about 1½ cups for 4 (4-inch) square Belgian waffles and spreading evenly. Cook according to manufacturer's instructions, then transfer directly onto oven rack to keep warm. (Don't stack waffles; they will stay crisp if kept in 1 layer.)

Serve waffles topped with pineapple and sprinkled with remaining ½ cup (coarsely chopped) pecans.

Cooks' notes:
• Batter can be chilled up to 1 day.
• Pecans can be toasted and chopped 1 day ahead.
PHOTO ON PAGE 61

VANILLA BROWN SUGAR SYRUP

Makes about 1⅓ cups
Active time: 5 min   Start to finish: 50 min (includes cooling)

½ vanilla bean
¼ cup strained fresh pineapple juice, squeezed
   with your hands from pineapple rind
   (reserved from topping for pecan waffles;
   recipe precedes)
1½ cups packed dark brown sugar
1½ cups water
3 tablespoons unsalted butter
⅛ teaspoon salt

Halve vanilla bean and scrape seeds into a 2-quart heavy saucepan, then add pod and remaining ingredients. Bring to a boil, stirring until sugar is dissolved, then boil until syrupy and reduced to about 1⅓ cups, about 20 minutes. Cool to warm and discard vanilla bean pod.

Cooks' note:
• Syrup can be made 3 days ahead and chilled, covered. Reheat over low heat.

egg dishes

STRIPED OMELET

Serves 8
Active time: 1 hr   Start to finish: 2 hr

3 medium red bell peppers
3 tablespoons olive oil
1 tablespoon finely chopped fresh basil
2 lb red or green Swiss chard, center ribs
    and stems discarded
¼ cup finely chopped shallot
13 large eggs
⅜ teaspoon salt
½ cup plus 3 tablespoons crème fraîche or
    heavy cream
6 oz coarsely grated white sharp Cheddar
    (1½ cups)

Special equipment: **a nonstick 12- by 4- by
2½-inch loaf pan (8-cup capacity) or
9- by 2-inch round cake pan**

Roast and sauté peppers:
Roast bell peppers on racks of gas burners over high heat, turning with tongs, until skins are charred, 6 to 8 minutes. (Alternatively, broil peppers on rack of a broiler pan about 5 inches from heat, turning occasionally, 15 to 25 minutes.) Transfer to a bowl and let stand, tightly covered, until cool. Peel peppers, discarding stems and seeds, and finely chop.

Heat 1½ tablespoons oil in a 10-inch heavy skillet over moderately high heat until hot but not smoking, then sauté peppers, stirring frequently, until tender and excess liquid is evaporated, 5 to 10 minutes. Stir in basil and salt and pepper to taste. Transfer to a bowl and cool.

Cook chard:
Cook chard leaves in a 4- to 6-quart pot of boiling salted water (see Tips, page 8), uncovered, until tender, 2 to 3 minutes. Drain in a colander and rinse under cold water to stop cooking. Squeeze handfuls of chard to remove excess moisture, then finely chop.

Cook shallot in remaining 1½ tablespoons oil in clean skillet over moderate heat, stirring occasionally, until softened and just beginning to brown, 4 to 5 minutes. Add chard and cook, stirring occasionally, until mixture looks dry, 2 to 3 minutes, then stir in salt and pepper to taste and cool.

Prepare egg mixtures and bake omelet:
Put oven rack in middle position and preheat oven to 450°F. Oil loaf pan.

Break 4 large eggs into each of 2 bowls, then add ⅛ teaspoon salt and pepper to taste to each and whisk to combine eggs in each bowl. Whisk 3 tablespoons crème fraîche into 1 bowl of eggs until smooth, then stir in bell pepper mixture. Whisk ¼ cup crème fraîche into other bowl of eggs until smooth, then stir in chard mixture.

Pour bell pepper eggs into loaf pan and bake in a hot water bath (see Tips, page 8) in oven until firm to the touch, 18 to 20 minutes (about 13 minutes if using round cake pan).

Pour chard eggs into loaf pan and continue to bake until layer is firm, 18 to 20 minutes more (about 13 minutes if using round cake pan).

While chard layer bakes, break remaining 5 eggs into a bowl, then add remaining ⅛ teaspoon salt and pepper to taste and whisk to combine. Whisk in Cheddar and remaining ¼ cup crème fraîche, then pour cheese eggs into loaf pan and bake until layer is lightly browned and slightly puffed, about 20 minutes (about 16 minutes if using round cake pan). Transfer loaf pan to a rack and cool omelet 5 minutes.

Invert a long platter over loaf pan and invert omelet onto platter. Serve hot, warm, or at room temperature.

PHOTO ON PAGE 90

CREAMY SCRAMBLED EGGS WITH SPINACH

Serves 4
Active time: 15 min   Start to finish: 15 min

8 large eggs
1 teaspoon chopped fresh tarragon or
    ¼ teaspoon dried, crumbled
1 tablespoon unsalted butter
¾ lb baby spinach, coarsely chopped
2 oz cold cream cheese, cut into ½-inch cubes

Whisk together eggs and tarragon in a bowl and season with salt and pepper. Melt butter in a 12-inch nonstick skillet over moderate heat, then cook spinach, stirring occasionally, until just wilted.

Add egg mixture and cream cheese and cook, stirring slowly, until eggs are just set, about 3 minutes.

KALE AND POTATO SPANISH TORTILLA

Serves 6
Active time: 1 hr   Start to finish: 1¾ hr

The potatoes are poached in olive oil as they often are in Spain—only some oil is absorbed; the rest is drained off.

   1 lb boiling potatoes
   1 cup olive oil
   1 large onion, chopped
1½ teaspoons salt
   1 lb kale, center ribs discarded
   7 large eggs

Peel potatoes and cut into ⅓-inch dice (2¼ cups). Heat oil in a 10-inch nonstick skillet over moderate heat until hot but not smoking, then reduce heat to moderately low. Cook potatoes, chopped onion, and 1 teaspoon salt, stirring occasionally, until potatoes are tender, about 20 minutes.

Blanch kale while potatoes cook:
Cook kale in a 4- to 6-quart pot of boiling salted water (see Tips, page 8) until wilted, 2 to 3 minutes. Drain in a colander and immediately transfer to a bowl of cold water to stop cooking. Drain again, squeezing handfuls to extract excess moisture, then coarsely chop.

Add kale to potato mixture and cook, stirring occasionally, until kale is tender, about 5 minutes. Drain vegetables in colander set over a bowl, reserving drained oil, and cool 10 minutes.

Lightly beat eggs in a large bowl, then stir in vegetable mixture, 1 tablespoon drained oil, and remaining ½ teaspoon salt.

Add 1 tablespoon drained oil to skillet, then add egg mixture and cook over low heat, covered, until sides are set but center is still loose, about 12 minutes. Remove from heat and let stand, covered, 15 minutes.

Shake skillet gently to make sure tortilla is not sticking (if it is sticking, loosen with a heatproof plastic spatula). Slide tortilla onto a large flat plate, then invert skillet over tortilla and flip it back into skillet. Round off edge of tortilla with plastic spatula and cook over low heat, covered, 10 minutes more. Slide tortilla onto a plate and serve warm, cut into wedges.

PHOTO ON PAGE 52

SPINACH AND CHEESE STRATA

Serves 6 to 8
Active time: 30 min   Start to finish: 10 hr (includes chilling)

   1 (10-oz) package frozen spinach, thawed
1½ cups finely chopped onion (1 large)
   3 tablespoons unsalted butter
   1 teaspoon salt
   ½ teaspoon black pepper
   ¼ teaspoon freshly grated nutmeg
   8 cups cubed (1 inch) French or Italian bread (½ lb)
   6 oz coarsely grated Gruyère (2 cups)
   2 oz finely grated Parmigiano-Reggiano (1 cup)
2¾ cups whole milk
   9 large eggs
   2 tablespoons Dijon mustard

Squeeze handfuls of spinach to remove as much liquid as possible, then finely chop.

Cook onion in butter in a large heavy skillet over moderate heat, stirring, until soft, 4 to 5 minutes. Add ½ teaspoon salt, ¼ teaspoon pepper, and nutmeg and cook, stirring, 1 minute. Stir in spinach, then remove from heat.

Butter a 3-quart gratin dish or other shallow ceramic baking dish. Spread one third of bread cubes in gratin dish and top evenly with one third of spinach mixture. Sprinkle with one third of each cheese. Repeat layering twice (ending with cheeses).

Whisk together milk, eggs, mustard, remaining ½ teaspoon salt, and remaining ¼ teaspoon pepper in a large bowl and pour evenly over strata. Chill strata, covered with plastic wrap, at least 8 hours (for bread to absorb custard).

Put oven rack in middle position and preheat oven to 350°F. Let strata stand at room temperature for 30 minutes.

Bake strata, uncovered, until puffed, golden brown, and cooked through, 45 to 55 minutes. Let stand 5 minutes before serving.

Cooks' note:
• Strata can be chilled up to 1 day.

PHOTO ON PAGE 108

sandwiches

APPLE CHEDDAR MELTS WITH WATERCRESS

Serves 2
Active time: 20 min   Start to finish: 20 min

These sandwiches make a savory lunch or, served with a bowl of soup, a perfect Sunday supper. We prefer Madras curry powder for this recipe because its subtle, sweet flavor complements the apple and cheese particularly well.

4 slices whole-wheat bread, lightly toasted
2 tablespoons unsalted butter, softened
½ teaspoon curry powder
1 Granny Smith apple, halved, cored, and thinly sliced
1 bunch watercress (8 oz), trimmed and coarse stems discarded
½ lb extra-sharp white Cheddar, thinly sliced

Preheat broiler.

Arrange toasts in 1 layer in a shallow baking pan. Mash together butter and curry powder and spread on toasts. Arrange apple slices on toasts, then top with watercress and cover evenly with cheese. (Tuck watercress under cheese to prevent it from burning.)

Broil sandwiches about 6 inches from heat until cheese is melted and lightly browned, 3 to 5 minutes.

CHICKEN PARMESAN HEROS AND EGGPLANT PARMESAN HEROS

Serves 8
Active time: 1½ hr   Start to finish: 2 hr

3 tablespoons olive oil
1 small onion, finely chopped
2 garlic cloves, chopped
2 (28-oz) cans whole tomatoes in purée, puréed in a blender until smooth
2 teaspoons salt
¾ teaspoon black pepper
1 (1¼-lb) eggplant, cut crosswise into ¼-inch-thick rounds
6 skinless boneless chicken breast halves (2 lb total)
2 cups all-purpose flour

3½ cups fine fresh bread crumbs (from firm white sandwich bread), lightly toasted
3 oz finely grated Parmigiano-Reggiano (1 cup)
5 large eggs, lightly beaten
2 cups vegetable oil
4 (12-inch-long) loaves Italian bread, halved lengthwise
1 lb fresh mozzarella, thinly sliced

Make tomato sauce:

Heat olive oil in a 4- to 5-quart heavy saucepan over moderately high heat until hot but not smoking, then sauté onion, stirring occasionally, until golden, about 5 minutes. Add garlic and sauté, stirring, 1 minute. Add tomato purée, ½ teaspoon salt, and ¼ teaspoon pepper and simmer, uncovered, stirring occasionally, until slightly thickened, about 30 minutes.

Prepare eggplant and chicken:

Toss eggplant slices with 1 teaspoon salt in a colander set over a bowl, then let stand 30 minutes.

While eggplant drains, gently pound chicken breasts to ⅓-inch thickness between 2 sheets of plastic wrap using a flat meat pounder or a rolling pin. Season with salt and pepper.

Stir together flour, remaining ½ teaspoon salt, and remaining ½ teaspoon pepper in a shallow bowl, then stir together bread crumbs and Parmigiano-Reggiano in another shallow bowl.

Dredge eggplant slices in flour, shaking off excess, then dip in egg, letting excess drip off, and dredge in bread crumbs until evenly coated. Transfer eggplant to sheets of wax paper, arranging slices in 1 layer. Coat chicken in same manner, transferring to wax paper.

Put oven racks in upper and lower thirds of oven and preheat oven to 400°F.

Heat vegetable oil in a deep 12-inch heavy skillet over moderately high heat until hot but not smoking, then fry eggplant 4 slices at a time, turning over once, until golden brown, 2 to 3 minutes per batch. Transfer with tongs to paper towels to drain.

Fry chicken 3 pieces at a time, turning over once, until golden brown and just cooked through, about 6 minutes per batch. Transfer with tongs to paper towels to drain.

Arrange bottom halves of bread loaves on a large baking sheet and tops on another large baking sheet, all with cut sides up. Spread ¼ cup tomato sauce on each top and bottom. Divide chicken between 2 bottom halves, then divide eggplant between remaining

2 bottom halves, overlapping slices slightly. Top each (open-faced) sandwich with ¼ cup tomato sauce and one fourth of mozzarella.

Bake open-faced sandwiches in lower third of oven until cheese melts, about 3 minutes. When cheese begins to melt, put tops of loaves in upper third of oven and bake until edges are golden, 3 to 4 minutes (watch tops closely; they burn easily). Put tops on bottoms to make sandwiches, then slice into serving pieces.

Cooks' note:
• **Tomato sauce can be made 3 days ahead and chilled, covered. Reheat before using.**
PHOTO ON PAGE 50

TARRAGON SHALLOT EGG SALAD SANDWICHES

Makes 6 sandwiches
Active time: 25 min   Start to finish: 45 min

For egg salad
8 large eggs
½ cup mayonnaise
3 tablespoons finely chopped shallot
1½ tablespoons finely chopped fresh tarragon, or to taste
2 teaspoons tarragon vinegar or white-wine vinegar
¼ teaspoon salt, or to taste
¼ teaspoon black pepper, or to taste
For sandwiches
  Mayonnaise for spreading on bread (optional)
12 slices seedless rye bread or 6 kaiser rolls
3 cups tender pea shoots (3 oz) or shredded lettuce

Make egg salad:
Cover eggs with cold water by 1 inch in a 2-quart heavy saucepan and bring to a rolling boil, partially covered. Reduce heat to low and cook eggs, covered completely, 30 seconds. Remove pan from heat and let eggs stand in hot water, covered, 15 minutes. Transfer

eggs with a slotted spoon to a bowl of ice and cold water and let stand 5 minutes (to cool). Peel eggs and finely chop.

Stir together eggs and remaining salad ingredients in a bowl with a fork.
Make sandwiches:
Spread some mayonnaise (if using) on bread and make sandwiches with egg salad and pea shoots.

Cooks' note:
• **Egg salad can be made 1 day ahead and chilled, covered.**
PHOTO ON PAGE 6

ITALIAN SAUSAGE AND PEPPER HEROS

Serves 4
Active time: 40 min   Start to finish: 45 min

Don't skip the green bell peppers when making these sandwiches. They give just the right balance to the pepper mixture, slightly cutting the sweetness of their red and orange companions.

3 tablespoons olive oil
1 large onion (1 lb), halved lengthwise and thinly sliced crosswise
3 assorted bell peppers such as red, green, and orange, cut lengthwise into thin strips
3 large garlic cloves, thinly sliced
½ teaspoon salt
¼ teaspoon black pepper
½ lb hot Italian sausage links
½ lb sweet Italian sausage links
1 (12- to 14-inch) loaf Italian bread, cut crosswise into 4 pieces, then halved horizontally

Heat oil in a 12-inch heavy skillet over moderately high heat until hot but not smoking, then cook onion, bell peppers, garlic, salt, and pepper, stirring occasionally, until onion is golden, about 15 minutes.

While peppers cook, preheat broiler. Prick sausages all over with a fork, then broil on rack of a broiler pan 3 to 5 inches from heat, turning over once, until golden brown and cooked through, 10 to 12 minutes.

Transfer sausages to a cutting board and let stand 5 minutes, then halve lengthwise.

Make 4 sandwiches using bread, pepper mixture, and sausages.

PASTA AND GRAINS

pasta

BUCKWHEAT CRÊPE NOODLES WITH CHIVE BUTTER

Serves 8
Active time: 1½ hr   Start to finish: 2 hr

Buckwheat—which grows well in cold climates—has a solid place in French-Canadian cuisine. Buckwheat crêpes can be traced back to Brittany, and buckwheat pancakes are a regular part of a Canadian breakfast. These "noodles," made from savory crêpes, are a contemporary twist on this classic dish.

For crepes
3 cups whole milk
4 large eggs
1 cup buckwheat flour
½ cup all-purpose flour
1 teaspoon salt
¼ teaspoon black pepper
⅓ cup finely chopped fresh flat-leaf parsley
5 tablespoons unsalted butter, melted
For chive butter
½ stick (¼ cup) unsalted butter, softened
⅓ cup finely chopped fresh chives

Make crepes and cut into noodles:
Blend milk, eggs, flours, salt, and pepper in a blender, scraping down sides occasionally, until smooth, then add parsley and 3 tablespoons butter and blend just until incorporated.

Lightly brush a 10-inch nonstick skillet with some remaining butter and heat over moderate heat until hot. Fill a ¼-cup measure three-fourths full of batter, then pour into skillet, tilting and rotating skillet to coat bottom. (If batter sets before skillet is coated, reduce heat slightly for next crepe.) Cook just until underside is set and lightly browned, 10 to 15 seconds, then loosen crepe with a heatproof plastic spatula and flip over with your fingers. Cook crepe until other side is just cooked through, about 15 seconds more. Transfer crepe to a large sheet of wax paper. Make more crepes in same manner, lightly brushing skillet with more butter as needed between batches and stacking crepes in 2 piles.

Transfer crepe stacks to a cutting board and cut each stack into ½-inch-wide strips, then separate strips into noodles.

Make chive butter and assemble dish:
Put oven rack in upper third of oven and preheat oven to 350°F. Generously butter a baking pan.

Mash together butter and chives with a fork in a small bowl, then add salt and pepper to taste.

Spread noodles in baking pan and reheat in oven until hot, about 15 minutes.

Melt chive butter (along with any remaining melted butter from crepes) in a small saucepan, then drizzle over noodles. Gently transfer noodles to a warmed serving bowl (noodles are delicate).

Cooks' notes:
• Crêpes can be made (but not cut into noodles) 2 days ahead and chilled, wrapped well in wax paper and then foil. Bring to room temperature before cutting.
• Chive butter can be made 3 days ahead and chilled, covered.
PHOTO ON PAGE 102

EGGPLANT LASAGNE WITH PARSLEY PESTO

Serves 8
Active time: 1¾ hr   Start to finish: 2¾ hr

There will be about ¾ cup of parsley pesto left over after making this lasagne.

For béchamel
1 garlic clove, minced
3 tablespoons unsalted butter
5 tablespoons all-purpose flour
5 cups whole milk
1 Turkish or ½ California bay leaf
1 teaspoon salt
⅛ teaspoon white pepper
For pesto and ricotta mixture
1⅓ cups hazelnuts (5½ oz), toasted (see Tips, page 8) and loose skins rubbed off in a kitchen towel

4 cups loosely packed fresh flat-leaf parsley
    leaves (from ¾ lb)
3 oz finely grated Parmigiano-Reggiano
    (1½ cups; see Tips, page 8)
⅔ cup plus ¼ cup olive oil
2 garlic cloves, finely chopped
2 teaspoons salt
1¼ teaspoons black pepper
1 large egg
1 (15-oz) container whole-milk ricotta
    For lasagne
4 lb medium eggplants (4), cut crosswise
    into ⅓-inch-thick slices
6 tablespoons olive oil
1 teaspoon salt
¾ teaspoon black pepper
9 (7- by 3½-inch) oven-ready lasagne noodles
    (sometimes called "no-boil"; 6 oz)
1½ oz finely grated Parmigiano-Reggiano

Make béchamel:

Cook garlic in butter in a 3-quart heavy saucepan over moderately low heat, stirring, 1 minute. Add flour and cook roux, whisking, 3 minutes. Add milk in a stream, whisking. Add bay leaf and bring to a boil over moderately high heat, whisking constantly, then reduce heat and simmer, whisking occasionally, until liquid is reduced to about 4 cups, about 10 minutes. Whisk in salt and white pepper, then remove from heat and discard bay leaf. Cover surface of sauce with wax paper until ready to use.

Make pesto and ricotta mixture:

Coarsely chop ⅓ cup hazelnuts and reserve for sprinkling over lasagne.

Purée parsley, Parmigiano-Reggiano, ⅔ cup oil, garlic, 1 teaspoon salt, 1 teaspoon pepper, and remaining cup hazelnuts in a food processor until pesto is smooth, about 1 minute.

Whisk egg in a bowl, then stir in ricotta, 1 cup parsley pesto, remaining teaspoon salt, and remaining ¼ teaspoon pepper until combined well.

Stir together ¼ cup pesto and remaining ¼ cup oil in a small bowl for drizzling over lasagne.

Roast eggplant for lasagne:

Put oven racks in upper and lower thirds of oven and preheat oven to 450°F. Oil 2 large baking sheets.

Brush eggplant with oil on both sides, then arrange in 1 layer on baking sheets and sprinkle with salt and pepper. Bake eggplant, switching position of sheets halfway through baking and turning slices over once,

until tender, 20 to 25 minutes total.

Assemble lasagne:

Move oven rack to middle position and reduce oven temperature to 425°F. Lightly oil a 13- by 9- by 2-inch glass or ceramic baking dish (3 quart) and line a larger shallow baking pan with foil.

Spread 1 cup béchamel in baking dish and cover with 3 pasta sheets, leaving spaces between sheets. Drop 1 cup ricotta mixture by spoonfuls over pasta, spreading evenly (layer will be thin), then top with 1 layer of eggplant, cutting rounds to fit if necessary. Make 1 more layer each of béchamel, pasta, ricotta, and eggplant. Spread with 1 cup béchamel and cover with remaining 3 pasta sheets. Spread remaining cup ricotta mixture over pasta, then spread ricotta with remaining cup béchamel and top with remaining eggplant in 1 layer (you may have a few slices left over). Sprinkle Parmigiano-Reggiano over eggplant and scatter with reserved chopped hazelnuts.

Tightly cover baking dish with oiled foil (oiled side down), then set dish in foil-lined pan (to catch drips) and bake lasagne 30 minutes. Remove foil and bake until golden and bubbling, 10 to 15 minutes more. Let lasagne stand 15 to 20 minutes before serving.

Serve lasagne drizzled with pesto.

Cooks' notes:
- Lasagne can be assembled 2 hours ahead and chilled, covered. Bring to room temperature before baking.
- Lasagne can be baked 1 day ahead and cooled completely, then chilled, covered. Let stand at room temperature 1 hour, then heat in a preheated 350°F oven, covered, until hot, 30 to 40 minutes.

PHOTO ON PAGE 95

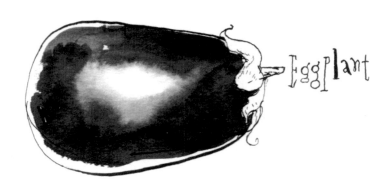
Eggplant

FETTUCCINE ALFREDO

Serves 4 (main course)
Active time: 10 min   Start to finish: 25 min

In Rome, this pasta would be served as a first course, but we prefer it as a main course. Traditionally, Romans don't use heavy cream in this dish, so you won't find any here either.

    5 tablespoons unsalted butter, cut into
        tablespoon pieces
   12 oz dried egg fettuccine
    ¼ teaspoon salt, or to taste
    2 oz finely grated Parmigiano-Reggiano
        (1 cup; see Tips, page 8)

Put oven rack in middle position and preheat oven to 250°F.

Melt butter in a heatproof serving bowl in oven, about 5 minutes.

Cook fettuccine in a 6- to 8-quart pot of boiling salted water (see Tips, page 8) until al dente. Reserve ½ cup pasta cooking water, then drain fettuccine in a colander. Immediately toss fettuccine with butter and salt in bowl, then add ¾ cup cheese little by little, tossing constantly and adding enough of cooking water to keep pasta moist. Season with salt and pepper to taste, then sprinkle with remaining cheese.

LINGUINE WITH COLLARD GREENS AND BACON

Serves 4 to 6 (main course)
Active time: 50 min   Start to finish: 50 min

   10 bacon slices (½ lb), chopped
    ¾ cup pine nuts (¼ lb)
    ¼ lb shallots, finely chopped (¾ cup)
    6 garlic cloves, minced
    1 teaspoon dried hot red pepper flakes
    2 tablespoons olive oil
    3 lb collard greens, stems and center ribs
        discarded and leaves chopped
    ¼ teaspoon salt
    2 cups water
    1 lb dried linguine
    1 lb grape or cherry tomatoes, quartered
    1 cup Parmigiano-Reggiano shavings, made
        with a vegetable peeler

Cook bacon in a 5-quart heavy pot over moderate heat, stirring occasionally, until crisp, about 5 minutes, then transfer with a slotted spoon to paper towels to drain. Pour off all but 3 tablespoons bacon fat from pot. Add pine nuts to pot and cook over moderate heat, stirring, until golden, about 2 minutes. Transfer nuts with slotted spoon to paper towels to drain and season with salt.

Add shallots to pot and cook over moderate heat, stirring, until softened, about 4 minutes. Add garlic and red pepper flakes and cook, stirring, 1 minute. Add oil and half of collard greens and cook, stirring, until slightly wilted, about 1 minute. Add remaining greens and salt and continue to cook, stirring, until greens are crisp-tender, about 2 minutes more. Add water and cover pot, then simmer greens, stirring occasionally, until just tender, about 15 minutes.

While collard greens simmer, cook linguine in a 6- to 8-quart pot of boiling salted water (see Tips, page 8) until al dente. Drain linguine in a colander.

Add drained linguine and tomatoes to pot with greens and cook over moderately high heat, stirring constantly, 1 minute. Season pasta with salt and pepper and serve topped with bacon, pine nuts, and cheese shavings.

LEMON POPPY SEED NOODLES

Serves 6
Active time: 10 min   Start to finish: 25 min

    6 oz wide egg noodles
   1½ teaspoons poppy seeds
   1½ tablespoons unsalted butter
    ½ teaspoon finely grated fresh lemon zest
    2 tablespoons finely chopped fresh chives

Cook noodles in a large pot of boiling salted water (see Tips, page 8) until tender.

While noodles cook, lightly toast poppy seeds in a dry small skillet over moderately low heat, stirring, until just fragrant, about 2 minutes.

Reserve ½ cup cooking water and drain noodles in a colander. Add butter and zest to warm pot and swirl until melted. Add noodles and toss, adding enough of reserved cooking water to keep noodles moist, then stir in poppy seeds, chives, and salt and pepper to taste.

Each serving about 140 calories and 5 grams fat

PHOTO ON PAGE 107

ORZO WITH SUMMER SQUASH AND TOASTED HAZELNUTS

Serves 8
Active time: 40 min   Start to finish: 40 min

People who turn their noses up at rice often find this tiny pasta irresistible.

1½ cups orzo (10 oz)
3 tablespoons unsalted butter
3 tablespoons olive oil
1 cup finely chopped shallot (6½ oz)
2 medium zucchini (1½ lb total), cut into ⅓-inch dice
2 medium yellow squash (1 lb total), cut into ⅓-inch dice
1 teaspoon salt
½ teaspoon black pepper
¾ cup hazelnuts (4 oz), toasted (see Tips, page 8), loose skins rubbed off in a kitchen towel, and nuts coarsely chopped
½ cup chopped fresh flat-leaf parsley
½ cup chopped fresh basil
2 teaspoons finely grated fresh lemon zest

Cook orzo in a 4- to 5-quart pot of boiling salted water (see Tips, page 8) until al dente. Reserve ½ cup cooking water, then drain orzo in a colander.

While orzo cooks, heat butter and oil in a deep 12-inch heavy skillet over moderately high heat until foam subsides, then sauté shallot, stirring, until golden, about 5 minutes. Add zucchini, yellow squash, salt, and pepper and sauté, stirring occasionally, until vegetables are just tender, about 5 minutes. Remove from heat and stir in nuts, parsley, basil, and zest.

Add cooked orzo to skillet and stir gently. If mixture seems dry, moisten with some reserved pasta water. Season with salt and pepper. Serve warm or at room temperature.

PHOTO ON PAGE 88

PENNE ALLA GORGONZOLA

Serves 6 (main course)
Active time: 15 min   Start to finish: 25 min

1 lb penne (preferably ridged)
3 tablespoons unsalted butter
1 tablespoon thinly sliced fresh sage or 1 teaspoon dried sage, crumbled
1 cup whole milk
½ lb Gorgonzola *dolce* or Saga Blue, rind discarded and cheese cut into pieces (2 cups)
¼ teaspoon black pepper
⅛ teaspoon freshly grated nutmeg
2 oz finely grated Parmigiano-Reggiano (1 cup; see Tips, page 8)

Cook pasta in a 6- to 8-quart pot of boiling salted water (see Tips, page 8), stirring occasionally, until al dente, 10 to 12 minutes.

While pasta boils, heat butter in a 12-inch heavy skillet over moderate heat until foam subsides, then cook sage, stirring, 1 minute. Add milk and Gorgonzola and cook, stirring and breaking up cheese, until sauce is smooth, about 2 minutes (sauce will be thin). Reduce heat to low and stir in pepper, nutmeg, and salt to taste.

Reserve ½ cup cooking water and drain pasta. Add pasta and Parmigiano-Reggiano to sauce, stirring to coat. Thin with a little reserved cooking water if necessary.

CORIANDER NOODLES WITH ZUCCHINI AND CARROTS

Serves 4 (main course) or 6 (side dish)
Active time: 20 min   Start to finish: 30 min

1 lb spaghetti
¼ cup vegetable oil
½ teaspoon dried hot red pepper flakes
2½ teaspoons ground coriander
1½ teaspoons finely grated peeled fresh ginger
¼ cup soy sauce
¼ teaspoon salt
½ lb zucchini (1 medium), coarsely shredded
½ lb carrots (3 medium), coarsely shredded
6 scallions (1 bunch), thinly sliced diagonally
1 tablespoon Asian sesame oil

Cook spaghetti in a 6- to 8-quart pot of boiling salted water (see Tips, page 8) until al dente. Drain in a colander, then rinse well under cold water and transfer to a large bowl.

Heat vegetable oil with red pepper flakes in a small saucepan over moderate heat until hot, then whisk in coriander, ginger, soy sauce, and salt (sauce will sizzle). Add sauce to spaghetti along with remaining ingredients and toss until combined well. Serve at room temperature.

PASTA PRIMAVERA

Serves 6
Active time: 1 hr   Start to finish: 1½ hr

1 oz dried morel mushrooms
1½ cups warm water
½ lb asparagus, trimmed and cut into 1-inch pieces
¼ lb green beans (preferably *haricots verts*), trimmed and cut into 1-inch pieces
¾ cup frozen baby peas, thawed
2 teaspoons minced garlic
   Rounded ½ teaspoon dried hot red pepper flakes
4 tablespoons extra-virgin olive oil
1½ pt grape tomatoes
1 tablespoon balsamic vinegar
3 tablespoons water
1 lb spaghettini (thin spaghetti)
½ stick (¼ cup) unsalted butter
⅔ cup heavy cream
1 teaspoon finely grated fresh lemon zest
2 oz finely grated Parmigiano-Reggiano (1 cup; see Tips, page 8)
¼ cup finely chopped fresh flat-leaf parsley
¼ cup finely chopped fresh basil
⅓ cup pine nuts (1½ oz), lightly toasted (see Tips, page 8)

Garnish: **Parmigiano-Reggiano shavings**

Prepare vegetables:
   Soak morels in warm water in a small bowl 30 minutes. Lift mushrooms out of water, squeezing excess liquid back into bowl. Pour soaking liquid through a sieve lined with a dampened paper towel into a small bowl and reserve. Rinse morels thoroughly to remove grit, then squeeze dry. Discard any tough stems. Halve small morels lengthwise and quarter larger ones.
   Cook asparagus and beans in a 6- to 8-quart pot of boiling salted water (see Tips, page 8), uncovered, 3 minutes. Add peas and cook until beans and asparagus are just tender, about 1 to 2 minutes more. Immediately transfer vegetables with a large slotted spoon to a bowl of ice and cold water to stop cooking, reserving hot water in pot for cooking pasta. Drain cooled vegetables in a colander.
   Cook 1 teaspoon garlic and a rounded ¼ teaspoon red pepper flakes in 2 tablespoons oil in a 10- to 12-inch heavy skillet over moderately low heat, stirring, just until garlic is fragrant, about 1 minute. Add drained vegetables and salt and pepper to taste and cook, stirring, 2 minutes, then transfer to a bowl. Reserve skillet.

Cook tomatoes:
   Cut half of tomatoes into quarters and halve remainder lengthwise, keeping quarters and halves separate. Cook remaining teaspoon garlic and remaining rounded ¼ teaspoon red pepper flakes in remaining 2 tablespoons oil in skillet over moderately low heat, stirring, just until garlic is fragrant, about 1 minute. Add quartered tomatoes with salt and pepper to taste and simmer, stirring occasionally, until tomatoes are softened, about 3 minutes. Add halved tomatoes, vinegar, and water and simmer, stirring occasionally, until sauce is thickened and halved tomatoes are softened, 3 to 4 minutes. Keep tomatoes warm.

Cook spaghettini and assemble dish:
   While tomatoes cook, return water in pot to a boil and cook spaghettini until al dente. Drain in a colander.
   Immediately add butter, cream, zest, and morels to empty pasta pot and simmer gently, uncovered, 2 minutes. Stir in cheese and add pasta, tossing to coat and adding as much of reserved morel soaking liquid as necessary (½ to ⅔ cup) to keep pasta well coated. Add green vegetables, parsley, basil, pine nuts, and salt and pepper to taste and toss gently to combine.
   Serve pasta topped with tomatoes and Parmigiano-Reggiano shavings.

PHOTO ON PAGE 109

Spaghetti

grains

FRIED GARLIC GRITS

Serves 8
Active time: 1½ hr   Start to finish: 4½ hr (includes chilling)

We tested this recipe with stone-ground and regular "old-fashioned" grits; we liked the stone-ground best here because of its pronounced corn flavor. If you already have the "old-fashioned" type on hand, it's a fine substitute. Simply follow our procedure and disregard the cooking instructions on the package.

4½ cups water
3 tablespoons unsalted butter
4 garlic cloves, minced
1½ teaspoons salt
½ teaspoon black pepper
1 cup coarse stone-ground white grits
2 cups all-purpose flour
2 large eggs, lightly beaten with 2 tablespoons
   water
2 cups plain fine dry bread crumbs
6 cups vegetable oil

Special equipment: **a deep-fat thermometer**

Line a lightly oiled 13- by 9- by 2-inch baking pan lengthwise with a 24-inch-long sheet of wax paper, letting excess hang over ends.

Bring water, butter, garlic, salt, and pepper to a boil in a 4- to 5-quart heavy pot, then slowly stir in grits. Reduce heat and cook at a bare simmer, covered, stirring frequently, until thickened, about 40 minutes. Remove lid and simmer grits, stirring frequently, until very thick and tender, 10 to 15 minutes. Cool grits in pot 10 minutes, then pour into lined baking pan, smoothing top, and cool completely. Chill grits, covered with plastic wrap, until firm, at least 3 hours.

Discard plastic wrap and transfer grits on wax paper to a work surface, then pat dry. Cut grits into 8 (4½- by 3¼-inch) rectangles, then diagonally halve each rectangle to form 2 triangles.

Put flour, eggs, and bread crumbs in separate shallow dishes. Dredge 1 grits triangle in flour, knocking off excess, then dip in egg, letting excess drip off, and dredge in bread crumbs. Transfer coated triangle to a large baking sheet. Coat remaining grit triangles in same manner.

Put oven rack in middle position and preheat oven to 300°F.

Heat oil in a 5- to 6-quart heavy pot over moderately high heat until it registers 375°F on thermometer. Fry triangles in 4 batches, stirring gently, until crisp and golden brown, 1 to 2 minutes, then transfer with a slotted spoon to paper towels to drain. Return oil to 375°F between batches. Keep grits hot on a rack set in a baking pan in oven while frying other batches.

Cooks' notes:
• Grits can be chilled in baking pan up to 2 days.
• Grits triangles can be fried 1 hour ahead and kept at room temperature on a rack in a baking pan. Reheat, uncovered, in middle of a preheated 375°F oven 5 to 8 minutes.
PHOTO ON PAGE 71

CREAMY POLENTA

Makes about 10 cups (serving 8 to 10)
Active time: 15 min   Start to finish: 1 hr

We love Marcella Hazan's "no-stirring" method for polenta—the following recipe is based on the one in her book Essentials of Classic Italian Cooking. *It does require some stirring, but not the constant attention of traditional methods.*

8 cups water
2 teaspoons salt
2 cups polenta (not quick-cooking) or yellow
   cornmeal (10 oz)

Bring water to a boil with salt in a 4-quart heavy saucepan, then add polenta in a thin stream, whisking. Cook over moderate heat, whisking, 2 minutes. Reduce heat to low and simmer polenta, covered, stirring for 1 minute after every 10 minutes of cooking, 45 minutes total. Remove from heat and serve warm.

Cooks' note:
• Polenta can be made 20 minutes ahead and kept, covered, at room temperature (do not let stand longer or it will solidify).
PHOTO ON PAGE 59

WILD RICE, APPLE, AND DRIED-CRANBERRY STUFFING

Serves 8 to 10
Active time: 1¼ hr   Start to finish: 2¾ hr

4 cups water
1 cup wild rice
1½ teaspoons salt
½ lb crusty white bread, cut into ½-inch
    cubes (6 cups)
1 stick (½ cup) unsalted butter, plus
    2 tablespoons melted unsalted butter
    or reserved fat from turkey
2 cups diced (⅓ inch) onion
2 cups diced (⅓ inch) celery
2 cups diced (⅓ inch) apple
¼ cup finely chopped fresh flat-leaf parsley
2 tablespoons finely chopped fresh sage or
    1½ teaspoons dried, crumbled
2 teaspoons finely chopped fresh marjoram
    or ½ teaspoon dried, crumbled
1 teaspoon finely chopped fresh thyme or
    ¼ teaspoon dried, crumbled
½ teaspoon black pepper
1 cup dried cranberries (5 oz)
1 cup turkey stock (page 181) or
    chicken broth

Bring water to a boil in a 2-quart heavy saucepan, then add rice and ½ teaspoon salt. Reduce heat to low and cook, covered, until rice is tender and most grains are split open, 1 to 1¼ hours (not all liquid will be absorbed). Drain well in a colander and spread out in a baking pan to cool completely.

Put oven rack in upper third of oven and preheat oven to 350°F.

Spread bread cubes in a shallow baking pan and bake until dry, about 20 minutes.

Melt 1 stick butter in a large nonstick skillet over moderate heat, then cook onion and celery, stirring, until softened, about 8 minutes. Add apple and cook, stirring, until crisp-tender, about 5 minutes. Stir in herbs, pepper, and remaining teaspoon salt and cook, stirring, 2 minutes. Transfer to a large bowl and toss with rice, bread, and dried cranberries.

Increase oven temperature to 450°F and butter a shallow 3-quart baking dish (13 by 9 inches).

Spread stuffing evenly in baking dish and drizzle with turkey stock and melted butter. Bake stuffing, covered tightly with foil, until heated through, about 20 minutes. Remove foil and bake until top is browned, 10 to 15 minutes more.

Cooks' note:
• Stuffing can be assembled (without drizzling with stock and melted butter), but not baked, 1 day ahead and cooled, uncovered, then chilled, covered. Bring to room temperature before proceeding.
PHOTO ON PAGE 98

QUINOA WITH MANGO AND CURRIED YOGURT

Serves 6 (side dish)
Active time: 20 min   Start to finish: 45 min

⅓ cup plain yogurt
1 tablespoon fresh lime juice
2 teaspoons curry powder
1 teaspoon finely grated peeled fresh ginger
¾ teaspoon salt
¼ teaspoon black pepper
2 tablespoons vegetable or peanut oil
1⅓ cups quinoa (7½ oz)
1 lb firm-ripe mango, peeled, pitted, and cut
    into ½-inch chunks (2 cups)
1 red bell pepper, cut into ¼-inch dice
1 fresh jalapeño chile, seeded (if desired for
    less heat) and minced
⅓ cup chopped fresh mint
½ cup salted roasted peanuts (2½ oz),
    chopped

Whisk together yogurt, lime juice, curry powder, ginger, salt, and pepper in a large bowl. Add oil in a slow stream, whisking until combined.

Rinse quinoa in a bowl using 5 changes of water, rubbing grains and letting them settle before pouring off water (if quinoa does not settle, drain in a large sieve after each rinsing).

Cook quinoa in a 4- to 5-quart pot of boiling salted water (see Tips, page 8) 10 minutes. Drain in a large sieve and rinse under cold water.

Set sieve with quinoa over a saucepan containing 1½ inches boiling water (sieve should not touch water) and steam quinoa, covered with a kitchen towel and lid, until fluffy and dry, 10 to 12 minutes. Toss quinoa with curried yogurt and remaining ingredients in a large bowl. Serve warm or at room temperature.

GINGER FRIED RICE
WITH SHIITAKE MUSHROOMS

Serves 6 (side dish)
Active time: 35 min   Start to finish: 35 min

This recipe is a great use for cold leftover rice. Order extra rice with Chinese takeout or make a double batch of your own one night—you can keep it, chilled, up to 1 week.

    2 tablespoons plus 1 teaspoon vegetable oil
    1 large egg, beaten with 1 tablespoon water
 1½ tablespoons minced peeled fresh ginger
    3 scallions, white and green parts chopped
        separately
  ¾ teaspoon kosher salt
  ½ lb fresh shiitake mushrooms, stems
        discarded and caps thinly sliced
    3 cups cold cooked white rice
  ½ teaspoon Asian sesame oil

Heat a wok or a 12-inch nonstick skillet over moderate heat until hot, then add ½ teaspoon vegetable oil and swirl around wok. Add half of egg mixture and swirl wok to coat bottom with a thin layer about 5 inches in diameter. When egg crêpe is set, about 45 seconds, transfer with a wide metal spatula to a plate to cool. Make another egg crêpe with another ½ teaspoon vegetable oil and remaining egg mixture in same manner. Stack crêpes, roll into a cylinder, and cut crosswise into ¼-inch-wide strips, then unroll.

Heat remaining 2 tablespoons vegetable oil in wok over high heat until it begins to smoke. Add ginger, white part of scallions, and kosher salt and stir-fry until fragrant, about 30 seconds. Add shiitakes and stir-fry until tender, 3 to 5 minutes. Crumble rice into wok and stir-fry until lightly browned, 10 to 15 minutes. Remove from heat and add scallion greens, egg strips, and sesame oil, tossing to combine.

FUYU PERSIMMON RICE PILAF

Serves 4
Active time: 15 min   Start to finish: 40 min

  ¼ cup finely chopped shallot
    1 tablespoon olive oil
    1 cup long-grain white rice
    1 tablespoon finely chopped peeled
        fresh ginger
  ¼ teaspoon cinnamon
    1 cup low-sodium chicken broth
  ¾ cup water
  ½ lb firm-ripe Fuyu persimmons, peeled,
        seeded if necessary, and chopped
  ½ cup finely chopped fresh cilantro
        Fresh lemon juice to taste

Cook shallot in oil in a 1½- to 2-quart heavy saucepan over moderate heat, stirring occasionally, until golden, 2 to 5 minutes. Reduce heat to low, then add rice, ginger, and cinnamon and cook, stirring, 1 minute. Add broth and water and bring to a boil. Reduce heat to low and cook, covered, until rice is tender, about 20 minutes. Remove pan from heat and let stand, covered, 5 minutes.

Fluff rice with a fork and stir in persimmons, cilantro, lemon juice, and salt and pepper to taste. Serve warm.

VEGETABLES AND BEANS

vegetables

BEETS AND CARAMELIZED ONIONS WITH FETA

Serves 4 (first course or side dish)
Active time: 20 min   Start to finish: 45 min

*This dish is a particularly good accompaniment
to beef or lamb.*

2 tablespoons cider vinegar
1 teaspoon Dijon mustard (preferably
   whole-grain or coarse-grain)
¼ teaspoon black pepper
¾ teaspoon salt
5 tablespoons olive oil
1 lb onions (2 medium), quartered lengthwise,
   then cut crosswise into 1-inch pieces
2 (15-oz) cans small whole beets, drained and
   quartered (or halved if very small)
3 oz crumbled feta (½ cup)
¼ cup pine nuts (1 oz), toasted (see Tips,
   page 8) and coarsely chopped

Whisk together vinegar, mustard, pepper, and
½ teaspoon salt in a large bowl, then add 3 tablespoons
oil in a slow stream, whisking until combined well.

Cook onions with remaining ¼ teaspoon salt in
remaining 2 tablespoons oil in a 12-inch heavy skillet
over moderate heat, stirring occasionally, until golden
brown, 18 to 20 minutes. Add onions to dressing along
with beets and cheese, stirring gently to combine. Serve
sprinkled with pine nuts.

SHREDDED BRUSSELS SPROUTS WITH MAPLE HICKORY NUTS

Serves 8 to 10
Active time: 30 min   Start to finish: 30 min

¾ cup hickory nut halves or coarsely chopped
   pecans (3 oz)
½ stick (¼ cup) unsalted butter

1 tablespoon pure maple syrup
1 teaspoon salt
2 lb Brussels sprouts, any discolored leaves
   discarded and stem ends left intact
¼ teaspoon black pepper
1 tablespoon cider vinegar

Special equipment: **a Japanese Benriner or other
adjustable-blade slicer**

Put oven rack in middle position and preheat oven
to 350°F.

Toast nuts in a small shallow baking pan until fragrant and a few shades darker, about 10 minutes.

While nuts toast, melt 1 tablespoon butter and stir
together with syrup and ½ teaspoon salt.

Add maple glaze to hot nuts and toss to coat.

Holding each Brussels sprout by stem end, cut into
very thin slices with slicer. Toss slices in a bowl to separate layers.

Heat remaining 3 tablespoons butter in a 12- to
13-inch nonstick skillet over moderately high heat until
foam subsides, then sauté shredded sprouts with pepper
and remaining ½ teaspoon salt, stirring, until sprouts
are wilted but crisp-tender, 3 to 5 minutes. Add vinegar
and sauté, stirring, 1 minute. Add hickory nuts and any
glaze in baking pan and sauté, stirring, 1 minute.

Cooks' notes:
• Nuts can be glazed 1 day ahead and cooled, then kept,
  covered, at room temperature.
• Brussels sprouts can be sliced 1 day ahead and chilled
  in a sealed plastic bag lined with paper towels.
PHOTO ON PAGE 97

SPICED CARROTS

Serves 6
Active time: 15 min   Start to finish: 20 min

¼ teaspoon ground cumin
¼ teaspoon paprika
   Pinch of cayenne
1 teaspoon olive oil
2 teaspoons honey

¼ teaspoon salt

1¼ lb carrots, cut into ¼-inch-thick
    matchsticks

1½ teaspoons fresh lemon juice

1½ tablespoons coarsely chopped fresh
    flat-leaf parsley

Cook spices in oil in a small nonstick skillet over low heat, stirring, until fragrant, about 2 minutes. Remove from heat and cool slightly, then stir in honey and salt.

Cook carrots in a 4-quart saucepan of boiling salted water (see Tips, page 8) until tender, 4 to 5 minutes, then drain in a colander.

Toss warm carrots in a bowl with spiced oil and lemon juice. Just before serving, toss with parsley and salt to taste. Serve warm or at room temperature.

Each serving about 51 calories and 1 gram fat

PURÉE DE CAROTTES ET POMMES DE TERRE
Carrot and Potato Purée

Serves 8
Active time: 30 min   Start to finish: 1 hr

1½ lb carrots, cut into ½-inch pieces

2½ lb large Yukon Gold potatoes

½ cup heavy cream

3 tablespoons unsalted butter

1 teaspoon fine sea salt

Special equipment: **a potato ricer or a food mill
fitted with medium disk**

Cook carrots in a 6-quart pot of boiling salted water (see Tips, page 8), uncovered, until very tender, 20 to 25 minutes.

While carrots boil, peel potatoes and cut into ½-inch pieces.

Transfer cooked carrots with a slotted spoon to a food processor. Add potatoes to boiling water and cook, uncovered, until tender, about 10 minutes, then drain in a colander.

While potatoes cook, purée carrots in food processor with ¼ cup cream until smooth, about 2 minutes.

Heat butter and remaining ¼ cup cream in pot over moderate heat, stirring, until butter is melted, then force potatoes through ricer into pot. Add carrot purée, sea salt, and pepper to taste and stir until combined well.

Cooks' note:
- Carrot and potato purée can be made 1 day ahead and chilled, covered. Reheat in a microwave or double boiler.

PHOTO ON PAGE 48

SAUTÉED COLLARD GREENS

Serves 8
Active time: 30 min   Start to finish: 30 min

A long cooking time for collard greens is a southern tradition. We sliver ours, then sauté them only for a minute, which renders them crisp-tender but allows the greens to keep their color and full flavor.

**3 lb collard greens, leaves halved lengthwise
    and stems and center ribs discarded**

2 tablespoons vegetable oil

Stack several collard leaf halves and roll up tightly into a cigar shape. Cut crosswise into very thin slices (no wider than ⅛ inch). Roll and slice remaining leaves in same manner.

Heat oil in a 12-inch heavy skillet over moderately high heat until hot but not smoking, then sauté greens, tossing with tongs, just until they are bright green, about 1 minute. Season with salt and pepper.

Cooks' note:
- Collards can be thinly sliced 6 hours ahead and chilled in a sealed plastic bag.

PHOTO ON PAGE 71

CORN AND HARICOTS VERTS IN LIME SHALLOT BUTTER

Serves 6
Active time: 30 min   Start to finish: 30 min

¼ cup finely chopped shallot
2 tablespoons unsalted butter
¾ lb *haricots verts* or other thin green
   beans, trimmed and cut crosswise into
   ¼-inch pieces
3 cups corn (from 6 ears)
1 teaspoon salt
1 teaspoon finely grated fresh lime zest
½ teaspoon fresh lime juice, or to taste

Cook shallot in butter in a 12-inch heavy skillet over moderate heat, stirring, until softened, about 3 minutes. Add beans, corn, and salt and cook, stirring, until vegetables are tender, about 6 minutes. Remove from heat and stir in lime zest and lime juice.
PHOTO ON PAGE 83

GLAZED CHESTNUTS AND HARICOTS VERTS

Serves 8
Active time: 1 hr   Start to finish: 1 hr

Sortilège is a blend of Canadian whiskey and maple syrup. Here it infuses the chestnuts with maple flavor and picks up the sweetness of the green beans.

⅓ cup finely chopped shallot
½ stick (¼ cup) unsalted butter
1 (14- to 15-oz) jar whole roasted chestnuts
½ cup chicken broth
¼ cup Sortilège maple liqueur or ¼ cup
   Canadian whiskey stirred together with
   1 tablespoon pure maple syrup
2 lb haricots verts or other thin green beans,
   trimmed

Cook shallot in 2 tablespoons butter in a 10-inch heavy skillet over moderate heat, stirring occasionally, until lightly browned, about 5 minutes. Add chestnuts, broth, and liqueur and simmer, swirling skillet occasionally, until liquid is evaporated and chestnuts are glazed, 3 to 5 minutes. Season with salt and pepper, then remove from heat and keep warm.
Cook beans in a 6- to 8-quart pot of boiling salted water (see Tips, page 8), uncovered, until crisp-tender, 4 to 5 minutes. Drain in a colander, then transfer beans with tongs to a large bowl of ice and cold water to stop cooking. Drain well.
Heat remaining 2 tablespoons butter in a 12-inch heavy skillet over moderately high heat until lightly browned. Add beans and toss until heated through, about 2 minutes. Season with salt and pepper.
Serve beans topped with chestnuts.

Cooks' notes:
• Chestnuts can be glazed 2 days ahead and chilled, covered. Stir in 3 tablespoons additional chicken broth or water and reheat over low heat.
• Haricots verts can be boiled 1 day ahead and chilled in a sealed plastic bag lined with paper towels. Bring to room temperature before proceeding.
PHOTO ON PAGE 102

EGGPLANT ROLLS WITH SPICY TOMATO SAUCE

Serves 4 (main course) or 8 (first course)
Active time: 45 min   Start to finish: 45 min

1 garlic clove, minced
¼ teaspoon dried hot red pepper flakes
7 tablespoons olive oil
1½ lb plum tomatoes, chopped
½ teaspoon sugar
1 teaspoon salt
1 (1¼-lb) eggplant
12½ oz ricotta (preferably fresh; 1½ cups)
1½ oz finely grated Parmigiano-Reggiano
   (½ cup; see Tips, page 8)
3 tablespoons finely chopped fresh basil
¼ teaspoon black pepper

Special equipment: a well-seasoned ridged grill
   pan or a gas grill (see cooks' note, below)

Make sauce:
Cook garlic and red pepper flakes in 1 tablespoon oil in a 2-quart heavy saucepan over moderate heat, stirring, until garlic is golden, about 30 seconds. Add tomatoes, sugar, and ½ teaspoon salt and simmer, uncovered, stirring occasionally, until slightly thickened, 15 to 20 minutes.
Grill eggplant while sauce cooks:
Heat grill pan over high heat until hot. Peel 2-inch-

wide strips of skin from opposite sides of eggplant and discard. Holding a knife parallel to a peeled side, cut eggplant lengthwise into 8 (⅓-inch-thick) slices.

Brush both sides of slices with 3 tablespoons oil (total), then season with salt and pepper.

Grill eggplant slices in batches, turning over once and brushing grilled sides with some of remaining oil, until golden brown and tender, about 4 minutes, then transfer to a tray.

Assemble eggplant rolls:

Stir together cheeses, 2 tablespoons basil, pepper, and remaining ½ teaspoon salt. Divide cheese mixture among slices (3 to 4 tablespoons per slice), leaving an ⅛-inch border along edge. Roll up each slice, beginning with a short end, and serve rolls topped with sauce and sprinkled with remaining tablespoon basil.

Cooks' note:
• Eggplant can be grilled using a gas grill. Preheat all burners on high, covered, 10 minutes, then reduce heat to medium. Grill eggplant on lightly oiled grill rack, covered with lid, turning over once, until tender and grill marks appear, 4 to 5 minutes total.

WILD MUSHROOM POTATO GRATIN

Serves 8
Active time: 45 min   Start to finish: 2 hr

For a more elegant presentation, we cut out rounds from the gratin with a 4-inch cookie cutter.

½ lb fresh wild or exotic mushrooms such as chanterelles or shiitakes (discard shiitake stems), trimmed and coarsely chopped
2½ tablespoons unsalted butter
¾ lb fresh cremini mushrooms, trimmed and sliced ¼ inch thick
1½ teaspoons minced garlic
3 lb russet (baking) potatoes
1½ cups heavy cream
1½ cups whole milk
1½ teaspoons salt
½ teaspoon white pepper
¼ teaspoon freshly grated nutmeg
2 oz finely grated Gruyère (1 cup)

Special equipment: a 15- by 10- by 2-inch oval gratin dish or other 3-qt shallow baking dish

Put oven rack in middle position and preheat oven to 400°F.

Cook chanterelles or shiitakes with salt and pepper to taste in 1 tablespoon butter in a large nonstick skillet over moderate heat, stirring, until liquid mushrooms give off is evaporated and mushrooms are tender, about 8 minutes, then transfer to a bowl. Cook cremini in remaining 1½ tablespoons butter in skillet, stirring, until liquid is evaporated and mushrooms are tender, about 8 minutes, then transfer to bowl with wild mushrooms. Toss mushrooms with 1 teaspoon garlic.

Peel potatoes and cut crosswise into ⅛-inch-thick slices (preferably with an adjustable-blade slicer). Bring potatoes, cream, milk, salt, white pepper, nutmeg, and remaining ½ teaspoon garlic to a boil in a 4- to 6-quart heavy pot, stirring once or twice, then remove pot from heat.

Butter gratin dish. Transfer half of potatoes to gratin dish with a slotted spoon, spreading evenly. Spread mushrooms evenly over potatoes, then top with remaining potatoes. Pour cooking liquid over potatoes and sprinkle with cheese.

Bake gratin until top is golden brown and potatoes are tender, 45 to 55 minutes. Let stand 10 minutes before serving.

Cooks' note:
• Instead of using ½ lb of 1 type of wild or exotic mushroom, you could use ¼ lb each of 2 types.
PHOTO ON PAGE 92

SAUTÉED KALE

Serves 1 (with leftovers)
Active time: 30 min   Start to finish: 30 min

1 lb kale, tough stems and center ribs
   discarded and leaves cut into 1-inch-wide
   strips (8 cups)
2 tablespoons olive oil
1 small red onion, halved lengthwise and
   thinly sliced crosswise
1 garlic clove, minced
   Pinch of dried hot red pepper flakes
1 tablespoon red-wine vinegar, or to taste
¼ teaspoon salt

Cook kale in a 6-quart pot of boiling salted water, uncovered, stirring occasionally, until just tender, about 10 minutes, then drain in a colander.

Heat oil in a 12-inch heavy skillet over moderately high heat until hot but not smoking, then sauté onion, stirring occasionally, until softened, 6 to 8 minutes. Add garlic and red pepper flakes and sauté, stirring, until garlic is fragrant, about 1 minute. Reduce heat to moderate, then add kale and cook, stirring occasionally, until heated through. Remove from heat and stir in vinegar and salt.

Cooks' note:
• Sautéed kale keeps, chilled in an airtight container, 3 days.

CREAMED PEARL ONIONS

Serves 8 to 10
Active time: 1¼ hr   Start to finish: 2 hr

3 lb white pearl onions
2 tablespoons unsalted butter
1 teaspoon sugar
¾ teaspoon salt
5 whole cloves
   About 4 cups water
½ cup heavy cream
¼ cup finely chopped fresh flat-leaf parsley

Blanch onions in a large pot of boiling water 2 minutes, then drain and peel.

Heat butter in a deep 12-inch heavy skillet over moderate heat until foam subsides, then cook onions,

stirring occasionally, until golden in patches, about 8 minutes. Add sugar, salt, cloves, and enough water to cover onions and simmer, covered, until onions are tender but not falling apart, 25 to 30 minutes. Boil onions, uncovered, until liquid is reduced to about ½ cup, about 20 minutes more.

Stir in cream and simmer, stirring, until slightly thickened, about 5 minutes. Discard cloves, then season with salt and pepper. Stir in parsley just before serving.

Cooks' notes:
• Onions can be blanched and peeled 2 days ahead and chilled, covered.
• Creamed pearl onions can be made 1 day ahead and chilled, covered. Reheat in a heavy saucepan over low heat, or in a microwave, stirring occasionally.

THREE PEA STIR-FRY

Serves 4 (side dish)
Active time: 30 min   Start to finish: 30 min

It may seem odd that we use frozen green peas, but, sadly, even the best fresh ones can taste starchy by the time they make it to the supermarket.

1 tablespoon vegetable oil
1 large garlic clove, minced
1 tablespoon finely chopped peeled
   fresh ginger
¼ teaspoon dried hot red pepper flakes
6 oz sugar snap peas, trimmed and cut
   diagonally into 1-inch pieces
6 oz snow peas, trimmed and cut
   diagonally into 1-inch pieces
1 cup frozen green peas
1 teaspoon soy sauce
1 teaspoon Asian sesame oil
1 tablespoon sesame seeds, toasted
   (see Tips, page 8)

Heat vegetable oil in a 12-inch nonstick skillet over moderately high heat until hot but not smoking, then stir-fry garlic, ginger, and red pepper flakes until fragrant, about 1 minute. Add sugar snaps and snow peas and stir-fry until crisp-tender, about 3 minutes. Add frozen peas and stir-fry until hot, about 2 minutes. Remove from heat, then stir in soy sauce and sesame oil. Sprinkle with sesame seeds and season with salt.

SNAP PEAS AND CARROTS

Serves 1
Active time: 15 min   Start to finish: 15 min

½ lb baby carrots (from 1 bunch), trimmed
  and peeled
¼ cup water
½ cup sugar snap peas, strings removed and
  snap peas halved lengthwise diagonally
1 tablespoon fresh orange juice
¼ teaspoon sugar
½ tablespoon unsalted butter

Special equipment: **parchment paper**

Put carrots, water, and salt and pepper to taste in
an 8-inch skillet, then cover with a round of buttered
parchment paper (buttered side down; parchment
should be touching carrots) and simmer until carrots are
crisp-tender, about 2 minutes. Remove parchment. Add
snap peas and increase heat to high, then cook until
peas are crisp-tender and liquid is reduced to about
1 teaspoon, about 1½ minutes. Add orange juice, sugar,
and butter, swirling skillet to coat carrots and peas, and
cook until liquid is reduced to a syrupy glaze, about
30 seconds. Season with salt and pepper.

PHOTO ON PAGE 111

POTATO AND PARMESAN CAKE

Serves 4 (side dish)
Active time: 15 min   Start to finish: 40 min

*These potatoes, oven-crisped on the outside and tender
inside, go especially well with red meat.*

2 tablespoons unsalted butter, melted
1 tablespoon extra-virgin olive oil
1 lb Yukon Gold potatoes
¾ teaspoon salt
¼ teaspoon black pepper
½ oz finely grated Parmigiano-Reggiano
  (¼ cup; see Tips, page 8)

Special equipment: **a Japanese Benriner or other
  adjustable-blade slicer**

Put oven rack in middle position and preheat oven
to 450°F.

Stir together butter and oil in a cup. Peel potatoes,
then thinly slice using slicer and toss with 2 tablespoons butter mixture, salt, and pepper in a large bowl.

Heat remaining butter mixture in a 10-inch heavy
ovenproof nonstick skillet over moderately high heat.
Spread one third of potatoes evenly in skillet. Toss
remaining potatoes with cheese and spread evenly over
first layer of potatoes in skillet, pressing with a spatula.
Cook 3 minutes, then transfer skillet to oven and roast,
uncovered, pressing top occasionally with spatula, until
potatoes are tender and top is starting to brown, 20 to
25 minutes.

Invert potato cake onto a cutting board and cut
into wedges.

GARLIC MASHED POTATOES

Serves 1
Active time: 10 min   Start to finish: 1 hr

*We roasted a whole head of garlic for this recipe even
though it's more than you need—the leftover cloves
can be used in a puréed soup, rubbed on bread, mixed
with green vegetables or a salad dressing, or mashed
with mayonnaise.*

1 head garlic, left unpeeled
1 teaspoon olive oil
1 large Yukon Gold potato (½ lb)
2 tablespoons half-and-half or milk
1 tablespoon unsalted butter

Put oven rack in middle position and preheat oven
to 450°F.

Cut off and discard top ½ inch of garlic head,
exposing cloves. Rub garlic all over with oil and season
with salt and pepper, then wrap tightly in foil. Roast
garlic until tender when center of a clove is pierced
with tip of a paring knife, about 40 minutes.

Peel potato and cut into 1-inch pieces, then cover
with cold salted water (see Tips, page 8) in a small
saucepan. Bring to a boil, then reduce heat and simmer,
uncovered, until potato is tender, 8 to 10 minutes. Pour
off water, then add half-and-half, butter, and 2 or
3 peeled roasted garlic cloves (reserve remaining roasted garlic for another use). Mash with a potato masher
to desired consistency and season with salt and pepper.

PHOTO ON PAGE 111

GARLIC ROASTED POTATOES

Serves 8
Active time: 15 min   Start to finish: 1½ hr

Do not use a dark aluminum baking pan (including nonstick) for this recipe because the potatoes will burn (see Tips, page 8).

3 tablespoons olive oil
1 tablespoon minced garlic
4½ lb large yellow-fleshed potatoes such as
   Yukon Gold
1 teaspoon kosher salt

Put oven rack in lower third of oven and preheat oven to 375°F.

Stir together oil and garlic in a large bowl. Peel potatoes and diagonally cut crosswise into ½-inch-thick slices, discarding ends. Toss slices with garlic oil, then arrange in 1 layer in a large shallow baking pan (1 inch deep) and sprinkle with kosher salt.

Roast potato slices until undersides are golden brown and crisp, about 1 hour. Turn potatoes over with a metal spatula and roast until tender, about 15 minutes more.

Season potatoes with salt and transfer, crusted sides up, to a platter.

PHOTO ON PAGE 63

SALT ROASTED POTATOES

Serves 1
Active time: 5 min   Start to finish: 40 min

2 teaspoons olive oil (preferably extra-virgin)
½ teaspoon kosher salt
½ lb small (1½-inch) white or Yukon Gold
   potatoes (about 5), scrubbed well

Put oven rack in middle position and preheat oven to 425°F.

Stir together oil and kosher salt in a small shallow baking dish or pie plate. Add potatoes and rub with oil mixture to coat.

Roast potatoes until tender when pierced with a sharp paring knife, 30 to 35 minutes.

PHOTO ON PAGE 110

POTATO PARSNIP PURÉE

Serves 8 to 10
Active time: 30 min   Start to finish: 1½ hr

2 lb parsnips, peeled and cut into 1-inch
   pieces
2 lb russet (baking) potatoes, peeled and cut
   into 2-inch pieces
1 tablespoon plus ½ teaspoon salt
1 cup heavy cream
½ stick (¼ cup) unsalted butter
¼ teaspoon black pepper

Special equipment: **a potato ricer or a food mill
   fitted with medium disk**

Cover parsnips and potatoes with cold water by 1 inch in a 6- to 8-quart pot, then add 1 tablespoon salt and bring to a boil, partially covered. Reduce heat and simmer vegetables, partially covered, until very tender but not falling apart, 30 to 40 minutes.

Meanwhile, bring cream, butter, pepper, and remaining ½ teaspoon salt to a simmer in 4-quart heavy saucepan over moderate heat.

Drain vegetables in a colander, then force warm vegetables through ricer into cream mixture. Stir to combine well.

Cooks' note:
• Potato parsnip purée can be made 1 day ahead and chilled in a baking dish, covered. Bring to room temperature and reheat, covered, in a preheated 450°F oven until hot, about 20 minutes, or in a microwave.

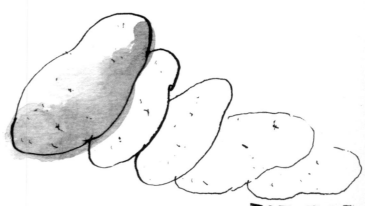

POTATOES

SCALLOPED BUTTERNUT SQUASH

Serves 8
Active time: 40 min   Start to finish: 1½ hr

This recipe is based on a delicious dish made by Laura DaMiano, a Quebecois chef. She loves the flavor of butternut squash paired with Oka cheese, a mild, semisoft cow's-milk cheese. Mild Cheddar can be used as a substitute.

1 teaspoon salt
Rounded ¼ teaspoon black pepper
5½ to 6 lb butternut squash
5 oz Oka cheese or mild Cheddar, rind discarded and cheese coarsely grated on large holes of a box grater (1⅓ cups)
1½ cups heavy cream
3 fresh thyme sprigs

Special equipment: **a Japanese Benriner or other adjustable-blade slicer; parchment paper; a 2½-inch round cookie cutter (optional)**

Put oven rack in lower third of oven and preheat oven to 350°F. Generously butter a 13- by 9-inch glass baking dish (3-quart capacity).

Stir together salt and pepper in a small bowl. Cut off necks of squash, reserving bottoms for another use (you will have about 3 pounds necks). Peel squash and very thinly slice crosswise with slicer.

Layer one third of squash slices, overlapping, in baking dish and sprinkle with some of salt and pepper mixture. Sprinkle with half of cheese, then layer half of remaining squash slices on top and sprinkle with some of salt and pepper mixture. Top with remaining cheese and remaining squash slices, then sprinkle with remaining salt and pepper.

Bring cream and thyme sprigs to a simmer in a small saucepan over moderate heat. Discard thyme and pour cream evenly over squash. Put a sheet of parchment paper on surface of squash and poke a few holes in parchment with a knife. Bake squash until tender, about 45 minutes.

Discard parchment and let squash stand 10 minutes before serving. If desired, cut rounds from squash with cookie cutter and transfer to plates with a spatula.

Cooks' note:
• Squash can be baked (but not cut into rounds) 2 days ahead and cooled, uncovered, then chilled, covered. If

cutting rounds, cut them out while gratin is cold, then transfer to a buttered baking sheet and reheat in lower third of a preheated 350°F oven 15 minutes. If leaving gratin whole, reheat in middle of a 350°F oven 25 minutes.

PHOTO ON PAGE 103

GRILLED SCALLIONS WITH LEMON

Serves 4
Active time: 10 min   Start to finish: 40 min
(includes soaking skewers)

12 large scallions (10 oz total), trimmed, leaving most of greens attached
½ teaspoon olive oil
¼ teaspoon salt
⅛ teaspoon black pepper
½ lemon

Special equipment: **2 (8-inch) wooden skewers, soaked in water for 30 minutes**

Prepare grill for cooking. If using a charcoal grill, open vents on bottom of grill, then light charcoal. Charcoal fire is hot when you can hold your hand 5 inches above rack for 1 to 2 seconds. If using a gas grill, preheat burners on high, covered, 10 minutes.

Toss scallions with oil, salt, and pepper in a large bowl. Line up scallions side by side on a work surface and thread skewers, 1 at a time, crosswise through all scallions to form a solid rectangle. (Skewers should be inserted about 2 inches from each end.)

Grill scallions on lightly oiled grill rack, uncovered, turning over once or twice, until softened and charred in patches, 4 to 5 minutes total. Transfer scallions to a platter and squeeze lemon evenly over them, then remove skewers.

Cooks' note:
• If you aren't able to grill outdoors, cook scallions (without skewers) in a hot lightly oiled well-seasoned ridged grill pan over moderately high heat.

Each serving about 52 calories and 1 gram fat

GARLIC CREAMED SPINACH

Serves 1
Active time: 10 min   Start to finish: 10 min

¼ cup water
5 oz baby spinach (6 cups)
3 tablespoons heavy cream
1 garlic clove, lightly smashed and peeled
  Scant ⅛ teaspoon freshly grated nutmeg
⅛ teaspoon salt
⅛ teaspoon black pepper

Bring water to a boil in a 2-quart heavy saucepan over moderate heat, then add spinach in handfuls and cook, tossing, until wilted, 2 to 3 minutes. Transfer to a sieve set over a bowl and press on spinach with back of a wooden spoon to remove excess liquid. Discard liquid.

Add cream, garlic, nutmeg, salt, and pepper to saucepan and boil until reduced to 1 tablespoon, about 2 minutes. Discard garlic and add spinach to cream mixture, tossing until coated and heated through.

PHOTO ON PAGE 110

MOLASSES HORSERADISH SWEET-POTATO SPEARS

Serves 8 to 10
Active time: 25 min   Start to finish: 45 min

We strongly recommend using light-colored metal (including nonstick) shallow baking pans (1 large or 2 small) for this recipe. When we used dark baking pans, the potatoes blackened before they were completely cooked through.

3 lb medium sweet potatoes, peeled and each
  cut lengthwise into 8 spears
¼ cup vegetable oil
1¼ teaspoons salt
5 tablespoons unsalted butter
⅓ cup molasses (not robust or blackstrap)
⅓ cup bottled horseradish (including
  juice; 3 oz)

Put oven rack in lower third of oven and preheat oven to 450°F.

If potato spears are very long, halve them diagonally. Toss potatoes with oil and ¾ teaspoon salt in a large bowl, then spread in 1 layer in a large shallow baking pan (1 inch deep). Roast, turning once or twice, until tender, 18 to 22 minutes. (Leave oven on.)

While potatoes roast, bring butter, molasses, horseradish (with juice), and remaining ½ teaspoon salt to a boil in a small heavy saucepan, stirring, then reduce heat and simmer, stirring occasionally, until slightly thickened and reduced to about ¾ cup, about 5 minutes.

Transfer mixture to a blender and purée 30 seconds (use caution when blending hot liquids). Pour glaze through a fine-mesh sieve into a heatproof bowl, pressing on and discarding solids. Drizzle glaze over cooked sweet potatoes and gently toss until coated.

Just before serving, bake glazed sweet potatoes until hot, 3 to 5 minutes.

Cooks' note:
• Sweet potatoes can be roasted 2 hours ahead. Toss with glaze and reheat just before serving.
PHOTO ON PAGES 96 AND 97

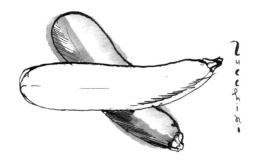

MASHED SWEET POTATOES WITH SAGE BUTTER

Serves 4
Active time: 15 min   Start to finish: 35 min

1½ lb sweet potatoes (2 large), peeled and cut
  into ½-inch pieces
½ teaspoon salt
3 tablespoons unsalted butter, softened
2 teaspoons chopped fresh sage

Cover sweet potatoes with water in a 2-quart heavy saucepan and add salt. Cook, covered, over moderately high heat until tender, 15 to 20 minutes. Reserve ¼ cup cooking liquid, then drain sweet potatoes in a colander. Transfer sweet potatoes and reserved cooking liquid to a bowl and mash with a potato masher.

Mash together butter, sage, and salt and pepper to taste, then stir half of sage butter into sweet potatoes. Serve potatoes topped with remaining sage butter.

ROASTED TOMATOES

Serves 4
Active time: 5 min   Start to finish: 1¼ hr

4 large plum tomatoes (1 lb), trimmed and halved lengthwise
½ teaspoon salt
¼ teaspoon black pepper

Put oven rack in middle position and preheat oven to 375°F.

Arrange tomatoes, cut sides up, in 1 layer in an 8- to 9-inch glass baking dish and sprinkle with salt and pepper.

Roast until skins are wrinkled and beginning to brown, about 50 minutes. Keep warm, covered with foil, until ready to serve.

Each serving (2 tomato halves) about 22 calories and less than 1 gram fat

FRIED BABY ZUCCHINI WITH CHEESE-STUFFED BLOSSOMS

Serves 4
Active time: 25 min   Start to finish: 35 min

The myzithra *cheese often used to stuff zucchini blossoms in Greece comes in two forms: soft and dried salted. We substituted fresh ricotta for the soft one with very good results. We've also given ricotta salata as an alternative for the salted* myzithra.

12 baby zucchini with blossoms attached
⅔ cup whole-milk ricotta (preferably fresh)
2 oz coarsely grated salted *myzithra* cheese or ricotta salata (⅔ cup)
1 large egg yolk
½ teaspoon dried oregano, crumbled
About 1 cup extra-virgin olive oil

Special equipment: **a deep-fat thermometer**

Keeping blossoms attached to zucchini, carefully open blossoms and remove pistil from each. Trim stem ends of zucchini, then, beginning ¼ inch from blossom end, cut a 2-inch slit lengthwise through center of each zucchini, ending ¼ inch from stem end (slits will help zucchini cook evenly).

Stir together cheeses, yolk, and oregano in a small bowl until combined well, then season with pepper. Gently open each blossom and fill with 1 to 2 rounded teaspoons of cheese mixture (depending on blossom size), then gently twist end of blossom to enclose filling. (You may have leftover filling.)

Heat ⅓ inch oil in a 10-inch heavy skillet until it registers 360°F on thermometer (see cooks' note, below), then fry zucchini (with blossoms attached) in 2 batches, turning once, until golden, 1 to 2 minutes per batch. Transfer with tongs to paper towels to drain. (Return oil to 360°F between batches.) Serve zucchini warm or at room temperature.

Cooks' note:
• **To take the temperature of a shallow amount of oil, put bulb in skillet and turn thermometer facedown, resting end against edge of skillet. Check temperature frequently.**
PHOTO ON PAGE 73

SAUTÉED ZUCCHINI RIBBONS

Serves 4
Active time: 25 min   Start to finish: 25 min

2 lb medium zucchini (4)
2 tablespoons olive oil
1 garlic clove, smashed
½ teaspoon salt
¼ teaspoon black pepper
2 teaspoons finely grated fresh lemon zest

Special equipment: **a Japanese Benriner or other adjustable-blade slicer**

Cut zucchini lengthwise into ⅛-inch-thick slices with slicer. Heat 1 tablespoon oil in a 12-inch heavy skillet over moderately high heat until hot but not smoking, then sauté garlic, stirring, until golden, about 2 minutes. Discard garlic with a slotted spoon.

Add half of zucchini to garlic oil and sauté, turning and stirring frequently, until just tender but not golden, about 5 minutes. Sprinkle with ¼ teaspoon salt and ⅛ teaspoon pepper. Transfer to a platter using tongs.

Heat remaining tablespoon oil over moderately high heat, then sauté and season remaining zucchini in same manner and transfer to platter. Sprinkle zucchini with zest and toss gently using tongs.

RATATOUILLE

Serves 8 to 10 (side dish)
Active time: 50 min   Start to finish: 2 hr

2½ lb tomatoes (4 large)
  8 large garlic cloves, thinly sliced
  1 cup chopped fresh flat-leaf parsley
 20 fresh basil leaves, torn in half
  1 cup plus 2 tablespoons extra-virgin olive oil
  2 lb eggplant, cut into 1-inch cubes
2¼ teaspoons salt
  2 large onions (1½ lb total), quartered
     lengthwise and thinly sliced crosswise
  3 assorted bell peppers (green, red, and/or
     yellow; 1½ lb total), cut into 1-inch pieces
  4 medium zucchini (2 lb), quartered
     lengthwise and cut crosswise into
     ¾-inch-thick pieces
  ½ teaspoon black pepper

Garnish: **Parmigiano-Reggiano shavings and
    fresh basil**

Cut an X in bottom of each tomato with a sharp paring knife and blanch together in a 4-quart pot of boiling water 1 minute. Transfer tomatoes with a slotted spoon to a cutting board and, when cool enough to handle, peel off skin, beginning from scored end, with paring knife.

Coarsely chop tomatoes and transfer to a 5-quart heavy pot with garlic, parsley, basil, and ⅓ cup oil. Simmer, partially covered, stirring occasionally, until tomatoes break down and sauce is slightly thickened, about 30 minutes.

While sauce simmers, toss eggplant with ½ teaspoon salt in a large colander and let stand in sink 30 minutes.

Meanwhile, cook onions in 3 tablespoons oil with ¼ teaspoon salt in a 12-inch heavy skillet over moderate heat, stirring occasionally, until softened, 10 to 12 minutes. Transfer onions with a slotted spoon to a large bowl, then add 3 tablespoons oil to skillet and cook bell peppers with ¼ teaspoon salt over moderate heat, stirring occasionally, until softened, about 10 minutes. Transfer peppers with slotted spoon to bowl with onions. Add 3 tablespoons oil to skillet and cook zucchini with ¼ teaspoon salt over moderate heat, stirring occasionally, until just tender, 6 to 8 minutes. Transfer zucchini with slotted spoon to bowl with vegetables.

While zucchini cook, pat eggplant cubes dry. Add remaining oil (about ¼ cup) to skillet and cook eggplant over moderate heat, stirring occasionally, until softened, 10 to 12 minutes.

Add vegetables, remaining teaspoon salt, and black pepper to tomato sauce and simmer, covered, stirring occasionally, until vegetables are very tender, about 1 hour. Cool, uncovered, and serve warm or at room temperature.

Cooks' note:
• Ratatouille can be made 2 days ahead and chilled, covered. Bring to room temperature or reheat before serving.

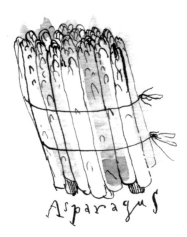

Asparagus

SPRING VEGETABLE SAUTÉ

Serves 8
Active time: 40 min   Start to finish: 40 min

  ½ lb fresh or 2 oz dried morel mushrooms
     (preferably small)
  2 lb fresh fava beans, shelled (2 cups)
  ½ stick (¼ cup) unsalted butter, softened
1½ lb thin asparagus, cut diagonally into
     1½-inch pieces
  1 lb sugar snap peas, trimmed
  4 bunches scallions (white and pale green
     parts only), trimmed and cut into
     2½-inch lengths
  2 tablespoons chopped fresh mint

If using dried morels, soak in warm water to cover 30 minutes. Agitate fresh or dried morels in water to dislodge grit, then lift from water, squeezing out excess, and pat dry with paper towels. Whether using fresh or dried, leave small morels whole and halve or quarter larger ones.

Cook beans in a 4-quart saucepan of boiling salted water (see Tips, page 8) 3 minutes, then transfer with a slotted spoon or skimmer to a colander and rinse under cold water. Peel skins from beans with your fingers. (Keep water simmering, covered.)

Heat 2 tablespoons butter in a 12-inch nonstick skillet over moderately high heat until foam subsides, then sauté morels, stirring, until tender, about 4 minutes. Season with salt and pepper. Remove from heat and let stand, covered.

Return water in saucepan to a boil, then cook asparagus, sugar snaps, and scallions until crisp-tender, 1½ to 2 minutes. Add beans and immediately drain well in colander. Add vegetables and remaining 2 tablespoons butter to morels and toss to combine. Stir in mint and salt and pepper to taste and serve immediately.

Cooks' notes:
• Dried morels can be soaked and patted dry 1 day ahead and chilled, covered.
• Fava beans can be cooked and peeled 1 day ahead and chilled, covered.
• Be aware that fava beans can cause a potentially fatal reaction in some people of Mediterranean, African, and Pacific Rim descent.
• Asparagus, sugar snaps, and scallions can be trimmed and cut 1 day ahead and chilled in sealed plastic bags lined with dampened paper towels.

PHOTO ON PAGE 63

beans

BLACK BEANS WITH CILANTRO

Serves 4
Active time: 10 min   Start to finish: 2 hr

¼ lb dried black beans (⅔ cup), picked over and rinsed
1 small onion, finely chopped (½ cup)
2 fresh cilantro sprigs
½ tablespoon olive oil
6 cups cold water
¼ teaspoon salt, or to taste

Bring beans, onion, cilantro sprigs, oil, and water to a boil in a 2-quart heavy saucepan. Reduce heat and simmer, partially covered, until beans are just tender, about 1¼ hours. Add salt and simmer, uncovered, until liquid is evaporated to just below level of beans. Season with salt and discard cilantro sprigs.

Cooks' notes:
• If you don't have time to cook dried beans, rinse and drain a 19-ounce can of cooked black beans. Cook onion in oil in a small heavy skillet over moderately low heat, stirring, until softened, then stir in beans, cilantro, salt, and ¼ cup water and simmer, stirring, until beans are heated through.
• Beans can be cooked 1 day ahead and cooled, uncovered, then chilled, covered. Reheat beans before serving.

Each serving about 135 calories and 2 grams fat
PHOTO ON PAGE 106

BLACK-EYED PEAS WITH DILL

Serves 4
Active time: 10 min   Start to finish: 1¼ hr

2 cups water
2 fresh dill sprigs plus 2 tablespoons chopped dill leaves
2 large scallions, white and pale green parts cut into 1-inch pieces and dark green parts chopped
½ teaspoon salt
¼ cup extra-virgin olive oil
1 (10-oz) package frozen black-eyed peas

Accompaniment: lemon wedges

Bring water, dill sprigs, white and pale green parts of scallions, salt, and 2 tablespoons oil to a boil in a 2-quart heavy saucepan, covered. Reduce heat to moderately low, then add peas and simmer, covered, stirring occasionally, until peas are tender, 30 to 35 minutes.

Cool, uncovered, then transfer mixture with any liquid to a serving dish and stir in chopped dill, scallion greens, and remaining 2 tablespoons oil.

Cooks' note:
• Black-eyed peas can be cooked, cooled, and dressed 1 day ahead and chilled, covered. Bring to room temperature before serving.

PHOTO ON PAGE 73

BABY LIMA BEANS AND CORN IN CHIVE CREAM

Serves 6 to 8 (side dish)
Active time: 15 min   Start to finish: 30 min

4 bacon slices, cut crosswise into
    ½-inch-wide pieces
1 medium onion, chopped
1 green bell pepper, cut into ½-inch dice
1 (10-oz) package frozen baby lima beans
1 (10-oz) package frozen corn kernels
1 cup water
½ teaspoon salt
¼ teaspoon black pepper
½ cup heavy cream
2 tablespoons chopped fresh chives
1 tablespoon chopped fresh flat leaf parsley

Cook bacon in a 10-inch nonstick skillet over moderate heat, stirring occasionally, until crisp. Transfer bacon with a slotted spoon to paper towels to drain, then cook onion and bell pepper in fat in skillet over moderate heat, stirring frequently, until vegetables are softened, 5 to 6 minutes.

Add lima beans, corn, water, salt, and pepper, then simmer, covered, until vegetables are tender, about 8 minutes. Increase heat to high and add cream, then boil, uncovered, until liquid is reduced by about half, 7 to 10 minutes. Stir in herbs and salt to taste. Serve sprinkled with bacon.

GREEK-STYLE LIMA BEANS

Serves 4
Active time: 10 min   Start to finish: 30 min

Serve these beans with bread to sop up the juices.

1 (10-oz) package frozen baby lima beans
1 cup water
3 tablespoons extra-virgin olive oil
2 tablespoons chopped fresh flat-leaf parsley
1 tablespoon minced garlic
½ teaspoon salt

Cook lima beans, water, 2 tablespoons oil, 1 tablespoon parsley, garlic, and salt in a 2-quart heavy saucepan, tightly covered, over moderate heat, stirring occasionally, until beans are tender, 17 to 20 minutes.

Season with salt and pepper and transfer to a bowl. Serve sprinkled with remaining tablespoon parsley and drizzled with remaining tablespoon oil.

GRILLED TOFU AND SAUTÉED ASIAN GREENS

Serves 2 (main course)
Active time: 25 min   Start to finish: 25 min

Pressing excess moisture out of your tofu will increase its firmness and its ability to absorb the marinade.

1 (14-oz) block firm tofu, drained
¼ cup low-sodium soy sauce
1 teaspoon Asian sesame oil
1½ teaspoons packed dark brown sugar
1½ teaspoons finely grated peeled fresh ginger
1 small garlic clove, minced
¼ teaspoon Tabasco or dried hot red
    pepper flakes
1 tablespoon plus 1 teaspoon vegetable oil
2 (5-oz) bags Asian greens or baby spinach

Cut tofu crosswise into 6 slices. Arrange in 1 layer on a triple layer of paper towels and top with another triple layer of towels. Weight with a shallow baking pan or baking sheet and let stand 2 minutes. Repeat weighting with dry paper towels 2 more times.

Stir together soy sauce, sesame oil, brown sugar, ginger, garlic, Tabasco, and 1 tablespoon vegetable oil in a glass pie plate. Add tofu in 1 layer and marinate, turning over every couple of minutes, 8 minutes total.

Heat a lightly oiled well-seasoned ridged grill pan over moderately high heat until hot but not smoking. Lift tofu from marinade with a slotted spatula (reserve marinade) and grill, turning over once carefully with spatula, until grill marks appear and tofu is heated through, 4 to 6 minutes total.

While tofu grills, heat remaining teaspoon vegetable oil in a 12-inch skillet over moderately high heat until hot but not smoking, then sauté greens, tossing with tongs, until beginning to wilt. Add reserved marinade and sauté, tossing, until greens are just wilted, about 1 minute. Lift greens from skillet with tongs, letting excess marinade drip off, and divide between 2 plates.

Serve greens with tofu slices.

SALADS

main course salads

CHICKEN SALAD WITH GRAPES AND WALNUTS

Serves 4 to 6
Active time: 35 min   Start to finish: 35 min

4 cups cubed (½ inch) cooked chicken (1¾ lb)
1 cup walnuts, toasted (see Tips, page 8) and chopped
1 celery rib, cut into ¼-inch-thick slices
2 tablespoons finely chopped shallot
2 cups halved seedless red grapes
¾ cup mayonnaise
3 tablespoons tarragon vinegar
2 tablespoons finely chopped fresh tarragon
½ teaspoon salt
½ teaspoon black pepper

Toss together all ingredients in a large bowl until combined well.

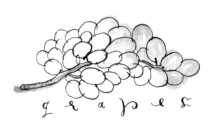

CHICKEN AND WILD RICE SALAD

Serves 4 to 6
Active time: 30 min   Start to finish: 1½ hr

4 cups water
1 cup wild rice
1½ teaspoons salt, or to taste
½ cup plus 2 tablespoons olive oil
¼ cup Sherry vinegar
2 tablespoons Dijon mustard
½ teaspoon black pepper
4 cups cubed (½ inch) cooked chicken (1¾ lb)
2 celery ribs, cut into ¼-inch-thick slices
1 medium red onion, finely chopped (1 cup)
2 Granny Smith apples, cut into ½-inch cubes

Bring water to a boil in a 2-quart heavy saucepan, then add rice and 1 teaspoon salt. Reduce heat to low and cook, covered, until rice is tender and most grains are split open, 1 to 1¼ hours. Drain well and cool.

Whisk together oil, vinegar, mustard, remaining ½ teaspoon salt, and pepper.

Combine rice with remaining ingredients in a large bowl, then gently toss with vinaigrette.

THAI-STYLE CRAB SALAD IN PAPAYA

Serves 4 (light main course)
Active time: 20 min   Start to finish: 20 min

Look for Gold or Strawberry papayas. Their sweet flavor complements this tangy crab salad beautifully.

¼ cup rice vinegar (not seasoned)
3 tablespoons sugar
2 tablespoons water
4 teaspoons Asian fish sauce
½ teaspoon salt
½ cup chopped green bell pepper
½ cup chopped red bell pepper
1½ teaspoons minced fresh *serrano* chile (including seeds)
2 tablespoons chopped fresh cilantro
½ lb jumbo lump crabmeat, picked over
2 ripe small papayas, halved lengthwise and seeded

Accompaniment: **lime wedges**

Whisk together vinegar, sugar, water, fish sauce, and salt in a bowl until sugar is dissolved. Add bell peppers, chile, cilantro, and crabmeat and toss gently to combine.

Serve crab salad mounded in papaya halves.

ISLAND PORK TENDERLOIN SALAD

Serves 6 to 8 (main course)
Active time: 1¼ hr   Start to finish: 1¼ hr

For pork
2 teaspoons salt
½ teaspoon black pepper
1 teaspoon ground cumin
1 teaspoon chili powder
1 teaspoon cinnamon
2 pork tenderloins (2¼ to 2½ lb total)
2 tablespoons olive oil
For glaze
1 cup packed dark brown sugar
2 tablespoons finely chopped garlic
1 tablespoon Tabasco
For vinaigrette
3 tablespoons fresh lime juice
1 tablespoon fresh orange juice
1 tablespoon Dijon mustard
1 teaspoon curry powder, toasted
    (see Tips, page 8)
½ teaspoon salt
¼ teaspoon black pepper
½ cup olive oil
For salad
3 navel oranges
5 oz baby spinach, trimmed (6 cups)
4 cups thinly sliced Napa cabbage
    (from 1 medium head)
1 red bell pepper, cut lengthwise into thin
    strips
½ cup golden raisins
2 firm-ripe California avocados

Special equipment: **an instant-read thermometer**

Prepare pork:
Put oven rack in middle position and preheat oven to 350°F.
Stir together salt, pepper, cumin, chili powder, and cinnamon, then coat pork with spice rub.
Heat oil in an ovenproof 12-inch heavy skillet over moderately high heat until just beginning to smoke, then brown pork, turning, about 4 minutes total. Leave pork in skillet.
Make glaze and roast pork:
Stir together brown sugar, garlic, and Tabasco and pat onto top of each tenderloin. Roast until thermome-ter inserted diagonally in center of each tenderloin registers 140°F, about 20 minutes. Let pork stand in skillet 10 minutes. (Temperature will rise to about 155°F while standing.)
Make vinaigrette while pork roasts:
Whisk together juices, mustard, curry powder, salt, and pepper, then add oil in a stream, whisking until emulsified.
Prepare salad ingredients while pork stands:
Cut peel, including white pith, from oranges with a sharp knife, then cut oranges crosswise into ¼-inch-thick slices. Toss spinach, cabbage, bell pepper, and raisins in a large bowl with about ¼ cup vinaigrette. Halve, pit, and peel avocados, then cut diagonally into ¼-inch-thick slices.
Assemble salad:
Cut pork at a 45-degree angle into ½-inch-thick slices. Line a large platter with dressed salad and arrange sliced pork, oranges, and avocados in rows on top. Drizzle some vinaigrette over avocados and oranges. Pour any juices from skillet over pork.

PHOTO ON PAGE 109

THAI-STYLE TOMATO AND SHRIMP SALAD

Serves 4 to 6
Active time: 45 min   Start to finish: 45 min

If you can't find Thai anise basil and Thai lemon basil, you can substitute Italian basil and lemon balm (the latter is available at farmers markets and specialty produce stores).

1 lb large shrimp in shell
    (21 to 25 per lb), peeled
2 limes
3 small fresh lemongrass stalks,
    1 or 2 outer leaves discarded
2 tablespoons fresh lime juice
¼ cup finely chopped red bell pepper
3 scallions, sliced crosswise ¼ inch thick
2 (3-inch) fresh green chiles such as Thai
    or *serrano*, minced (including seeds)
3 to 4 teaspoons Asian fish sauce
1 tablespoon sugar
½ teaspoon salt
2 lb beefsteak tomatoes, cut into
    1-inch wedges
¾ lb cucumbers, peeled and cut into
    1-inch pieces

½ cup loosely packed fresh Thai anise
    basil leaves
½ cup loosely packed fresh Thai lemon
    basil leaves
½ cup loosely packed fresh cilantro leaves

Cook shrimp in a 4-quart saucepan of boiling salted water (see Tips, page 8) until just cooked through, 1 to 2 minutes, then drain in a colander and cool.

Cut peel and white pith from limes with a sharp knife and discard. Cut lime segments free from membranes, then finely chop enough segments to measure ¼ cup. Mince enough lemongrass from bottom 6 inches of stalks to measure 2 tablespoons total.

Stir together chopped lime, minced lemongrass, lime juice, bell pepper, scallions, chiles, fish sauce (to taste), sugar, and salt until sugar is dissolved. Toss shrimp, tomatoes, and cucumbers with dressing and top with herbs.

STEAK SALAD WITH SHALLOTS AND RED WINE

Serves 4
Active time: 30 min   Start to finish: 30 min

1½ teaspoons salt
 1 teaspoon black pepper
½ teaspoon ground cumin
 2 (1½-inch-thick) boneless top loin steaks
    (10 oz each)
 2 tablespoons olive oil
½ lb large shallots, thinly sliced lengthwise
    (2 cups)
½ cup dry red wine
¼ cup red-wine vinegar
 1 tablespoon packed dark brown sugar
 3 tablespoons unsalted butter
 1 head escarole (1 lb), torn into 1-inch
    pieces (6 cups)

Special equipment: **an instant-read thermometer**

Stir together salt, pepper, and cumin in a small bowl. Pat steaks dry and sprinkle spice mixture evenly on both sides, rubbing to adhere.

Heat oil in a 10- to 12-inch heavy skillet over moderate heat until hot but not smoking, then cook steaks, turning over once, until thermometer inserted horizontally into a steak registers 115°F, about 12 minutes total. Transfer steaks to a cutting board and let stand, loosely covered, 10 minutes. (Beef will continue to cook as it stands.)

Add shallots to skillet and cook over moderate heat, stirring frequently, until just softened, about 3 minutes. Stir in wine, vinegar, and brown sugar and cook 3 minutes. Add butter and cook, whisking constantly, until butter is incorporated and sauce is slightly thickened. Pour any meat juices accumulated on cutting board into sauce.

Cut steaks into ¼-inch slices and serve over escarole. Spoon shallots and sauce over steak.

Shrimp

SMOKED-TROUT AND WHITE BEAN SALAD

Serves 4 (main course)
Active time: 10 min   Start to finish: 20 min

 5 tablespoons extra-virgin olive oil
 3 tablespoons minced shallot
¼ teaspoon finely grated fresh lemon zest
 2 tablespoons fresh lemon juice
½ teaspoon salt
¼ teaspoon black pepper
 1 (15- to 19-oz) can white beans, rinsed
    and drained
 2 smoked-trout fillets (½ lb total),
    skinned and flaked
 1 bunch watercress (6 oz), tough stems
    discarded
 1 head Bibb lettuce, torn into bite-size pieces

Bring oil, shallot, zest, juice, salt, and pepper to a simmer in a 2-quart heavy saucepan, then stir in beans. Remove from heat and let stand, uncovered, 10 minutes for beans to absorb flavor.

Toss together trout, watercress, lettuce, and bean mixture in a serving bowl.

GRILLED TUNA SALADE NIÇOISE

Serves 6
Active time: 1 hr   Start to finish: 1½ hr

For dressing
¼ cup red-wine vinegar
2½ tablespoons minced shallot
2 teaspoons Dijon mustard
1 large garlic clove, minced and mashed to
　　a paste with ½ teaspoon salt
　Rounded ½ teaspoon anchovy paste
1 cup extra-virgin olive oil
1½ teaspoons minced fresh thyme
1½ tablespoons finely chopped fresh basil
　For salad
¾ lb green beans (preferably *haricots verts*),
　　trimmed
1½ lb small (1- to 2-inch) potatoes (preferably
　　Yukon Gold)
1½ lb (1-inch-thick) tuna steaks
　Vegetable oil for brushing
¼ cup drained bottled capers
¾ lb Boston lettuce (2 heads), leaves separated
　　and large ones torn into pieces
1 pt cherry or grape tomatoes
⅔ cup Niçoise or other small brine-cured
　　black olives
4 hard-boiled large eggs, quartered
3 tablespoons finely chopped fresh flat-leaf
　　parsley and/or basil

Make dressing:
Whisk together vinegar, shallot, mustard, garlic paste, and anchovy paste in a small bowl until combined well, then add oil in a slow stream, whisking until emulsified. Whisk in thyme, basil, and salt and pepper to taste.

Make salad:
Cook beans in a 4- to 6-quart pot of boiling salted water (see Tips, page 8), uncovered, until crisp-tender, 3 to 4 minutes, then immediately transfer with a slotted spoon to a bowl of ice and cold water to stop cooking. Add potatoes to boiling water and simmer, uncovered, until tender, 15 to 20 minutes, then drain in a colander. Halve potatoes while still warm (peel if desired) and toss with 2 tablespoons dressing in a bowl, then cool.

Prepare grill for cooking. If using a charcoal grill, open vents on bottom of grill, then light charcoal. Charcoal fire is medium-hot when you can hold your hand 5 inches above rack for 3 to 4 seconds. If using a gas grill, preheat burners on high, covered, 10 minutes, then reduce heat to moderately high.

Brush tuna with oil and season with salt and pepper, then grill on lightly oiled rack, uncovered, turning over once, until browned on outside but still pink in center, 6 to 8 minutes total. Let tuna stand 3 minutes, then break into large (3-inch) pieces. Transfer tuna to a large platter and drizzle with 2 to 3 tablespoons dressing and top with capers.

Transfer potatoes to platter with tuna, reserving bowl. Drain beans and pat dry. Toss beans in bowl with 1 tablespoon dressing and salt and pepper to taste, then transfer to platter. Toss lettuce leaves in bowl with 2 tablespoons dressing and salt and pepper to taste, then transfer to platter. Toss cherry tomatoes in bowl with 1 tablespoon dressing and salt and pepper to taste, then transfer to a serving platter.

Arrange olives and eggs on platter and sprinkle salad with parsley and/or basil. Serve salad with remaining dressing on the side.

Cooks' notes:
• If you're unable to grill outdoors, tuna can be cooked in a hot lightly oiled well-seasoned ridged grill pan.
• Beans and potatoes can be cooked 1 hour ahead and kept at room temperature. Toss potatoes with dressing while warm and let stand. Do not dress beans until just before serving.

PHOTO ON PAGE 108

LAYERED TACO SALAD

Serves 6
Active time: 45 min   Start to finish: 45 min

For dressing
¼ cup fresh lime juice
½ cup chopped fresh cilantro
1 teaspoon sugar
1 tablespoon chili powder
¼ teaspoon ground cumin
½ teaspoon salt
¼ teaspoon black pepper
½ cup olive oil
　For beef
1 medium onion, chopped
3 garlic cloves, finely chopped
1 to 2 fresh *serrano* chiles, finely chopped
　　(including seeds)

1 tablespoon chili powder
2 teaspoons ground cumin
2 tablespoons olive oil
1½ lb ground chuck
1 (8-oz) can tomato sauce
½ teaspoon salt
¼ teaspoon black pepper
For salad
1 (½-lb) firm-ripe California avocado
1 head iceberg lettuce, thinly sliced (8 cups)
1 large tomato (½ lb), chopped
¼ lb coarsely grated extra-sharp
 Cheddar (1½ cups)
1 (15- to 19-oz) can black beans,
 drained and rinsed
1 (6-oz) can sliced pitted California black
 olives, drained

Accompaniment: **tortilla chips**

Make dressing:
 Whisk together lime juice, cilantro, sugar, chili powder, cumin, salt, and pepper, then add oil in a stream, whisking until emulsified.
Cook beef:
 Cook onion, garlic, chiles (to taste), chili powder, and ground cumin in oil in a 12-inch heavy skillet over moderate heat, stirring occasionally, until onion is well softened, about 6 minutes. Add beef and cook, stirring occasionally and breaking up lumps, until meat is no longer pink, about 5 minutes, then spoon off any excess fat from skillet.
 Add tomato sauce, salt, and pepper to beef and cook, stirring, until slightly thickened, about 3 minutes. Remove from heat.
Assemble salad:
 Peel and pit avocado, then cut into ½-inch pieces.
 Spread lettuce over bottom of a shallow 4-quart dish. Spoon beef mixture evenly over lettuce and continue making layers with tomatoes, cheese, beans, avocado, and olives. Drizzle dressing over salad.

salads with greens

ARUGULA WITH LEMON AND OLIVE OIL

Serves 6
Active time: 10 min   Start to finish: 10 min

3 oz baby arugula (6 cups)
1 teaspoon fresh lemon juice
⅛ teaspoon salt
2 tablespoons olive oil

 Toss together arugula, lemon juice, and salt in a bowl. Drizzle with oil and toss to combine well.
PHOTO ON PAGE 78

ESCAROLE SALAD WITH FRIED SHALLOTS AND PRUNES

Serves 6
Active time: 20 min   Start to finish: 20 min

1 cup olive oil
6 oz shallots, thinly sliced (1⅓ cups)
1 tablespoon fresh lemon juice
¼ teaspoon salt
⅛ teaspoon black pepper
½ cup packed pitted prunes (5 oz), finely
 chopped
1 head escarole (1 lb), tough ribs and outer
 leaves discarded and inner leaves and
 tender ribs cut crosswise into ½-inch-wide
 strips (8 cups)

 Heat oil in a 1-quart heavy saucepan over moderate heat until hot but not smoking, then fry shallots in 3 batches, stirring frequently and being careful not to burn, until golden brown, 3 to 4 minutes. Transfer shallots as browned with a slotted spoon to paper towels to drain. (Shallots will crisp as they cool.) Transfer 3 tablespoons shallot oil from pan to a cup for dressing and reserve remainder for another use.
 Whisk together lemon juice, salt, and pepper in a large bowl, then add shallot oil in a slow stream, whisking until combined. Add prunes, escarole, half of shallots, and salt to taste, then toss well to coat. Sprinkle with remaining shallots.

ESCAROLE, FENNEL, AND ORANGE SALAD

Serves 8 (first course)
Active time: 25 min   Start to finish: 25 min

2 navel oranges (1 lb total)
2 medium fennel bulbs (sometimes called
    anise; 1¾ lb total), stalks discarded
    and bulbs halved lengthwise
1½ tablespoons white-wine vinegar
½ teaspoon salt
¼ teaspoon black pepper
¼ cup olive oil
2 heads escarole (2 lb total), dark outer
    leaves discarded and pale green and yellow
    inner leaves torn into bite-size pieces

Finely grate enough zest from 1 orange (see Tips, page 8) to measure 1 tablespoon. Cut peel, including all white pith, from both oranges with a paring knife. Cut segments free from membranes, then cut segments crosswise into ½-inch pieces.

Cut out and discard core of each fennel bulb, then cut bulbs crosswise into thin slices.

Whisk together vinegar, zest, salt, and pepper in a small bowl until salt is dissolved, then add oil in a stream, whisking until combined well.

Toss escarole, fennel, and oranges with dressing in a large bowl until combined well. Season with salt and pepper.

Cooks' notes:
• Orange segments can be cut 2 hours ahead and
  chilled, covered.
• Escarole can be washed and torn 1 day ahead and
  chilled in sealed plastic bags lined with dampened
  paper towels.

PHOTO ON PAGES 94 AND 95

FRISÉE, ESCAROLE, AND ENDIVE SALAD

Serves 8 to 10
Active time: 20 min   Start to finish: 20 min

When dressing a salad in the classic Italian style, each ingredient is tossed individually with the greens in a specific order, rather than being whisked together.

½ lb frisée (French curly endive) or chicory,
    white and pale green ribs and leaves cut
    into bite-size pieces (6 cups)
1 lb escarole, white and pale green ribs and
    leaves cut into bite-size pieces (4 cups)
1 lb red or green Belgian endive, trimmed
    and cut crosswise into ½-inch-thick slices
    (4 cups)
¾ teaspoon kosher salt, or to taste
3 tablespoons extra-virgin olive oil, or to
    taste
1 tablespoon red-wine vinegar, or to taste

Toss greens with kosher salt in a large salad bowl. Drizzle oil over greens and toss to coat well. Sprinkle vinegar over greens and toss again.

MIXED GREEN SALAD
WITH TARRAGON VINAIGRETTE

Serves 8
Active time: 30 min   Start to finish: 30 min

4 teaspoons Sherry vinegar
1 tablespoon minced shallot
½ teaspoon Dijon mustard
½ teaspoon salt
¼ teaspoon black pepper
¼ cup extra-virgin olive oil
2 teaspoons finely chopped fresh tarragon
½ lb frisée (French curly endive), torn into
    bite-size pieces
1 head Boston lettuce (1 lb), torn into
    bite-size pieces
1 bunch arugula (½ lb), coarse stems
    discarded
1 bunch watercress (½ lb), coarse stems
    discarded

Whisk together vinegar, shallot, mustard, salt, and pepper in a small bowl, then add oil in a slow stream, whisking until emulsified. Whisk in tarragon.

Toss greens with dressing in a large bowl and season with salt and pepper.

Cooks' note:
• Greens can be washed, trimmed, and torn 1 day ahead and chilled in a sealed plastic bag lined with paper towels.

BACON AND LETTUCE SALAD

Serves 8
Active time: 20 min   Start to finish: 20 min

10 thick-cut slices meaty smoked bacon (½ lb),
  cut crosswise into 2-inch-long pieces
2 tablespoons white balsamic vinegar
1 tablespoon finely chopped shallot
½ teaspoon Dijon mustard
¼ teaspoon salt
⅛ teaspoon black pepper
3 tablespoons extra-virgin olive oil
1½ lb Boston lettuce (3 heads), torn into
  bite-size pieces (16 cups)

Cook bacon pieces in a 12-inch nonstick skillet over moderate heat, stirring, just until crisp. Transfer with a slotted spoon to paper towels. Discard fat from skillet.

Whisk together vinegar, shallot, mustard, salt, and pepper in a large bowl, then add oil in a slow stream, whisking until emulsified. Add lettuce and bacon and toss well.

Cooks' note:
• Lettuce can be washed and torn 1 day ahead and chilled in a sealed plastic bag lined with paper towels.
PHOTO ON PAGE 90

PARSLEY, RADICCHIO, AND NAPA CABBAGE SALAD WITH LEMON VINAIGRETTE

Serves 8
Active time: 15 min   Start to finish: 15 min

1½ tablespoons fresh lemon juice
1 teaspoon finely grated fresh lemon zest
¼ teaspoon sugar
¼ teaspoon salt
¼ teaspoon black pepper
⅓ cup plus 1 tablespoon olive oil

6 cups thinly sliced Napa cabbage (½ lb;
  from 1 head)
4½ cups loosely packed fresh flat-leaf parsley
  leaves (3 large bunches)
2 cups thinly sliced radicchio (¼ lb)

Whisk together lemon juice, zest, sugar, salt, and pepper until sugar is dissolved, then add oil in a slow stream, whisking until emulsified.

Just before serving, toss cabbage, parsley, and radicchio in a large bowl with just enough dressing to coat, then season with salt and pepper.

RED LEAF LETTUCE, WATERCRESS, AND CUCUMBER SALAD WITH BUTTERMILK DRESSING

Serves 6
Active time: 15 min   Start to finish: 15 min

For dressing
½ cup well-shaken low-fat buttermilk
2 tablespoons low-fat sour cream
1 tablespoon mayonnaise
¾ teaspoon finely chopped fresh tarragon or
  ¼ teaspoon dried, crumbled
½ teaspoon minced garlic, mashed to a paste
  with ¼ teaspoon salt
¼ teaspoon dry mustard, or to taste
For salad
½ cup finely chopped red onion
1 small head red leaf lettuce (½ lb), torn
  into pieces
1 bunch watercress, coarse stems discarded
1 cup thinly sliced seedless cucumber (usually
  plastic-wrapped)

Make dressing:
Whisk together all dressing ingredients in a small bowl with salt and pepper to taste.
Make salad:
Soak onion in 1 cup cold water 10 minutes, then drain well in a sieve.

Toss lettuce, watercress, and cucumber together in a bowl and divide among 6 plates. Spoon dressing over, then sprinkle salads with onion.

Each serving about 50 calories and 3 grams fat
PHOTO ON PAGE 107

SALADE DE CRESSON ET ENDIVE
Watercress and Belgian Endive Salad

Serves 8
Active time: 10 min   Start to finish: 10 min

5¼ teaspoons white-wine vinegar
1 garlic clove, minced
⅛ teaspoon fine sea salt
⅛ teaspoon black pepper
⅓ cup olive oil
3 large bunches watercress sprigs (9 oz), coarse stems discarded
1½ lb Belgian endives, cut crosswise into ½-inch-wide pieces

Whisk together vinegar, garlic, sea salt, and pepper in a bowl until salt is dissolved, then add oil in a slow stream, whisking until emulsified. Toss watercress and endive with just enough dressing to coat in a large bowl, then season with salt and pepper.

FUYU PERSIMMON AND AVOCADO SALAD

Serves 6 (first course)
Active time: 20 min   Start to finish: 20 min

The miso dressing—which has the body of an egg yolk dressing without all the fat—lends depth of flavor to sweet persimmon and creamy avocado.

2 tablespoons fresh lemon juice
4 teaspoons water
1½ tablespoons sweet white miso (fermented soybean paste)
¼ teaspoon black pepper
⅛ teaspoon salt
⅓ cup olive oil
3 firm-ripe California avocados (1½ lb total)
1 lb firm-ripe Fuyu persimmons, peeled, halved lengthwise, seeded if necessary, and thinly sliced crosswise
2 bunches watercress (6 oz total), coarse stems discarded

Blend together lemon juice, water, miso, pepper, and salt in a blender until smooth. With motor running, add oil in a slow stream in 3 batches, blending until emulsified after each addition. Season with salt and black pepper.

Halve, pit, and peel avocados, then thinly slice crosswise. Gently toss together avocados, persimmons, and 6 tablespoons dressing. Toss watercress with just enough dressing to coat (about 3 tablespoons) in another bowl.

Divide persimmon mixture among 6 plates and top with watercress.

WILTED MIXED GREENS

Serves 4
Active time: 30 min   Start to finish: 1½ hr (includes draining)

There is a tradition in Crete of gathering wild greens and using them not only in vegetable or salad dishes but also as stuffings for savory turnovers. Cretans make use of tiny leeks, wild fennel, purslane, and milk-wort, as well as the more familiar greens. We have substituted a mixture of the varieties of tender greens available at most supermarkets. You can even use prepackaged mixes, such as baby Asian salad or baby braising mix.

1½ lb mixed tender or baby greens such as young chard, kale, mustard greens, spinach, beet greens, dandelion, and arugula, coarse stems discarded and leaves coarsely chopped (20 cups)
2 tablespoons red-wine vinegar
½ teaspoon salt
3 tablespoons extra-virgin olive oil

Cook greens in a 6- to 8-quart pot of boiling salted water (see Tips, page 8), uncovered, until wilted and tender, about 3 minutes. Drain greens in a colander, then immediately plunge into a large bowl of very cold water to stop cooking. Once cooled, drain in colander, tossing occasionally, 1 hour.

Just before serving, whisk together vinegar, salt, and oil in a bowl until combined well. Add greens and toss to coat.

Cooks' note:
• Greens can be cooked and drained (but not dressed) 1 day ahead and chilled, covered. Bring to room temperature before proceeding.
PHOTO ON PAGE 73

WILTED ASIAN GREENS

Serves 6
Active time: 10 min   Start to finish: 10 min

Tatsoi, mizuna, and pea shoots are available at Asian markets as well as at some specialty foods shops and farmers markets. If you have trouble finding any of these greens, packaged organic baby Asian salad mix (such as Earthbound Farm brand) is an excellent substitute and can be found at most supermarkets. (Buy three 5-ounce packages.)

¼ cup rice vinegar (not seasoned)
3 tablespoons soy sauce
2½ teaspoons sugar
1½ teaspoons finely grated peeled fresh ginger
1½ teaspoons Asian sesame oil
6 cups pea shoots or pea sprouts (3 oz)
6 cups *tatsoi* (3 oz)
6 cups *mizuna* (3 oz)

Heat vinegar, soy sauce, sugar, ginger, and sesame oil in a small saucepan over moderately low heat, stirring, until sugar is dissolved (do not let boil). Pour hot dressing over greens in a large bowl and toss well. Serve immediately.

PHOTO ON PAGE 84

vegetable salads and slaws

ANTIPASTO SALAD

Serves 8
Active time: 20 min   Start to finish: 45 min
(includes cooling onion)

For vinaigrette
3 tablespoons red-wine vinegar
1 small garlic clove, minced
½ teaspoon sugar
½ teaspoon salt
⅛ teaspoon black pepper
6 tablespoons extra-virgin olive oil
For salad
2 cups water
3 tablespoons red-wine vinegar
2 tablespoons sugar
1 teaspoon salt

1 medium red onion, halved lengthwise and thinly sliced crosswise
2 hearts of romaine (12 oz total), torn into bite-size pieces
1 cup loosely packed fresh flat-leaf parsley leaves
1 (8-oz) jar roasted red peppers, rinsed, drained, and cut lengthwise into ¼-inch-thick strips
2 (6-oz) jars marinated artichoke hearts, drained
1 cup assorted brine-cured olives
1 cup drained bottled *peperoncini* (5 oz)
½ lb cherry tomatoes, halved

Make vinaigrette:
Whisk together all vinaigrette ingredients in a small bowl until combined well.
Make salad:
Bring water, vinegar, sugar, and salt to a boil in a 1-quart heavy saucepan, then add onion and simmer until crisp-tender, about 3 minutes. Drain and cool.

Spread romaine on a large platter and scatter with parsley, peppers, artichokes, olives, *peperoncini*, tomatoes, and onion. Whisk vinaigrette again and drizzle over salad.

Cooks' notes:
• Vinaigrette can be made 1 day ahead and chilled, covered.
• Onion can be pickled 1 day ahead and chilled, covered.

PHOTO ON PAGE 51

Romaine

GREEN BEAN SALAD WITH TUNA SAUCE AND OLIVES

Serves 4 (side dish)
Active time: 25 min   Start to finish: 25 min

The tuna sauce for this salad is based on the Northern Italian tonnato—*a summer sauce served over chilled veal roast. Use white tuna for an attractive sauce.*

  1 lb green beans, trimmed
  1 (3-oz) can white tuna packed in oil,
     drained and flaked
  ¼ cup extra-virgin olive oil
  2 tablespoons water
1½ teaspoons fresh lemon juice
  1 teaspoon anchovy paste
  2 tablespoons Niçoise or other small brine-
     cured black olives
  2 tablespoons fresh flat-leaf parsley leaves

Cook beans in a large pot of boiling salted water (see Tips, page 8), uncovered, until crisp-tender, 4 to 5 minutes. Drain in a colander and immediately transfer to a large bowl of ice and cold water to stop cooking. When beans are cold, drain and pat dry, then arrange on a platter and season with salt.

Purée tuna with olive oil, water, lemon juice, and anchovy paste in a blender, scraping down sides as necessary, until very smooth. Season sauce with salt and pepper and spoon over beans. Scatter olives and parsley leaves on top.

BEET AND PARSLEY SALAD

Serves 4
Active time: 25 min   Start to finish: 25 min

2 medium beets without greens
1 cup fresh flat-leaf parsley leaves
¼ teaspoon salt, or to taste
¼ teaspoon sugar, or to taste
⅛ teaspoon black pepper
2 teaspoons extra-virgin olive oil
2 teaspoons balsamic vinegar

Special equipment: **a Japanese Benriner or other adjustable-blade slicer**

Trim and peel raw beets, then cut into very thin slices (1/16 inch thick) with slicer. Make small stacks of slices and cut each stack with a sharp knife into very thin strips (1/16 inch thick).

Toss beets with parsley, salt, sugar, and pepper in a serving bowl until sugar is dissolved. Add oil and toss to coat. Sprinkle vinegar on salad and toss again. Serve immediately.

  Cooks' note:
  • Beets can be cut and parsley leaves removed from stems 8 hours ahead and chilled separately, wrapped in dampened paper towels in a sealed plastic bag.

Each serving about 63 calories and 3 grams fat

ROASTED BUTTERNUT SQUASH AND SPINACH SALAD WITH TOASTED ALMOND DRESSING

Serves 6 (first course)
Active time: 20 min   Start to finish: 1¼ hr

  1 (2- to 2¼-lb) butternut squash, peeled,
     seeded, and cut into ½-inch cubes
     (4 cups)
5½ tablespoons extra-virgin olive oil
  ¾ cup whole almonds with skins (3½ oz),
     very coarsely chopped
  2 teaspoons fresh lemon juice
  ½ lb spinach, coarse stems discarded
     (10 cups)

Put oven rack in middle position and preheat oven to 450°F.

Toss squash with 1½ tablespoons oil in a shallow baking pan and spread cubes in 1 layer. Season with salt and pepper and roast, stirring once halfway through roasting, until squash is just tender and pale golden, about 30 minutes total. Cool in pan on a rack until warm, about 15 minutes.

While squash roasts, cook almonds in remaining 4 tablespoons oil in a 10-inch skillet over moderately low heat, stirring constantly, until golden, about 3 minutes, then season with salt and pepper. Pour almonds and oil into a fine-mesh sieve set over a large bowl and cool until warm, about 10 minutes.

When almonds and oil have cooled, whisk lemon juice into oil in bowl until combined well, then season with salt and pepper. Add squash, spinach, and half of almonds to dressing and toss gently to coat.

Divide salad among 6 salad plates and sprinkle with remaining almonds.

WARM POTATO SALAD WITH LEMON AND DILL

Serves 4 to 6
Active time: 15 min   Start to finish: 40 min

Soaking the red onion in cold water mellows its flavor.

- 2 lb small yellow-fleshed potatoes such as Yukon Gold
- 1 small red onion, finely chopped (⅓ cup)
- 2 tablespoons fresh lemon juice
- ¾ teaspoon salt
- ½ cup sour cream
- ⅓ cup mayonnaise
- ¼ cup chopped fresh dill

Cover potatoes with salted cold water by 1 inch (see Tips, page 8) and bring to a boil, then reduce heat and simmer, uncovered, until potatoes are tender, 15 to 20 minutes. Reserve ¼ cup cooking water, then drain potatoes in a colander.

While potatoes boil, soak onion in cold water 15 minutes, then drain in a sieve and pat dry.

When potatoes are just cool enough to handle, peel and quarter, then toss with lemon juice and salt in a large bowl.

Whisk together onion, sour cream, mayonnaise, dill, and reserved cooking water in a bowl until well blended. Whisk in salt and pepper to taste, then add to potatoes and toss to coat. Serve warm.

WARM CAULIFLOWER SALAD

Serves 6
Active time: 15 min   Start to finish: 25 min

- 1 small garlic clove
- ½ teaspoon kosher salt
- 1 flat anchovy fillet, rinsed
- 2 tablespoons drained bottled capers, rinsed
- 1½ tablespoons fresh lemon juice
- ¼ teaspoon black pepper
- ¼ cup extra-virgin olive oil
- 1 head cauliflower (1¾ lb), cut into 1½-inch florets
- ¼ cup firmly packed fresh flat-leaf parsley leaves

Mince garlic and mash to a paste with kosher salt using a large heavy knife, then add anchovy and capers and finely chop. Transfer mixture to a large bowl and whisk in lemon juice and pepper, then add oil in a slow stream, whisking until combined well.

Cook cauliflower in a 4-quart saucepan of boiling salted water (see Tips, page 8) until crisp-tender, 4 to 5 minutes. Drain well in a colander, then toss hot cauliflower with dressing. Cool cauliflower to warm, tossing occasionally, then add parsley and toss to coat. Serve immediately.

Cooks' note:
- Dressing can be made 2 hours ahead and kept at room temperature.

PHOTO ON PAGE 52

butternut squash

SWEET-POTATO SALAD WITH MUSTARD VINAIGRETTE

Serves 6
Active time: 15 min   Start to finish: 40 min

2½ lb sweet potatoes (2 large)
 1 tablespoon Dijon mustard
 4 teaspoons white-wine vinegar
 ¼ teaspoon salt
 ¼ cup olive oil
 4 scallions, thinly sliced

Peel potatoes and halve lengthwise. Cut lengthwise into ¾-inch-thick wedges, then cut wedges crosswise into 1-inch pieces. Steam potatoes in a steamer over boiling water in a large pot, covered, until just tender, 10 to 12 minutes.

While potatoes steam, whisk together mustard, vinegar, and salt in a large bowl, then add oil in a slow stream, whisking until emulsified.

Add hot potatoes to dressing and gently toss to combine well. Cool salad to room temperature, about 15 minutes. Add scallions and salt to taste and gently toss to combine well.

Cooks' note:
• Salad (without scallions) can be made 2 hours ahead. Toss in scallions just before serving.

PHOTO ON PAGE 78

Heirloom Tomatoes

CUCUMBER, JICAMA, AND PICKLED GINGER SALAD

Serves 4
Active time: 20 min   Start to finish: 35 min

2 teaspoons white-wine vinegar
 ½ teaspoon sugar
 ¼ teaspoon salt
 2 tablespoons olive oil
 1 seedless cucumber (1¼ lb; usually plastic-wrapped), cored and cut into ⅛-inch-thick matchsticks
 ½ lb jicama, peeled and cut into ⅛-inch-thick matchsticks (2 cups)
 2 tablespoons drained bottled pickled ginger, finely chopped

Whisk together vinegar, sugar, and salt in a small bowl until sugar is dissolved, then add oil in a slow stream, whisking until emulsified. Toss together cucumber, jicama, ginger, and dressing in a bowl until combined well, then let stand, covered and chilled, 15 minutes.

HEIRLOOM TOMATOES WITH BACON, BLUE CHEESE, AND BASIL

Serves 6
Active time: 40 min   Start to finish: 40 min

6 slices firm white sandwich bread
 ¼ lb sliced bacon (5 slices)
 6 tablespoons olive oil
 ¼ cup finely chopped shallot
 3 tablespoons Sherry vinegar
 4 assorted medium heirloom tomatoes (2 lb total), cut into ¼- to ⅓-inch-thick slices
 30 small fresh basil leaves
1½ oz blue cheese (preferably Maytag Blue), crumbled, at room temperature

Special equipment: **a 3-inch round cookie cutter**
Garnish: **very small heirloom cherry or currant tomatoes**

Cut 1 round from each bread slice with cutter.
Cook bacon in a 10-inch heavy skillet over moderate heat until crisp, then transfer to paper towels to

drain. Pour off bacon fat from skillet and reserve fat (do not clean skillet).

Heat 1½ tablespoons oil in skillet over moderate heat until hot but not smoking, then toast 3 bread rounds, turning over once, until golden brown, about 3 minutes total. Transfer toasts to a rack to cool and season with salt and pepper. Toast remaining 3 bread rounds in 1½ tablespoons more oil in same manner.

Cook shallot in 2 tablespoons reserved bacon fat and remaining 3 tablespoons oil in a small heavy saucepan over moderate heat, stirring, until softened, about 2 minutes. Add vinegar and simmer, whisking, until emulsified, about 1 minute. Season dressing with salt and pepper and keep warm, covered.

Crumble bacon. Arrange bread rounds on 6 plates and divide tomato slices among them, stacking slices and sprinkling some basil and bacon between slices. Sprinkle cheese and remaining basil and bacon over and around tomatoes. Spoon some of warm bacon dressing over and around tomatoes and season with salt and pepper.

Cooks' notes:
• Toasts can be made 3 hours ahead and kept in an airtight container at room temperature.
• Dressing can be made 1 hour ahead and chilled, covered. Reheat before proceeding.
• Tomatoes can be sliced 1 hour ahead and kept, covered, at room temperature.
PHOTO ON PAGE 83

WINTER WHITE SALAD

Serves 4 to 6 (first course)
Active time: 20 min   Start to finish: 20 min

1 tablespoon whole-grain or coarse-grain mustard
2 tablespoons white-wine vinegar
½ cup heavy cream
½ teaspoon salt
¼ teaspoon white pepper
½ medium head cauliflower (¾ lb), stems discarded and florets cut lengthwise into ¼-inch slices (3 cups)
2 Belgian endives, leaves separated and cut diagonally into ½-inch pieces
1 small head Napa cabbage (½ lb), greenish outer leaves discarded and pale inner leaves cut crosswise into 1-inch pieces (5 cups loosely packed)
1 small onion, finely chopped and soaked in cold water 10 minutes, then drained

Whisk together mustard, vinegar, cream, salt, and white pepper in a large bowl until blended.

Blanch cauliflower in a 2- to 3-quart saucepan of boiling salted water (see Tips, page 8) 30 seconds, then drain and transfer to a bowl of ice and cold water to stop cooking. Drain well again and add to dressing in bowl. Add endives, cabbage, and onion, tossing to coat. Season with salt and pepper.

SAUCES AND CONDIMENTS

condiments

TOMATO ORANGE MARMALADE

Makes 3 (½-pint) jars
Active time: 40 min   Start to finish: 1 day

This recipe has a small yield, so it's not necessary to sterilize and process the jars if you plan on keeping the marmalade in the refrigerator and eating it within a few weeks. But if you want to make larger batches, process the jars according to the procedures that follow.

3 lb ripe beefsteak tomatoes
3 cups sugar
2 juice oranges, quartered, seeded, and
    sliced crosswise ⅛ inch thick
1 lemon, quartered, seeded, and sliced
    crosswise ⅛ inch thick
⅛ teaspoon salt

Special equipment: 3 (½-pint) canning jars
    (optional) with lids and screw bands;
    a wide 5- to 6-quart heavy pot (at least
    9½ inches in diameter)

If desired, sterilize jars, lids, and screw bands.
Chill 2 small plates (for testing marmalade).
Cut an X in bottom of each tomato with a sharp paring knife and blanch together in a 4-quart pot of boiling water 1 minute. Transfer tomatoes with a slotted spoon to a cutting board and, when cool enough to handle, peel off skin, beginning from a scored end, with paring knife. Chop tomatoes, reserving any juices.

Cook all ingredients, including reserved juices from tomatoes, in pot over moderate heat, stirring frequently, until sugar is dissolved, about 6 minutes. Simmer, stirring frequently as marmalade thickens (to prevent scorching) and adjusting heat as needed, until the marmalade tests done, 50 minutes to 1¼ hours. Begin testing for doneness after 50 minutes: Drop a spoonful of marmalade on a chilled plate, then tilt; it should remain in a mound and not run (if necessary, remove pot of marmalade from heat while testing).

If not processing, cool marmalade, uncovered, then chill in an airtight container (preferably glass).

If processing, drain jars upside down on a clean kitchen towel 1 minute, then invert. Ladle marmalade into jars, leaving ¼ inch of space at top. Run a thin knife between marmalade and jar to eliminate air bubbles.

Seal, process, and store filled jars (and boil marmalade in jars 10 minutes).

Let marmalade stand in jars at least 1 day for flavors to develop.

Cooks' note:
• Marmalade keeps, chilled, 3 weeks.

TO STERILIZE JARS

Wash jars, lids, and screw bands in hot soapy water, then rinse well. Dry screw bands.

Put jars on a rack in a boiling-water canner or a deep 8- to 10-quart pot and add enough water to cover by 2 inches. Bring to a boil, covered with lid, and boil 10 minutes. Heat lids in water to cover in a small saucepan until an instant-read or candy thermometer registers 180°F (do not let boil). Keep jars and lids submerged in hot water, covered, until ready to use.

TO SEAL, PROCESS, AND STORE FILLED JARS

Wipe off rims of filled jars with a clean damp kitchen towel. Firmly screw on lids with screw bands.

Put sealed jars on a rack in a boiling-water canner or a deep 8- to 10-quart pot and add enough water to cover by 2 inches. Bring to a boil, covered. Boil jars of marmalade 10 minutes, then transfer with tongs to a towel-lined surface to cool. Jars will seal (if you hear a ping, that signals that the vacuum formed at the top has made the lid concave) and marmalade will thicken as it cools.

After jars have cooled 12 to 24 hours, press center of each lid to check that it's concave, then remove screw band and try to lift lid with your fingertips. If you can't, the lid has a good seal.

Store in a cool dry place.

APRICOT CHUTNEY

Makes about 3 cups
Active time: 15 min   Start to finish: 1 hr (includes cooling)

2 garlic cloves, finely chopped
2 teaspoons finely chopped peeled fresh
  ginger
1 tablespoon vegetable oil
1 teaspoon mustard seeds
¾ cup dried apricots (6 oz), finely chopped
⅓ cup dried currants (1½ oz)
¾ cup water
⅓ cup red-wine vinegar
¼ cup sugar
¾ teaspoon salt

Cook garlic and ginger in oil in a 1-quart heavy saucepan over moderate heat, stirring, until golden, 1 to 2 minutes. Add mustard seeds and cook, stirring, until fragrant, about 1 minute. Add all remaining ingredients and simmer, partially covered, stirring occasionally, until almost all liquid is absorbed, about 20 minutes (chutney should be moist). Cool to room temperature.

OLIVE CAPER RELISH

Makes about 1½ cups
Active time: 10 min   Start to finish: 10 min

This relish is an appealing condiment and makes a quick hors d'oeuvre—spread toasts with goat cheese and top with the relish.

1 cup pimiento-stuffed green olives
  (5 oz), rinsed well
⅔ cup pitted Kalamata olives (3 oz),
  rinsed well
3 tablespoons drained bottled capers,
  rinsed well
1½ tablespoons extra-virgin olive oil
1 large garlic clove, minced
1 teaspoon red-wine vinegar or fresh
  lemon juice
⅛ teaspoon dried oregano or thyme, crumbled
⅛ teaspoon dried hot red pepper flakes

Pulse all ingredients together in a food processor until coarsely chopped.

BLACK OLIVE MAYONNAISE

Makes about ¾ cup
Active time: 5 min   Start to finish: 1 hr (includes chilling)

Serve on cold roast beef or with crudités.

⅔ cup mayonnaise
2 tablespoons black olive paste or tapenade
½ teaspoon fresh lemon juice

Stir together all ingredients. Chill, covered, 1 hour (for flavors to develop).

BASIL GARLIC MAYONNAISE

Makes about 1 cup
Active time: 10 min   Start to finish: 1¼ hr (includes chilling)

Top steak, chicken, or fish with this sauce, or toss it with warm potatoes. It's also great in a tomato or tuna sandwich.

1 cup coarsely chopped fresh basil
1 garlic clove, smashed
¼ teaspoon salt
⅛ teaspoon cayenne
¾ cup mayonnaise

Pulse basil, garlic, salt, and cayenne in a food processor until finely chopped. Add mayonnaise and blend until smooth. Chill, covered, 1 hour (for flavors to develop).

ROASTED-PEPPER AND ALMOND MAYONNAISE

Makes about 1 cup
Active time: 10 min Start to finish: 1¼ hr
(includes chilling)

This romesco-*style sauce is good on grilled fish or vegetables as well as burgers.*

- ½ cup mayonnaise
- ¼ cup drained bottled roasted red peppers, chopped
- ¼ cup salted roasted almonds
- 1 garlic clove, smashed
- 2 teaspoons Sherry vinegar, or to taste
- ⅛ teaspoon cayenne

Blend all of the ingredients in a blender or food processor until smooth. Chill, covered, 1 hour (for flavors to develop).

JELLIED CRANBERRY SAUCE

Makes about 3½ cups
Active time: 30 min   Start to finish: 13 hr
(includes chilling)

Intensely flavored and vibrant red, this jelly bears no resemblance to the stuff in the can—it's definitely worth the effort. Though we call for 4 bags of cranberries, the yield is only 3 cups because all the solids get strained out. You'll be happy if you have any extra cranberry sauce when you make sandwiches with leftover turkey.

- 4 (12-oz) bags cranberries, thawed if frozen
- 3 cups sugar
- 3⅓ cups cold water
- 2 tablespoons unflavored gelatin (from three ¼-oz envelopes)

Special equipment: **a 3½-cup nonreactive decorative mold or 10 individual (⅓-cup) decorative molds**

Bring cranberries, sugar, and 3 cups water to a boil in a 4- to 5-quart heavy saucepan, stirring until sugar is dissolved, then reduce heat and simmer, partially covered, stirring occasionally, until all berries have burst, 10 to 15 minutes. Pour into a large fine-mesh sieve set over a 2-quart glass measure or a bowl and let stand until all juices have drained through, about 30 minutes. If necessary, press on solids until there is enough juice to measure 3 cups, then discard solids.

Stir together gelatin and remaining ⅓ cup water and let stand 1 minute to soften. Bring 1 cup drained cranberry liquid to a simmer in a small saucepan, then add gelatin mixture and stir until just dissolved. Add gelatin mixture to remaining cranberry liquid and stir well. Pour cranberry sauce into lightly oiled mold and chill, covered with plastic wrap, until firmly set, at least 12 hours.

To unmold, run tip of a thin knife between edge of mold and cranberry sauce. Tilt mold sideways and tap side of mold against a work surface, turning it, to evenly break seal and loosen cranberry sauce. Keeping mold tilted, invert a plate over mold, then invert cranberry sauce onto plate.

Cooks' notes:
- Cranberry sauce can be chilled in mold up to 2 days.
- Cranberry sauce can be unmolded 1 hour ahead and chilled or kept at room temperature.

PHOTO ON PAGE 98

PICKLED RED ONIONS

Makes about 1 cup
Active time: 10 min   Start to finish: 20 min

This is the traditional condiment for chicken pibil
*(see chicken legs recipe, page 176). The onions turn a
beautiful pink if they are made 1 day ahead.*

    1 cup boiling-hot water
    1 medium red onion, halved lengthwise,
        then very thinly sliced lengthwise
    1 fresh *habanero* or Scotch bonnet chile,
        halved, seeded, and deveined, then
        thinly sliced
    ¼ cup fresh orange juice
    ¼ cup fresh lime juice
    1 teaspoon dried oregano (preferably
        Mexican), crumbled
    ½ teaspoon salt

Pour boiling water over onion in a small bowl and
let stand until softened, about 10 minutes. Drain onion
well and return to bowl. Stir in remaining ingredients.

Cooks' note:
• Pickled onions keep, covered and chilled, 1 week.

Each serving about 28 calories and less than 1 gram fat
PHOTO ON PAGE 106

ANGLED LOOFAH
BREAD-AND-BUTTER PICKLES

Makes 6 cups
Active time: 10 min   Start to finish: 1¼ hr
(plus 2 days for marinating)

Try to buy young loofah (no longer than 12 inches).

    1 angled loofah (½ lb)
    2 tablespoons kosher salt
    2 cups ice cubes
    1 cup cider vinegar
    ½ cup water
    ¾ cup sugar
    1 teaspoon mustard seeds
    ½ teaspoon celery seeds
    ¼ teaspoon turmeric
    1 medium sweet onion (½ lb), thinly sliced
        crosswise and separated into rings

Scrub loofah and peel only the ridges, then cut
diagonally into ½-inch-thick slices. Toss loofah with
kosher salt in a bowl, then cover with ice and let stand
2 hours. Drain and remove any unmelted ice.

Bring vinegar, water, sugar, mustard seeds, celery
seeds, and turmeric to a boil in a 1-quart nonreactive
saucepan, stirring until sugar is dissolved. Add loofah
and onion, then reduce heat and simmer, uncovered,
5 minutes.

Transfer pickles with liquid to a 1-quart heatproof
glass or ceramic bowl and cool to room temperature.
Chill, covered, at least 2 days (for flavors to develop)
and up to 1 month.

Cooks' note:
• We don't recommend processing these pickles.
  Additional heating gives the loofah a mushy texture.

SALSA VERDE

Makes about ¾ cup
Active time: 20 min   Start to finish: 20 min

Serve this sauce with roasted meat, fish, or chicken.

    ⅓ cup coarsely crumbled firm white
        sandwich bread
    2 tablespoons red-wine vinegar
    2 tablespoons drained bottled capers,
        finely chopped
    1 garlic clove, minced and mashed to
        a paste with ¼ teaspoon salt
    ½ teaspoon anchovy paste
    ½ teaspoon Dijon mustard
    ⅓ cup finely chopped fresh flat-leaf parsley
    1½ tablespoons finely chopped fresh mint
    1 tablespoon finely chopped fresh tarragon,
        or to taste
    7 tablespoons extra-virgin olive oil

Mash together bread crumbs, vinegar, capers, garlic
paste, anchovy paste, and mustard using a mortar and
pestle (or whisk together in a bowl).

Add herbs, oil, and salt and pepper to taste, then
stir (or whisk) until combined well.

SOUR CHERRY SALSA

Makes about 2 cups
Active time: 15 min   Start to finish: 45 min

This spicy-sweet salsa makes a great accompaniment to grilled pork, chicken, or duck.

2¼ cups fresh or frozen pitted sour
  cherries (¾ lb)
1 tablespoon sugar
3 tablespoons finely chopped red onion
1 large fresh jalapeño chile, finely chopped,
  including seeds (1½ tablespoons)
2 tablespoons fresh lime juice
¼ cup chopped fresh cilantro
½ teaspoon salt

If using fresh cherries, coarsely chop, then stir together with sugar in a small bowl until sugar is dissolved, about 5 minutes. If using frozen cherries, thaw in a small bowl, reserving any juices in bowl, then coarsely chop and stir together with sugar in same bowl. Stir in onion, jalapeño, lime juice, cilantro, and salt and let stand at room temperature 30 minutes (for flavors to develop).

Cooks' note:
• This salsa is best the day it is made but will keep, covered and chilled, 1 day.

dessert sauces and toppings

BLACKBERRY SYRUP

Makes about 1⅓ cups
Active time: 10 min   Start to finish: 45 min

4½ cups blackberries (1½ lb)
1 cup sugar
½ cup water

Bring berries, sugar, and water to a boil in a 2- to 3-quart heavy saucepan over moderately high heat, stirring until sugar is dissolved. Reduce heat and simmer, uncovered, stirring occasionally, until fruit is soft, about 30 minutes.

Pour mixture through a fine-mesh sieve into a bowl, pressing gently on and then discarding solids. Serve syrup at room temperature.

CHOCOLATE SYRUP

Makes about 1½ cups
Active time: 10 min   Start to finish: 30 min

This syrup is delicious over ice cream or it can be used as a base for an intense hot chocolate; simply heat 1 cup milk with ⅓ cup syrup.

1 cup water
½ cup sugar
⅔ cup unsweetened cocoa powder
  (preferably Dutch-process)
¼ teaspoon salt
1 teaspoon vanilla

Bring water and sugar to a boil, whisking until sugar is dissolved. Whisk in cocoa and salt and simmer, whisking, until slightly thickened, about 3 minutes. Remove from heat and stir in vanilla, then cool (syrup will continue to thicken as it cools).

BURNT-SUGAR PECAN RUM SAUCE

Makes about 2 cups
Active time: 35 min   Start to finish: 35 min

1 cup sugar
2 tablespoons water
½ cup heavy cream
1 tablespoon dark rum
¾ cup pecan pieces (2½ oz), toasted
  (see Tips, page 8)

Cook sugar in a dry 2-quart heavy saucepan over moderate heat, undisturbed, until it begins to melt. Continue to cook, stirring occasionally with a fork, until sugar is melted into a deep golden caramel.

Tilt pan and carefully pour in water, then cream and rum (mixture will bubble up and steam vigorously). Cook over moderately low heat, stirring, until caramel is dissolved. Stir in pecans and serve sauce warm.

DESSERTS

cakes

BLUEBERRY CRUMB CAKE

Serves 8 to 12
Active time: 15 min   Start to finish: 1¼ hr

3 cups all-purpose flour
1 cup plus 2 tablespoons sugar
2 teaspoons baking powder
¾ teaspoon baking soda
¾ teaspoon salt
¾ teaspoon cinnamon
Rounded ¼ teaspoon freshly grated nutmeg
1½ sticks (¾ cup) plus 2 tablespoons cold
    unsalted butter, cut into ½-inch cubes
2 large eggs, lightly beaten
1 cup sour cream
1½ teaspoons vanilla
3 cups fresh blueberries (15 oz)

Put oven rack in middle position and preheat oven to 375°F. Butter a 13- by 9- by 2-inch baking pan.

Whisk together flour, 1 cup sugar, baking powder, baking soda, salt, cinnamon, and nutmeg in a bowl. Blend 1½ sticks butter into flour with your fingertips or a pastry blender just until mixture resembles coarse meal with some small (roughly pea-size) butter lumps.

Transfer 1½ cups flour mixture to another bowl for crumb topping. Add remaining 2 tablespoons butter and remaining 2 tablespoons sugar to crumb topping, then blend with your fingertips until large lumps form.

Whisk together eggs, sour cream, and vanilla, then add to remaining flour mixture, stirring until just combined. Fold in blueberries and spread batter in baking pan, distributing berries evenly. Sprinkle batter evenly with crumb topping.

Bake until cake is golden and a wooden pick or skewer inserted in center comes out clean, 40 to 45 minutes. Cool cake in pan on a rack 20 minutes before cutting.

Cooks' note:
• This crumb cake is best eaten the day it is made.
PHOTO ON PAGE 90

MINI CHOCOLATE CUPCAKES

Makes 12 cupcakes (serves 4)
Active time: 25 min   Start to finish: 1¼ hr

These cupcakes have such a rich, chocolaty flavor, you would never know there were dates in the batter if you hadn't baked them yourself.

⅓ cup water
⅓ cup pitted dates, coarsely chopped
¼ cup unsweetened Dutch-process
    cocoa powder
1 oz fine-quality bittersweet chocolate
    (not unsweetened), coarsely chopped
3 tablespoons packed light brown sugar
1 large egg
¼ teaspoon vanilla
¼ teaspoon baking soda
2 tablespoons all-purpose flour
    Vegetable oil cooking spray
1 teaspoon confectioners sugar for dusting

Special equipment: **a mini-muffin pan with 12 (⅛-cup) muffin cups (preferably nonstick)**

Put oven rack in middle position and preheat oven to 325°F.

Bring water and dates just to a boil in a 1-quart heavy saucepan, then transfer mixture to a food processor and add cocoa powder and chocolate, pulsing once to combine. Let cool 2 minutes, then add brown sugar, egg, vanilla, baking soda, and a pinch of salt, then purée until smooth. Add flour and pulse just until incorporated.

Spray muffin cups with cooking spray. (If pan is not nonstick, line sprayed bottoms with rounds of wax paper, then spray paper.) Spoon batter into cups, dividing it evenly, and bake until a wooden pick or skewer comes out clean, 18 to 22 minutes.

Cool cupcakes in pan on a rack 10 minutes, then turn out onto rack (remove wax paper, if using) and cool completely, right side up. Just before serving, sprinkle tops lightly with confectioners sugar.

Each serving (3 cupcakes) about 177 calories and 4 grams fat

MAPLE WALNUT BÛCHE DE NOËL

Serves 8
Active time: 1¼ hr   Start to finish: 3½ hr
(includes making buttercream and brittle)

Cakes resembling Yule logs are very popular at Christmastime in Canada and the United States. Though you'll often see them in bakery windows decorated with marzipan woodland animals and meringue mushrooms, we went with a simpler but more elegant look.

   1¼ cups walnuts (4½ oz), toasted (see
       Tips, page 8) and cooled
   ¼ cup cake flour (not self-rising)
   ½ teaspoon salt
   ¼ teaspoon cinnamon
   ⅓ cup plus 4 tablespoons sugar
   4 large eggs, warmed in a bowl of hot
       water 5 minutes and then separated
   1½ tablespoons Canadian whiskey
   ½ teaspoon vanilla
   ½ stick (¼ cup) unsalted butter, melted
       and cooled
       Maple meringue buttercream (recipe
       follows)
       Walnut brittle (page 229)

Put oven rack in middle position and preheat oven to 350°F. Butter a 15- by 10- by 1-inch baking pan and line bottom with wax paper or parchment. Butter paper and dust with flour, knocking out excess.

Pulse toasted walnuts, flour, salt, cinnamon, and 2 tablespoons sugar in a food processor until nuts are finely chopped.

Beat together yolks, whiskey, vanilla, and ⅓ cup sugar in a large bowl with an electric mixer at high speed until thick and pale and forms a ribbon that takes 2 seconds to dissolve when beaters are lifted, 5 to 8 minutes in a standing mixer or 8 to 12 minutes with a handheld. Fold in nut mixture in 4 batches.

Beat whites with a pinch of salt in another bowl with cleaned beaters at medium speed until they just hold soft peaks. Add remaining 2 tablespoons sugar ½ tablespoon at a time, beating, and continue to beat until whites just hold stiff peaks.

Fold one fourth of whites into yolk mixture to lighten, then fold in remaining whites gently but thoroughly. Stir ½ cup batter into butter in a small bowl until combined, then fold butter mixture into batter gently but thoroughly. Spread batter evenly in baking pan and rap once on counter to help eliminate air bubbles.

Bake cake until firm to the touch, pale golden, and beginning to pull away from sides of pan, 12 to 16 minutes. Cool cake in pan on a rack 15 minutes, then loosen sides with a knife. Put a sheet of foil over cake and invert rack over foil, then flip cake onto rack and remove wax paper. Cool completely.

Slide cake (on foil) off rack, then spread 1¼ cups buttercream evenly over cake and sprinkle with chopped brittle. Using foil as an aid, roll up cake, jelly-roll style, beginning with a short end. Carefully transfer cake with a long metal spatula to a platter and remove foil.

Frost cake with about 1½ cups buttercream, then chill cake until frosting is firm, about 30 minutes. (If you plan to finish assembling cake within 1 hour, keep remaining ¼ cup buttercream at room temperature. If not, chill remaining buttercream, covered.)

Cut a thin slice from one end of log (to make end even), then, starting about a ½ inch in from cut edge, cut a diagonal piece from same end of cake. Arrange piece on side of cake to resemble a cut branch, using a bit of remaining buttercream to glue piece to "log" and cover seam. Arrange shards of walnut brittle decoratively on cake.

   Cooks' note:
   • **Frosted cake (uncut and without brittle shards) can be made 3 days ahead and chilled, covered. Bring to room temperature before serving. Chill remaining buttercream, covered, then bring to room temperature before using. If buttercream seems lumpy, beat with electric mixer until smooth.**
   PHOTO ON PAGE 103

MAPLE MERINGUE BUTTERCREAM

Makes about 3 cups
Active time: 20 min   Start to finish: 35 min

We found that Grade A dark amber maple syrup (in addition to maple sugar) gave this frosting the deep, rich taste we wanted. Curiously, Grade B syrup didn't give us as flavorful a result.

   2 large egg whites, at room temperature
       for 30 minutes
       Scant ¼ teaspoon cream of tartar
   ⅛ teaspoon salt
   2 tablespoons maple sugar

⅔ cup pure maple syrup (preferably
    Grade A dark amber)
2 sticks (1 cup) unsalted butter, cut into
    tablespoon pieces and softened

Special equipment: **a candy thermometer**

    Beat egg whites with cream of tartar and salt in a large bowl with an electric mixer at medium speed until they just hold soft peaks. Add maple sugar 1 teaspoon at a time, beating, and continue to beat until whites just hold stiff peaks.

    Boil syrup in a small heavy saucepan over moderate heat, undisturbed, until it reaches soft-ball stage (registering 238 to 242°F on thermometer), about 3 to 7 minutes. Immediately remove from heat and slowly pour hot syrup in a slow stream down side of bowl into egg whites, beating constantly at high speed. Beat meringue, scraping down side of bowl occasionally with a rubber spatula, until meringue is cool to the touch, about 6 minutes. (It's important that meringue be fully cooled before proceeding.)

    With mixer at medium speed, add butter 1 tablespoon at a time, beating well after each addition. (If buttercream looks soupy after some butter is added, meringue is too warm: Chill bottom of bowl in a larger bowl of ice and cold water for a few seconds before continuing to beat in remaining butter.) Continue beating until buttercream is smooth. (Mixture may look curdled before all butter is added but will come together before beating is finished.)

    Cooks' notes:
• Buttercream can be made 1 week ahead and chilled, covered, or 1 month ahead and frozen. Bring to room temperature (do not use a microwave) and beat with an electric mixer before using.
• The egg whites in this recipe will not be fully cooked, which may be of concern if there is a problem with salmonella in your area. You may want to use either pasteurized egg whites in the carton or reconstituted powdered egg whites.

WALNUT BRITTLE

Makes about 2 cups (½ cup chopped plus shards)
Active time: 15 min   Start to finish: 30 min

½ cup walnuts (2 oz), toasted
    (see Tips, page 8), cooled, and
    finely chopped with a knife
1 cup sugar
¼ cup water

Special equipment: **a nonstick bakeware liner such as Silpat (optional)**

    Shake nuts in a sieve to remove nut powder (this will make for a clearer brittle.) Line a baking sheet with nonstick pad or with an oiled sheet of foil.

    Heat sugar and water in a deep 2-quart heavy saucepan over moderately low heat, stirring slowly with a fork, until melted and pale golden. Cook caramel without stirring, gently swirling pan, until golden. Stir in walnuts, then immediately pour caramel onto baking sheet, tilting sheet to spread caramel as thin as possible. Cool brittle completely at room temperature.

    Coarsely chop enough brittle to measure ½ cup, then break remainder into shards for decorating cake.

    Cooks' note:
• Brittle can be made 1 week ahead and kept in an airtight container at room temperature.

FRESH APRICOT UPSIDE-DOWN CAKE

Serves 8
Active time: 20 min   Start to finish: 1¾ hr

For topping
 1 stick (½ cup) unsalted butter
 ¾ cup packed light brown sugar
 10 or 11 small (2- to 2¼-inch) fresh apricots
    (1¼ lb), halved lengthwise and pitted
 For cake
 1¾ cups all-purpose flour
 1½ teaspoons baking powder
 ½ teaspoon baking soda
 ½ teaspoon salt
 1 stick (½ cup) unsalted butter,
    softened
 ¾ cup granulated sugar
 1½ teaspoons vanilla extract
 ¼ teaspoon almond extract
 2 large eggs at room temperature for
    30 minutes
 ¾ cup well-shaken buttermilk

Special equipment: **a 10-inch well-seasoned
    cast-iron or heavy nonstick skillet
    (at least 2 inches deep)**

Put oven rack in middle position and preheat oven
to 375°F.
 Make topping:
 Heat butter in skillet over moderate heat until foam
subsides. Reduce heat to low and sprinkle brown sugar
evenly over butter, then cook, undisturbed, 3 minutes
(not all of sugar will be melted). Remove skillet from
heat and arrange apricot halves, cut sides down, close
together on top of brown sugar.
 Make cake batter:
 Sift together flour, baking powder, baking soda,
and salt into a small bowl.
 Beat together butter, sugar, and extracts in a large
bowl with an electric mixer at medium speed until pale
and fluffy, 2 to 3 minutes in a standing mixer or 3 to
4 minutes with a handheld. Beat in eggs 1 at a time,
then beat until mixture is creamy and doubled in volume, 2 to 3 minutes.
 Reduce speed to low and add flour mixture and buttermilk alternately in 3 batches, beginning and ending
with flour mixture, and mixing until just combined.
Gently spoon batter over apricots, spreading evenly.

Bake cake:
 Bake cake until golden brown and a wooden pick
or skewer inserted in center comes out clean, 40 to
45 minutes.
 Wearing oven mitts, immediately invert a large
plate over skillet and, keeping plate and skillet firmly
pressed together, invert cake onto plate. Carefully lift
skillet off cake and, if necessary, replace any fruit that
is stuck to bottom of skillet. Cool to warm or room
temperature.

CRANBERRY COFFEECAKE

Serves 6 to 8
Active time: 15 min   Start to finish: 1¾ hr

 2 cups fresh or thawed frozen cranberries
 1¾ cups granulated sugar
 2 cups all-purpose flour
 2 teaspoons baking powder
 ¾ teaspoon salt
 1 stick (½ cup) unsalted butter, softened
 2 large eggs
 1 teaspoon vanilla
 ½ cup whole milk

Garnish: **confectioners sugar**

Put oven rack in middle position and preheat
oven to 350°F. Generously butter a 9- by 5- by 3-inch
loaf pan.
 Pulse cranberries with ½ cup granulated sugar in a
food processor until finely chopped (do not purée).
Transfer to a sieve and let drain while making batter.
 Sift together flour, baking powder, and salt. Beat
together butter and remaining 1¼ cups granulated sugar
in a large bowl with an electric mixer at medium-high
speed until light and fluffy, about 5 minutes with a
standing mixer or about 8 minutes with a handheld.
Add eggs 1 at a time, beating well after each addition,
then beat in vanilla. Reduce speed to low and add flour
mixture and milk alternately in batches, beginning and
ending with flour and mixing until just incorporated.
 Spread one third of batter evenly in loaf pan, then
spoon half of drained cranberries evenly over batter,
leaving a ½-inch border along sides. Top with another
third of batter and remaining cranberries, leaving a
½-inch border along sides, then cover with remaining
batter. Bake until golden brown and a wooden pick or

skewer inserted in center comes out clean, 1 to 1¼ hours. Cool cake in pan on a rack 30 minutes.

Invert cake onto rack. Serve warm or at room temperature.

Cooks' note:
• Coffeecake can be made 1 day ahead. Cool completely, then store in a cake keeper or wrapped in foil at room temperature. If desired, warm in a preheated 350°F oven 15 minutes before serving.

PHOTO ON PAGE 56

cookies and bars

DULCE DE LECHE CHEESECAKE SQUARES

Makes 64 (1-inch) petits fours

Active time: 45 min Start to finish: 9¾ hr (includes chilling)

Wheatmeal crackers (sometimes called digestive biscuits) have a flavor similar to graham crackers. For this particular recipe, we prefer Carr's brand wheatmeal crackers, which are available at supermarkets and labeled as "whole wheat crackers." (Don't use Carr's Wheatolos, which are a bit too sweet.)

For crust
3½ oz wheatmeal crackers (sometimes called digestive biscuits), crumbled (1 cup)
2 tablespoons sugar

3 tablespoons unsalted butter, melted
For filling
1 teaspoon unflavored gelatin (from a ¼-oz envelope)
¼ cup whole milk
8 oz cream cheese, softened
2 large eggs
⅜ teaspoon salt
1 cup dulce de leche (12½ oz)
For glaze
3 oz fine-quality bittersweet chocolate (not unsweetened), coarsely chopped
½ stick (¼ cup) unsalted butter, cut into pieces
2 teaspoons light corn syrup

Make crust:
Put oven rack in middle position and preheat oven to 325°F. Line bottom and sides of an 8-inch square baking pan with 2 sheets of foil (crisscrossed), leaving a 2-inch overhang on all sides.

Finely grind crackers with sugar and a pinch of salt in a food processor. With motor running, add butter, blending until combined. Press mixture evenly onto bottom of baking pan. Bake 10 minutes, then cool in pan on a rack 5 minutes.

Make filling:
Sprinkle gelatin over milk in a small bowl and let stand 2 minutes to soften.

Beat together cream cheese, eggs, salt, and gelatin mixture in a bowl with an electric mixer at medium speed until well combined, about 2 minutes, then stir in dulce de leche gently but thoroughly. Pour filling over crust, smoothing top, then bake in a hot water bath (see Tips, page 8) in oven until center is just set, about 45 minutes. Cool cheesecake completely in pan on rack, about 2 hours. Chill, covered, at least 6 hours.

Glaze cake within 2 hours of serving:
Heat all of the glaze ingredients in a double boiler or a small metal bowl set over a saucepan of barely simmering water, stirring until smooth, then pour over cheesecake, tilting baking pan to coat top evenly. Chill, uncovered, 30 minutes.

Lift cheesecake from pan using foil overhang and cut into 1-inch squares with a thin knife, wiping off knife after each cut.

Cooks' note:
• Cheesecake (without glaze) can be chilled up to 3 days.
PHOTO ON PAGE 104

HONEY CHEESECAKE SQUARES

Makes 25 (1½-inch) squares
Active time: 25 min   Start to finish: 4 hr
(includes chilling)

6 (4¾- by 2½-inch) graham crackers
2½ tablespoons sugar
3 tablespoons unsalted butter, melted
8 oz cream cheese, softened
1 large egg
2 tablespoons milk
2 teaspoons finely grated fresh lemon zest
1 tablespoon fresh lemon juice
¼ cup mild honey

Put oven rack in middle position and preheat oven to 325°F.

Crumble graham crackers into a food processor, then finely grind with sugar and a pinch of salt. With motor running, add butter, then press mixture evenly over bottom of an ungreased 8-inch square baking pan.

Bake 10 minutes, then cool 5 minutes.

Meanwhile, blend cream cheese, egg, milk, zest, and lemon juice in cleaned food processor. Add honey and blend filling well.

Pour filling over crust and bake until slightly puffed and set, about 30 minutes.

Cool cheesecake in pan on a rack, then chill, covered, until cold, at least 3 hours. Cut into squares.

DARK CHOCOLATE COOKIES

Makes about 36 cookies
Active time: 20 min   Start to finish: 1 hr

¾ cup all-purpose flour
¾ cup unsweetened cocoa powder
½ teaspoon baking soda
½ teaspoon salt
1½ sticks (¾ cup) unsalted butter, softened
1 cup sugar
2 large eggs
1 teaspoon vanilla

Put oven rack in middle position and preheat oven to 375°F.

Whisk together flour, cocoa, baking soda, and salt in a bowl.

Beat together butter and sugar in a large bowl with an electric mixer at medium speed until pale and fluffy, about 3 minutes, then beat in eggs and vanilla until combined. Reduce speed to low, then add flour mixture and mix just until combined.

Drop level tablespoons of dough about 2 inches apart onto ungreased baking sheets and bake in batches until puffed and set, about 12 minutes. Transfer cookies to a rack to cool.

PB&J CRUMBLE BARS

Makes 24 bars
Active time: 30 min   Start to finish: 1¾ hr

¾ stick (6 tablespoons) unsalted butter, softened
6 tablespoons peanut butter
½ cup packed light brown sugar
1 large egg
1½ cups all-purpose flour
½ teaspoon salt
½ cup grape jelly

Put oven rack in middle position and preheat oven to 350°F. Line a 9-inch square baking pan with foil.

Beat together butter, peanut butter, and brown sugar in a large bowl with an electric mixer at medium speed until fluffy, about 2 minutes. Add egg and beat until combined. Reduce speed to low, then add flour and salt and mix until a dough forms.

Reserve 1 cup dough for topping. Press remaining dough evenly onto bottom of baking pan. Spread jelly in an even layer on top of dough, then coarsely crumble reserved dough over jelly layer. Bake until top is golden, 30 to 35 minutes. Cool completely in pan on a rack, about 45 minutes, then cut into bars.

CHOCOLATE ORANGE PETITS FOURS

Makes about 32 petits fours
Active time: 30 min   Start to finish: 1¾ hr

For cookie base
1 cup all-purpose flour
⅔ cup packed dark brown sugar
2 tablespoons unsweetened cocoa powder
½ teaspoon salt
7 oz fine-quality bittersweet chocolate (not unsweetened), finely chopped
½ stick (¼ cup) unsalted butter, cut into tablespoon pieces
2 large eggs
2 teaspoons finely grated fresh orange zest
For topping
½ cup chilled heavy cream
1 teaspoon sugar
4 navel orange segments, membranes discarded from each and fruit cut into ¼-inch pieces

Special equipment: 2 (12-inch-long) sheets of parchment paper; a 1½-inch round fluted cookie cutter

Make cookie base:
Whisk together flour, brown sugar, cocoa powder, and salt in a bowl.

Melt chocolate and butter in a metal bowl set over a saucepan of barely simmering water, stirring occasionally, until smooth. Remove bowl from heat and stir in eggs, zest, and flour mixture until just combined. (Dough will be soft.)

Roll out dough between parchment sheets into an 8-inch round (½ inch thick). Transfer round (still in parchment) to a large baking sheet and chill until firm, at least 1 hour, or freeze at least 30 minutes.

Put oven rack in middle position and preheat oven to 350°F. Butter a large baking sheet.

Remove top sheet of parchment paper and replace it loosely. Flip over paper-enclosed round and discard paper now on top. Cut out about 20 cookies with cookie cutter and arrange about 1 inch apart on baking sheet. Reroll scraps between parchment sheets and cut out 12 more cookies (chill or freeze dough as needed if it becomes too soft to handle).

Bake cookies until matte (dough will start out shiny and turn dull), about 10 minutes, then transfer with a spatula to a rack to cool completely. (Cookies will have a fudgy consistency.)

Top cookies:
Beat cream and sugar with an electric mixer until it just holds stiff peaks. Top each cookie with ½ teaspoon cream and a piece of orange.

Cooks' notes:
• Dough can be chilled, wrapped well in plastic wrap, up to 1 day or frozen 1 week.
• Baked cookies (without topping) can be made 2 days ahead and kept in an airtight container at room temperature.
PHOTO ON PAGE 64

ORANGE SHORTBREAD

Makes 12 cookies
Active time: 10 min   Start to finish: 1 hr

1 stick (½ cup) unsalted butter, softened
¼ cup superfine granulated sugar
1 teaspoon finely grated fresh orange zest
⅛ teaspoon salt
1 cup all-purpose flour
1 tablespoon coarse sugar (optional)

Put oven rack in middle position and preheat oven to 375°F.

Blend together butter, superfine sugar, zest, and salt in a bowl with a fork. Sift flour into butter mixture and blend with fork until mixture forms a soft dough.

Transfer dough to an ungreased large baking sheet and pat into a 10- by 5-inch rectangle. Prick dough all over with fork and sprinkle with coarse sugar (if using), pressing it gently into dough with your fingertips to adhere. Score dough crosswise with back of a knife into 6 rectangles (do not cut all the way through), then score each rectangle into 2 triangles.

Bake shortbread until edges are golden but center is pale, 12 to 17 minutes. Cool on baking sheet on a rack 10 minutes, then cut into 12 triangles along scored lines while still warm. Transfer triangles with a long spatula to a rack to cool completely.

Cooks' notes:
• Shortbread can be made 3 days ahead and kept in an airtight container at room temperature.
• Shortbread keeps 1 week.
PHOTO ON PAGE 55

WHOOPIE PIES

Makes 8 individual desserts
Active time: 30 min   Start to finish: 1 hr

We prefer Droste brand Dutch-process cocoa for this recipe because it gives the cakes a richer chocolate flavor. Though whoopie pies can be served on the same day they're made, we think the cakes are much better a day after baking.

For cakes
2 cups all-purpose flour
⅔ cup Dutch-process cocoa powder
1¼ teaspoons baking soda
1 teaspoon salt
1 cup well-shaken buttermilk
1 teaspoon vanilla
1 stick (½ cup) unsalted butter, softened
1 cup packed brown sugar
1 large egg
For filling
1 stick (½ cup) unsalted butter, softened
1¼ cups confectioners sugar
2 cups marshmallow cream such as Marshmallow Fluff
1 teaspoon vanilla

Make cakes:
Put oven racks in upper and lower thirds of oven preheat oven to 350°F. Butter 2 large baking sheets.

Whisk together flour, cocoa, baking soda, and salt in a bowl until combined. Stir together buttermilk and vanilla in a small bowl.

Beat together butter and brown sugar in a large bowl with an electric mixer at medium-high speed until pale and fluffy, about 3 minutes in a standing mixer or 5 minutes with a handheld, then add egg, beating until combined well. Reduce speed to low, then add flour mixture and buttermilk alternately in batches, beginning and ending with flour, scraping down side of bowl occasionally, and mixing until smooth.

Spoon ¼-cup mounds of batter about 2 inches apart onto baking sheets. Bake in upper and lower thirds of oven, switching position of sheets halfway through baking, until tops are puffed and cakes spring back when touched, 11 to 13 minutes. Transfer with a metal spatula to a rack to cool completely.

Make filling:
Beat together softened butter, confectioners sugar, marshmallow, and vanilla in a bowl with electric mixer at medium speed until smooth, about 3 minutes.

Assemble pies:
Spread a rounded tablespoon filling on flat sides of half of cakes and top with remaining cakes.

Cooks' notes:
• Cakes can be made 3 days ahead and kept, layered between sheets of wax paper, in an airtight container at room temperature.
• Filling can be made 4 hours ahead and kept, covered, at room temperature.
PHOTO ON PAGE 51

PISTACHIO APRICOT OATMEAL COOKIES

Makes 18 large cookies
Active time: 20 min   Start to finish: 45 min

1 stick (½ cup) unsalted butter, softened
¾ cup packed light brown sugar
¼ cup granulated sugar
¼ teaspoon vanilla
1 large egg
¾ cup all-purpose flour
½ teaspoon baking soda
¼ teaspoon salt
⅛ teaspoon cinnamon
1½ cups old-fashioned rolled oats (not quick-cooking)
⅓ cup dried apricots (2 oz), cut into ¼-inch pieces
⅓ cup shelled pistachios (1½ oz; not dyed red), coarsely chopped

Put oven racks in upper and lower thirds of oven and preheat oven to 350°F. Butter 2 baking sheets.

Beat together butter and sugars in a large bowl with an electric mixer at medium-high speed until fluffy, about 2 minutes, then beat in vanilla. Add egg and beat until combined well. Stir together flour, baking soda, salt, and cinnamon in a small bowl, then add to dough and mix at low speed until just combined. Fold in oats, apricots, and pistachios.

Spoon rounded tablespoons of dough about 2 inches apart onto baking sheets. Bake cookies, switching position of sheets halfway through baking, until golden brown, 16 to 18 minutes total. Transfer cookies with a spatula to racks. (Cookies will crisp as they cool.)

SPICED TUILES

Makes about 30 cookies
Active time: 45 min   Start to finish: 1¼ hr

½ stick (¼ cup) unsalted butter
¼ cup packed light brown sugar
 3 tablespoons light corn syrup
¼ cup all-purpose flour
½ teaspoon ground cinnamon
¼ teaspoon ground cardamom
⅛ teaspoon salt

Special equipment: **a small offset spatula; a long rolling pin (2 inches in diameter)**

Bring butter, brown sugar, and corn syrup to a boil in a 1- to 1½-quart heavy saucepan over moderate heat, stirring. Add flour and cook, stirring constantly, until dough is slightly thickened, about 1 minute. Stir in cinnamon, cardamom, and salt and cool to warm, 15 to 20 minutes.

While dough cools, put oven rack in middle position and preheat oven to 375°F. Lightly butter a large baking sheet.

Drop teaspoons of dough about 3 inches apart onto baking sheet and pat each into a 2½-inch round with your fingertips. Bake until golden and most of bubbling has subsided, 6 to 8 minutes (cookies will spread to about 3 inches).

Let cookies stand on baking sheet until just firm enough to hold their shape, about 2 minutes. Gently loosen cookies 1 at a time with offset spatula and immediately drape over rolling pin. (If cookies become too brittle to drape onto rolling pin, return baking sheet to oven for a few seconds to soften.) Cool cookies completely on rolling pin, about 1 minute, then transfer to a platter. Make and shape more spiced tuiles with remaining dough.

Cooks' note:
• Cookies can be made 3 days ahead and kept, layers separated with wax paper, in an airtight container at room temperature.

WALNUT THINS

Makes about 80 small cookies
Active time: 1 hr   Start to finish: 1 hr

Over the past century, pecans have become closely associated with the South. However, walnuts were actually the pecan's predecessor in the Lowcountry, and were far more popular in earlier times.

½ stick (¼ cup) unsalted butter, softened
⅓ cup packed light brown sugar
⅛ teaspoon salt
 1 large egg
½ teaspoon vanilla
¼ cup all-purpose flour
 1 cup walnuts (4 oz), minced, lightly toasted (see Tips, page 8), and cooled

Put oven rack in middle position and preheat oven to 425°F. Generously butter 2 baking sheets.

Beat together butter, brown sugar, and salt in a bowl with an electric mixer until light and fluffy, about 3 minutes, then beat in egg and vanilla until just combined. Sift flour over batter, then fold in. Fold in walnuts.

Drop level ½ teaspoons batter about 2 inches apart onto baking sheets and pat into 1½-inch rounds with back of a fork. (To keep fork from sticking to batter, dip fork in water, then tap off excess water onto a paper towel.)

Bake cookies in batches until pale golden around edges, 5 to 7 minutes. Carefully loosen hot cookies with a metal spatula and transfer to a rack to cool. (If cookies become too firm to remove without breaking, return to oven for a few seconds to soften.)

Cooks' note:
• Cookies can be made 2 days ahead and kept, layered between sheets of wax paper, in an airtight container at room temperature.
PHOTO ON PAGE 71

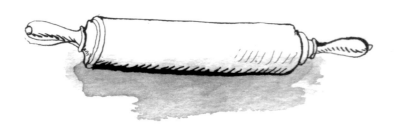

pies and tarts

THREE-BERRY PIE WITH VANILLA CREAM

Serves 8
Active time: 40 min   Start to finish: 6 hr
(includes making dough and cooling pie)

1 cup granulated sugar
3 tablespoons cornstarch
2 tablespoons quick-cooking tapioca
¼ teaspoon salt
3 cups fresh blackberries (¾ to 1 lb)
2 cups fresh raspberries (½ to ¾ lb)
2 cups fresh blueberries (½ to ¾ lb)
  Pastry dough (recipe follows)
1 large egg, lightly beaten
1 tablespoon sanding or granulated sugar

Special equipment: **a 9-inch metal or glass pie
  plate (4-cup capacity)**
Accompaniment: **vanilla cream (recipe below)**

Put oven rack in middle position, then put a large baking sheet on rack and preheat oven to 450°F.

Whisk together granulated sugar, cornstarch, tapioca, and salt, then toss with berries.

Roll out 1 piece of dough (keep remaining piece chilled) on a lightly floured surface with a lightly floured rolling pin into a 13-inch round and fit into pie plate. Trim edge, leaving a ½-inch overhang. Chill shell while rolling out dough for top crust.

Roll out remaining chilled piece of dough on lightly floured surface with floured rolling pin into an 11-inch round.

Spoon filling into shell, then cover pie with pastry round and trim with kitchen shears, leaving a ½-inch overhang. Press edges together, then crimp edge decoratively. Brush top of pie with egg and sprinkle all over with sanding sugar. Cut 3 steam vents in top crust with a small sharp knife.

Bake pie on hot baking sheet 15 minutes, then reduce oven temperature to 375°F and continue to bake until crust is golden brown and filling is bubbling, about 45 minutes more.

Cool pie on a rack at least 3 hours before serving to allow juices to thicken slightly (filling will still be juicy).

PHOTO ON PAGE 89

PASTRY DOUGH

Makes enough for 1 double-crust 9-inch pie
Active time: 10 min   Start to finish: 1¼ hr

2½ cups all-purpose flour
1½ sticks (¾ cup) cold unsalted butter, cut into
  ½-inch cubes
¼ cup cold vegetable shortening
½ teaspoon salt
4 to 6 tablespoons ice water

Special equipment: **a pastry or bench scraper**

Blend together flour, butter, shortening, and salt in a bowl with your fingertips or a pastry blender (or pulse in a food processor) until most of mixture resembles coarse meal with some small (roughly pea-size) butter lumps. Drizzle evenly with 4 tablespoons ice water and gently stir with a fork (or pulse in food processor) until incorporated.

Squeeze a small handful: If it doesn't hold together, add more ice water, 1 tablespoon at a time, stirring (or pulsing) until incorporated, then test again. (Do not overwork mixture, or pastry will be tough.)

Turn out mixture onto a lightly floured surface and divide into 8 portions. With heel of your hand, smear each portion once or twice in a forward motion to help distribute fat. Gather dough together with scraper and press into 2 balls, then flatten each into a 5-inch disk. Wrap disks separately in plastic wrap and chill until firm, at least 1 hour.

Cooks' note:
• **Dough can be chilled up to 1 day.**

VANILLA CREAM

Makes about 2 cups
Active time: 5 min   Start to finish: 5 min

½ vanilla bean, halved lengthwise, or
  1 teaspoon vanilla extract
1 cup chilled heavy cream
2 tablespoons sugar

Scrape seeds from vanilla bean with tip of a knife into a bowl. Add cream and sugar and beat with an electric mixer until cream just holds soft peaks.

GALETTE DE POMMES AU CALVADOS
Apple and Calvados Tart

Serves 8
Active time: 45 min   Start to finish: 3¾ hr
(includes making pastry dough and applesauce)

All-butter pastry dough (recipe follows)
1¾ lb Gala apples
2 teaspoons fresh lemon juice
⅓ cup plus ½ tablespoon granulated sugar
    Calvados applesauce (page 238)
3 tablespoons unsalted butter, cut into
    ½-inch pieces
1½ tablespoons apple jelly
1 cup chilled heavy cream
1 tablespoon confectioners sugar
1½ tablespoons Calvados

Special equipment: **a large baking sheet (at least 14 inches wide); parchment paper**

Line large baking sheet with parchment. Roll out pastry on a lightly floured surface with a floured rolling pin into a rough 16-inch round (⅛ inch thick), then transfer carefully to baking sheet. Loosely fold in edge of pastry where necessary to fit on baking sheet, then chill, covered loosely with plastic wrap, 30 minutes.

Put oven rack in middle position and preheat oven to 425°F.

While pastry chills, peel and core apples, then cut into ⅛-inch-thick slices. Toss slices with lemon juice and ⅓ cup granulated sugar.

Put baking sheet with pastry on a work surface and unfold any edges so pastry is flat. Spread applesauce over pastry, leaving a 2-inch border, and top sauce with sliced apples, mounding slightly. Fold edges of dough over filling, partially covering apples (center will not be covered) and pleating dough as necessary. Dot apples with butter, then brush pastry edge lightly with water and sprinkle with remaining ½ tablespoon granulated sugar. Bake *galette* until pastry is golden and apples are tender, 40 to 45 minutes.

While *galette* bakes, melt apple jelly in a very small saucepan over moderately low heat, stirring.

Slide baked *galette* on parchment onto a rack, then brush with melted jelly and cool *galette* until warm or room temperature.

Beat together cream and confectioners sugar in a bowl with an electric mixer until cream just holds soft peaks, then beat in Calvados. Serve *galette* topped with dollops of Calvados cream.

Cooks' note:
• *Galette* can be made 8 hours ahead and kept at room temperature.
PHOTO ON PAGE 49

ALL-BUTTER PASTRY DOUGH

**Makes enough for a 12-inch single-crust *galette*
or a 9-inch double-crust pie**
Active time: 15 min   Start to finish: 1¼ hr

Though this pastry dough is very good when made with regular butter, it really shines when you use the richest butter possible, such as Plugrá or Land O Lakes Ultra Creamy Butter.

2½ cups all-purpose flour (not unbleached)
2 teaspoons sugar
¾ teaspoon salt
2 sticks (1 cup) cold unsalted butter, cut
    into ½-inch cubes
9 to 12 tablespoons ice water

Special equipment: **a pastry or bench scraper**

Whisk together flour, sugar, and salt in a bowl, then blend in butter with your fingertips or a pastry blender (or pulse in a food processor) just until most of mixture resembles coarse meal with small (roughly pea-size) butter lumps. Drizzle evenly with 9 tablespoons ice water and gently stir with a fork (or pulse in food processor) until incorporated.

Squeeze a small handful: If it doesn't hold together, add more ice water, 1 tablespoon at a time, stirring (or pulsing) until just incorporated, then test again. (Do not overwork mixture, or pastry will be tough.)

Turn out mixture onto a lightly floured surface and divide into 8 portions. With heel of your hand, smear each portion once or twice in a forward motion to help distribute fat. Gather dough together with scraper and press into a ball, then flatten into a 6-inch disk. Chill dough, wrapped in plastic wrap, until firm, at least 1 hour.

Cooks' note:
• Dough can be chilled up to 1 day. Let stand at room temperature 20 minutes before rolling out.

CALVADOS APPLESAUCE

Makes about 1¼ cups
Active time: 10 min   Start to finish: 1 hr (includes cooling)

1 lb Gala apples
½ cup water
½ cup sugar
½ teaspoon finely grated fresh lemon zest
⅛ teaspoon cinnamon
2 tablespoons Calvados

Peel and core apples, then cut into 1-inch pieces. Bring apples, water, sugar, zest, and cinnamon to a boil in a 2-quart heavy saucepan, stirring occasionally, then reduce heat and simmer, covered, 15 minutes.

Remove lid and simmer until most of liquid is evaporated, 5 to 10 minutes. Add Calvados and simmer, stirring occasionally, 1 minute. Mash apples with a potato masher or a fork to a coarse sauce, then cool.

Cooks' note:
• Applesauce can be made 3 days ahead and chilled, covered.

BRANDIED SOUR CHERRY AND PEAR TARTLETS

Makes 16 tartlets
Active time: 2 hr   Start to finish: 3½ hr

For pastry
3½ cups all-purpose flour
1 teaspoon salt
2 sticks (1 cup) cold unsalted butter, cut into ½-inch cubes
½ cup cold vegetable shortening
3 tablespoons sugar
8 to 10 tablespoons ice water
3 tablespoons whole milk
For filling
1½ lb firm-ripe pears (3)
2 cups dried sour cherries (10 oz)
½ cup brandy
½ cup water
3 tablespoons sugar
2 tablespoons cornstarch

Special equipment: **a pastry or bench scraper; a 3½-inch fluted round cookie cutter; small (½- to ¾-inch) decorative cutters; a 4-inch fluted or plain round cutter; 16 (3¼- to 3½- by ⅝-inch) fluted round nonstick tartlet pans**

Make pastry:
Blend together flour, salt, butter, shortening, and 2 tablespoons sugar with your fingertips or a pastry blender in a large bowl (or pulse in a food processor, then transfer to a large bowl) just until most of mixture resembles coarse meal with small (roughly pea-size) butter lumps. Drizzle evenly with ½ cup ice water and gently stir with a fork until incorporated.

Squeeze a small handful: If it doesn't hold together, add more ice water, 1 tablespoon at a time, stirring until just incorporated, then test again. (Do not overwork mixture, or pastry will be tough.)

Turn out mixture onto a lightly floured surface and divide into 8 portions. With heel of your hand, smear each portion once or twice in a forward motion to help distribute fat. Gather dough together with scraper and divide into 2 balls, one slightly larger than the other, then flatten each into a 5- to 6-inch disk. Chill, wrapped in plastic wrap, until firm, at least 1 hour.

Make filling while pastry chills:
Peel, halve, and core pears. Cut pears into ¼-inch dice, then stir together with remaining filling ingredients in a 3-quart heavy pot. Bring to a boil, stirring, then reduce heat and simmer, uncovered, stirring occasionally, until thick, about 10 minutes. Transfer filling to a shallow dish and cool to room temperature.

Make tartlet tops:
Roll out smaller disk of dough into a 13-inch round (about ⅛ inch thick) on a floured surface with a floured rolling pin, lifting up dough carefully and flouring surface as necessary to keep dough from sticking.

Line a baking sheet with wax paper. Cut out as many rounds as possible (about 12) with 3½-inch fluted cutter, transferring as cut to baking sheet. Chill rounds until firm, about 10 minutes, before decorating. Gather dough scraps and chill 20 to 30 minutes, then reroll, cut, and chill additional 3½-inch rounds (reroll scraps only once) for a total of 16.

Cut out shapes from rounds with decorative cutters or a sharp paring knife, leaving a ½-inch border around edge, and reserve cutout pieces if desired for additional decoration. Brush tops lightly with milk. Lightly press reserved cutouts (if using) onto decorated rounds and brush lightly with milk. Sprinkle remaining tablespoon sugar evenly over tops and chill while making bottoms.

Put oven rack in middle position and preheat oven to 375°F.

Make tartlet bottoms:

Roll out larger disk of dough into a 15-inch round (about ⅛ inch thick) on floured surface with floured rolling pin, lifting up dough carefully and flouring surface as necessary to keep dough from sticking. Cut out as many rounds as possible (about 12) with 4-inch cutter. Gather dough scraps and chill 20 to 30 minutes, then reroll and cut additional 4-inch rounds (reroll scraps only once) for a total of 16. Fit each 4-inch round into a tartlet pan (don't trim). Fill each tartlet with 3 tablespoons cooled filling and brush edge of pastry lightly with milk. Place decorated tops over filling in each tartlet, then press each top lightly around edge to help seal edges and trim pastry if necessary.

Bake tartlets:

Bake tartlets on a large baking sheet until golden, 20 to 25 minutes. Transfer tartlets to a rack and cool 10 minutes. To remove tartlets from pans, cover 1 hand with a folded kitchen towel and invert tartlets 1 at a time onto towel, reinverting them onto a platter. Serve warm or at room temperature.

Cooks' notes:
- **Disks of pastry dough can be chilled up to 1 day. Let stand at room temperature about 20 minutes to soften slightly before rolling out.**
- **Filling can be made 1 day ahead and cooled, uncovered, then chilled, covered.**
- **Assembled tartlets (unbaked) can be made 1 week ahead and frozen, wrapped well in plastic wrap. Do not thaw before baking.**
- **Tartlets can be baked 1 day ahead and kept, loosely covered, at room temperature. Reheat in a preheated 350°F oven until warm, 10 to 15 minutes.**
- **Instead of 16 tartlets, you can make 1 (10-inch) tart. Use slightly larger decorative cutouts, if desired, and bake longer, about 50 to 60 minutes total.**

PHOTO ON PAGE 98

CANDIED KUMQUAT AND RICOTTA TART

Serves 8 to 12
Active time: 1¾ hr   Start to finish: 2¾ hr
(includes making pastry shell)

4 cups fresh kumquats (1½ lb with leaves; 1 lb without)
1 cup water
2 cups plus 2 tablespoons sugar
1 teaspoon fennel seeds, lightly toasted (see Tips, page 8)
⅔ cup ricotta
⅓ cup sour cream
1 (12- to 13-inch) baked sweet tart shell (page 240)

Special equipment: **an electric coffee/spice grinder**

Thinly slice kumquats crosswise with a sharp knife, discarding seeds.

Bring water and 2 cups sugar to a boil in a 2-quart heavy saucepan, stirring until sugar is dissolved, then simmer syrup, uncovered, 5 minutes. Stir in kumquats and simmer gently 10 minutes. Drain and cool kumquats in a sieve set over a bowl, then return drained syrup to pan and boil until reduced to about 1⅓ cups, 3 to 5 minutes.

Finely grind fennel seeds in coffee/spice grinder, then transfer to a bowl and whisk together with ricotta, remaining 2 tablespoons sugar, and a pinch of salt just until ricotta is slightly smoother. Whisk in sour cream until just combined and spread evenly over bottom of tart shell.

Arrange kumquats as evenly as possible over ricotta using your fingers or a small spoon, separating slices as necessary with a skewer, then brush kumquats with some of reduced syrup.

Remove side of tart pan.

Cooks' notes:
- **Kumquats can be candied 1 day ahead and chilled in syrup (before reducing), covered. Warm mixture before proceeding.**
- **Ricotta filling can be made 1 day ahead and chilled, covered.**
- **Tart can be assembled 2 hours ahead and kept at room temperature.**

PHOTO ON PAGE 60

BAKED SWEET TART SHELL

Makes 1 (12- to 13-inch) tart shell
Active time: 30 min Start to finish: 1¼ hr

2⅓ cups all-purpose flour
⅓ cup sugar
¾ teaspoon salt
1¾ sticks (¾ cup plus 2 tablespoons) cold
    unsalted butter, cut into ½-inch cubes
3 large egg yolks
1 teaspoon vanilla

Special equipment: a pastry or bench scraper;
    1 (12- to 13-inch) round fluted tart pan
    (1 inch deep) with removable bottom; pie
    weights or raw rice

Pulse together flour, sugar, salt, and butter in a food processor until most of mixture resembles coarse meal with small (roughly pea-size) butter lumps. Add yolks and vanilla and pulse just until incorporated and mixture begins to clump.

Turn out mixture onto a lightly floured surface and divide into 6 portions. With heel of your hand, smear each portion once or twice in a forward motion to help distribute fat. Gather dough together into a ball with scraper and transfer to tart pan. Pat out ball with floured fingertips onto bottom and up side of tart pan in an even ¼-inch layer. (If mixture sticks to your fingers, spread a sheet of plastic wrap over it and pat through plastic wrap.) Prick bottom of shell all over with a fork, then chill until firm, at least 30 minutes.

Put oven rack in middle position and preheat oven to 375°F.

Line shell with foil and fill with pie weights. Bake on or over a large sheet of foil (to catch any drips of butter) until sides are set and edges are light golden, about 20 minutes. Carefully remove foil and weights and bake shell until bottom is golden and sides are golden brown, 14 to 16 minutes more. Cool shell completely in pan on a rack before filling.

Cooks' note:
• Unbaked tart shell can be chilled, wrapped tightly
  in plastic wrap, up to 1 day, or frozen 1 week.

FRESH FIG TART WITH ROSEMARY CORNMEAL CRUST AND LEMON MASCARPONE CREAM

Serves 6
Active time: 1¼ hr Start to finish: 1¾ hr

For crust
1½ cups all-purpose flour
½ cup yellow cornmeal (not stone-ground)
1 tablespoon sugar
¼ teaspoon salt
1 stick (½ cup) cold unsalted butter, cut into
    tablespoon pieces
1½ tablespoons finely chopped fresh rosemary
4 to 5 tablespoons ice water
For filling
⅓ cup sour cream
8 oz mascarpone cheese (1 cup)
¼ cup sugar
1½ teaspoons finely grated fresh lemon zest
⅛ teaspoon salt
2 tablespoons red-currant jelly
1 tablespoon honey
1½ lb fresh figs

Special equipment: an 11¼- by 8- by 1-inch
    rectangular or 10-inch round fluted tart
    pan (1 inch deep) with a removable
    bottom

Make crust:
Pulse together flour, cornmeal, sugar, and salt in a food processor. Add butter and rosemary and pulse until mixture resembles coarse meal with some small (roughly pea-size) butter lumps. Drizzle evenly with 4 tablespoons ice water and pulse until just incorporated.

Gently squeeze a small handful: If it doesn't hold together, add more water, ½ tablespoon at a time, pulsing after each addition and continuing to test.

Press dough evenly onto bottom and up sides of tart pan with floured fingers. Smooth dough with a small offset metal spatula or back of a spoon (floured if necessary), then roll a rolling pin over top of pan to trim dough flush with rim. Chill crust until firm, about 30 minutes.

Put oven rack in middle position and preheat oven to 400°F.

Bake crust until center and edges are golden, 25 to 30 minutes (don't worry if bottom of crust cracks), then cool in pan on a rack.

Prepare filling and assemble tart:

Whisk together sour cream, mascarpone, sugar, zest, and salt in a bowl.

Heat jelly and honey in a small saucepan over moderately low heat, whisking, until jelly is melted, about 4 minutes, then cool glaze slightly.

Remove side of tart pan and spread mascarpone cream in shell. Cut figs lengthwise into ¼-inch-thick slices and arrange decoratively over cream. Brush figs with honey glaze.

Cooks' notes:
• Crust can be made 1 day ahead and kept, covered, at room temperature.
• Mascarpone mixture can be made 1 day ahead and chilled, covered.
• Tart can be assembled 1 hour ahead and kept, loosely covered, at room temperature.
PHOTO ON PAGE 83

COCONUT CREAM TART

Makes 1 (9-inch) tart
Active time: 30 min   Start to finish: 6¼ hr
(includes cooling and chilling)

For crust
7½ oz shortbread cookies such as Lorna
   Doone, finely ground (2 cups)
1¼ cups sweetened flaked coconut (3 oz)
½ stick (¼ cup) unsalted butter, melted
For coconut custard
1 cup whole milk
5 tablespoons cornstarch
1 cup heavy cream
1 cup well-stirred canned cream of coconut
   (not coconut milk) such as Coco López
2 large eggs, lightly beaten
½ teaspoon coconut extract
For cream topping
1 cup chilled heavy cream
¼ cup sour cream
1 teaspoon sugar

Special equipment: a 9-inch round fluted tart pan
   (1 inch deep) with removable bottom

Make crust:

Put oven rack in middle position and preheat oven to 350°F.

Pulse cookie crumbs, coconut, and butter in a food processor until coconut is finely ground, then press evenly onto bottom and up side of tart pan. Bake until golden, about 16 minutes, then cool completely in pan on a rack.

Make custard:

Stir together whole milk and cornstarch until combined well.

Bring heavy cream and cream of coconut to a boil in a heavy saucepan over moderate heat, whisking occasionally. Whisk cornstarch mixture, then add to cream in a stream, whisking. Boil custard, whisking constantly, 1 minute. Remove from heat and immediately whisk in eggs and coconut extract.

Pour custard into cooled crust and smooth top. Cover custard with a round of wax paper (to prevent a skin from forming) and cool to room temperature, about 1 hour. Chill tart until set, at least 4 hours.

Make topping:

Beat together cream, sour cream, and sugar with an electric mixer until it just holds stiff peaks. Remove wax paper from tart and spread cream evenly over tart.

Cooks' notes:
• Tart (without cream topping) can be chilled up to 8 hours (the crust will begin to soften if chilled longer).
• Tart can be topped with whipped cream 2 hours ahead and chilled.
PHOTO ON PAGE 65

SOUR CHERRY CROSTATA

Serves 8
Active time: 1½ hr   Start to finish: 5 hr (includes cooling)

This beautiful tart features a pastry the Italians call pasta frolla—the texture of the dough is more like cookie dough than traditional French-style pastry. The lattice crust is surprisingly easy to make because it doesn't require weaving the strips.

For pastry
1½ sticks (¾ cup) unsalted butter, softened
⅓ cup plus 1 tablespoon sugar
1 large egg, lightly beaten
1 teaspoon vanilla
2¼ cups all-purpose flour
½ teaspoon salt
2 teaspoons finely grated fresh lemon zest (see Tips, page 8)
For filling
3 tablespoons unsalted butter, cut into pieces
5¼ cups fresh or frozen (not thawed) sour cherries (1¾ lb), pitted
¾ cup plus 1 tablespoon sugar
2 tablespoons cold water
3 tablespoons cornstarch

Special equipment: **a 9- by 1-inch fluted round tart pan with removable rim**

Make pastry dough:
Beat together butter and ⅓ cup sugar with an electric mixer at medium speed until pale and fluffy, about 3 minutes. Reserve 1 tablespoon beaten egg, chilled, for egg wash and beat remaining egg into butter mixture, then add vanilla, beating well. Reduce speed to low and mix in flour, salt, and zest until mixture just forms a dough.

Halve dough and form each half into a 5- to 6-inch disk. Wrap disks in plastic wrap and chill until firm, at least 30 minutes.

Make filling:
Heat butter in a 12-inch nonstick skillet over moderate heat until foam subsides, then add fresh or frozen cherries with any juices and sugar and simmer, stirring, until sugar is dissolved. (Cherries will exude juices.) Continue to simmer until cherries are tender but not falling apart, about 8 minutes. Stir together water and cornstarch to form a thick paste, then stir into simmering filling and boil, stirring frequently, 2 minutes. Cool

filling quickly by spreading it in a shallow baking pan and chilling until lukewarm, about 15 minutes.

Assemble and bake crostata:
Roll out 1 piece of dough (keep remaining piece chilled) between 2 sheets of wax paper into a 12-inch round. Remove top sheet of paper and invert dough into tart pan. Trim overhang to ½ inch and fold inward, then press dough against side of pan to reinforce edge. Chill tart shell.

Roll out remaining piece of dough in same manner and remove top sheet of paper, then cut dough into 10 (1-inch-wide) strips and slide dough, still on wax paper, onto a baking sheet. Chill strips until firm, about 5 minutes.

Line a large baking sheet with foil. Put oven rack in middle position, then put baking sheet on rack and preheat oven to 375°F.

Spread filling in chilled tart shell and arrange 5 strips 1 inch apart across filling, pressing ends onto edge of tart shell. Arrange remaining 5 strips 1 inch apart diagonally across first strips to form a lattice with diamond-shaped spaces. Trim edges of all strips flush with edge of pan. Brush lattice top with reserved beaten egg. Sprinkle *crostata* with remaining tablespoon sugar.

Bake *crostata* on baking sheet until pastry is golden and filling is bubbling, about 1 hour. (If lattice and edges look too brown after 30 minutes, loosely cover with foil.)

Cool *crostata* completely in pan on a rack, 1½ to 2 hours, (to allow juices to thicken).

Cooks' note:
• *Crostata* is best the day it is made but can be made 1 day ahead and kept, covered with foil, at room temperature.

frozen desserts

CANTALOUPE, HONEYDEW, AND ALMOND BOMBE

Serves 8 to 10
Active time: 1¼ hr   Start to finish: 12½ hr (includes freezing)

This dessert is a trompe l'oeil, resembling the peel, rind, and flesh of a cantaloupe.

1⅓ cups sugar
1⅓ cups water
 3 cups cubed (½ inch) ripe cantaloupe
 ¼ cup fresh lime juice
 2 cups cubed (½ inch) ripe honeydew melon
  Vegetable oil for brushing mold
 1 pt superpremium vanilla ice cream, slightly
  softened
1½ cups slivered almonds (7 oz), toasted
  (see Tips, page 8) and cooled
 ⅛ teaspoon almond extract

Special equipment: **an ice cream maker; a 7- to 8-cup decorative metal mold in the shape of a half-melon or a 2-qt metal bowl**

Make sorbets:
Bring sugar and water to a boil in a 1-quart heavy saucepan, stirring until sugar is dissolved. Remove from heat and cool syrup.

Purée cantaloupe with 2 tablespoons lime juice in a blender, then transfer to a bowl and stir in 1 cup sugar syrup. Purée honeydew with remaining 2 tablespoons lime juice in cleaned blender, then transfer to another bowl and stir in remaining cup sugar syrup. Chill both mixtures, covered, until cold, about 2 hours.

Freeze sorbets separately in an ice cream maker. Transfer to airtight containers and freeze until firm but still spreadable, about 30 minutes.

Assemble bombe:
Lightly brush mold with vegetable oil and freeze mold 30 minutes. While mold chills, put vanilla ice cream in refrigerator 20 minutes to soften.

Pulse almonds in a food processor until finely ground (do not grind to a paste).

Stir together almonds, ice cream, and almond extract until blended. Spread evenly onto bottom and up sides of chilled mold. (If ice cream begins to melt,

freeze 10 minutes.) Freeze ice cream until firm, about 30 minutes.

Spread honeydew sorbet in an even layer over ice cream and freeze until sorbet is firm, about 20 minutes.

Fill center with cantaloupe sorbet, pressing in firmly, and smooth top. Cover mold with plastic wrap and freeze until hardened, at least 8 hours.

To serve, unwrap mold and invert bombe onto a chilled serving platter. Wet a kitchen towel with hot water, quickly wring it dry, and drape over pan 30 seconds. Lift off pan, then peel off plastic wrap and put bombe in refrigerator 10 minutes to soften.

Cooks' notes:
• Sorbets can be made 2 days ahead of assembling bombe. Soften in refrigerator before using.
• Assembled bombe can be frozen up to 3 days.

CHOCOLATE SORBET

Makes about 1 qt
Active time: 15 min   Start to finish: 8¼ hr
(includes chilling and freezing)

1¼ cups sugar
 3 cups water
 ¾ cup unsweetened cocoa powder,
  preferably Dutch-process
 ¼ teaspoon salt
 1 teaspoon vanilla

Special equipment: **an ice cream maker**

Cook sugar in a dry 2-quart heavy saucepan over moderate heat, undisturbed, until it begins to melt. Continue to cook, stirring occasionally with a fork, until sugar is melted into a deep golden caramel. Add water (caramel will harden and steam vigorously) and cook over moderately low heat, stirring, until caramel is dissolved.

Add cocoa and salt, whisking until dissolved, then transfer to a bowl and cool, stirring occasionally. Stir in vanilla, then chill, covered, until cold (about 2 hours).

Freeze in ice cream maker, then transfer to an airtight container and put in freezer to harden.

APRICOT FROZEN YOGURT

Makes about 1½ qt
Active time: 30 min   Start to finish: 7½ hr
(includes chilling and freezing)

We highly recommend using California apricots for this recipe—their intense flavor and color give this frozen yogurt a real boost that's missing when it's made with the Turkish variety.

1½ cups sugar
1¾ cups cold water
  2 cups packed soft dried California
     apricots (10 oz)
  1 (32-oz) container whole-milk plain
     yogurt (3½ cups)
2½ teaspoons unflavored gelatin (from
     a ¼-oz envelope)

Special equipment: **an ice cream maker**

Bring sugar and 1 cup cold water to a boil in a 2½- to 3-quart heavy saucepan over moderately high heat, stirring until sugar is dissolved. Add apricots, then reduce heat and simmer, covered, until plump and very soft, 25 to 30 minutes. Drain apricots in a sieve set over a bowl, then return syrup to pan. Cook syrup over moderate heat, swirling pan occasionally, until a deep caramel, 4 to 5 minutes. (Syrup will bubble, so remove from heat periodically to check color.)

Carefully add ½ cup cold water to caramel (mixture will bubble up and steam vigorously), then cook over moderate heat, stirring, until caramel is dissolved. Purée apricots and caramel in a food processor until almost smooth, then cool to room temperature.

Whisk together apricot purée and yogurt in a large bowl until combined well and chill, covered, until cold, about 4 hours.

Sprinkle gelatin over remaining ¼ cup cold water in a very small saucepan and let stand 1 minute to soften. Heat gelatin over moderate heat, stirring, until dissolved, then immediately whisk into apricot mixture.

Freeze apricot mixture in ice cream maker. Transfer mixture to an airtight container and put in freezer to harden.

Cooks' note:
• Frozen yogurt can be made 1 week ahead.

CHERRY TORTONI

Serves 10
Active time: 1 hr   Start to finish: 6 hr (includes freezing)

The tart cherries brighten the classic flavor of almond in this tortoni.

2¼ cups fresh or frozen (not thawed) pitted
     sour cherries (¾ lb)
  ½ cup plus ⅓ cup sugar
  2 tablespoons Di Saronno Amaretto or
     other almond-flavored liqueur
1½ teaspoons cornstarch
  1 tablespoon cold water
1½ cups sliced almonds, toasted (see Tips,
     page 8) and cooled
1¼ cups fine vanilla-wafer crumbs
     (from about 40 wafers)
  ½ stick (¼ cup) unsalted butter, melted
  4 large egg whites
  ½ teaspoon cream of tartar
1⅓ cups chilled heavy cream
  2 tablespoons sweet Marsala wine or
     sweet Sherry
  ¾ cup coarsely ground *amaretti* cookies
     (from about 20 one-inch cookies)

Special equipment: **a 9- to 9½-inch springform pan; an instant-read thermometer**

Cook cherries:
If using frozen cherries, thaw, reserving juices. Simmer cherries, ½ cup sugar, and liqueur in a 2- to 3-quart heavy saucepan, uncovered, stirring occasionally, until cherries are soft, about 5 minutes. Whisk together cornstarch and water until combined, then whisk into cherry mixture and boil 1 minute. Transfer to a shallow bowl and chill, uncovered, 1 hour.

Make crust:
Butter springform pan. Pulse 1 cup almonds in a food processor until finely ground (do not pulse to a paste). Transfer to a bowl and stir in wafer crumbs and butter with a fork until combined well. Pat crumb mixture evenly onto bottom and 1½ inches up side of springform pan, then freeze while making filling, about 30 minutes.

Make tortoni filling:
Beat egg whites with remaining ⅓ cup sugar, cream of tartar, and a pinch of salt in a metal bowl set over a saucepan of simmering water using a handheld electric

mixer at medium-high speed until whites just hold soft peaks and thermometer registers 170°F, about 5 minutes. Remove metal bowl from saucepan and continue to beat whites until they just hold stiff peaks, about 2 minutes more.

Beat cream with sweet Marsala in another bowl at medium speed until it just holds stiff peaks. Fold in *amaretti* and half of whites gently but thoroughly. Fold in remaining whites and pour into crust in pan, smoothing top.

Drain cherries in a sieve set over a bowl and reserve juices. Scatter cherries evenly over top of tortoni, then swirl cherries into tortoni with tip of a sharp knife for a marbled effect. Sprinkle top of tortoni with remaining ½ cup toasted sliced almonds and freeze, loosely covered, until firm, at least 4 hours.

Let stand in pan at room temperature 10 minutes to soften slightly before serving. Carefully remove side of pan, then cut cherry tortoni into wedges and serve with cherry juices.

Cooks' note:
• Tortoni can be frozen up to 1 week.

CHOCOLATE GELATO

Makes about 1 qt
Active time: 20 min   Start to finish: 5 hr
(includes chilling and freezing)

There are no eggs in this recipe—it's the cornstarch that gives the gelato a smooth, silky texture. Fine-quality chocolate provides its rich flavor.

　3 cups whole milk
¼ cup sugar
　3 tablespoons cornstarch
　　Scant ¼ teaspoon salt
　7 oz fine-quality bittersweet chocolate
　　(not unsweetened), finely chopped

Special equipment: an ice cream maker

Bring 2¼ cups milk just to a boil in a 4-quart heavy saucepan over moderate heat. While milk heats, whisk together sugar, cornstarch, salt, and ¼ cup (cold) milk in a bowl until smooth, then whisk into boiling milk and bring to a boil over moderate heat, whisking. Boil, whisking frequently, 3 minutes (mixture will be very thick). Remove from heat.

Bring remaining ½ cup (cold) milk just to a boil in a 1-quart heavy saucepan over moderate heat. Pour hot milk over chocolate in a bowl and let stand until chocolate is melted, about 1 minute, then whisk until smooth. Stir into cornstarch-milk mixture and force through a fine-mesh sieve into a bowl. Cool slightly, stirring frequently to prevent a skin from forming, then cover surface with wax paper and chill until cold, at least 1½ hours.

Freeze mixture in ice cream maker, then transfer to an airtight container and freeze until hardened, about 3 hours. Let soften 5 minutes before serving.

Cooks' note:
• Gelato keeps 1 week.

MEXICAN CHOCOLATE ICE CREAM

Makes about 1½ qt
Active time: 40 min   Start to finish: 2½ hr (includes freezing)

　½ vanilla bean
11 oz Mexican chocolate (3½ disks; preferably
　　Ibarra), coarsely chopped
3¾ cups half-and-half
　3 large eggs
　　Scant ¼ teaspoon salt

Special equipment: an instant-read thermometer;
an ice cream maker

Halve vanilla bean lengthwise and scrape seeds into a 3-quart heavy saucepan. Add chocolate and half-and-half and bring to a boil over moderate heat, whisking. Remove from heat.

Lightly beat eggs with salt in a bowl, then add hot chocolate mixture in a slow stream, whisking. Transfer custard to cleaned saucepan and cook over moderately low heat, stirring constantly with a wooden spoon, until custard registers 175°F on thermometer, 1 to 5 minutes. Immediately pour through a fine-mesh sieve into a metal bowl. Put bowl in a larger bowl of ice and cold water and cool, stirring occasionally.

Freeze custard in ice cream maker. Transfer ice cream to an airtight container and freeze until hardened, about 1 hour.

Cooks' note:
• Ice cream keeps 4 days.
PHOTO ON PAGE 55

FROZEN MANGO RASPBERRY TERRINE

Serves 10 to 12

Active time: 40 min   Start to finish: 11½ hr (includes freezing)

We discovered that store-bought mango sorbet and ice cream were so good we could do little to improve upon them. But most store-bought raspberry sorbet lacked the color, tang, and true berry flavor of homemade.

For raspberry sorbet
⅔ **cup sugar**
1 **cup water**
15 **oz fresh raspberries (3 cups)**
1½ **tablespoons fresh lemon juice**
For terrine
2 **pt mango sorbet**
2 **pt superpremium mango ice cream**

Special equipment: **an ice cream maker;**
          a 12- by 4½- by 3-inch loaf pan or
          other 8-cup mold
Accompaniment: **diced mango (optional)**

Make sorbet:
Bring sugar and water to a boil in a 1-quart heavy saucepan, stirring until sugar is dissolved. Remove from heat and cool syrup.

Purée raspberries and lemon juice in a food processor, then force through a fine-mesh sieve into a bowl, discarding seeds. Stir in sugar syrup and chill, covered, until cold, about 2 hours.

Freeze sorbet in ice cream maker. Transfer to an airtight container and freeze until slightly firmer but still spreadable, about 30 minutes.

Assemble terrine:
Line loaf pan with 3 pieces of plastic wrap (1 lengthwise and 2 crosswise), leaving at least a 2-inch overhang on all sides. Freeze pan 10 minutes.

While raspberry sorbet is in freezer, soften mango sorbet and mango ice cream in refrigerator.

Mash mango sorbet in a bowl with a spoon until spreadable but not melted. Mash ice cream in another bowl in same manner.

Evenly spread 1¾ cups mango sorbet in bottom of loaf pan (preferably with a small offset metal spatula), then top with 1¾ cups mango ice cream and half of raspberry sorbet. (If sorbets or ice cream become too soft for spreading, freeze 10 minutes between layering.) Repeat layering with 1¾ cups mango sorbet, 1¾ cups mango ice cream, and remaining raspberry sorbet (pan

will be full). Cover top of terrine with plastic-wrap overhang, then wrap pan with more plastic wrap and freeze until terrine is hardened, at least 8 hours.

To serve, unwrap pan, then open overhang and invert pan onto a chilled serving platter. Wet a kitchen towel with hot water, quickly wring it dry, and drape over pan 30 seconds. Lift off pan from terrine and peel off plastic wrap.

Cooks' notes:
• Raspberry sorbet can be made 3 days ahead. Soften in refrigerator about 30 minutes before using.
• Assembled terrine can be frozen up to 3 days.

Ice cream

FROZEN MOCHA RUM PARFAITS

Serves 8

Active time: 50 min   Start to finish: 4 hr (includes freezing)

6 **oz fine-quality bittersweet chocolate**
   (not unsweetened), chopped
⅔ **cup strong brewed coffee**
3 **tablespoons plus 2 teaspoons dark rum**
3 **large eggs**
¾ **cup granulated sugar**
2 **cups chilled heavy cream**
1½ **tablespoons confectioners sugar**

Special equipment: **an instant-read thermometer**

Melt chocolate in coffee in a metal bowl set over a large saucepan of barely simmering water, stirring until smooth, then stir in 3 tablespoons rum. Remove bowl from heat.

Beat together eggs, granulated sugar, and a pinch of salt in a large metal bowl with a handheld electric mixer until combined well. Set bowl over saucepan of simmering water and beat mixture until tripled in volume, very thick, and registers 160°F on thermometer, about 6 minutes. Remove bowl from heat, then beat in chocolate mixture. Chill until cool, about 10 minutes.

Beat 1 cup cream in a bowl with cleaned beaters until it just holds stiff peaks, then fold into chocolate mixture. Divide among 8 (8-ounce) stemmed glasses and freeze, covered with plastic wrap, until set, at least 3 hours.

Before serving, let parfaits stand at room temperature 15 minutes to soften slightly.

While parfaits stand, beat remaining cup cream with confectioners sugar until it just holds stiff peaks, then beat in remaining 2 teaspoons rum and spoon onto parfaits.

Cooks' note:
• Parfaits can be frozen up to 1 day.
PHOTO ON PAGE 71

FROZEN PASSION-FRUIT MERINGUE CAKE

Serves 8 to 10
Active time: 1½ hr   Start to finish: 7 hr (includes freezing)

For meringue layers
**4 large egg whites at room temperature
    for 30 minutes
1 cup sugar**
For passion-fruit mousse and cream
**1 stick (½ cup) unsalted butter, cut
    into pieces
½ teaspoon cornstarch
¾ cup thawed frozen passion-fruit pulp
¾ cup plus 2 tablespoons sugar
1 whole large egg
6 large egg yolks
1½ cups chilled heavy cream**

Special equipment: **a 15- by 12-inch sheet of
    parchment paper; a pastry bag with a
    ⅓-inch plain tip and an ⅛-inch plain tip;
    a long thin platter or a foil-wrapped
    cardboard rectangle (at least 15 by
    4 inches)**

Make meringue layers:
Put oven rack in middle position and preheat oven to 275°F. Lightly butter a large baking sheet.

Draw 3 (14- by 3-inch) rectangles, about ¾ inch apart, on parchment. Turn paper over (rectangles will be visible) and put it on baking sheet.

Beat whites with a pinch of salt in a large bowl with an electric mixer at medium speed until they hold soft peaks. Beat in sugar, 1 tablespoon at a time, then increase speed to high and continue beating until whites hold stiff glossy peaks, about 4 minutes with a standing mixer or 8 to 10 minutes with a handheld. Transfer meringue to pastry bag fitted with ⅓-inch tip and fill in rectangles completely. Gently smooth tops, then bake until firm and very pale golden, 45 to 60 minutes. Slide meringue layers (on parchment) onto a large rack. Cool completely, then carefully peel off parchment.

Make mousse and cream while meringues bake:
Melt butter with cornstarch, passion-fruit pulp, and ¾ cup sugar in a 2-quart heavy saucepan over moderately low heat, stirring until sugar is dissolved.

Whisk together whole egg and yolks in a large bowl until combined, then add butter mixture in a stream, whisking. Transfer mixture to saucepan and cook over moderately low heat, whisking constantly, until thick enough to hold mark of whisk and first bubble appears on surface, 3 to 5 minutes. Transfer curd immediately to a metal bowl set in a larger bowl of ice and cold water and cool, stirring occasionally, until cold.

Beat cream with remaining 2 tablespoons sugar with electric mixer until it just holds stiff peaks. Fold 2 cups whipped cream into curd gently but thoroughly to form a mousse (for filling and icing).

Transfer ¾ cup whipped cream to a small bowl and reserve, chilled, for cream layer. Fold ½ cup mousse into remaining whipped cream, then transfer to cleaned pastry bag fitted with ⅛-inch tip and reserve, chilled, for decorative icing.

Assemble cake and freeze:
Arrange 1 meringue layer, flat side down, on platter and spread evenly with ¾ cup mousse. Cover with another meringue layer and spread evenly with reserved whipped cream. Cover with remaining meringue layer, flat side up, and spread remaining mousse evenly over top and sides of cake, smoothing with a cake spatula. Pipe icing decoratively on top of cake, then freeze, uncovered, until firm, at least 3 hours.

About 1 hour before serving, put cake in refrigerator to soften slightly.

Cooks' note:
• Cake can be frozen up to 2 days. Once cake is firm, cover with plastic wrap; remove plastic wrap before softening in refrigerator.

VANILLA-BEAN ICE CREAM

Makes about 1½ qt
Active time: 20 min Start to finish: 4 hr (includes freezing)

2 cups heavy cream
1 cup whole milk
¾ cup sugar
⅛ teaspoon salt
3 vanilla beans, split lengthwise
2 large eggs

Special equipment: **an instant-read thermometer;**
an ice cream maker

Combine cream, milk, sugar, and salt in a heavy saucepan. Scrape seeds from vanilla beans with tip of a knife into cream mixture, then drop in pods. Heat cream mixture just to a boil.

Whisk eggs in a large bowl, then add hot cream mixture in a slow stream, whisking. Pour mixture into saucepan and cook over moderately low heat, stirring constantly, until slightly thickened and registers 170°F on thermometer (do not let boil).

Pour custard through a fine-mesh sieve into a clean metal bowl, then cool, stirring occasionally. Chill, covered, until cold, at least 3 hours.

Freeze custard in ice cream maker. Transfer to an airtight container and put in freezer to harden.

Cooks' notes:
• **To cool custard quickly after straining, set bowl in a larger bowl of ice and cold water and stir until chilled.**
• **Custard can be chilled up to 24 hours.**

Bananas

fruit finales

BAKED APPLE

Serves 1
Active time: 15 min Start to finish: 1 hr

1 small apple (¼ lb) such as Empire,
    McIntosh, or Gala
1 teaspoon fresh lemon juice
1 tablespoon unsalted butter, melted
2 tablespoons apricot jam
2 tablespoons brandy
1 teaspoon packed light brown sugar
⅛ teaspoon ground allspice
1 (3-inch) cinnamon stick

Put oven rack in middle position and preheat oven to 450°F.

Peel and core apple, leaving it whole, then turn it on its side and slice into ¼-inch-thick rounds. Reassemble to form a whole apple and brush with some of lemon juice. Put apple into a shallow 4-inch round or oval baking dish.

Stir together butter, jam, brandy, brown sugar, allspice, and remaining lemon juice in a small bowl. Spoon 2 teaspoons of mixture into core of apple. Pour rest of mixture over outside of apple and bake, basting once or twice, 25 minutes.

Reduce oven temperature to 350°F. Insert cinnamon stick into core of apple and bake, basting frequently, until apple is tender and well browned and juices are thick and syrupy, about 20 minutes more.

PHOTO ON PAGE 111

LADY APPLES IN APPLE ICE WINE GELÉE

Serves 8
Active time: 15 min Start to finish: 4¼ hr (includes chilling)

Apple ice wine gets its particular sweetness and deep golden color from frozen apples.

1 lemon
2¾ lb lady apples (24 to 28)
1½ cups apple ice wine, or ¾ cup unfiltered
    apple cider stirred together with ¾ cup
    dry white wine
¾ cup sugar

Remove 2 (4- by 1-inch) strips of zest from lemon with a vegetable peeler, then halve lemon crosswise.

Peel top ½ inch of each apple, leaving stem and rest of skin intact. Rub cut side of a lemon half over peeled part of apples. Arrange apples, stem ends up, in 1 layer in a 12-inch heavy skillet. Add zest and ice wine to skillet, then sprinkle sugar over apples. Bring to a simmer over moderate heat, swirling skillet occasionally, then reduce heat to low and cover skillet. Poach until apples are tender but still hold their shape, 20 to 50 minutes, depending on ripeness of apples. Check apples frequently after 20 minutes and transfer as cooked to a bowl.

Discard zest and spoon cooking liquid over apples. Chill, covered, until cold, at least 3 hours (liquid will gel slightly). Bring apples to room temperature just before serving.

Cooks' note:
• Apples can be chilled up to 3 days.

APRICOT GINGER PEAR PARFAITS

Serves 6
Active time: 30 min   Start to finish: 1¼ hr

6 firm-ripe pears (3 lb)
5 oz dried apricots (preferably California;
     1 heaping cup)
4 teaspoons finely grated peeled fresh ginger
½ cup water
2 to 3 tablespoons sugar
4 (4- by 1-inch) strips fresh lemon zest
1 (3-inch) piece cinnamon stick
2 tablespoons fresh lemon juice
1 (8-oz) container nonfat vanilla yogurt

Special equipment: **a food mill fitted
     with medium disk**
Garnish: **diced fresh pear and dried
     apricot slivers**

Peel 4 pears (2 pounds) and coarsely chop (including cores), then transfer to a 3- to 4-quart heavy saucepan. Add apricots, ginger, water, 2 tablespoons sugar, zest, cinnamon stick, and 1 tablespoon lemon juice and simmer, covered, until pears are very tender, about 20 minutes. Discard cinnamon stick and force mixture through food mill into a bowl. If desired, stir in up to 1 tablespoon additional sugar and cool sauce.

While sauce cools, peel, core, and finely dice (⅓ inch) remaining 2 pears (1 pound), then toss with remaining tablespoon lemon juice in a bowl.

Spoon ¼ cup sauce into each of 6 (8-ounce) glasses and top each serving with 2 tablespoons diced pear. Then spread 2 tablespoons yogurt in each glass and top with 2 more tablespoons diced pear and ¼ cup sauce.

Cooks' note:
• Sauce can be made 1 day ahead and chilled, covered.

Each serving about 230 calories and 1 gram fat
PHOTO ON PAGE 107

CARAMELIZED BANANA WITH RUM SAUCE

Serves 1
Active time: 10 min   Start to finish: 10 min

2 teaspoons unsalted butter
1 banana, halved lengthwise, then crosswise
2 teaspoons packed brown sugar
2 tablespoons rum (preferably dark)
2 teaspoons water
⅛ teaspoon freshly grated nutmeg
⅛ teaspoon cinnamon
2 tablespoons sliced or chopped nuts, toasted
     (see Tips, page 8)

Accompaniment: **vanilla ice cream**

Melt butter in a 10-inch heavy skillet over moderately high heat until foam subsides, then sauté banana, cut sides down, shaking skillet, 1 minute. Remove skillet from heat (away from flame) and sprinkle brown sugar around banana, then pour rum around banana. Return skillet to heat and continue to sauté, shaking skillet occasionally, until sugar begins to melt, about 30 seconds.

Add water, nutmeg, cinnamon, and a pinch of salt and cook over moderate heat, shaking skillet occasionally, until sauce is slightly thickened, 1 to 2 minutes.

Serve banana hot, sprinkled with nuts.

ORANGE, GRAPEFRUIT, AND GRAPE COMPOTE

Serves 6
Active time: 30 min   Start to finish: 30 min

6 navel oranges
2 large grapefruit
6 tablespoons sugar
½ lb seedless green grapes (1⅓ cups),
    quartered lengthwise

Finely grate zest from 2 oranges and 1 grapefruit into a small bowl and stir in sugar.

Cut peel, including all white pith, from all oranges and grapefruit with a sharp knife, then, working over a large bowl, cut segments free from membranes, letting segments fall into bowl. Squeeze enough juice from membranes to measure ½ cup, then add to citrus segments with grapes and 3 tablespoons citrus sugar. Toss fruit gently and serve with remaining sugar on the side.

Cooks' note:
• Compote can be made 1 day ahead and chilled, covered. Keep remaining citrus sugar in a sealed plastic bag at room temperature.
PHOTO ON PAGE 57

CHERRIES IN SPICED WINE SYRUP

Serves 4
Active time: 20 min   Start to finish: 3 hr

Spoon these cherries over ice cream or pound cake, or serve them topped with whipped cream and biscotti.

1 Turkish or ½ California bay leaf
4 whole cloves
4 whole black peppercorns
3 (3- by ½-inch) strips fresh lemon zest
1½ cups red Zinfandel
½ cup kirsch or other cherry-flavored brandy
½ cup water
½ cup sugar
3 cups fresh or frozen (not thawed) pitted
    sour cherries (1 lb)
1 (3-inch) cinnamon stick
1 vanilla bean, halved lengthwise

Special equipment: **a 4-inch square of cheese-cloth; kitchen string; a 1-qt jar with lid**

Wrap bay leaf, cloves, peppercorns, and zest together in cheesecloth and tie into a bundle with kitchen string.

Bring wine, kirsch, water, sugar, and cheesecloth bag to a boil in a 4-quart heavy saucepan. Add fresh or frozen cherries with any juices, cinnamon stick, and vanilla bean and simmer, uncovered, until cherries are tender but still hold their shape, 3 to 4 minutes.

Drain cherries in a sieve set over a bowl. Return cooking liquid to pan along with vanilla bean, cinnamon stick, and cheesecloth bag and boil until reduced to about 1¼ cups, about 12 minutes. Cool liquid slightly and then discard vanilla bean, cinnamon stick, and cheesecloth bag. Transfer cherries and cooled liquid to jar and chill, covered, at least 2 hours (to allow flavors to develop).

Cooks' note:
• Cherries can be kept in jar, chilled, up to 1 month.

NECTARINE AND BLACKBERRY COBBLER

Serves 6
Active time: 20 min   Start to finish: 1 hr

1¼ cups plus ½ teaspoon sugar
1 tablespoon cornstarch
2¼ lb nectarines (7 medium), pitted and
    cut into ½-inch-thick wedges
¾ lb blackberries (2½ cups)
2 cups all-purpose flour
2 teaspoons baking powder
¾ teaspoon salt
1¼ sticks (10 tablespoons) cold unsalted
    butter, cut into ½-inch cubes
¾ cup whole milk

Special equipment: **a 12- by 10- by 2-inch baking dish or other shallow 2½-qt baking dish (no deeper than 2 inches)**
Accompaniment: **lightly sweetened whipped cream**

Put oven rack in middle position and preheat oven to 425°F. Butter baking dish.

Whisk together 1¼ cups sugar and cornstarch in a large bowl, then add nectarines and blackberries and toss to combine well. Transfer to baking dish and bake until hot, 10 to 15 minutes.

While fruit bakes, whisk together flour, baking powder, and salt in another large bowl, then blend in butter with your fingertips or a pastry blender until mixture resembles coarse meal. Add milk and stir just until a dough forms.

Drop dough onto hot fruit mixture in 6 mounds, then sprinkle dough with remaining ½ teaspoon sugar. Bake cobbler until top is golden, 25 to 35 minutes.

PHOTO ON PAGE 79

berries

BRANDIED POACHED PEACHES

Serves 8

Active time: 20 min   Start to finish: 1 hr

⅔ cup sugar
½ cup fresh orange juice
2 cups water
5 (4-inch-long) strips fresh orange zest (see
  Tips, page 8)
½ vanilla bean, halved lengthwise
8 firm-ripe small peaches (2 to 2½ lb total)
1½ to 2 tablespoons brandy or Cognac

Bring sugar, orange juice, water, zest, and vanilla bean to a boil in a 4-quart heavy saucepan, stirring until sugar is dissolved. Add peaches, stem ends up. Cover pan and reduce heat, then poach peaches at a bare simmer 8 minutes. Turn peaches over and continue to poach, covered, until tender, 7 to 8 minutes more.

Transfer peaches with a slotted spoon to a bowl or shallow dish to cool, reserving poaching liquid in saucepan. Lift out vanilla bean pod and scrape seeds into poaching liquid, then boil liquid until reduced to about 1 cup, 10 to 15 minutes. Pour syrup through a sieve into a small bowl or glass measure and cool. Stir in brandy (to taste).

Peel peaches and serve whole with syrup.

Cooks' note:
• Peaches can be poached and peeled 2 days ahead. Pour syrup over peaches and chill, covered. Bring to room temperature before serving.

PHOTO ON PAGE 93

MANGOES FLAMBÉ

Serves 4

Active time: 10 min   Start to finish: 15 min

4 (1-lb) firm-ripe mangoes
6 tablespoons turbinado sugar
  such as Sugar in the Raw
⅓ cup dark rum

Preheat broiler. Line a large shallow baking pan (1 inch deep) with foil.

Wash and dry mangoes. Remove 2 flat sides of each mango with a sharp knife, cutting lengthwise alongside pit and cutting as close to pit as possible so that mango flesh is in 2 large pieces (reserve remaining fruit for another use). Make a crosshatch pattern with a small sharp knife, cutting across fruit down to skin at ½-inch intervals and being careful not to pierce through. Grasp fruit at both ends and turn inside out to make flesh side convex.

Arrange fruit, skin side down, in baking pan and sprinkle evenly with 4 tablespoons turbinado sugar (total). Broil 5 inches from heat until fruit is golden brown (it will not brown evenly), about 5 minutes. Arrange fruit on a large platter.

Cook rum with remaining 2 tablespoons sugar in a small heavy saucepan over moderately low heat, stirring, until sugar is dissolved. Remove from heat, then carefully ignite rum with a kitchen match and pour, still flaming, over warm mangoes. Serve immediately.

PEAR, BLUE CHEESE, AND FIG NAPOLEONS

Serves 4 (cheese course)
Active time: 10 min   Start to finish: 10 min

2 firm-ripe pears
3 to 4 oz firm blue cheese (about ⅔ cup), crumbled
3 to 4 soft dried figs, stemmed and finely chopped (about ⅓ cup)

Cut each pear lengthwise into 10 (⅛- to ¼-inch-thick) slices (5 from one side, then 5 more from opposite side), avoiding core and discarding rounded outermost slices.

Layer 4 pear slices with cheese and fig on each of 4 plates, beginning with largest pear slices, and ending with smallest.

Sprinkle any remaining cheese and chopped fig around napoleons.

BRANDIED BAKED PEARS

Serves 6
Active time: 20 min   Start to finish: 1¼ hr

6 firm Bosc or Bartlett pears
¼ cup packed light brown sugar
2 tablespoons unsalted butter
½ cup water
¼ cup plus 1 teaspoon brandy
¼ cup chilled heavy cream

Special equipment: **a melon-ball cutter**

Put oven rack in middle position and preheat oven to 450°F.

Peel and halve pears, leaving stems intact, then core with melon-ball cutter and toss with brown sugar in a large bowl.

Melt butter in a 3-quart shallow baking dish in oven, about 1 minute, then add pears, turning to coat with butter. Add water to dish and bake pears, turning over occasionally, until tender and edges of pears are caramelized, 30 to 50 minutes, depending on ripeness.

Transfer pears with a slotted spoon to a plate, then add ¼ cup brandy to baking dish and stir with a heat-proof rubber spatula to dissolve any caramelized juices. Return pears to dish.

Whisk cream in a bowl just until thick (before soft peaks form), then whisk in remaining teaspoon brandy. Serve pears with brandy sauce and drizzle with brandied cream.

Cooks' notes:
• Brandied baked pears can be baked 1 hour ahead and kept, loosely covered, at room temperature. Reheat, covered, in a preheated 350°F oven until warm, 10 to 15 minutes.
• Brandied cream can be made 1 hour ahead and chilled, covered. Stir before serving.

Each serving about 222 calories and 8 grams fat

ROASTED PEARS WITH ALMOND CRUNCH

Serves 6
Active time: 15 min   Start to finish: 1 hr

For almond crunch
1 large egg white
3 tablespoons sugar
¾ cup sliced almonds (2½ oz; preferably with skins)
For pears
3 firm Bosc pears
1 tablespoon unsalted butter, softened
¼ cup sugar
2 tablespoons Di Saronno Amaretto or other almond-flavored liqueur
½ cup water

Make almond crunch:
Put oven rack in middle position and preheat oven to 350°F. Butter a baking sheet.

Whisk together egg white and sugar, then add almonds, stirring until coated. Spread in a thin layer on baking sheet and bake until golden, 15 to 25 minutes. Cool on baking sheet on a rack, then break into pieces.

Increase oven temperature to 425°F.
Roast pears:
Halve pears lengthwise and core (preferably with a melon-ball cutter). Spread butter on bottom of a 9-inch square baking pan and sprinkle with ¼ cup sugar. Arrange pears, cut sides up, on sugar, then brush cut sides with 1 tablespoon Amaretto.

Roast pear halves, uncovered, until barely tender, about 25 minutes. Add water, remaining tablespoon Amaretto, and a pinch of salt to baking pan, then baste pears with pan juices. Roast pears, basting twice with pan juices, until tender, about 15 minutes more.

Serve pears warm or at room temperature and drizzle with pan juices and top with almond crunch.

Cooks' notes:
- Almond crunch can be made 4 days ahead and kept in a sealed plastic bag at room temperature.
- Pears can be roasted 1 hour ahead and kept, covered, at room temperature.

RASPBERRIES AND BLACKBERRIES IN RED-WINE SYRUP

Serves 8

Active time: 20 min   Start to finish: 45 min

The nutty, slightly spicy flavor of the sweet red wine works well with the berries in this dish.

½ cup sugar
2 cups sweet red wine (preferably
    Manischewitz Extra Heavy Malaga)
3 cups raspberries (13½ oz)
3 cups blackberries (13½ oz)

Accompaniment: **almond meringues (recipe follows)**

Cook sugar in a 3-quart dry heavy saucepan over moderately low heat, stirring slowly with a fork (to help sugar melt evenly), until melted and pale golden. Cook caramel without stirring, swirling pan, until deep golden. Remove pan from heat and carefully add wine (mixture will bubble up and caramel will harden), then simmer until caramel is dissolved and syrup is reduced to about 1½ cups, 8 to 10 minutes. Cool red-wine syrup to room temperature.

Divide berries among 8 serving bowls, then spoon syrup over berries.

Cooks' notes:
- To cool syrup quickly, pour into a metal bowl set in a larger bowl of ice and cold water and stir occasionally.
- Syrup can be made 2 days ahead and chilled, covered. Bring to room temperature before using.

PHOTO ON PAGE 67

ALMOND MERINGUES

Makes 8

Active time: 45 min   Start to finish: 2½ hr

This recipe makes more meringue than you'll need for 8 servings. You can pipe the extra into sticks and bake them to eat as a snack.

3 large egg whites
¾ cup superfine granulated sugar
⅓ cup sliced almonds, lightly toasted
    (see Tips, page 8), cooled, and
    coarsely crushed

Special equipment: **parchment paper; a pastry bag fitted with a ⅜-inch plain tip**

Put oven racks in upper and lower thirds of oven and preheat oven to 225°F.

Beat whites with a pinch of salt in a bowl with an electric mixer at high speed until they hold soft peaks. Add ½ cup superfine sugar a little at a time, beating, then continue to beat at high speed until whites hold stiff, glossy peaks, 1 to 3 minutes. Fold in remaining ¼ cup sugar gently but thoroughly.

Line 2 baking sheets with parchment paper. Put a small dab of meringue on all 4 corners of each sheet, then turn paper over, pressing on corners to adhere parchment to baking sheets.

Spoon meringue into pastry bag. You will be making 4 lattice cookies on each sheet, so work in 1 quadrant for each: Pipe 4 (4-inch-long) diagonal lines, about ⅜ inch apart, then pipe 4 (4-inch-long) parallel lines diagonally across original 4 lines, ⅜ inch apart, to form a lattice. Make 3 more lattice meringues on same baking sheet, about 1 inch apart. Sprinkle half of almonds over meringues. Pipe 4 more lattice meringues on second baking sheet in same manner, then sprinkle with remaining almonds.

Bake meringues in upper and lower thirds of oven, switching position of sheets halfway through baking, until crisp and pale golden, about 1 hour total.

Cool meringues completely on sheets on racks, about 1 hour, then carefully peel from parchment.

Cooks' note:
- Meringues can be made 3 days ahead and kept in an airtight container at room temperature.

PHOTO ON PAGE 67

TEQUILA AND LIME BAKED PINEAPPLE

Serves 4
Active time: 20 min   Start to finish: 1¼ hr

3 tablespoons tequila (preferably *reposado*
   or *añejo*)
3 tablespoons fresh lime juice
2 tablespoons sugar
1 (3-lb) pineapple (labeled "extra sweet")

Stir together tequila, lime juice, and sugar until
sugar is dissolved.

Peel pineapple with a large sharp knife, keeping
crown of leaves attached and trim bottom. Remove
eyes from pineapple in spiral channels with a sharp paring knife: Cut along each side of diagonal row of eyes
that spirals down pineapple, forming a V-shaped channel about ¼ inch deep underneath eyes. Cut out channel
and eyes, flicking out strip of eyes with knife tip, and
repeat procedure with remaining rows of eyes.

Put oven rack in middle position and preheat oven
to 425°F.

Lay pineapple on its side, then, beginning at base
and moving upward, carefully cut pineapple lengthwise
in half through leaves, keeping leaves attached. Cut out
core from each half and pull out some of long inner-
most leaves so no leaves are longer than about 7 inches.

Arrange pineapple halves, flat sides down, in a
glass or ceramic 13- by 9-inch baking dish, then pierce
all over and all the way through with a skewer.

Stir tequila mixture and spoon over pineapple. Lay
a sheet of wax paper over pineapple and bake, basting
with juices every 10 minutes, until pineapple is tender
and slightly caramelized, about 50 minutes. Halve
pineapple halves lengthwise and serve with any juices
remaining in baking dish.

Cooks' note:
• Pineapple can be baked 3 hours ahead. Reheat,
  covered with wax paper, in a preheated 350°F oven
  until heated through, 15 to 20 minutes.

Each serving about 138 calories and less than 1 gram fat

PHOTO ON PAGE 106

custards, puddings, and mousses

PERSIMMON FOOL

Serves 4 (makes about 2¼ cups)
Active time: 20 min   Start to finish: 8½ hr (includes chilling)

2 teaspoons unflavored gelatin (from one
   ¼-oz envelope)
1 tablespoon water
2 cups Hachiya persimmon purée (recipe
   follows)
2 tablespoons sugar
1½ teaspoons fresh lemon juice
½ cup chilled heavy cream
6 oz firm-ripe Fuyu persimmons

Sprinkle gelatin over water in a small heatproof cup
and let stand 1 minute to soften. Stir together persimmon purée, sugar, lemon juice, and a pinch of salt in a
bowl until sugar is dissolved.

Melt softened gelatin in cup set in a saucepan of
simmering water, then stir into persimmon purée. Beat
cream in another bowl with an electric mixer until it
just holds stiff peaks, then gently fold into purée.
Divide fool among 4 stemmed glasses and chill,
covered, at least 8 hours (it will set softly).

Just before serving, peel Fuyu persimmons,
seeding if necessary, chop and sprinkle over fool.

Cooks' note:
• Persimmon fool can be chilled up to 24 hours.

HACHIYA PERSIMMON PURÉE

Makes about 2 cups
Active time: 5 min   Start to finish: 5 min

It's important to look for very ripe Hachiya persimmons—they are incredibly astringent and tannic when not at their peak. The fruit should feel like a water balloon when squeezed and appear almost translucent.

2 lb very ripe Hachiya persimmons

Discard dried green or brown calyx from persimmons, then force persimmons 1 at a time through a medium-mesh sieve into a bowl using a rubber spatula, pressing hard on solids. (Discard solids.)

Cooks' note:
• Purée keeps, chilled, 3 days (cover surface with a round of wax paper, then cover bowl with plastic wrap) or frozen 1 month in an airtight container.

RHUBARB SABAYON WITH STRAWBERRIES

Serves 6
Active time: 25 min   Start to finish: 25 min

1 cup chopped fresh rhubarb stalks (2 large ribs)
½ cup sugar
1 cup orange Muscat wine such as Essensia
1 qt fresh strawberries, trimmed and quartered
2 large eggs

Special equipment: **an instant-read thermometer**

Bring rhubarb, sugar, and wine to a simmer in a small heavy saucepan, stirring until sugar is dissolved, then simmer, uncovered, until rhubarb is tender and begins to fall apart, about 5 minutes. Purée in a blender until smooth (use caution when blending hot liquids).

Divide strawberries among 6 glasses.

Beat eggs in a large deep metal bowl with a handheld electric mixer at medium-high speed 1 minute, then add hot rhubarb purée in a stream, beating constantly. Put bowl over a saucepan of simmering water and beat until mixture is tripled in volume, very thick, and registers 160°F on thermometer, about 6 minutes. Remove from heat and ladle sabayon over strawberries. Serve immediately.

HACHIYA PERSIMMON BREAD PUDDING

Serves 6 to 8
Active time: 15 min   Start to finish: 1½ hr

2 cups whole milk
1½ cups Hachiya persimmon purée (recipe this page)
¾ cup packed dark brown sugar
3 large eggs
¼ cup raisins
1 teaspoon vanilla
⅛ teaspoon salt
8 cups cubed (1 inch) challah or soft white Italian bread (from a 1¼-lb loaf)
½ cup walnuts (2 oz), coarsely chopped and toasted (see Tips, page 8)
1½ tablespoons unsalted butter, cut into ½-inch cubes

Accompaniment: **whipped cream**

Whisk together milk, persimmon purée, brown sugar, eggs, raisins, vanilla, and salt in a large bowl, then stir in bread and let mixture stand at room temperature 15 minutes.

Put oven rack in middle position and preheat oven to 375°F. Butter a shallow 8-inch square (2 quart) glass or ceramic baking dish.

Stir walnuts into bread pudding, then spoon pudding into baking dish, spreading evenly. Dot with butter. Bake pudding until golden, puffed, and set, 35 to 40 minutes. Cool to warm in pan on a rack, about 20 minutes.

Cooks' note:
• Bread pudding can be made 1 day ahead and cooled completely, uncovered, then chilled, covered. Reheat, uncovered, in a preheated 350°F oven until warm.

PISTACHIO BLANCMANGES

Serves 8

Active time: 1 hr   Start to finish: 7¼ hr (includes chilling)

Blancmange is a jellied molded pudding (similar to panna cotta) that is made with almonds and milk and served cold, often with a fruit sauce. Though it dates back to medieval times, blancmange became part of Thomas Jefferson's dessert repertoire after he encountered it during his years in Paris. Following his lead as an innovator, we made this version with pistachios instead of almonds, which gives the pudding a beautiful pale green hue and terrific flavor.

1½ cups shelled unsalted pistachios
    (not dyed red; 7 oz)
1¾ cups whole milk
⅛ teaspoon almond extract
1¾ teaspoons unflavored gelatin
    (from a ¼-oz envelope)
2 tablespoons cold water
½ cup sugar
1 cup chilled heavy cream

Special equipment: **8 (4-oz) oval or round metal molds or ceramic ramekins; a thin fine-weave kitchen towel (not terry cloth)**
Accompaniment: **brandied poached peaches (page 251)**
Garnish: **chopped unsalted pistachios**

Put oven rack in middle position and preheat oven to 350°F. Oil molds and line bottom of each with an oval of wax paper.

Spread pistachios on a baking sheet and toast until nuts are fragrant but not colored, 4 to 5 minutes. Transfer to a bowl and cool completely. Rub off and discard any skins.

Blend nuts with milk in a blender or food processor 2 minutes. Rinse kitchen towel under cold water and wring out as much water as possible. Line a large sieve with towel, then set sieve over a bowl or large glass measure and pour pistachio mixture into towel. Wrap towel up and around mixture and, working over sieve, squeeze pistachio milk (about 1 cup) from towel into bowl, discarding ground pistachios. Stir in almond extract and a pinch of salt.

Sprinkle gelatin over cold water in a very small bowl or a cup and let stand 1 minute.

Heat pistachio milk and sugar in a small saucepan over moderately low heat, stirring, until sugar is dissolved. Add gelatin mixture and cook, stirring, until gelatin is dissolved. Transfer to a metal bowl set in a larger bowl of ice and cold water and cool, stirring constantly, just until mixture is the consistency of raw egg white. Remove bowl from ice water.

Beat cream in another bowl with an electric mixer until it just holds stiff peaks, then whisk one fourth of cream into pistachio mixture to lighten. Fold in remaining cream gently but thoroughly and spoon mixture into molds. Chill blancmanges, covered with plastic wrap, until set, at least 6 hours.

Working with 1 blancmange at a time, run tip of a thin knife between each custard and metal mold. Tilt mold sideways and tap side of mold against a work surface, turning it, to evenly break seal and loosen custard. Keeping mold tilted, invert a dessert plate over mold, then invert blancmange onto plate.

Cooks' notes:
• Blancmanges (in molds) can be chilled up to 2 days.
• If you're short on time, it's not necessary to turn blancmanges out onto plates—they can be eaten out of the molds.

PHOTO ON PAGE 93

PUMPKIN GINGER RICE PUDDING

Serves 8 to 10

Active time: 1¾ hr   Start to finish: 2½ hr

Caramelizing the top of this pudding adds an extra depth of flavor, but it's equally delicious without doing it. A blowtorch works best here; the broiler didn't give us the uniform browning we wanted.

1 (1½- to 2-lb) piece pumpkin or butternut
    squash, halved and seeded
1 tablespoon unsalted butter
⅔ cup plus 2 teaspoons granulated sugar
⅔ cup long-grain white rice
½ teaspoon salt
5 cups whole milk
8 large egg yolks
1 teaspoon vanilla
¼ cup finely chopped crystallized ginger (2 oz)
2 tablespoons turbinado sugar such as Sugar
    in the Raw (optional)

Special equipment: **a blowtorch (optional)**

Bake pumpkin:

Put oven rack in middle position and preheat oven to 450°F.

Arrange each piece of pumpkin, cut side up, on a sheet of foil. Top each with ½ tablespoon butter and 1 teaspoon granulated sugar. Wrap separately in foil and bake, cut sides up, in a shallow baking pan until flesh is tender, about 1 hour.

Open foil and cool pumpkin slightly, then scoop flesh into a food processor and purée until smooth. Reduce oven temperature to 350°F.

Cook rice while pumpkin bakes:

Heat rice, salt, 4 cups milk, and remaining ⅔ cup granulated sugar in a 2- to 3-quart heavy saucepan over moderate heat, stirring, until very hot. Transfer to a large metal bowl set over a large saucepan of simmering water (or to a double boiler) and cook over low heat, covered, stirring occasionally, until rice is tender and most of milk is absorbed, 1 to 1¼ hours. (Add more simmering water to saucepan if necessary.) Remove pan from heat and keep rice warm, covered.

Make pudding:

Butter a 2-quart flameproof shallow baking dish (not glass). Lightly whisk yolks in a large bowl, then whisk in vanilla, ginger, 1⅓ cups pumpkin purée (reserve remainder for another use), and remaining cup milk. Gradually stir in warm rice, then pour mixture into baking dish. Set baking dish in a roasting pan and bake pudding in a hot water bath (see Tips, page 8), uncovered, in oven until set, 50 minutes to 1 hour.

If caramelizing pudding, sprinkle evenly with turbinado sugar, then move blowtorch flame evenly back and forth over sugar until sugar is melted and caramelized. Serve warm or at room temperature.

Cooks' notes:
- Pumpkin can be baked and puréed 2 days ahead and cooled, uncovered, then chilled, covered.
- Pudding can be baked (but not caramelized) 1 day ahead and cooled, uncovered, then chilled, covered. Bring to room temperature before caramelizing or serving.

MANGO CRÈME BRÛLÉE

Serves 6
Active time: 25 min   Start to finish: 5 hr (includes chilling)

5 large egg yolks
⅓ cup granulated sugar
⅛ teaspoon salt
1 vanilla bean, halved lengthwise
2 cups heavy cream
1½ cups diced (¼ inch) firm-ripe mango (from 1½ lb)
3 tablespoons turbinado sugar such as Sugar in the Raw

Special equipment: **6 (4-oz) flameproof ramekins**

Put oven rack in middle position and preheat oven to 325°F.

Whisk together yolks, granulated sugar, and salt in a bowl until combined well. Using tip of a knife, scrape seeds from vanilla bean into heavy cream in a 2-quart saucepan, then add pod. Heat over moderate heat until hot but not boiling. Discard pod and add cream to egg mixture in a slow stream, whisking until combined.

Spoon ¼ cup mango into each ramekin. Pour custard through a fine-mesh sieve into a bowl, then ladle over mango. Arrange ramekins in a roasting pan and bake in a hot water bath (see Tips, page 8) in oven until custards are just set, 35 to 40 minutes. Transfer custards with tongs to a rack to cool, then chill, uncovered, at least 4 hours.

Preheat broiler.

Sprinkle turbinado sugar evenly over custards and broil in a shallow baking pan 5 to 7 inches from heat until sugar is caramelized, 2 to 3 minutes.

Cooks' note:
- A blowtorch can be used to caramelize the sugar topping instead of the broiler.

ginger

COCONUT FLANS WITH COFFEE CARAMEL

Serves 6
Active time: 20 min   Start to finish: 5½ hr (includes chilling)

2½ teaspoons instant-espresso powder
 3 tablespoons water
 ⅔ cup plus ½ cup sugar
 1 (13- to 14-oz) can unsweetened
   coconut milk, stirred well
1¼ cups whole milk
 3 whole large eggs
 2 large egg yolks
 ⅛ teaspoon salt

Special equipment: **6 (6-oz) ramekins**

Preheat oven to 325°F.

Stir together instant-espresso powder and water until powder is dissolved.

Cook ½ cup sugar with a pinch of salt in a 1½- to 2-quart heavy saucepan over moderate heat, undisturbed, until it begins to melt. Continue to cook, stirring occasionally with a fork, until sugar is melted into a deep golden caramel.

Remove caramel from heat and whisk in espresso (mixture will steam and bubble vigorously). Once bubbles begin to subside, immediately divide mixture among ramekins, tilting to coat bottoms, and let stand until hardened, about 10 minutes.

While caramel hardens, bring coconut milk and whole milk just to a simmer over moderate heat, stirring, then remove from heat. Whisk together whole eggs, yolks, salt, and remaining ⅔ cup sugar in a large bowl, then add warm milk mixture in a stream, whisking. Pour custard through a fine-mesh sieve into a 1-quart glass measure.

Divide custard among ramekins. Arrange ramekins in a small roasting pan lined with a folded kitchen towel (bottom only). Bake custards in a hot water bath (see Tips, page 8), uncovered, in middle of oven until custards are set around edges but still tremble slightly in centers, about 1¼ hours.

Run a thin knife around side of each flan to loosen, then transfer ramekins to a rack and cool completely. Chill, covered, until cold, at least 4 hours. ·

To unmold, invert small plates over ramekins and invert flans onto plates.

Cooks' note:
• Flans can be chilled in ramekins up to 2 days.

PHOTO ON PAGE 85

pastries

APPLE TURNOVERS

Makes 6 pastries
Active time: 20 min   Start to finish: 1 hr

1 large apple, peeled, cored, and cut
   into ¼-inch dice
3 tablespoons dried cranberries
3 tablespoons apple jelly, heated
1 tablespoon cornstarch
⅛ teaspoon cinnamon
1 frozen puff pastry sheet (from a
   17¼-oz package), thawed
1 large egg, lightly beaten
2 tablespoons cold unsalted butter,
   cut into ½-inch cubes
1 tablespoon sugar

Put oven rack in lower third of oven and preheat oven to 400°F. Butter a large baking sheet.

Stir together apple, cranberries, jelly, cornstarch, and cinnamon in a bowl.

Roll out pastry on a lightly floured surface into a 12- by 9-inch rectangle. Cut into 6 (roughly 4-inch) squares. Divide apple mixture among squares, leaving a 1-inch border, and lightly brush egg on border. Dot filling with butter. Fold each pastry into a triangle, enclosing filling, and crimp edges with a fork. Cut 2 small steam vents in top of each turnover. Brush tops lightly with more egg and sprinkle with sugar. Bake on baking sheet until puffed and golden, about 20 minutes. Cool turnovers to warm.

FRIED PASTRY SPIRALS WITH HONEY, SESAME, AND WALNUTS

Makes 10 pastries (serving 4 to 6)
Active time: 1 hr   Start to finish: 2 hr

For pastry
1½ **cups all-purpose flour plus additional for kneading**
¾ **teaspoon salt**
1 **tablespoon raki, ouzo, or other anise-flavored liqueur**
1 **tablespoon fresh lemon juice**
 About 4 cups extra-virgin olive oil
½ **cup water**
2 **tablespoons finely chopped walnuts**
2 **tablespoons sesame seeds**
 For syrup
1 **cup water**
⅔ **cup sugar**
½ **cup mild honey**
2 **(4- by 1-inch) strips fresh lemon zest**
2 **(4- by 1-inch) strips fresh orange zest**

Special equipment: **a fluted pastry wheel (optional); a deep-fat thermometer; a long-handled metal 2- or 3-prong kitchen fork; a regular stainless-steel fork**

Make pastry dough:
Stir together flour and salt in a bowl, then make a well in center and add raki, lemon juice, ¾ teaspoon oil, and water. Stir until a soft dough forms. Turn out dough onto a floured surface and knead, working in just enough additional flour to keep dough from sticking, until dough is smooth and elastic, 8 to 10 minutes. Wrap dough in plastic wrap and let stand at room temperature 1 hour.

Make syrup while pastry stands:
Bring water, sugar, honey, and zests to a boil in a 2-quart heavy saucepan, stirring until sugar is dissolved. Reduce heat and simmer 5 minutes. Cool syrup.

Form and fry spirals:
Dust a dry kitchen towel with flour. Halve dough. Roll out 1 half into a roughly 18- by 11-inch (paper-thin) rectangle on floured surface with a floured rolling pin, rotating rectangle and turning over occasionally and dusting with just enough flour to keep dough from sticking. Cut rectangle lengthwise into 5 (2-inch-wide) strips using pastry wheel or a sharp knife, then transfer strips to kitchen towel, gently stretching strips to 20 inches as you transfer them. Roll out remaining dough and make 5 more strips in same manner.

Heat 1 inch oil in a deep 12-inch heavy skillet until it registers 375°F on thermometer (see cooks' note, below). Working with 1 strip at a time, carefully slip one third of strip into hot oil (holding rest of strip aloft in one hand), then, using your other hand, hook end of strip (in oil) between tines of long-handled fork. Rotate fork, tilting it upright to be perpendicular to skillet and wrapping dough into beginning of spiral. As dough in oil begins to puff, continue to gradually lower uncooked part of strip into oil, rotating fork to wrap pastry around fork in a loose spiral (this will take about 30 seconds total). Using regular fork, gently hold end of strip against spiral. Turn spiral over using both forks and fry until pale golden, about 30 seconds more. Transfer spiral to paper towels to drain. Fry remaining 9 pastry strips in same manner. (Return oil to 375°F between spirals.)

Assemble pastries:
Toast walnuts and sesame seeds in a dry small skillet over moderately low heat, stirring constantly, until seeds are golden, about 3 minutes. Transfer to a bowl to cool.

Reheat syrup until warm, then discard zests. Arrange spirals on a large platter and drizzle syrup over them, then sprinkle with walnut mixture.

Cooks' notes:
• **To take the temperature of a shallow amount of oil, put bulb in skillet and turn thermometer facedown, resting other end against rim of skillet. Check temperature frequently.**
• **Pastries can be fried and drizzled with syrup 1 day ahead and kept, loosely covered with foil, at room temperature.**
• **Syrup and nut mixture can be made 2 days ahead and kept separately, covered, at room temperature.**
• **This frying oil can be strained through a paper-towel-lined sieve into a bowl and reused for frying once more.**
PHOTO ON PAGE 72

BEVERAGES

alcoholic

BEACHCOMBER

Makes 1 drink
Active time: 5 min   Start to finish: 5 min

1½ oz light rum (3 tablespoons)
½ oz triple sec (1 tablespoon)
1 tablespoon fresh lime juice
1 teaspoon maraschino liqueur or kirsch
Sparkling water to taste

Garnish: **a maraschino cherry**

Shake all ingredients except sparkling water in a cocktail shaker with 1 cup ice cubes, then strain into a tall glass filled with ice cubes. Add sparkling water and stir.

FROZEN MANGO DAIQUIRI

Makes 2 drinks
Active time: 15 min   Start to finish: 2½ hr
(includes freezing mango)

3 oz amber rum (¼ cup plus 2 tablespoons)
1½ cups (1-inch) cubes of firm-ripe mango
(from two 1-lb mangoes), frozen
3 tablespoons fresh lime juice
1 oz triple sec (2 tablespoons)
4 teaspoons superfine granulated sugar
2 cups ice cubes

Blend all ingredients in a blender until smooth.

RHUBARB COLLINS

Makes about 16 drinks
Active time: 45 min   Start to finish: 3½ hr (includes chilling)

The tangy flavor of seasonal rhubarb complements the taste of gin surprisingly well. You can double the quantities for a bigger batch.

4 lb rhubarb stalks, trimmed and cut into
½-inch pieces
2 cups sugar
6 cups water
¾ to 1 cup fresh lime juice
1 (750-ml) bottle gin (optional)
⅓ cup Cointreau or other clear orange liqueur
(2½ oz; optional)
2 (1-liter) bottles seltzer water, chilled
16 small lime wedges

Bring rhubarb, sugar, and water to a boil in a 5- to 6-quart heavy pot, stirring until sugar is dissolved, then reduce heat and simmer, partially covered, until rhubarb falls apart, about 15 minutes. Remove from heat and cool 15 minutes. Pour mixture into a large fine-mesh sieve set over a large bowl and drain 15 minutes, then press gently on and discard solids. (There will be about 8 cups syrup.) Skim off any foam and cool syrup to room temperature. Pour syrup into 1 or 2 pitchers and chill, uncovered, until cold, about 2 hours.

Stir in lime juice (to taste), then gin and Cointreau (if using).

Fill glasses with ice and add rhubarb gin mixture, stopping about 1 inch from rim. Top off with seltzer. Run a wedge of lime around rim of each glass, then squeeze into drink.

Cooks' notes:
• Rhubarb syrup (without lime juice, gin, or Cointreau) can be made 1 day ahead and chilled, covered, or frozen 1 week.
• Lime juice, gin, and Cointreau can be stirred into rhubarb syrup 4 hours ahead and chilled, covered.
PHOTO ON PAGE 76

BLUE HAWAIIAN

Makes 2 drinks
Active time: 5 min   Start to finish: 5 min

3 oz light rum (¼ cup plus 2 tablespoons)
2 oz blue Curaçao (¼ cup)
½ cup unsweetened pineapple juice
¼ cup well-stirred canned cream of coconut
    (not coconut milk) such as Coco López
3 cups ice cubes

Garnish: **a pineapple wedge**

Blend all ingredients in a blender until smooth.

MOSCOW MULE

Makes 1 drink
Active time: 5 min   Start to finish: 5 min

This drink was dreamed up in Los Angeles in the 1940s by businessman John Martin, who was desperately trying to sell Smirnoff vodka. It so happened that Jack Morgan, owner of the Cock'n Bull, was trying to sell a ginger beer he had recently concocted. The two got together and tracked down a company that had a surplus of mugs, and they had a logo of a kicking mule stamped onto them. A drink was born ...

1½ oz vodka (3 tablespoons)
1 tablespoon fresh lime juice
⅔ cup ginger beer, chilled

Garnish: **a lime slice**

Fill a 12-ounce glass three-fourths full with ice cubes. Add vodka, lime juice, and ginger beer and gently stir.

HERBAL WHITE SANGRIA

Makes about 8 cups
Active time: 15 min   Start to finish: 8¼ hr (includes steeping)

⅔ cup superfine granulated sugar
⅔ cup water
1 cup green seedless grapes (7 oz)
20 fresh thyme sprigs (preferably lemon thyme)
¼ cup fresh lemon juice

2 teaspoons green cardamom pods, crushed
2 (750-ml) bottles fruity white wine, such as
    dry Riesling

Garnish: **small (pesticide-free) edible flower blossoms such as Johnny-jump-ups or garden pea blossoms**

Stir together sugar and water in a bowl until sugar is dissolved. Crush grapes in a 2-quart pitcher or bowl with a potato masher, then add sugar syrup and remaining ingredients. Steep, covered and chilled, at least 8 hours.

Pour sangria through a fine-mesh sieve into a clean pitcher. Serve over ice.

Cooks' note:
• Sangria can be steeped up to 1 day.

GARNET PUNCH
Cranberry Rosemary Cocktail

Serves 16 (makes about 2¼ qt)
Active time: 15 min   Start to finish: 4 hr (includes chilling)

1½ lb fresh or frozen cranberries (6 cups;
    thawed if frozen)
2 cups sugar
1 tablespoon finely chopped fresh rosemary
4½ cups water
1 (750-ml) bottle vodka (3 cups)

Garnish: **fresh rosemary sprigs (leaves stripped except for top 1 inch)**

Simmer cranberries, sugar, rosemary, and water in a 4-quart heavy saucepan over moderately low heat, uncovered, stirring occasionally, until cranberries have burst and are very soft and liquid is slightly syrupy, about 30 minutes.

Pour syrup through a fine-mesh sieve into a bowl, gently stirring cranberries but not pressing on them, then discard berries. Chill syrup, uncovered, until cold, at least 3½ hours.

Just before serving, stir together vodka and syrup in a pitcher. Serve over ice in 6- to 8-ounce glasses.

Cooks' note:
• Syrup can be chilled, covered, up to 3 days.
PHOTO ON PAGE 104

TANGERINE MIMOSAS

Makes 6 drinks
Active time: 15 min   Start to finish: 15 min

**3 cups fresh tangerine juice (from 10 to
12 large tangerines), chilled
1 (750-ml) bottle sparkling white wine, chilled**

Divide juice among 6 stemmed glasses and top off with sparkling wine.

PHOTO ON PAGE 61

MINT JULEPS

Makes 8 drinks
Active time: 10 min   Start to finish: 10 min

Mint juleps are traditionally made one at a time, crushing the mint in a silver julep cup. We've adapted the recipe to make a large batch.

**1½ cups bourbon or sour mash whiskey (12 oz)
8 teaspoons superfine granulated sugar,
   or to taste
1 cup fresh mint leaves
12 cups crushed ice**

Garnish: **fresh mint sprigs**

Stir together bourbon and 4 teaspoons sugar until sugar is dissolved. Lightly crush mint leaves with remaining 4 teaspoons sugar in a metal bowl with back of a spoon until sugar is dissolved, about 5 minutes. Add 4 cups crushed ice, then add ¾ cup bourbon mixture and stir well.

Divide mixture among 8 (12-ounce) glasses with a ladle. Add enough of remaining 8 cups ice to almost fill glasses, then add remaining ¾ cup bourbon and stir well.

PHOTO ON PAGE 70

MAI TAI

Makes 1 drink
Active time: 5 min   Start to finish: 5 min

**1 oz dark rum (2 tablespoons)
1 oz amber rum (2 tablespoons)
2 tablespoons fresh orange juice
½ oz Cointreau or triple sec (1 tablespoon)
1 tablespoon fresh lime juice
1 teaspoon orgeat syrup or 1 drop pure
   almond extract
1 teaspoon superfine granulated sugar
   Dash of grenadine**

Garnish: **an orange slice**

Shake all ingredients in a cocktail shaker with 1 cup ice cubes, then strain into a glass filled with ice cubes.

non-*alcoholic*

FRESH TOMATO JUICE COCKTAIL

Makes about 6 cups
Active time: 30 min   Start to finish: 3 hr

*Try this refreshing drink on a sizzling-hot summer day.
Add a splash of aquavit (we like Linie brand), then
serve on the rocks with a parsley sprig, and you have
a Norwegian Mary. As with any fresh-squeezed juice,
this is best served the day it's made.*

3 lb beefsteak tomatoes, quartered
1 small fennel bulb (sometimes called anise;
   ½ lb), stalks cut off and discarded,
   reserving fronds, and bulb chopped
2 celery ribs with leaves, chopped
1 cup loosely packed fresh flat-leaf parsley
   sprigs, chopped
2 teaspoons fine sea salt, or to taste

Special equipment: **3 (20-inch) squares of
cheesecloth**

Finely chop all ingredients in batches in a food
processor, transferring to a large bowl. Let stand at
room temperature, loosely covered, 1½ hours.

Line a large sieve with layered cheesecloth squares
and set over a large nonreactive pot. Carefully pour
tomato mixture into center of cheesecloth, then gather
up edges of cheesecloth to form a large sack and, working over sieve, squeeze solids to extract as much juice
as possible. Discard solids.

Chill juice until cold, about 1 hour, and stir before
serving. (Juice will be pale in color but flavorful.)

CAFÉ AU LAIT

Serves 6
Active time: 5 min   Start to finish: 15 min

6 cups steaming-hot milk
3 cups hot brewed strong coffee (preferably
   New Orleans–style with chicory)

Blend milk in 2 batches in a blender until frothy
(use caution when blending hot liquids). Divide coffee
among 6 large cups and top off with hot milk.
PHOTO ON PAGE 61

guides to the text

CREDITS

We gratefully acknowledge the photographers listed below. With a few exceptions, their work was previously published in *Gourmet*.

Sang An: Tarragon Shallot Egg Salad Sandwiches, p. 6. Flavors of the American Heartland, pp. 96-99. All Photographs © 2003.

Quentin Bacon: Grilled Spiced-Rubbed Skirt Steak, p. 6. Table setting, p. 44. A Pretty Grill, pp. 78-79. Winter Light, pp. 100-103. All Photographs © 2003.

Mary Ellen Bartley: It's a Kick, pp. 50-51. All Photographs © 2003.

Beatriz Da Costa: A Passover Seder, pp. 66-67. All Photographs © 2003.

Miki Duisterhof: Fruit centerpiece, p.2. French Connection, pp. 46-49. The Virginian, pp. 92-93. All Photographs © 2003.

Rob Fiocca: Rhubarb Collins, p. 6. Light Fantastic, pp. 74-77. Brunch and All That Jazz, pp. 90-91. All Photographs © 2003.

Lisa Hubbard: A Weekend in the Country, pp. 52-61. Island Elegance, pp. 68-71. All Photographs © 2003.

Richard Gerhard Jung: Masterfeast, pp. 14-23. All Photographs © 2003.

John Kernick: Woman at Ditirambo, p. 11. Piazza Farnese, pp. 12-13. Campo de' Fiori market, p. 30. All Photographs © 2003.

Rita Maas: Green Beans with Lemon and Oil, p. 36. Vignarola, p. 39. All Photographs © 2003.

John Midgley: Thanks for the Memory, pp. 94-95. All Photographs © 2003.

Paolo Nobile: Wendy Artin's Still Life With Flavor, pp. 24-29. All Photographs © 2003.

Tina Rupp: Forecast: Chile and Crisp, pp. 84-85. All Photographs © 2003.

Mikkel Vang: Sophisticated Rhythm, pp. 104-105. All Photographs © 2003.

George Whiteside: Under a Mediterrean Sky, pp. 72-73. All Photographs © 2003.

Anna Williams: Shellfish and Watermelon Ceviche, p. 6. Spring Fling, pp. 62-65. Lazy Days, pp. 80-83. Smiles of a Summer Day, pp. 86-89. Heirloom Tomatoes with Bacon, Blue Cheese, and Basil, p. 112. All Photographs © 2003.

Romulo Yanes: Gnocchetti all'Amatriciana, front jacket. Individual Zucchini Frittatas with Pecorino and Chives, p. 32. Pizza Bianca, p. 34. Cacio e Pepe, p. 35. Gnocchetti all'Amatriciana, p. 41. Cooking Class photos, p. 43. Low-Fat: Mood Mexico, p. 106. Low-Fat: Comforting Resolution, p. 107. Six One-Dish Dinners, pp. 108-109. Dinner for One: Major Flavors, p. 110. Dinner for One: Tray Chic, p. 111. All Photographs © 2003.

Index icon illustrations: Tobie Giddio © 2002.
Tobie Giddio/www.cwc-i.com

SOURCES

Below are sources for the sometimes hard-to-find ingredients and cookware.

INGREDIENTS

Achiote (annatto) seeds—Latino markets, the spice section of some supermarkets, and Kitchen/Market (888-468-4433); purchase seeds that are a bright, brick-red color—dull brown seeds are too old.

Asian fish sauce (such as Thai *nam pla* or Vietnamese *nuoc mam*)—Asian markets and EthnicGrocer.com (866-438-4642).

Beef stock—some butcher shops and specialty foods shops.

Black truffle butter—some specialty foods shops and D'Artagnan (800-327-8246).

Buckwheat flour—natural foods stores and some supermarkets.

Cajun seasoning—BlueChef (Bluechef.com), The Spice Hunter (800-444-3061; spicehunter.com), and McCormick (AASpices.com).

Cardamom pods—Indian markets, specialty foods shops, and Kalustyan's (800-352-3451; kalustyans.com).

Chayotes—Latino markets and some supermarkets.

Chinese rice wine —Asian markets and Uwajimaya (800-899-1928).

Chinese rock sugar—Asian markets and Uwajimaya (800-899-1928).

Coarse stone-ground white grits—specialty foods shops and Hoppin' John's (800-828-4412; hoppinjohns.com).

Confit duck legs—some specialty foods shops and D'Artagnan (800-327-8246).

Cooked Virginia country ham—Edwards (800-222-4267).

Cotija cheese—cheese shops, Latino markets, and some specialty foods shops.

Dried *ancho* chiles—Mexican markets, many supermarkets, and Chile Today–Hot Tamale (800-468-7377).

Dried edible lavender flowers—Penzeys (800-741-7787) and Kalustyan's (800-352-3451).

Dried epazote—Kitchen/Market (212-243-4433).

Dried-porcini bouillon cubes—some specialty foods shops and Dean & DeLuca (877-826-9246).

Dulce de leche—specialty foods shops and Cooking.com.

Flaky sea salt—specialty foods shops and Salt Works (800-353-7258).

Flaxseeds—natural foods stores and some supermarkets.

French green lentils—specialty foods shops and some supermarkets.

Frozen passion-fruit pulp—Latino markets and some supermarkets.

Greek whole-milk yogurt—Greek and Middle Eastern markets, natural foods stores, and some supermarkets.

Habanero or Scotch bonnet chiles—specialty produce markets and Latino markets.

Hickory nut halves—some specialty foods shops and American Spoon Foods (888-735-6700).

Hulled (green) pumpkin seeds—natural foods stores and some supermarkets.

Instant-espresso powder—specialty foods shops, many supermarkets, and The Baker's Catalogue (800-827-6836).

Lemongrass stalks—Asian markets and some supermarkets.

Mexican chocolate—specialty foods shops, some supermarkets, and Kitchen/Market (212-243-4433).

Mild Spanish chorizo—Latino markets, specialty foods shops, and some supermarkets.

Mirin—Asian markets, specialty foods shops, and Uwajimaya (800-889-1928).

Orgeat syrup—Fortunes Coffee Roastery Inc. (888-327-5282).

Pecorino Romano—Volpetti (011-39-06-574-2352; volpetti.com), Il Forteto Cacio Di Fossa (available at Citarella; 866-248-2735), Sini Fulvi (available at DiPalo Dairy; 212-226-1033), and Columbo (available at Todaro Brothers; 212-532-0633).

Pure almond paste—specialty foods shops and many supermarkets.

Quinoa—specialty foods shops, natural foods stores, and EthnicGrocer.com (866-438-4642).

Radish sprouts or baby pea shoots—specialty produce markets and some Asian markets.

Ras-el-hanout—specialty foods shops and Kalustyan's (800-352-3451).

Rice flour—the Latino section of many supermarkets, natural foods stores, Kalustyan's (800-352-3451), and The Baker's Catalogue (800-827-6836).

Rice-paper rounds (sometimes labeled "spring roll wrappers")—Asian markets and EthnicGrocer.com (866-438-4642).

Salted *myzithra* cheese—Greek markets, specialty foods shops, and Ninth Avenue Cheese Market (212-397-4700).

Semolina (sometimes labeled "semolina flour"; resembles fine yellow cornmeal)—Italian markets, natural foods stores, and some supermarkets.

Sorrel—farmers markets and some specialty produce markets.

Sortilège maple liqueur—Laird & Co. (877-438-5247).

Sweet or hot Spanish smoked paprika—specialty foods shops, some supermarkets, and The Spanish Table (505-986-0243) and Tienda.com (888-472-1022).

Sweet white *miso*—Asian markets and Uwajimaya (800-889-1928).

Vermicelli rice-stick noodles—Asian markets and EthnicGrocer.com (866-438-4642).

Wasabi paste—Asian markets, specialty foods shops, some supermarkets, and Uwajimaya (800-899-1928).

White *arepa* flour—Latino markets, some supermarkets, and Kitchen/Market (212-243-4433).

White or black truffle oil—specialty foods shops and D'Artagnan (800-327-8246).

Whole roasted chestnuts—some supermarkets and specialty foods shops.

COOKWARE

Baba au rhum molds—some cookware shops and Bridge Kitchenware (800-274-3435 or 212-838-1901).

Blowtorch—cookware shops and A Cook's Wares (800-915-9788).

Small decorative cutters — specialty bakeware shops and Bridge Kitchenware (800-274-3435 or 212-838-1901).

Fluted round nonstick tartlet pans—specialty bakeware shops and Bridge Kitchenware (800-274-3435 or 212-838-1901).

Fluted tart pan (13½ by 4-inch rectangular) —cookware shops and Fante's Kitchen Wares Shop (fantes.com).

Japanese Benriner—Asian markets, some cookware shops, and Uwajimaya (800-889-1928).

Leaf-shaped cookie cutters (1¼- to 1½-inch)—Sweet Celebrations (800-328-6722).

Loaf pan (12- by 4½- by 3-inch)—some cookware shops, The Baker's Catalogue (800-827-6836), and A Cook's Wares (800-915-9788).

Metal loaf pan (12- by 4- by 2½-inch) —some cookware shops and The Baker's Catalogue (800-827-6836).

Muffin-top pans—cookware shops and Cooking.com.

Scallop shells—Bridge Kitchenware (800-274-3435).

Silpat nonstick bakeware liner—cookware shops and Bridge Kitchenware (800-274-3435).

INDEX

Page numbers in *italics* indicate color photographs
⏲ indicates recipes that can be prepared in 30 minutes or less, active time
indicates recipes that are leaner/lighter

TABLE SETTING ACKNOWLEDGMENTS

Any items not credited are privately owned.

Masterfeast
Pages 14-15: Stone table—Treillage (212-535-2288).

Still Life with Flavor
Page 27: Bowl—Accaso (011-39-02-657-1865). Wineglasses—Abito Qui (011-39-02-290-02518; abitoqui@tiscali.it).
Page 26: Shallow plates—Nicola Fasano (011-39-099-566-1037; nicolefasano@libero.it).
Page 27: Plate—Accaso.
Page 28: Plate—Accaso.
Page 29: Dessert cup—Abito Qui.

More Recipes from Rome
Page 36: Off-white plate—Global Table (212-431-5839).
Page 39: "Flirt" conical green bowl—Bernardaud (800-884-7775).

The Menu Collection
Page 44: "Thistle" dinner plates, cups, and saucers—Calvin Klein (212-719-2600). Fontenille Pataud forks—Bergdorf Goodman (212-339-3000). Stemware—Riedel Crystal (riedelcrystal.com). Marina table lamp—Crate & Barrel (800-996-9960). Candlesticks—Simon Pearce (212-334-2393).

French Connection
Page 47: Small plates—Takashimaya New York (800-753-2038 or 212-350-0100).
Page 48: Courson "Blanc d'Ivorie" dinner plates —La Cafetière (646-486-0667).

It's a Kick
Page 50: LSA's disc lager glass—Lille (773-342-0563). "Bronze Collection" brown porcelain plate—Joseph Abboud Environments (800-999-0600). Plywood tray—ABC Carpet & Home (212-473-3000).
Page 51: Rectangular white platter—Jonathan Adler (212-941-8950). "Stingray" tray—Lille. Television—Sony Electronics (sonystyle.com). White ceramic chip and dip bowl, glass bowl, white bowl, and square white salad plate—Crate & Barrel (800-996-9960). Wood tray table—Aero (212-966-1500). Football—Best Sports Apparel (nflstore.net). Square white ceramic plate—Jonathan Adler.

A Weekend in the Country
Page 56: "Marcasite" coffeepot and "Wedgwood White" cups and saucers—Wedgwood USA (800-955-1550).
Pages 58-59: "Painswick" sterling silverware and "Flavia" and "Iona" wineglasses—William Yeoward Crystal (800-818-8484). Large decanter—Rosenthal (800-804-8070). "Nature" pasta bowls—Wedgwood USA. Teak salad bowl and rosewood twig servers—Global Table (212-431-5839).

Spring Fling
Page 62: Table and chairs—Dune (212-925-6171). Plates—Crate & Barrel (800-996-9960). Napkins and flatware—Takashimaya (800-753-2038 or 212-350-0100). Vases—End of History (212-647-7598). Tall glass by d. Ehrlich—Takashimaya. Verdant" plate—Calvin Klein (877-256-7373).
Page 64: Sea glass plate—ABC Carpet & Home (212-473-3000).

Bowls—La Cafetière (866-486-0667). Bread fork—Takashimaya. Carving set—Holland & Holland (212-752-7755).

A Passover Seder
Page 66: Wineglasses—Tuckahoe Trading Company (757-487-1815). Vases and flatware—Takashimaya (800-753-2038 or 212-350-0100). Fabric on table—Silk Trading Co. (212-966-5464). "Squash" napkins—Archipelago (212-334-9460).
Page 67: Christine Perrochon plate, carafe, and fork—Takashimaya. Bowls and spoons—Takashimaya.

Island Elegance
Page 70: Footed pitcher—Livingston Antiques (843-556-6162).
Page 71: "Edward" glassware—Williams-Sonoma (877-812-6235). "Chambord" dinner plate and "Bernadotte" wine goblets—Villeroy & Boch (800-845-5376). "Alton" pewter flatware—Williams-Sonoma.

Under a Mediterranean Sky
Page 73: Dinner plates by Christiane Perrochon and blue napkins—Takashimaya New York (800-753-2038).

Light Fantastic
Page 74: Mosquito nets—Acorn Trading (acorntrading.com.au). "Hotel" tablecloths—Williams-Sonoma (800-541-1262). Stainless-steel steamers—Kam Kuo Food Corp. (212-349-3097). Small, medium, and large glass cake stands—Dean & DeLuca (877-826-9246). Serving plates—Crate & Barrel (800-996-9960).

TABLE SETTING ACKNOWLEDGMENTS

Page 76: Iittalia "Aarne" Champagne glasses and Stelton "Cylinda-Line" stainless-steel tray—Moss (212-226-2190). "Accenti" plate—Rosenthal. "Trumpet" cordial glasses—Crate & Barrel. Resin place mat—Calvin Klein Home (800-294-7978).
Page 77: "Hotel" white napkin—Williams-Sonoma. "Loft" dipping bowl—Rosenthal (800-804-8070).

A Pretty Grill
Page 78: "Rialto" yellow napkin—La Cafetière (866-486-0667).

Lazy Days
Page 81: Gustavian round table and chairs—White on White (212-288-0909). Hurricane lamps—Global Table (212-431-5839)." Chaleur" dinner plate and "Pordamsa" salt and pepper bowls—Global Table.

Forecast: Chile and Crisp
Page 84: Silver-plate charger with folded edge, "Arpa" flatware, and "Egala" dinner plates—Armani Casa (212-334-1271).
Page 85: Limoges porcelain dessert plates and "Fiume" square tray—Armani Casa.

Smiles of a Summer Day
Page 86: White folding chairs, Swedish drop-leaf table, and white bowls—Treillage (212-535-2288). Pitcher, glasses, and flatware—Williams-Sonoma (800-541-2233). Plates—Pottery Barn (800-922-5507).

Brunch and All that Jazz
Page 90: Espresso cup—The Terence Conran Shop (866-755-9079). Yellow plate—Global Table (212-431-5839).
Page 91: "Mud" platter and "Chaleur" plates—Global Table. George Jensen flatware—Michael C. Fina (800-289-3462). Vases—Ted Muehling (212-431-3825). "Ete Comme Hiver" place mats—Hermes (800-441-4488). "Mud" plates and bowl—Global Table. AREA blue linen napkin—The Terence Conran Shop.

The Virginian
Page 92: Silver flatware—James Robinson (212-752-6166). "Monticello" goblets—Metropolitan Museum of Art (800-662-3397). "Thistle" wineglasses—Cristal Saint-Louis (800-238-5522).

Sterling jug—James Robinson. "A La Reine" plate—Bernardaud (212-725-0397). "Cornflower Garland" reproduction of Monticello plate—Mottahedeh (212-685-3050).

Thanks for the Memory
Page 94: Plates—Catherine Memmi (212-226-8200). Glasses and napkins—Armani Casa (212-334-1271). Forks and knives—Takashimaya (212-350-0100). Candlesticks—Ted Muehling (212-431-3825). "Edvard" white chairs—Ikea (908-289-4488). Shag rug—ABC Carpet & Home (212-473-3000).

Sophisticated Rhythm
Page 104: Glass—Takashimaya New York (212-350-0100). Cocktail napkin—Takashimaya.
Page 105: Ceramic dipping bowl by MUD—ABC Carpet & Home (212-473-3000).

Dinner for One: Tray Chic
Page 111: Stoneware TV dinner tray—Sur La Table (800-243-0852).